RISE with SAP towards a Sustainable Enterprise

Become a value-driven, sustainable, and resilient enterprise using RISE with SAP

Adil Zafar

Dharma Alturi

Sanket Taur

Mihir R. Gor

BIRMINGHAM—MUMBAI

RISE with SAP towards a Sustainable Enterprise

Copyright © 2023 Packt Publishing

Group Product Manager: Alok Dhuri

Publishing Product Manager: Harshal Gundetty

Senior Editor: Kinnari Chohan

Technical Editor: Maran Fernandes

Copy Editor: Safis Editing

Project Coordinator: Manisha Singh

Proofreader: Safis Editing

Indexer: Hemangini Bari

Production Designer: Joshua Misquitta

Developer Relations Marketing Executives: Rayyan Khan and Deepak Kumar

First published: February 2023

Production reference: 1270123

Published by Packt Publishing Ltd.

Livery Place

35 Livery Street

Birmingham

B3 2PB, UK.

ISBN 978-1-80181-274-0

`www.packt.com`

Authoring this book required a lot of effort and dedication, so you can imagine that without the support of our families and extended teams, it wouldn't have been possible. We authors want to say thank you to all the supporters (family, friends, and mentors) who helped us complete this book.

Adil Zafar would like to dedicate this book to his wife, Saira, and his three children, Naila, Haroon, and Hammad. Without the support of his family, he would not have been able to write this book. Adil would like to thank Mark Dudgeon for believing in him when he brought him to IBM to lead RISE with SAP. He would like to thank Joseph Msays for his counsel and for providing the opportunities in leading the RISE with SAP Premium Supplier program. He would also like to thank his IBM mentors, such as Allan Coulter, Andrew Worsley-Tonks, and many others, as well as his coach, Richard Maund for opening up new opportunities to him. Finally, he would like to also dedicate this book to his (late) parents. Without their prayers and guidance, he would not be the man he is today.

Dharma Atluri would like to dedicate this book to his wife, Swetha Ginjupalli, his lovely son, Abhinav Atluri, and nephew, Akhil Mallela, without whose support and patience during each weekend, it wouldn't have been a possibility. He would also like to thank A. B. Vijay Kumar and Joseph Msays for providing him the opportunity to be the chief architect for the RISE with SAP program, which allowed him to deep dive into RISE with SAP at the most granular level and get to know the intricate details of the dos and don'ts. Finally, he would like to thank his parents and in-laws for their blessings and understanding during his long absences away from them.

Mihir Gor would like to dedicate this book to his wife, Gopa, and his two children, Hemal and Devisha, as well as his parents and in-laws. All of them have stood by him as he's progressed in his career at IBM. He is passionate about driving sustainability solutions, developing new SAP thought leadership, and operating at the cutting edge of technology innovation. This book helped him to integrate all of his collective thinking into the RISE with SAP context and share this with the community. He would like to thank his IBM mentors, such as Allan Coulter, Mike James, Sheri Hinish, and many others, as well as his coach, Hayden Bamber, for opening up new opportunities to him. In the end, for him, the book was a team effort and the final credit really goes to his fellow authors, Dharma Atluri, Adil Zafar, and Sanket Taur for inviting him to contribute.

Sanket Taur would like to dedicate this book to his wife, Janhavi Taur, for her steadfast support and patience throughout the past year and the understanding of his awesome son, Sharvil Taur, who showed great character while Sanket was busy writing the book on weekends or away taking care of his father. He drew the inspiration to complete this book from his father, the late Dr. Machindra Bajirao Taur, who achieved the amazing feat of completing his doctorate while fighting cancer in its final stages, and also his autobiography before he bid us all farewell. Dr. M. B. Taur was an accomplished professor with an unwavering commitment to guiding and shaping the lives of thousands of his students. He would also like to express his gratitude to his mentor, Allan Coulter, CTO SAP IBM; Andrew Worsley-Tonks, SAP Leader, EMEA; his IBM colleagues; and the client teams he worked with who gave him the opportunity to garner the valuable experience that has been reflected in this book.

Contributors

About the authors

Adil Zafar is an associate partner with over 22 years of experience as a S/4HANA technical architect. He is also the global leader for RISE with SAP at IBM. Over the years, Adil has developed into an all-rounder with a hands-on approach to winning and delivering SAP consulting services. Adil is an experienced S/4HANA technical solutions architect, technical project manager, and delivery manager. He is an experienced team builder, managing teams both onshore and offshore.

Dharma Alturi is an executive architect and AI/ML evangelist at IBM. He has more than 20 years of experience working in hybrid-cloud-driven architectural deployments, both SAP and non-SAP. He leads the RISE with SAP program for IBM as a chief architect, a service integrator, and the core design lead for putting together the architecture on multiple hyper-scalers. He has provided strategic direction to clients globally regarding the adoption of RISE with SAP, helping clients achieve the vision of being an intelligent and sustainable enterprise. His recent contributions towards RISE with SAP, sustainability, and data intelligence-driven use cases have been recognized by a global audience on different forums.

Sanket Taur is a technology evangelist and speaker at events with SAP ASUG, SAP TechEd, and IBM. He is an associate partner and a global offering leader in intelligent and sustainable enterprise within IBM, leading service offerings with ecosystem partners such as SAP, Red Hat, AWS, and Microsoft. He helps global clients across industries to define and realize their digital strategies and business transformation goals using hybrid cloud platforms and technology-driven, innovative digital solutions. He has influenced C-suites and business leads to create new service propositions for their customers while bridging the gap between their business visions and outcomes with new business models, helping to monetize the investment in technology.

Mihir R. Gor is an IBM distinguished engineer with over 25 years of successful project delivery experiences across large, complex, and global SAP programs. He is the IBM SAP global sustainability innovation CTO, responsible for driving new SAP solutions that can meet his client's sustainability goals and objectives. He is a trusted advisor who engages C-suites to help develop their transformation roadmaps toward becoming intelligent, sustainable enterprises using the industry best practices, reference architectures, S/4HANA, and SAP BTP solutions that operate across a hybrid cloud ecosystem. He is an IBM consulting thought leader, a TOGAF enterprise architect, an AWS Cloud Certified Architect, SAP BTP-certified, and a member of the British Computer Society.

About the reviewers

Suma Rammohan is an author, speaker, and accomplished technologist with business acumen specializing in ERP, especially SAP S/4 HANA.

She has held multiple roles throughout her career – pre-sales/solution architecture, consulting, delivery, and so on. She has worked at large global companies such as SAP Labs, IBM, and Accenture. She is currently a senior principal enterprise architect and pre-sales lead at Capgemini, supporting European clients on their transformation journeys and focusing on mega-sized deals. She has a strong client-facing role, solving business problems via technical innovative solutions, creating enterprise solutions, and taking part in co-design workshops/discussions with clients.

Her key skills include enterprise architecture, technical solutions, Agile methodology, the journey to the cloud, delivery management, and technological innovation. Her SAP skills span RISE with SAP offerings for private and public clouds, two-tiered ERP architecture, S/4 HANA (migration and greenfield implementations), Enterprise HANA, BW/4HANA, and embedded analytics.

Haishan Qian is a technology visionary leader for large-scale and high-performance enterprise applications. His focus areas include IT strategy planning, new innovations, global system architecture, and business process improvements. Currently working as a lead solution architect at Apple Inc., he leads cross-functional teams and designs, builds, and implements various enterprise financial systems that support Apple's global business operations, including its digital media store, subscription services, retail, and finished goods. Haishan lives with his family in Palo Alto, California.

A. B. Vijay Kumar is an IBM Distinguished Engineer and chief technology officer focused on hybrid cloud management and platform engineering. He is responsible for providing technology strategies for managing complex application portfolios on hybrid cloud platforms using emerging tools and technologies.

He is an IBM Master Inventor who has issued more than 31 patents and has 30 pending in his name. He has more than 23 years of experience at IBM. He is recognized as a subject matter expert for his contribution to advanced mobility in automation and has led several implementations involving complex industry solutions. He specializes in mobile technologies; cloud technologies; containers; automotive technologies; sensor-based, machine-to-machine technologies; the IoT; and telematics.

Table of Contents

Part 2: The Journey with RISE with SAP

4

Intelligent Enterprise and Sustainable Design   85

5

Cloud with Silver Lining: Busting the Myth – Part 1   123

Part 3: The Way Forward: The Art of Possible

9

The Pilot: High Stakes   273

10

Going All In: A Leap of Faith   313

11

Innovation Unleashed: The Hunger Games   361

12

Digital Supremacy – the Path to Sustainable Growth   395

Preface

Welcome to the first comprehensive guide on *RISE with SAP towards a Sustainable Enterprise*! Since the launch of RISE with SAP as an offering in January 2021, clients and consultants alike have been trying to figure out what needs to be considered and the benefits the program can provide to help revolutionize their journey toward the cloud and toward being a sustainable enterprise. This book provides a practical perspective on the journey to the cloud and beyond, with RISE with SAP enabling your transformation into a value-driven intelligent, sustainable, and resilient enterprise. For the successful adoption of S/4HANA and RISE with SAP, three key components need to be considered:

- Identifying the problem statement and use cases that are value-adding for the business

- Building a strong business case by being aware of all the possible levers, such as process discovery, process mining, the adoption of best practices, the automation of testing, and data migration, along with sustainability-driven, intelligent, enterprise-based use cases

- Knowing more about what RISE with SAP provides, gaining insight into the roles and responsibilities involved, and ensuring you avoid any surprise costs as you proceed with and sustain the implementation

There are many different blogs and independent **points of view** (POVs) published by members of the SAP community. The focus of this book is to provide a journey map to you as a client or consultant, not just detailing what RISE with SAP is but also walking you through each of our three aforementioned key components and enabling you to handle each of them without any ambiguity. We will provide relevant information not just about the offering but also about relevant use cases for it and the options available on the market that apply to these use cases. We will also outline the lessons learned in different sections to ensure you can plan appropriately for your adoption of various technologies and RISE with SAP as an offering.

Who this book is for

This book is targeted at CXOs, IT owners, architects, process owners, cloud security consultants, administrators, and project managers who need a consolidated overview of the value of RISE with SAP and the other services connected to it. We'll cover different industry use cases, along with the benefits realized by adopting RISE with SAP, and the potential journey map to follow to achieve the most cost-optimized scenario. We also believe this book is relevant to all SAP-interested readers across all industries and technologies, even outside S/4HANA, so that they can understand its actual impact on the wider ecosystem.

Throughout the book, you will learn about the different trends in the industry today and the impact they have on business outcomes. We will talk about how being aware of these allows organizations to build a strong business case for RISE with SAP. You will understand what RISE with SAP is, along with the different services and products made available as part of the ecosystem around it. You will be informed on how to make the right choices and decisions when it comes to defining their use cases, scopes, and journey maps in order to achieve a sustainable enterprise.

Let's go through some key personas and how the book will help them:

- **IT owner/CXO/SAP architects/process owners**: These personas will be involved from the initial evaluation of the journey toward the cloud, along with security and other key decision factors. These also focus on TCO reduction while providing users with a strategic platform for both automating and infusing AI-enabled intelligent workflows into their daily activities.

- **CXO/IT Owner**: These personas will also be interested in identifying how their IT costs translate into business benefits. They will also need help with building the business case to either move toward S/4HANA with RISE with SAP or just their journey toward the cloud in general. These personas will be interested in understanding the security implications, along with the ROI, when it comes to the various services on offer.

- **SAP architects**: These personas will be interested in how the landscape architecture changes. What new services are available that can help the implementation, its management, and the business teams involved? What services will be part of the baseline model and what other additional or optional services should be opted for? What services should be requested of partners and how will monthly, quarterly, and yearly release cycles look after the move to RISE with SAP?

- **Process owners**: These personas will be interested in what value moving to RISE with SAP adds from a business process point of view. These personas will also want to understand the intelligent workflows and transformation options available and their potential.

We want to encourage our readers to take a deep dive into the concepts we introduce in this book and keep them in mind when adopting, implementing, and migrating or upgrading to S/4HANA, RISE with SAP, and beyond, building the necessary skills to meet your particular needs.

What this book covers

This reference book on RISE with SAP is both an overview and a detailed look at several topics related to trend evolutions and business challenges, and how organizations can build business cases to justify the adoption of RISE with SAP. The book also deep dives into RISE with SAP as an offering, explaining its different services and the dos and don'ts involved to prepare for the right service delivery. The structure of this book will guide you from a strategic level to a practical level, explaining each of the levers and different components to be considered. On an ongoing basis, you can pick up different chapters as needed and still learn about all the required details by reading through a chapter. You'll only need to jump to other chapters if more details are needed. However, we recommend that you start from the beginning and work through the chapters in order because some topics are built upon in later chapters to avoid the repetition of certain topics. *Chapter 1* and *Chapter 2* will provide you with the full context needed for the rest of the book.

To make the learnings more relevant and interesting we have introduced a business case: a hypothetical global electronics brand Spark4Life, facing unprecedented challenges due to the recent global upheavals. Every chapter helps you to go through the due diligence required for the pivotal decisions that need to be made at every stage of the transformation that Spark4Life sets out to take on. While doing so, we have given numerous examples and use cases helping solve the business challenges step by step. To ultimately bring it all together in the last few chapters to help you see how all the decisions (related to people, process and technology) taken in the previous chapters has helped turn the tide for Spark4Life and to reveal how the holistic transformation is greater than sum of its parts.

This book is organized into three parts; here's a quick overview of each:

In *Part I*, *Overview*, you will understand the need for innovation and the patterns evolving in the market both pre- and post-pandemic, along with the risks that businesses and clients need to prepare to face to survive in the market. We will then look at persona-based journeys for CXOs and businesses to identify how different LOBs need to evolve and how to manage expectations throughout this evolution. Furthermore, this part will set the context of how RISE with SAP, along with the industry solutions built around it, can help you achieve the objectives and the vision that you have initially set out. This part includes the following chapters:

- *Chapter 1, Truth and Dare: The CXO Challenges*

  This chapter provides an overview of various challenges faced by the CXOs in terms of the current market, financial aspects, regulation compliance, evolving technology, evolving customer perspectives, operational aspects, organizational aspects, and environmental aspects. You are given a glimpse of each of these ambits and how they impact the business operating model, with examples.

- *Chapter 2, Faith of Four: Vision of the Masters*

  Chapter 2 builds on the challenges mentioned in *Chapter 1* by walking you through the levers of change and various decisions to be made by CXOs to overcome these challenges in the context of a business transformation. This chapter goes through the perspective of CEOs, CFOs, CTOs/CIOs, and CSOs. It then sets the context of actual business challenges and the key objectives to address in both the short and long term. It then takes you through the typical issues within the landscape of an example organization and the different steps to go through to achieve what is needed, applying different levers such as S/4HANA adoption, the journey to the cloud using RISE with SAP, process mining/discovery, best practices, industry solutions, the relevance of data migration, and the adoption of different intelligent workflows, along with automation.

- *Chapter 3, Eureka Moment: The Missing Link*

  In *Chapter 3*, we expand upon one of the key components mentioned in *Chapter 2* – what RISE with SAP is, why RISE with SAP is useful, and the different options available within RISE with SAP, along with other alternate options beyond RISE with SAP. You will understand in detail how RISE with SAP as an offering can address business challenges and help achieve an organization's vision and objective, enabling value-driven outcomes. We will also dispel various myths around RISE with SAP to ensure that the right decisions can be made along the way. We will wrap up with a sample journey map for how a customer organization has evolved over different stages by leveraging RISE with SAP.

Next is *Part II, The Journey with RISE with SAP*. This part includes the following chapters:

- *Chapter 4, Intelligent Enterprise and Sustainable Design*

  Chapter 4 provides you with details about what steps can be considered by CXOs and how organizations can use the tools and services offered by RISE with SAP to help pave the roadmap toward becoming a sustainable enterprise. The chapter walks you through the basics of BTP, the design principles to follow from a shift-left POV, insight-driven approaches, the adoption of a clean core, and sustainable, intelligent workflow-based solutions.

- *Chapter 5, The Cloud with a Silver Lining: Busting the Myth – Part 1*

  Chapter 5 walks you through all the dimensions and parameters to be considered when building a business case for both the adoption of S/4HANA as part of the RISE with SAP offering and the different services under consideration. You will also get more information about the different industry trends to consider, as a follow-up to *Chapter 1*, and how RISE with SAP addresses these. You will then get insights into the architectural patterns of RISE with SAP, along with what is possible and what is not possible with RISE with SAP. We will wrap up by providing possible alternatives to RISE with SAP in case you are not yet ready for the journey to the cloud or the move toward S/4HANA but are still looking for managed services temporarily.

- *Chapter 6, The Cloud with a Silver Lining: Busting the Myth – Part 2*

  Chapter 6, as a continuation of the previous chapter, dives deeper into the different types of variants available within RISE with SAP and what they mean to you. The chapter then walks through the roles and responsibilities made available by SAP, defined as Standard, Additional, and Optional services, allowing you to make the right decision around the scope of services to select. You will also be given information on how to handle rollouts and upgrades as part of RISE with SAP and how daily life will change in terms of the application management services within the RISE with SAP offering. We will wrap up the chapter by introducing the **Cloud Application Service** (**CAS**) packages offered by SAP as part of RISE with SAP and how they complement the Standard, Additional, and Optional roles and responsibilities mentioned earlier.

- *Chapter 7, Back to the Drawing Board: Reimagined Processes*

  Chapter 7 provides an overview of how the design inputs across the different levers mentioned so far will influence the overall design and enable you to simulate and model new processes for future customer and employee experiences, changing existing processes and considering and introducing new processes. The chapter provides insight into how SAP Signavio Journey Modeler, for instance, can be used to design the **user experience** (**UX**), along with an organization's operating model and the relevant workflows. You will also see how the data within the landscape can be leveraged to generate value-driven insights for your business. You will then get information about how these insights can be consumed to orchestrate relevant, intelligent workflows that can eventually solve the challenges that we have previously identified.

- *Chapter 8, The Exodus: Data That Matters*

  Chapter 8 provides you with details on how important it is to plan your data migration to a target S/4HANA instance based on the type of migration activity planned as part of the move to the cloud (RISE with SAP). The chapter also provides an overview of why data governance and data quality are important aspects when it comes to safeguarding your investment in AI and intelligent workflow-based solutions. We finally wrap up the chapter by looking into SAP Activate Methodology and the adoption patterns available when it comes to data migration.

We'll conclude this book with *Part III, The Way Forward: Art of Possible*, which includes the following chapters:

- *Chapter 9, The Pilot: High-Stakes*

  Chapter 9 brings forward all the practices and best practices mentioned so far in the book to enable you to understand how these can help accelerate your transition toward becoming an intelligent and sustainable enterprise. You will be provided details on how the implementation/migration effort can be shifted left using the ready-to-use content from SAP and its partners. You will also be informed about the key dimensions of the UX strategy to be considered to achieve the desired business outcomes. Finally, we will wrap up the chapter by talking about the change and release management to be considered when deploying a pilot for either a region or a representative business unit before proceeding with a global rollout, which is termed "all in."

- *Chapter 10, All In: A Leap of Faith*

  Chapter 10 is about how to convert a successful pilot implementation into a global rollout, considering multiple localization- and regulation compliance-related requirements to make sure the solution is globally ready, including those of various processes that might be unique to certain countries. This chapter will provide you with insights into the factors to be considered when defining the instance strategy and the rollout strategy.

- *Chapter 11, Innovation Unleashed: A Hunger Game*

  Chapter 11 takes you beyond the initial implementation, providing information on why continuous innovation/improvement beyond the initial iteration is important for an organization to continue to evolve. This chapter will provide insight into how the cultural shift toward innovation within an organization plays a key role in this cycle. It will then provide a walk-through of the importance of enterprise agility and scalability as the key aspects to support an emerging operating model as trends progress. We will then explore the Web 3.0 and Industry 4.0 models, along with their importance to organizations driving intelligent solutions. We will wrap up the chapter with information on different business and commercial models to consider.

- *Chapter 12, Digital Supremacy: The Path to Sustainable Growth*

  In the final chapter of the book, we will summarize the findings from each of the chapters, along with the ongoing vision organizations can plan to differentiate themselves. You will also understand the steps you need to take to achieve the vision you have laid out and what to consider at different stages.

Download the color images

We also provide a PDF file that has color images of the screenshots and diagrams used in this book. You can download it here: `https://packt.link/pz5gp`.

Conventions used

> **Tips or important notes**
> Appear like this.

Get in touch

Feedback from our readers is always welcome.

General feedback: If you have questions about any aspect of this book, email us at `customercare@packtpub.com` and mention the book title in the subject of your message.

Errata: Although we have taken every care to ensure the accuracy of our content, mistakes do happen. If you have found a mistake in this book, we would be grateful if you would report this to us. Please visit `www.packtpub.com/support/errata` and fill in the form.

Piracy: If you come across any illegal copies of our works in any form on the internet, we would be grateful if you would provide us with the location address or website name. Please contact us at `copyright@packt.com` with a link to the material.

If you are interested in becoming an author: If there is a topic that you have expertise in and you are interested in either writing or contributing to a book, please visit `authors.packtpub.com`.

Share Your Thoughts

Once you've read *RISE with SAP towards a Sustainable Enterprise*, we'd love to hear your thoughts! Scan the QR code below to go straight to the Amazon review page for this book and share your feedback.

https://packt.link/r/1801812748

Your review is important to us and the tech community and will help us make sure we're delivering excellent quality content.

Download a free PDF copy of this book

Thanks for purchasing this book!

Do you like to read on the go but are unable to carry your print books everywhere?

Is your eBook purchase not compatible with the device of your choice?

Don't worry, now with every Packt book you get a DRM-free PDF version of that book at no cost.

Read anywhere, any place, on any device. Search, copy, and paste code from your favorite technical books directly into your application.

The perks don't stop there, you can get exclusive access to discounts, newsletters, and great free content in your inbox daily

Follow these simple steps to get the benefits:

1. Scan the QR code or visit the link below

https://packt.link/free-ebook/9781801812740

2. Submit your proof of purchase
3. That's it! We'll send your free PDF and other benefits to your email directly

Part 1: Overview

In *Part 1*, readers will understand the need for innovation and the patterns evolving in the market both pre- and post-pandemic, along with the risks that businesses and clients need to prepare to face to survive in the market. The reader will then look at persona-based journeys for CXOs and businesses to identify how different LOBs need to evolve and how to manage expectations throughout this evolution. Furthermore, this part will set the context of how RISE with SAP, along with the industry solutions built around it, can help you achieve the objectives and the vision that you have initially set out.

This part has the following chapters:

- *Chapter 1, Truth and Dare: The CXO Challenges*
- *Chapter 2, Faith of Four: Vision of the Masters*
- *Chapter 3, Eureka Moment: The Missing Link*

1

Truth and Dare –
The CxO Challenges

If one is asked the question of what is at the heart of any change for an organization, the response, more often than not, would be the *consumer*. Whether it relates to sustainable products, user experience, or value for money, the list is endless. While consumers come in all forms, such as end users, end consumers, wholesalers, and retailers, the outcome is the same. Consumers generate demand and cause a shift in the business ecosystem.

The example of the consumer is just one of many reasons businesses will react to challenges. Their reaction will be one of survival or adaption to change. In this chapter, we will look at what challenges businesses face on a day-to-day basis. To define a way forward, we will explore the characteristics of challenges in order to understand them, determine how to address them and find a solution, and examine how they impact the decision makers we know as the CxOs or the C-suite.

As you proceed to read through this book, you'll see that it has been designed to give real examples of challenges and provide solutions based on RISE with SAP as the platform to deliver a S/4HANA transformation. Although we appreciate that digital transformations can take many forms and scopes, our objective is to first provide you with an appreciation of the challenges businesses face and how they impact businesses, and how CxOs can react to those challenges in determining a solution.

The challenges impacting the day-to-day activities of a business can be defined in eight broad categories:

- The market
- Financial challenges
- Regulation compliance
- Technology evolution
- Evolving customer perspectives
- Operational challenges

- Organizational challenges
- Environmental challenges

Let's begin!

The market

There are external factors that affect businesses and how CXOs are compelled to make decisions to avert any short- and medium-term effects. Market-related effects are impacted by many factors, and this list is by no means exhaustive but only a glimpse into some of those issues.

Uncertainty about the future

If we all had a crystal ball or the ability to have knowledge of the future, it would help to weather the storm of change, but more importantly, thrive under such conditions. Alas, those prophetic abilities are in short supply, but there is a serious point to the uncertain future. It remains a constant threat to organizations' ability to deliver their services and products to market.

A business must determine ways in which to temper the constant flux in demand – changes in the market that can and do divert the organization's focus and can be exhausting and exacerbating. As the world becomes more uncertain, those organizations that can thrive under such conditions will have an advantage.

Trends

If we look at the last 3 years, during COVID-19, we can clearly see a surge of activity in conducting meetings remotely, with little or no travel. If we look at the impact of global warming, it can be seen as one of the direct causes of the increase in energy prices. The point we are making is that any trend has a *cause* and an *effect*.

In a similar fashion, whatever the trend we see, whether induced by technological advancements, environmental factors, or global health-related, it forces a shift in demand and supply, which invariably impacts the organization's ability to react.

Glocalization

According to Encyclopedia Britannica, the definition of glocalization has become more relevant than at any time before, where regional and global synergies are reflected at local levels. There has been a shift in developing global products and services at a global level that have local brand recognition, making them more relevant to the local market. For example, KFC is a global brand with common products available, but at the local level, you will find market-focused products.

If we look at this through the lens of an organization, it is acclimatizing its products and services created for the global market for its local market presence by adapting them to local cultures. For example, Frito-Lay, a division of PepsiCo, primarily uses the brand name "Lay's" in the United States and uses other brand names in certain other countries: Walkers in the UK and Ireland and Smith's in Australia.

The impact of localization is global and increases the challenges of ensuring the continuity of a brand, its quality, and the supply of its products and services.

The supply chain

There is a lack of supply chain diversity and the risk of multiple points of failure when relying on a globally distributed just-in-time supply chain. These are often broken, rigid, and have a myriad of regulations, increasing the threat of geo-political or climate-related disruption, with increased costs to sustain those supply chains, and making them less predictable. How do businesses protect their supply chain from becoming disrupted?

Financial challenges

The financial effect on a business is all too apparent, whether it's the effect of the rise in an interest rate in the US or the price of crude oil. The change in the value of the USD against the GBP determines the profitability of a company when it announces its results in USD. The value of a stronger USD gives a business greater purchasing power. In this section, we are going to understand the cost challenges businesses face.

CapEx versus OpEx

As is commonly understood, CapEx or **Capital Expenditures (CapEx)** derives from the purchases an organization makes that are for the long term or where the return on investment is seen over a long period of time. Conversely, **Operating Expenditures (OpEx)** are those expenses that are derived over a short period of time, that is, which are accounted for on a day-to-day, week-by-week, or month-by-month basis.

As consumers have adapted to the *pay-as-you-go* model of paying only on consumption of a service, the same has now happened with organizations where technology has moved rapidly in providing businesses a pay-as-you-go model for using traditional IT services heavily dependent on CapEx, and they can now be seen as IT as a service. The challenge here for organizations is to adapt to a differing financial model and accounting principles, along with managing those services.

Maintenance costs

The support and maintenance of infrastructure, whether bricks and mortar or hardware and applications, draw similar parallels. Both require constant maintenance, upgrades, and expansion as the business grows.

For IT applications that are at the core of supporting the operations of a business, two key challenges are always at the forefront:

- Keeping the existing systems going
- Adapting to new technologies without affecting the business

The question arises at what point do you stick to what you know and continue investing in existing initiatives and at what point do you divert and start to change the focus to new technologies?

The cost of living

It would have been unthinkable only a few years ago if the cost of living was quoted as a factor affecting decisions taken by the C-Suite. However, in recent times, it's seen as the measurement of everyday items, such as fuel, energy, groceries, mortgages, travel, and many other things.

What is the cause of this cost-of-living crisis? The slow emergence from COVID-19 impacted supplies of raw materials and thus caused a surge in costs. The geopolitical impact in Europe of the war in Ukraine impacted energy supplies from Russia. The effects of Brexit affected imports from EU countries and compounded the already depressing situation regarding the surge in the cost of living. All of these things converged, creating a crescendo of uncertainty, and limiting the already regressed business recovery.

The CPI inflation forecast published by the UK government's Office for Budget Responsibility provides an insight into the inflationary impact on the economy:

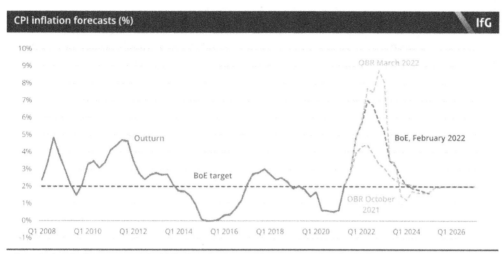

Source: Institute for Government analysis of Office for Budget Responsibility, Economic and Fiscal Outlook, October 2021 and March 2022 and Bank of England, Monetary Policy Report, February 2022. (cc) BY-NC

Figure 1.1: Inflation forecast in the United Kingdom issued by the Office for Budget Responsibility

The forecast nominal and real average earnings growth published provide an insight into the average earnings growth impact on the economy:

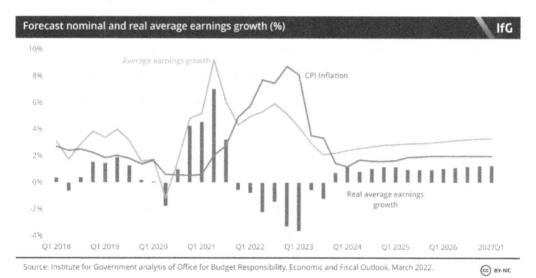

Source: Institute for Government analysis of Office for Budget Responsibility, Economic and Fiscal Outlook, March 2022. (cc) BY-NC

Figure 1.2: Earnings forecast in the United Kingdom issued by the Office for Budget Responsibility (https://www.instituteforgovernment.org.uk/publication/spring-statement-2022/cost-living-crisis)

Lack of investment

To some, a lack of investment in talent and innovation to support a business is an existential threat to its very survival. Looking at the last 3 years of the pandemic, the overnight adoption of remote working was like the flick of a switch. If your workforce is not ready to adopt change due to a lack of investment, then challenges are compounded. Similarly, if your organization is not set up to adopt new innovations, it will cause a huge upheaval when change is forced upon the organization. We have seen this with many tech companies that started sending thousands of laptops to their employees to cater to remote working. See this link to read more about it: `https://www.zdnet.com/article/` `coronavirus-how-we-got-10000-staff-remote-working-from-home-in-just-` `one-weekend/`.

The lack of the right talent has been steadily building up for years, and organizations are continually battling with attrition. We are now entering a digital era of accelerated change and organizations need to counter that with the right talent investment, not just in complex low-touch tech skills, but also basic tech skills just to keep up with all of the changes, such as working remotely and interacting using remote PMO tools such as Jira, Mural, Slack, and so on. If you don't keep up with change, then there is every chance the organization will fall further behind, due to not reacting to demand and changes in technology focus, and not harnessing new talent with the skills required.

The failure to innovate will almost certainly leave many organizations behind. The ONS carried out a survey on the impact of the coronavirus pandemic and other events on UK businesses and the economy. This survey was based on responses from the voluntary fortnightly business survey (BICS) about financial performance, workforce, prices, trade, and business resilience. The following figure shows the stark reality that up to 26% of businesses were either temporarily or permanently closed. It can be presumed that some of those closures were a result of inaction, lack of innovation, inflexibility in business processes, and a lack of agility in technology:

Figure 1.3: Impact of COVID-19 on businesses (https://www.ons.gov.uk/businessindustryandtrade/ business/businessservices/bulletins/businessinsightsandimpactontheukeconomy/8april2021)

The lack of investment in people and technology go hand in hand, and during times of economic, political, societal, and technological changes, it would be an unthinkable decision to not innovate and include technology within a business model, alongside the right talent to help accelerate the change from survival to prosperity. The COVID-19 pandemic is just one example of the myriad of challenges that impact businesses and how those challenges are met is the key to success. The number of businesses impacted by COVID-19 was beyond anyone's imagination. Almost a million UK businesses were at serious risk of bankruptcy before April 2021. See the report by Peter Lambert and John Van Reenen here: https://blogs.lse.ac.uk/businessreview/2021/02/02/a-wave-of-covid-related-bankruptcies-is-coming-to-the-uk-what-can-we-do-about-it/.

Recession

There is not a single person today who has not experienced a recession. The reality is that recession will impact every single person in some way, and this includes businesses. If you take the current economic situation in the United Kingdom, the country is facing its highest inflation since the conversion to decimal currency back in 1971. We are all experiencing the impact of inflation, with increased prices of basic consumer goods, including energy prices, along with higher interest rates.

Pensions and investment portfolios have most likely been impacted by inflation and the threat of a recession, and this is yet another challenge for businesses when they must cut back to survival mode as they brace themselves for a sharp decline in consumer confidence and spending. As a result of a recession, unemployment goes up because businesses have to cut back their workforce in order to manage the challenges of reduced consumer spending.

Return on investment

For a business to invest in any opportunity, it must consider the **return on investment** (**ROI**). However, it's important to first understand the expected outcome expected of the ROI. Here are some focus areas for a C-Suite to look at when considering ROI:

- Better customer experience and satisfaction and improved customer service and support
- Increased usability leads to increased sales
- Increased user satisfaction
- Improved/automated business processes
- Better access to data insights
- Improved digital executive dashboard
- Better forecasting
- Improved software vendor support
- Reduction in vendors and smoother service delivery

ROI is usually a metric that is used to understand the profitability of an investment. However, when it comes to understanding ROI in technology and solutions, it relies on measures made up of several other KPIs. Here are some examples:

- Revenue enhancement – where the investment results in increased sales

- Cost reduction – faster MRP runs and a reduction in operational and maintenance costs

- Cost avoidance – fewer outages and increased productivity

- Capital reduction – a shift from CapEx to OpEx

- Capital avoidance – divest investment from fixed assets

Accuracy cost estimation

Estimating the cost of a project or service being delivered is one of the most important functions in IT. The impact of a wrongly estimated IT program not only hurts the business financially but diverting key resources to the project means the loss of time on other initiatives, which would have otherwise driven growth.

With failed, overrun projects drawing away investment and resources away from the business, the challenges of cost estimation are largely centered around people, processes, and technology:

- Data-driven insight is critical to estimating the cost of a program

- Process adoption opportunities that would lead to greater returns and profitability

- Estimation requires strong and timely alignment across stakeholders

- ROI – time spent and the value generated in spending time on estimations

Regulation compliance

If you look at the history of regulations, they were created to protect – to protect businesses and consumers, to promote fairness and efficiency, and to encourage healthy competition.

Regulatory compliance exists to ensure that organizations not only comply with the legal statutes laid down by the local laws in a country but there are additional laws that pertain to specific industries that require additional rules in order to maintain those policies.

There are local, regional, and global laws for all organizations to follow and comply with, however, in order to maintain transparency both operationally and financially, organizations are adopting more consolidated sets of rules, policies, and compliances.

There are typically six types of regulations:

- Laws that impose burdens
- Laws that directly confer rights and/or provide protection
- Self-regulation
- Licensing bodies and inspectorates
- Economic regulators
- Regulators of public sector activities

In other words, regulations and compliance are where a set of rules and policies are set by a body that forms a part of external factors that are deemed necessary for businesses to comply with. These can be standardization, regulations, and legislation. These cannot be bypassed or ignored as they will invariably cause issues in the long run. For instance, non-compliance with the net-zero carbon footprint goal may preclude a business from entering a market in Singapore.

The topic of regulatory compliance is vast. For the purposes of understanding the challenges faced by businesses, there are three regulatory compliances that may specifically affect how businesses are able to function in specific regions and countries that would impact their IT solutions. Let's check them out in the following subsections.

GDPR

The **General Data Protection Regulation** (**GDPR**) centers around privacy and security laws of individuals and consumers and it is seen as the toughest privacy and security law in the world. Although the laws apply to companies in the **European Union** (**EU**), its impact in terms of obligations organizations have is vast and covers businesses situated anywhere in the world, so long as they target or collect data related to people in the EU.

The consequences of ignoring GDPR can mean heavy fines for a business, which could result in reputational and financial damage or even exclusion from carrying out any business in the EU. Fines can reach tens of millions of euros.

The CCPA

The **California Consumer Privacy Act** (**CCPA**) was inspired by the work carried out in the EU for GDPR, and in the state of California, businesses' privacy policies are required to include information on consumers' privacy rights. The world's largest and most successful electronic, big tech, financial services, and energy companies are headquartered in Silicon Valley, so where more appropriate to apply this act than the state where the impact is greatest?

Such laws, as described here, form the fundamental policy of businesses, and adherence is as essential as adhering to human rights laws pertaining to work and pay conditions.

Industry regulations

Industry regulations are rules and policies applied by an expert agency in that industry that govern the behavior of businesses. These regulations are supplemental to the fundamental laws applied across all businesses and organizations relating to privacy, security, and ordinary common law rules. In summary, these additional laws ensure there are no gaps in compliance with any laws governing industry-specific regulations.

Data residency

Whenever discussions are centered around business transformation, the subject of data residency is often not the most pressing issue to be addressed. However, it's a topic that causes the most concern when it comes to compliance with regulatory and taxation laws and perhaps for policy reasons imposed by the business itself. This is when businesses specifically ask for their data to reside in certain geographical locations.

Another contrasting aspect is the consideration of data localization where the law of the country requires that data created within a certain territory stays within that territory. For example, Russian federal law dictates that both Russian and foreign companies that manage and collect the personal data of Russian citizens must have the data stored locally within the Russian Federation.

Technology evolution

A recent IBV report stated that "An uneven response to the COVID-19 pandemic has taught us that to operate effectively in the presence of an unanticipated crisis, organizations need to be agile, robust, and secure. They need to be able to seamlessly engage customers and employees in both physical and digital domains. However, current events have been challenging —even painful—as industries and enterprises react and adapt."

Flexible adoption of new technology

Today, when we refer to the flexibility of adoption of technology, it is not just centered around IT infrastructure, that is, the hybrid cloud. There are also a number of other considerations, such as the adoption of new processes, techniques, and innovations, including AI and ML.

From a digital transformation perspective, there are four characteristics that need to underpin any transformation and the adoption of new technology:

- **Agile**: Based on the fundamental principle of keeping the core clean, standardizing business processes provides agility in extending the business processes and integrating with other solutions without disruption.

- **Flexible**: A cloud infrastructure inherently provides flexibility in terms of services that are on offer. That flexibility goes further into the application layer when you want to increase or reduce the number of services provided. This is even more critical when you want to scale as the needs of the business change.

- **Consumable**: Switch from CapEx to an OpEx financial cost mode to pay for a service, whether related to infrastructure, software, or services.

- **Software innovation**: Innovating at the speed of external innovation comes with its own challenges and businesses have never been able to truly master this, with the disruption of maintaining business as usual and at the same time bringing in new enhancements and innovation.

Technology strategy

With the backdrop of adopting new technologies, what are the challenges businesses face when considering digital transformation in the cloud?

- Business transformation rather than more of the same.

- Focusing on the value addition that the cloud brings. For example, opening up a technology platform to intelligent workflows accelerates moves to both enterprise platforms and the cloud.

- Innovating at the speed of external innovation. An enterprise platform must deliver new innovations without additional cost and with minimal impact.

- The number of options when adopting and adapting to the cloud when shifting core business processes, for example, hybrid migration in less time to preserve the investment.

- A consumption-based offering that compliments software application flexibility in delivering a complete solution.

- Greater emphasis on cost efficiencies, that is, lower TCO and shifting the cost model.

Emerging new technologies

With the emergence of Industry 4.0 technology (for instance, IoT, digital twins, and AI), products have become more connected, and OEMs and service providers now have ready access to products' and equipment's field performance data. This enables them to analyze, predict, and control the performance in order to maximize the efficiency at the customer's end.

Integrating and keeping up with the evolution of technology is yet another example of how businesses are under immense pressure to continually re-invent themselves to remain relevant both for consumers as well as for stakeholders.

Evolving customer perspectives

With the evolution of smart devices over the last two decades, fueled by the revolution of social media platforms, access to information is at the core of the evolving customer perspective.

Faster access to information, helping people to make informed decisions, and changing trends mean all of this has impacted the way businesses have had to adapt and react. At the same time, business are treating products/equipment not as CapEx anymore but as OpEx during the complete maintenance life cycle (from CapEx to OpEx).

Consistent customer service

A good customer experience is at the heart of business success and forms a key part of the business strategy to create and improve on a great customer experience through seamless, effective customer interaction.

Research by American Express found that the most common reason why customers take their business elsewhere is not that they are dissatisfied with the product or service they bought, but rather the post-sales customer service.

Read this to learn more: `https://www.americanexpress.com/en-us/business/trends-and-insights/articles/why-86-of-customers-quit-your-business/`.

The challenge of maintaining consistent customer service remains a volatile endeavor, with fluctuating demand and the quality of products and services making delivering a brand identity associated with customer satisfaction just one of many considerations businesses need to incorporate in their strategy.

Operational challenges

Operational challenges for businesses have become more acute in the last few years due to COVID-19; however, these pressures have always been present. The question remains as to what those operational challenges are and how you can determine where lies the greatest effort in overcoming them. Although operational issues cannot be bound to a mere few, the following are some challenges that have a wide impact on businesses through an IT lens.

Sustainable supply chain pressures

Every one of us has a story about how the pandemic impacted our daily lives, whether it was a lack of goods on the shelves, price increases for goods and services, a lack of availability of car parts, or a lack of critical medical services. All of these and so much more have been topics of discussion in our homes, in our businesses, and in every sphere of life.

Take any business today, and there will have been an impact on the supply chain, which can be determined by cause and effect. Take the motor industry as an example, which runs on the just-in-time approach. It cannot manage vast quantities of raw materials because the throughput would not change no matter how fast you delivered the raw material. Yet during the pandemic, we saw a lack of raw materials, which determined the pace at which cars could be manufactured.

Managing a myriad of factors, such as people, processes, partners, materials, services, and so on. determines how operationally effective a business is, and this is a key issue keeping our leaders awake at night.

Resourcing issues regarding raw materials, people, and skill gaps

There is a direct link between the cost of operations and the resources at a business's disposal. No matter what business you are in, cost control, especially within IT operations, plays a significant role in operational efficiency. The following factors impact operations:

- **The right talent**: It does not matter how advanced technology has become if you do not have the right talent to harness that technology to your advantage. A vastly underestimated aspect that businesses only started to learn about a few years ago is that developing and nurturing talent is at the core of a business's survival.

  If we look at attrition in just the last 2 years, the IT industry has seen a surge since the passing of the peak of the pandemic.

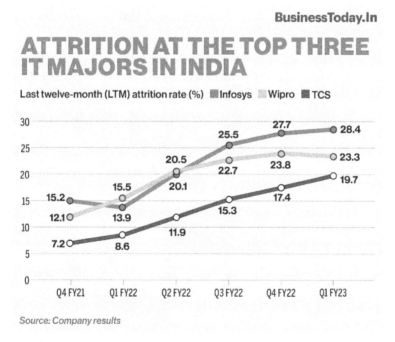

Figure 1.4: Attrition trend in the IT services industry in India due to COVID-19 (https://www.businesstoday.in/latest/corporate/story/why-infosys-tcs-wipro-and-other-indian-it-giants-are-facing-record-high-attrition-rates-346139-2022-09-01)

As we came out of the pandemic, we saw demand outstrip supply as the economy started to recover. Organizations' inability to be able to keep pace with demand, with the backdrop of attrition, was coupled with intense competition for skilled labor where the skilled workforce had a choice of taking up roles that suited their economic and personal circumstances better.

We saw the transportation and logistics sector hit particularly hard, with layoffs taking place due to the pandemic and then huge delays in the re-hiring process, which included following regulatory compliance and security protocols in hiring in sensitive sectors of the travel industry, causing numerous scheduled flights to be canceled as airlines were unable to cope with the demand: `https://www.mckinsey.com/capabilities/operations/our-insights/navigating-the-labor-mismatch-in-us-logistics-and-supply-chains`.

- **The availability of technology**: With the impending end of Moore's law, we cannot simply rely on the availability of faster computers to give businesses the edge they need to be operationally efficient. Although speed is one factor, the availability of the right technology and the ability to adopt it and harness it is a challenge businesses are facing. What good would Facebook be if we did not have smart devices?

    Taking it a step further, the availability of new and improved business application processes and solutions and adoption at pace is another challenge businesses are facing. After all, how is it possible to infuse efficiency without new technologies helping accelerate the pace of bringing in operational effectiveness?

- **The availability of services**: Since the launch of the smartphone, we have seen rapid changes in the services being developed and delivered to consumers. No one would have thought 20 years ago that the retail high street would no longer be required to purchase essential everyday items.

    When AWS was launched in early 2002, an internal paper was published that determined what Amazon's internal infrastructure should look like. It was suggested to sell it as a service and a business case was prepared for it. Two years later, Amazon implemented SAP for its internal businesses, and this gave rise to SAP applications being offered as a non-productive service to the masses. This also gave way to the pay-per-use model in consuming services.

If those services are not present, it is a hindrance to bringing in operation as a service. For businesses, the challenge remains adopting technology and services that are relevant today and can be adapted to suit the needs and requirements of the future.

The multi-vendor model

Traditional IT operations have been predicated on businesses interacting with multiple vendors and suppliers to deliver a service. For any IT solution, up to more than 10 suppliers can be seen interacting with the business. These can be suppliers of any of the following:

- Software licenses (OSs, databases, applications, security, network, storage)
- Hardware (laptops, servers, storage devices)
- Data centers (client-owned, vendor-owned, or in the cloud)
- Infrastructure service providers
- Implementation service providers
- Application-managed service providers
- Technical-managed service providers
- Network service providers

Each service contract will have different end dates, exit clauses, penalties, and SLAs. Managing the sheer complexity of services being delivered to the CIO's office requires a lot of resources. As mentioned earlier, it also means having the right talent to support the whole IT operation. A multi-vendor lock-in, unless carefully managed, could pose a risk to the business in delivering value, and instead increase the total cost of ownership.

The pressure is immense in ensuring operational efficiency is balanced with technological advancement without compromising IT services delivered to the business itself as well as to its consumers.

Choosing a SAP service provider

In the previous section, we mentioned the choice of services provided to businesses in supporting their IT operations and how we now see thousands of providers delivering those same services. If we look at SAP partners, then there are over 26,000 SAP partners who deliver valuable IT services. A list of SAP partners can be seen here: `https://www.sap.com/uk/partner/`.

What's the best way to choose a partner to deliver services? It all depends on the requirements, since many of them could be met through one or more similar services. So, what are the factors affecting the choice? It's important to note that organizations are looking to deliver value in any transformation, and there are three factors that will affect the outcome:

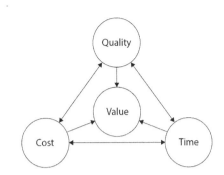

Figure 1.5: Factors affecting transformation value

- **Time**: How long does it take to deliver the service? In this case, it could be serviced by a partner to deliver an implementation of new business processes, or an upgrade to the software, for example, the efficiency with which new business processes are implemented via an upgrade from SAP ECC 6.0 to SAP S/4HANA varies from customer to customer. Typical timelines vary from 4-12 months.

- **Quality**: It's a misconception that IT operations must be of the highest quality. Just as we have the choice of buying a Rolls Royce or a VW Beetle, there are qualitative choices. These are usually determined by the category of partner you choose, experience in the particular industry, the talent pool, certifications, customer feedback, partner classification by vendor, brand, reputation, and so on.

- **Price**: Another misconception is that price is always a factor in determining your choice of partner to deliver a service. Wrong! You'll have heard the old saying "cheap and cheerful." Well, if you choose a cheap option, you will have to compromise on quality and time. Among the factors determining the value to the business, it requires a fine balance – if you compromise on one thing, you must give up on another. So, price is an important factor at a cost of quality or time.

Key considerations for businesses when opting for a cloud provider

When considering adopting cloud hosting providers for your business as the next evolutionary step in your transformation journey, along with improving operational efficiency, each provider is different in what services it offers, so careful consideration is needed.

Businesses may adopt the copycat approach and follow other organizations in similar industries, in the hope that it pays similar dividends. Is this the right approach? Can one company's adoption of the cloud mean another would share the same fate?

According to a recent IBV report, for many companies, the journey to the cloud lacks transparency. It states that there is often a perception that leaders presume their organization is faring better than expected when adopting cloud transformation. The recent survey states the contrary.

The IBV report provides a transformation index on the state of cloud transformation, shown in the following figure, which organizations can use to gauge how well they actually fare against industry norms. The index is built on the research of more than 3,000 C-Suite decision-makers across 12 countries and 23 industries.

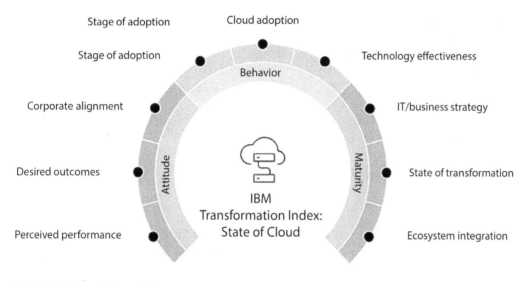

Figure 1.6: Transformation index (https://www.ibm.com/thought-leadership/institute-business-value/en-us/report/transformation-index)

Keeping the lights on

Delivering business continuity and resilience is at the back of the mind of every CIO, and whether its COVID-19, war in Europe, or the impact of climate change, those businesses that do not pay enough attention to this are faced with consequences that result in the following:

- Damage to the brand and reputation, where consumers lose confidence. It is now expected that the delivery of services should be uninterrupted.

- Financial loss because of unexpected downtime and breach of contract.

- Failure to repair consumer confidence can result in business closure.

Organizational challenges

It's said that culture and transformation are two sides of the same coin in an organization, intrinsically linked and going hand in hand when digital transformation is seen as a cultural change within the business. However, businesses that attempt to digitally transform to adopt new processes, new policies, and new approaches are faced with the challenge of transforming their own culture, attitude to technology, and people, since change is reflected in the needs of employees and customers. In this section, we will look at the factors affecting transformation, taking into account culture and people.

Transformation challenges – business- or IT-driven

A recent study, referenced here, revealed that some organizations' ability to carry out digital transformation and modernization programs was not geared up for the future.

Factors affecting transformation

Here are the list of factors affecting transformation:

- Talent shortage: we have already discussed the issues with attrition taking place due to the surge in demand since the pandemic. It's not only that there's a lack of skills but there's a lack of the right skills to help with the transformation.

- **Adversity to change**: It's a natural phenomenon that our initial reaction to any change is a negative one, and businesses are no different. It can sometimes feel like an uphill battle to change that mindset and move from a headwind to a tailwind toward transformation.

- **Re-skilling**: Investment is needed, as is the patience to re-skill the workforce to adapt to the new changes that the transformation will bring.

- **Cost impact on the bottom line**: This is one of the most critical factors in deciding whether the transformation will bring true ROI or TCO to, in effect, deliver the justification that it was all well worth it.

- **Lack of stakeholder buy-in**: If key sponsors are not aligned at the board level, then no amount of pushing from middle management will make this a success.

- **Business versus IT**: Transformation has always seen two opposing forces at work. More often than not, transformations are either business-led or IT-led, and the challenge remains to bring both together as no transformation can be a success without business or IT leaders.

- **Finding the right transformation partner**: Unless the business has the right skills, experience, and knowledge to carry out the business transformation it needs, finding the right implementation partner is vital. In the previous section, we discussed the challenges in finding the right partner.

- **Lack of business strategy**: It might seem strange to add business strategy as one of the factors affecting transformation, but if there is no clarity on how the organization would like to develop its business locally, regionally, or globally, it will become a hindrance to any investment in IT transformation.

- **Transformation fatigue**: Previous programs delivering business transformation can lead to resistance to change, and this is one of the key factors why innovating to the latest software and business process innovation is seen as more of the same.

Environmental challenges

Today's business leaders must balance the long-term future of their businesses and environments, the top line and green line, alongside the short-term need to preserve the bottom line. A sustainable enterprise is no longer a nice-to-have ethos for a business; it's a must and it's driven by consumers as they use their power of choice to move away from unsustainable, environmentally damaging products and services. In this section, we will look at not just sustainability challenges but additional external factors that are environmental.

Sustainability challenges

A report released by the **World Economic Forum** in early 2020 reported that 50% of Europeans and 75% of Chinese consider climate change a major threat to society (https://www.weforum.org/agenda/2020/01/climate-change-perceptions-europe-china-us/).

This was backed by **Pew Research**, which found similar concerns of the public in the US, putting the economy at the top but environmental issues being of significant concern and coming a close second (https://www.pewresearch.org/politics/2020/02/13/as-economic-concerns-recede-environmental-protection-rises-on-the-publics-policy-agenda/).

The IBV report also showed that 67% of organizations consider environmental issues of significant concern and they feature in strategic decision-making (https://www.ibm.com/thought-leadership/institute-business-value/en-us/report/sustainability-consumer-research).

In fact, we do not have to rely on surveys and research anymore; we only have to look at the news to see for ourselves that climate change is here and it has started to impact all our daily lives. We can no longer hope to find a solution in the coming years – we must act now.

Businesses are now expected to deliver on the Paris Accords and COP26, and for each proceeding year to rapidly real sustainable products and services that are delivered with minimal impact on the environment.

COVID-19

As the COVID-19 pandemic becomes part of the new normal, one cannot ignore the devastating impact it has had on everyone. Millions died. Millions more were left with the long-term effects of COVID, and millions of livelihoods were at stake.

We may never truly be able to estimate or even fathom the long-term impact of COVID-19 but it has changed the way we do business forever. The question remains how do businesses adapt to change and build resilience to external forces to weather the storm and then return even stronger?

We are already seeing predictions made in IBV research come true, where it stated that when organizations emerge from the pandemic, there will be an environment of more disruption. That change is already at full pace in a hyper-dynamic environment. Business leaders cannot sit back and need to push forward to use the fluid business environment to their advantage.

Political polarization

Since 2016, we have seen increased polarization in politics, swinging from the extreme right to the left wing of the political spectrum. Political uncertainty since Brexit has led to there being five prime ministers in the UK since the Brexit referendum, leading to poor decision-making, and other recent events have both directly and indirectly impacted the economy. Economic indicators resemble an ECG scan, making forecasting very hard for the CXO suite. The abolition of the 45p tax rate and a reduction in corporation tax, in the hope of putting more money into the pockets of the top 1% of consumers, resulted in a run on the GBP, and this led to interest rate hikes on UK gilts and pensions, leading to the Bank of England investing £65bn in propping up UK bonds in pension funds.

With such devastating effects on the economy, for consumers and businesses alike, what can business leaders do to protect their top and bottom line?

Impact of the war in Ukraine

The war in Ukraine is in its eighth month at the time of writing and the impact of the war has been seen to affect its closest service markets, particularly in Eastern Europe. An IDC paper analyzed the impact of the Russia-Ukraine war on the services market, as well as the global impact of the conflict, as of 2Q22. It presented its findings in the near-term IT services forecast pertaining to Russia, Central and Eastern Europe, and Western Europe, as well as IDC's assessment of how the crisis is affecting service providers sourcing locations.

Summary

In this chapter, we set out to understand what drives change in a business. It's universally agreed that "the customer is king," but change is orchestrated by effects on the business brought on by factors both internal and external, even though the consumer is at the heart of any changes.

We looked at eight levers of change that pose challenges for CXOs in a game of truth or dare on whether they believe such factors will truly test their business. These challenges have been laid out so that businesses can use them to test the capability of their organization and whether it would withstand the impact of change.

In the next chapter, we will look at some aspects of the levers of change impacting Spark4Life Ltd., the challenges it is facing, and how it is looking to overcome them in the context of business transformation.

2

Faith of Four –
Vision of the Masters

In the previous chapter, we looked at the challenges facing businesses and how each of the challenges plays a part in influencing decisions that decide the direction of the future of the organization. The purpose was to understand those challenges in the context of digital transformation. We now want to use the lens of digital transformation to see how the CxOs react to those challenges.

We are focusing on the Spark4Life Ltd fictional company's journey and, in particular, the four leaders: the CEO, CFO, CIO, and CSO. Each of these roles has a clear remit and responsibility to deliver for their consumers, shareholders, employees, vendors, suppliers, and partners. It's important to understand their individual personas to see what would drive them toward fulfilling their responsibilities.

As we progress through this chapter, we will look at the challenges facing Spark4Life Ltd and determine how it looked to overcome them in the context of business transformation. As stated in the previous chapter, without determining and understanding the issues and challenges, we cannot act to find the solution.

The following main topics will be covered in this chapter:

- The four masters
- The business challenge
- The way forward
- The phoenix transformation

Let us dive right in!

The four masters

The four key roles are typically found as part of the **Board of Directors** (**BoD**), along with the chairperson, non-executive directors, and other directors appointed by the shareholders. These roles are often misunderstood in terms of their scope and responsibility, and it's important to have an appreciation for the backdrop of Spark4Life Ltd, a fictitious company that is trying to transform itself, given the direction it has over the next few years and its commitment to its shareholders.

Chief Executive Officer (CEO)

Abhinav Haviland is the CEO of Spark4Life Ltd. He has been with the company since 2018 and has weathered the storm of COVID-19, where he saw a decline in the sales of white goods but an increase in personal products. The company's share price had started to recover to the pre-pandemic levels but another decline in profitability is around the corner due to the energy crisis and the war in Ukraine in Europe.

At the last AGM, the shareholders raised their concerns about what the company is doing to do regarding the impact on three areas:

- **Top-line growth** – provide better cashflow and help in bolstering the share price
- **Bottom-line growth** – introduce process and innovation efficiencies to cut costs
- **Green-line growth** – deliver impactful and meaningful processes, policies, and innovation that will deliver on the sustainability agenda agreed upon at COP26

Chief Finance Officer (CFO)

Damien Protus is the CFO of Spark4Life Ltd. He has been with the company since 2012 as a long-standing member of the board and has the backing of the shareholders and chairperson. He is seen as a safe pair of hands in delivering healthy EBITDA over the last 10 years.

With the COVID-19 pandemic and the unfortunate events in Ukraine, he has seen a sharp rise in the cost of goods and services being delivered to Spark4Life Ltd. This has already impacted the price of goods and services being delivered to consumers, wholesalers, and retailers.

The last AGM was the tipping point in how Spark4Life Ltd needed to evolve its business for the next five years and introduce new and innovative services, both with its products and its services, to increase the three key areas from the AGM, mentioned previously.

Chief Information/Technology Officer (CIO/CTO)

Patricia Askey is the CIO of Spark4Life Ltd and has been with the company since 2019. She brought in Kasper Haviland to modernize the company's approach to innovation and new services and to help drive automation into the business.

Patricia was a VP for SAP Consulting for 10 years prior to joining ABC Ltd, and before that, she delivered application and data center modernization for a Singapore-based electronics company.

Her remit is to deliver modernization for both business processes and technology, which will deliver on the three objectives laid out in the AGM. The AGM agreed to a five-year recovery plan, and Patricia must start to deliver on that plan.

Chief Sustainability Officer (CSO)

Tara Suri has recently been appointed as the CSO for Spark4Life Ltd. She has been with the company for over 10 years and has worked her way up through the ranks. She has built a reputation for having a *can-do, must-do, will-do* attitude and has been the driving force in introducing sustainability into Spark4Life Ltd's products and services, both from an environmental perspective and with her background in the supply chain.

Prior to joining Spark4Life Ltd, she spent 10 years as the director of supply chain management at a leading fashion retailer. Tara is acutely aware of the challenges in making sure that Spark4Life Ltd delivers and contributes back to the local and regional economies, but also leaves the least impact on its environment.

We are now going to focus on the business challenges facing Spark4Life Ltd while looking at the top-line, bottom-line, and green-line growth focuses they have set themselves.

The business challenge

At the first board meeting after the AGM, it was unanimously agreed that Damien Protus, the CFO, would lead the transformation program (which they named *phoenix*), to deliver on the three key objectives. Further details on how to deliver on the growth plan over the next five years were left to each of the CxO members to define.

Let's look at the business challenges facing Spark4Life Ltd today.

Top-line growth

With the rapid decline in sales, revenue, and after-sales services, there is increased pressure to improve profitability, cash flow, and share price. It was decided to review its current products and services and introduce new product lines and services going beyond its traditional white goods business and to grow its revenue by creating differentiating business models that would allow rapid innovation and time to market. It would also focus on industry-specific standardized processes and best practices to help increase the margin.

Bottom-line growth

Recently, there had been issues of personnel shortages, lack of field support, poor post-sale customer experience, different legacy information systems as a result of several company M&A initiatives and organic growth, and an increase in the cost of infrastructure to support the business. These led the board to focus on introducing new innovations, streamlining business processes and technologies to improve its **Return on Investment (ROI)**, innovation efficiencies, and at the same time, reducing its technical debt and being agile in a rapidly changing market. Introducing simplification, standardization, and intelligent automation across all mission-critical processes, it is hoped, will unlock new efficiency in the business.

Green-line growth

With the uncertainty in Europe over the war in Ukraine gathering pace and the global energy crisis gripping everyone, coupled with new legislation regarding carbon credit requirements across Europe and North America as an offset mechanism for carbon emissions, Spark4Life Ltd is shifting its operational paradigm by demanding innovative, circular economics for its sourcing and manufacturing. Moving forward, Spark4Life Ltd's partners and suppliers will be asked to track their sustainability metrics and have manual operational SOPs.

The board agreed to deliver impactful and meaningful processes, policies, and innovation to manage sustainability with company-wide transparency and controls. This will help to deliver on the company's sustainability agenda against the backdrop of challenges that have already been highlighted, which include the following:

- Encouraging investment in renewables
- Protecting and restoring ecosystems
- Mitigation through reducing emissions

Other focus areas

The board also asserted that, along with the three growth objectives, it wanted the following focus areas to be at the heart of any strategic decision:

- **Customer First**: By putting the customer first, it looks to elevate its brand reputation by delivering on the promises made on sales, service, and support. Better customer insight will help to deliver better after-sales service and support by investing in people, processes, and technology.
- **Cloud First**: Spark4Life Ltd has decided that *cloud first* would be the default operational infrastructure for business transformation. This will also allow moving from capital expenditure to operational expenditure and free up cash flow to develop new products and services. The introduction of a pay-as-you-consume model to integrate agility and flexibility, both financially and technically, will help to reduce its technical debt and to accelerate innovation.

- **Automation First**: The scope of *automation first* at Spark4Life Ltd is still in its incubation stage but the board is encouraged to prepare its business for the next 5 years. So, whether it is smart manufacturing, AI, smart procurement, or intelligent business process automation, the board will see its automation strategy mature in the next decade.

- **Sustainability First**: This is Spark4Life Ltd's bold new vision of balancing the long-term objective of protecting the planet with its short-term goal of helping to improve the top and bottom lines. It is clear that there will be no compromise on deviating from the 5-year plan on its sustainability commitments.

We will now look at how Spark4Life Ltd will chart a course forward in responding to those challenges.

The way forward

The outcome of the AGM and board meeting set in motion the future strategy for Spark4Life Ltd. But what of its current state of health? We saw a glimpse of what the challenges were but, in this section, we will delve deeper with a view to mapping a course on how to begin the transformation journey. By setting the context, we hope to gain a better understanding and realization of the decisions.

Uncertainty

There is concern about the decline in revenue, market share, and rising cost, coupled with a turbulent market, high attrition of its people, and the changes in regulations as it looks to open new markets.

Spark4Life Ltd, therefore, needs to create a differentiating business model that would allow rapid innovation and time to market. There is already a commitment to focus on industry-specific standardized processes and best practices to help increase margins and lower costs.

In 2019, the first act by the incoming CIO, Patricia Askey, was to start a companywide initiative to move its ERP systems and legacy applications to the cloud. With a heterogeneous landscape, each LoB within Spark4Life Ltd managed its own systems and processes, which ran in parallel to the SAP ECC 6.0 system (the core ERP application). Although migration of several legacy solutions to the cloud has been completed, spiraling costs for maintaining the systems remained the same; this was in part due to the supporting on-premises and cloud systems but also due to the business processes not capturing the benefits of the cloud migration.

Prior to the AGM, the office of the CIO commissioned a review of the business case, and it could not justify the value versus the costs, ROI, and effort required. The SAP ECC 6.0 was due to be migrated, but the program was put on hold until after the AGM and board meeting to decide on the next steps. The review also revealed that middle management was opposing the change, citing resistance to change. There was concern that modernizing the LoB solutions would mean relinquishing its IP and the business processes developed and matured over decades that gave Spark4Life Ltd its competitive advantage against its competitors, and would set it back if they were to move to a new solution.

Insights

At the behest of the CEO, the office of the CFO was tasked with spearheading, along with the CIO, the development of a strategic transformation roadmap as part of its recommendation to the board. This was subsequently and unanimously approved, giving Damien the remit to deliver on the plan over the next five years.

Several reports, reviews, and papers from leading organizations provided insight into how business, culture, and politics will shape the global, regional, and industry agendas over the next five years, including the following:

- **World Economic Forum** (**WEF**) is an international organization for public-private cooperation. The report by the WEF (`https://www3.weforum.org/docs/WEF_Future_of_Jobs_2020.pdf`) spoke of changing the workforce model, where half of all tasks will be carried out through automation, and how additional revenue will be generated through new innovations.

- **International Data Corporation** (**IDC**) is the premier global provider of market intelligence, advisory services, and events for the information technology, telecommunications, and consumer technology markets. The IDC elaborated on what the strategic priorities will be based on outcome-driven engagements and new business models: `https://www.idc.com/getdoc.jsp?containerId=US45599219`.

- **IBM Institute of Business Value** (**IBV**) provides expert analysis of the latest research and trends at the intersection of business and technology. IBM IBV provided analysis on people, processes, and technology with particular insight into intelligent workflows, automation, hybrid cloud, business process modernization, sustainability, and emerging technologies: `https://www.ibm.com/thought-leadership/institute-business-value/`.

- **IBM Insights on SAP**: An independent review providing insight into SAP based on its 50 years of experience with clients in the SAP ecosystem and where they continue to focus its SAP® software investments, particularly the SAP S/4HANA suite: `https://www.ibm.com/downloads/cas/DKPANXJZ`.

Yesterday's ERP

If we draw an analogy of car performance over the last three decades, you can certainly say that the cars of today are far more reliable, economical, integrated with technology, and sustainable. The same can be said for existing business models, processes, and innovations. Yesterday's ERP solutions cannot keep pace with the changing socio-economic, political, and environmental landscape that are key indicators of how the consumers' needs and perspectives are changing, and businesses need to be in step with those changes.

Yesterday's ERP can not keep pace with future business needs

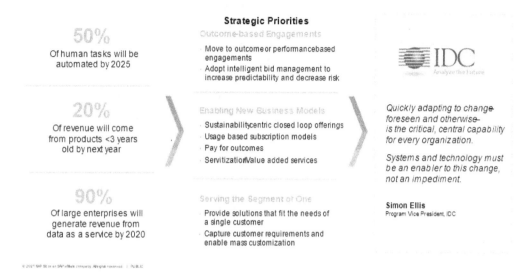

Figure 2.1 – Yesterday's ERP and its impact on future business needs

Whether it's automation, new revenue streams, greater data insight to make informed decisions, or creating brand loyalty as a result, it has now become imperative for Spark4Life Ltd to take the next step in this intelligent sustainable enterprise transformation. The following is an analysis of what customers are looking for when choosing a brand:

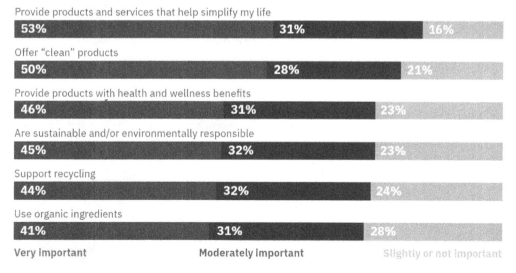

Figure 2.2 – The IBM Insights on SAP also revealed what customers are looking for when choosing a brand

Sustainability insight

The current ERP system cannot be used to measure or track sustainability, the business cannot act on what it cannot measure, and the organizations behind standards and frameworks are driving new reporting standards for non-financial disclosure as part of the auditable reporting requirements, which can only be achieved through the NextGen ERP platform. The following provides insight into the requirements and expectations of organizations on environmental sustainability:

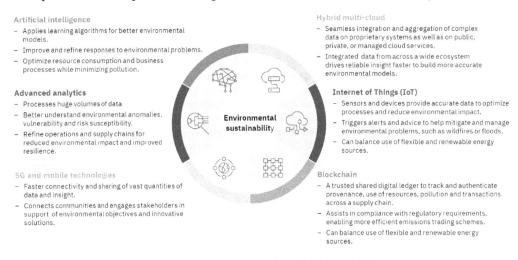

Artificial intelligence
- Applies learning algorithms for better environmental models.
- Improve and refine responses to environmental problems.
- Optimize resource consumption and business processes while minimizing pollution.

Advanced analytics
- Processes huge volumes of data
- Better understand environmental anomalies, vulnerability and risk susceptibility.
- Refine operations and supply chains for reduced environmental impact and improved resilience.

5G and mobile technologies
- Faster connectivity and sharing of vast quantities of data and insight.
- Connects communities and engages stakeholders in support of environmental objectives and innovative solutions.

Hybrid multi-cloud
- Seamless integration and aggregation of complex data on proprietary systems as well as on public, private, or managed cloud services.
- Integrated data from across a wide ecosystem drives reliable insight faster to build more accurate environmental models.

Internet of Things (IoT)
- Sensors and devices provide accurate data to optimize processes and reduce environmental impact.
- Triggers alerts and advice to help mitigate and manage environmental problems, such as wildfires or floods.
- Can balance use of flexible and renewable energy sources.

Blockchain
- A trusted shared digital ledger to track and authenticate provenance, use of resources, pollution and transactions across a supply chain.
- Assists in compliance with regulatory requirements, enabling more efficient emissions trading schemes.
- Can balance use of flexible and renewable energy sources.

Environmental sustainability

Figure 2.3 – Environmental sustainability insight

Environmental sustainability also reinforces the need for cloud, automation, data insights, and efficiencies, from a transparent supply chain to green IT, all aimed at addressing the ESG ambitions of Spark4Life Ltd, including its net zero transition plans. Digital transformation is the only path that will deliver exponential technology innovations that are unavailable in legacy ERP systems – **artificial intelligence (AI)**, 5G, **Internet of Things (IoT)**, cloud, blockchain, and others.

The next steps

In summary, the outcome of the Intelligent Sustainable Enterprise transformation is centered around six themes. They encompass all the objectives laid out by the business, and they now need to turn this transformation into reality.

Reality of today…

56%

Of CEOs say that enhanced operational agility and flexibility is their top priority for the nest 2-3 years[1]

74%

Of CEOs say that cloud computing will help them deliver the results they need over the next 2-3 years[1]

41%

Of CEOs say that they don't have enough skilled staff to keep up with changing technologies[1]

Organisations are still lacking the clarity in determining the best course to the Intelligent Sustainable Enterprise

Where do I start my Journey?

What is the best approach to S/4HANA?

How do I build Intelligence in my IT Systems?

How do I ensure my business processes remain optimal and relevant?

How to be a Sustainable Enterprise?

How to manage the Supply Chain Disruption?

Figure 2.4 – Challenges in becoming an Intelligent Sustainable Enterprise
(https://www.ibm.com/downloads/cas/DKPANXJZ)

In the next section, we will look at each of these themes and provide an overview. The following chapters will look at each of these themes in detail:

- How to start the journey
- How to adopt the approach to a new enterprise platform
- How to build an Intelligent Enterprise platform
- How to develop an optimal and relevant business process model
- How to build a sustainable enterprise
- How to create a sustainable supply chain

We now look forward to how Spark4Life Ltd will move forward with the transformation in the next section.

The phoenix transformation

As a global leader in consumer electronics manufacturing with a product portfolio ranging from household appliances to personal equipment such as computers and headphones, and certain medical equipment such as health monitors and watches, over the last 20 years, Spark4Life Ltd championed reliability, quality, and customer service. In a rapidly changing world, agility, flexibility, speed, and innovation are now key to winning new customers and staying ahead of the competition.

The next phase in Spark4Life Ltd's growth strategy is the development of new products and services and the streamlining of existing ones. However, this level of complexity cannot be supported by legacy ERP systems. This will require the realization of a major system transformation that would enable Intelligent Enterprise operations. Spark4Life Ltd also wants to become more efficient and even more flexible to be able to serve its customers more effectively while keeping costs under control.

Spark4Life Ltd is now ready to streamline all aspects of its business and accelerate its digital transformation to enable new customer services and business models.

How does Spark4Life Ltd take the first step?

It's important to not only have a clear strategy for transformation but also to understand and align that strategy internally across all business units within the organization. We know there are disagreements between business process owners and technology owners within Spark4Life Ltd. This is not a unique occurrence. Traditionally, IT, systems, and solutions have been within the remit of the IT department to deliver, however, a greater focus on the business process has diluted their involvement as it became more specialized, and hence LoB process owners emerged. They were now responsible for deciding what business processes would be defined and how, and how they would be developed for the business needs.

We know that the cloud migration of legacy systems had already started and before the core SAP ECC ERP system was to be migrated, the CIO halted the program.

With a renewed focus from the Board, it's clear that Spark4Life Ltd is now on a path to transforming its people, processes, and technology. To have access to exponential innovations and achieve the objectives of building an Intelligent Enterprise platform, it's vital that we look at where to start the journey. To take the first step into an intelligent sustainable transformation, you need to understand the journey, starting with the value advisory, then understanding the approach, and finally, looking at harnessing the exponential innovations:

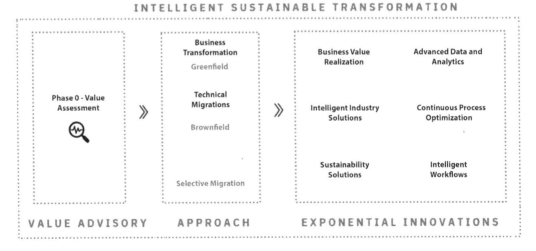

Figure 2.5 – Pathway to ERP transformation

What is value advisory?

Value advisory is also known as **value assessment**, and its purpose is to help clients to develop and align their strategic transformation plan. Service integrators and IT partners, including SAP, provide this service, which outlines the key ingredients required, enabled by technology and change, to build a foundation for success. In this section, we will provide the core components of value advisory with a view to how it will help Spark4Life Ltd in understanding its next steps, as described in the previous section.

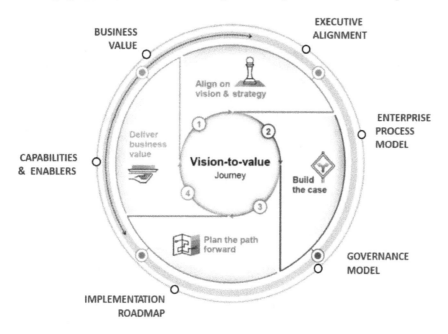

Figure 2.6 – Advisory Framework

(Source: https://assets.cdn.sap.com/sapcom/docs/2020/11/9a574b75-bb7d-0010-87a3-c30de2ffd8ff.pdf
https://www.ibm.com/services/resources/rapid-discovery)

SAP describes value advisory as vision-to-value; others describe it as building a foundation for transformation success for your business. The objective of any value assessment should be to determine the following:

- Aligning executives on vision and strategy:

  - Identifying senior influential executive personnel to participate

  - Conducting executive interviews to gain insight into key priorities, critical success factors, and transformation goals

- Building the case and defining the enterprise process model:

  - Functional workshops to review the **Business Process Hierarchy (BPH)**

  - Defining the impact of BPH in comparison with current-state operations

  - Finalizing Level 3 scope for the transformation by conducting BPH reviews with stakeholders

  - Mapping standard business process definitions to the in-scope processes

- Implementation roadmap and governance model:

  - Discovery session with business and IT stakeholders to evaluate and weigh priorities for moving to SAP S/4HANA. Leverage the S/4HANA Adoption Approach framework.

  - SAP Transformation Navigator mapping.

  - Defining an enterprise-wide roadmap for an SAP S/4HANA-enabled transformation program, including the creation of an instance strategy, new template, roll-outs across the enterprise, and implementation of digital transformation solutions (e.g., AI, blockchain, IoT, and analytics).

- Delivering business value, capabilities, and enablers:

  - Creating an outside-in estimate of business value with public data and KPI data

  - Identifying value pools and using the assumption of current performance to estimate the size of business benefits

  - Creating board-ready business cases and ROI by working with process owners

  - Working with client data and data contact

  - Working with process owners to refine benefit sizing and build ownership

  - Building a cost model and calculating ROI

Building a business case for transformation

An outcome of the value advisory is developing a business case for transformation. In *Chapter 6*, we will be discussing how Spark4Life Ltd can build a business case to adopt RISE with SAP, and the different points that organizations need to consider before finalizing the architecture of RISE with SAP. You will learn about the different considerations involved along with their impact and the associated options when considering RISE with SAP, including the following:

- Putting together a business case for RISE with SAP

- Industry trends influencing S/4HANA with RISE with SAP

- Understanding architectural patterns for RISE with SAP

- Exploring what is possible and what is not possible with RISE with SAP

- Looking into alternate options for RISE with SAP

Approaches

There are two main approaches when considering moving to S/4HANA, and these are briefly outlined next and further discussed in *Chapters 3* and *5*.

SAP S/4HANA deployment approach

As part of the value assessment, the deployment approach would be one of the value drivers. We will briefly discuss the options here, but we will look at them in more detail in *Chapter 3*.

SAP S/4HANA Public Cloud	SAP S/4HANA Private Cloud	SAP S/4HANA On-Premises
Customers who desire the following:	**Customers who desire the following:**	**Customers who require the following:**
• A complete, modern, native SaaS ERP solution with the full benefits of the public cloud • The fastest path to innovation and the lowest TCO • A clean cloud ERP solution without converting old/legacy ERP processes and configurations • To reimagine business processes and take advantage of standardized best practices	• Gradual transformation to a pure SaaS landscape at their own pace with a well-defined conversion methodology • Software, support, and technical managed services and infrastructure, from a single point of contact, with one set of SLAs • Full SAP S/4HANA functionality – 25 industries/64 countries – with the benefit of subscription-based, cloud economics • Ability to safeguard prior investments, including ECC customizations, configurations, and partner add-ons, such as SOLEXs and certified solutions	• Complete control and ownership of their application and data landscape • The ability to manage unique, customer-specific needs that cannot be addressed by public cloud or private cloud offerings • The utilization of their existing IT departments, infrastructure, budget, and IaaS vendor agreements • Specific compliance with industry- and country-specific regulatory requirements

Figure 2.7 – S/4HANA deployment approach

The choice of S/4HANA can follow three different deployment approaches (where to move):

- **On-Premises**:

  Typically, this is the option that offers the greatest flexibility for organizations in regulated industries where cloud hosting is not an option; organizations who want full control of the end-to-end stack; or organizations with specific requirements (e.g., customization, developments, and add-ons) that don't have to facilitate "fit to standard." This is based on the perpetual licensing model.

- **Public Cloud Edition**:

  This is for organizations that are new to SAP or are re-implementing (Greenfield) and want to move to SaaS with a full "fit to standard" approach, including SAP-approved add-ons.

- **Private Cloud Edition**:

  This is the optimal choice for organizations who want to move to SaaS but retain a level of flexibility and choice of adoption approach, and are more interested in the business outcomes than how and where the solution is hosted.

  A good fit would be existing organizations looking for migration with some degree of standardization.

Migration approach

Spark4Life Ltd knows it must adopt S/4HANA as its NextGen platform, but how to move from SAP ECC 6.0 to S/4HANA is where we explore the various transition paths:

Business Objectives	Purpose	Transition Paths
Business Model Innovation	**New Implementation / reimplementation** Re-engineering and process simplification based on latest innovations Implementing innovative business processes with pre-configured SAP Best Practice Industry Solutions Data Migration Greenfield Approach	New Implementation/ Greenfield
Business Process Optimization	**Value-driven data migration to the new platform** Value-driven data migration to the new platform Fit to standard Use Hybrid Migration to move Customizing, Customizing Repository and Data Protect part of IT investment by customers Take over historical data Migrate Configuration	Selective Migration
ERP Rapid Modernization	**Bring your business processes to the new platform** A complete technical in-place conversion of an existing SAP ECC software system to SAP S/4HANA Adoption of new innovations at your speed	System Conversion / Brownfield

Figure 2.8 – Adoption pathways to S/4HANA

Reasons why organizations would favor one migration option over the other

In this section, we will look at the characteristics of each of the migration options and compare the three options against each other. Referring to where Spark4Life Ltd is today, they have existing legacy non-SAP solutions alongside SAP ECC 6.0. We know that they have invested heavily in their existing SAP system and have heavy technical debt, both with bespoke customization and infrastructure.

It's important to note that data migration impacts all aspects of the migration approach. *Chapter 8* explains how important it is to plan the approach to data migration.

The value advisory will determine the best course when weighing up the options of abandoning the existing investment and focusing on the new functionality in SAP S/4HANA; it will be a discussion on ROI by the business process owners and TCO for the technology leaders. Here are some considerations for Spark4Life Ltd:

- **Greenfield**:

  - New implementation of industry-leading processes. Will help Spark4Life take advantage of adopting new business process models compared to what they have today.

  - Reengineering and process simplification accelerated by SAP best practices (reference solution, preconfigured template, etc). Adopting industry best practices is one of the key tenets of Spark4Life Ltd.

- **Brownfield**:

  - Enables S/4 HANA migration without reimplementation. Technical move to S/4HANA. This will help Spark4Life Ltd in keeping its existing IP address and investment.

  - Limited disruption for existing business processes.

  - All data will be migrated.

  - It will mean introducing new innovations at Spark4Life Ltd's pace, but it will also mean longer implementation timelines and costs to take advantage of the process enhancements in SAP S/4HANA and achieve full transformation.

- **Selective Migration**:

  - A selective migration approach will allow Spark4Life Ltd to stay with current business processes and move to S/4HANA innovations.

  - Harmonized business processes, organizational structures, and shared master data through consolidation.

  - As Spark4Life Ltd evolves through divestitures and M&A, it can carve out single entities of the company or merge SAP S/4HANA instances, respectively, and leverage process simplification and reduce technical and infrastructure debt.

Here are some key considerations when choosing a migration approach:

	Greenfield	Brownfield (System Conversion)	Selective Migration
Data	<ul><li>Migrate clean data</li><li>Efforts required to prepare data before migration to the greenfield system</li><li>Opportunity for a reduced data footprint</li><li>Allows for faster cutover</li></ul>	<ul><li>Unless data archiving is carried out by hand, there is often the issue of dealing with high data volume during the migration</li><li>Potential requirement for significant downtime, incompatible with business and operations</li><li>Old legacy data still present</li><li>Company code will need to be closed, in the source system, before conversion to S/4</li><li>The main tables were not updated after the financial close and only the cluster tables were updated through the Z-Program. Threw up inconsistency errors.</li></ul>	<ul><li>Allows for a controlled shortened downtime during cutover.</li><li>Can migrate data at own pace</li><li>Table-level data migration allows for selective data migration, thereby reducing volume</li><li>The two-step approach removes the dependency of converting with application and data</li><li>Reduce data footprint – harmonization</li><li>No impact of open company codes due to RESC and data migration carried out independently</li></ul>
Processes	<ul><li>New business process adoption quicker (e.g., Universal Journal, CV to Business Partners)</li><li>Fit-to-standard adoption opportunity</li><li>Reduce code footprint</li></ul>	<ul><li>No new processes introduced as it's a technical migration</li><li>Will require subsequent phases to realize the benefit</li><li>No innovation adoption</li></ul>	<ul><li>New business process adoption quicker (e.g., Universal Journal, CVI to Business Partners)</li><li>Fit-to-standard adoption opportunity</li><li>Reduce code footprint</li><li>Less maintenance of code</li></ul>

	Greenfield	Brownfield (System Conversion)	Selective Migration
Config | Customization | Interfaces	• Less maintenance of code • New adoption of business processes	• Leveraging several years of investment in configuration and customization • Complex interfaces and custom objects • Integration with a third party (e.g., warehouse management system)	• Custom code impact and remediation when moving from ECC to S/4 • Potential impact on unique configurations and customizations
New Functionality	• Fiori Apps for users to access and adopt • New adoption of integration platform	• Fiori Apps for users to access and adopt	• Adoption of new functionality is expected from the outset • Adoption of Intelligent Enterprise (e.g., SCP) and new ways of working with extensibility, IoT, and ML • Adopting ready-made assets in the cloud
Training	• Extensive adoption approach required since shifting to the new ERP platform • Abandoning old ways and adopting new ones	• Workforce already educated in the current SAP language and objects	• Functional changes still require retraining and change management • Adoption of a new extensibility approach (e.g., Classic versus In-App versus Side-by-Side
Testing	• Testing of new functionality against old ways of working • Creating new testing scripts	• Testing of current functionality against the newer application code-line. • Using existing testing scripts • Not much difference in the testing approach	• Testing of new functionality against old ways of working • Need to enhance existing testing scripts • Same testing approach

	Greenfield	Brownfield (System Conversion)	Selective Migration
Infrastructure	• Single landscape • Less complexity • Adopting a new deployment approach may lead to some operational challenges	• Complex infrastructure setup, possibly dual landscape • A new set of infrastructure setups with high availability and disaster recovery compared to the existing ones, which were standalone with high availability and disaster recovery • Redundant legacy data could impact the cost of storage, maintenance, backup, and restore	• Dual landscape required • Dual maintenance of ECC and S/4 environments becomes simpler
Timelines	• One step to adopting new innovations • Longer timelines if creating custom business processes • Faster go-live if adopting Fit-to-standard	• One-step technical conversion may mean longer downtime due to the approach • Additional phases are required after go-live to realize the benefit of new S/4HANA functionality and business processes • Multiple test cycles for each phase • Controlled and measured step forward in adopting the innovation roadmap • Will take longer to bring new innovations	• The two-step approach will also include the adoption of new innovations and business processes • Will also shorten the time taken to adopt S/4HANA functionality • Shorter cutover window required • For systems that are non-Unicode, rapid migration can carry out Unicode conversion and S/4HANA conversion in one step

Why RISE with SAP?

As mentioned previously, there are three deployment options available when moving to S/4HANA; however, considering the challenges and objectives of Spark4Life Ltd, it would be more strategic for them to move to a product that is based on a subscription-based consumption, as this would use a model that also provides the fully functional and industry capabilities along with access to exponential technologies such as AI, cloud integration, data analytics, and IoT.

Here are some key considerations:

Delivers Business Value

- Cloud First approach provides greater **flexibility**, **agility** and **resilience** in a rapidly changing market
- Clients can now deliver more value through focus on core business operations rather than worrying about IT operations.
- Reduce the number of vendors accountable when delivering Licenses, Cloud Infrastructure and Infrastructure Services

Delivers Strategic Value

- Transition to Cloud at customers pace
- Preserve investment in existing legacy ERP systems without re-inventing the solution
- Move from a Capital Expenditure (CapEx) to a Operational Expenditure (OpEx) to **lesser the upfront** investment
- Technology Platform delivered as a Service
- Protect against uncertainty
- Change at market speed

Delivers Technology Value

- Full ERP functional scope for 64 country versions in 39 languages, supporting 25 industries
- SAP Best Practice for ~30 countries
- **Full Extensibility Scope**
- Industry standard Security resilience
- **Low Cost of Ownership**
- **Delivers Innovation** at the speed of Innovation
- Core technology platform ready for Intelligent Workflows and Industry Solutions

Flexible Adoption

- Giving Clients flexible adoption options to MOVE to S/4HANA
- Implement without **long delivery timelines**
- Preserve investment in the legacy SAP ECC solution
- MOVE Clients to S/4HANA via **System Conversion** or Selective Migration
- Modifications of SAP Code allowed

Figure 2.9 – Key considerations of why to choose RISE with SAP

RISE with SAP – what's included?

This is an SAP S/4HANA **Software as a Service** (**SaaS**) cloud-based subscription offering that enables organizations to move their existing SAP ERP systems to S/4HANA with a choice of cloud infrastructure providers.

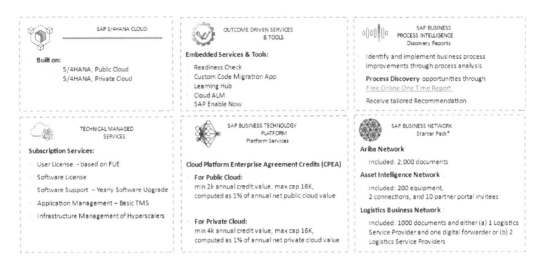

Figure 2.10 – Service offerings in SAP

To help organizations accelerate that journey to the cloud, it has bundled six service offerings within RISE with SAP:

- **Cloud Infrastructure Providers**: RISE with SAP provides the broadest cloud infrastructure providers, which include Microsoft Azure, AWS, GCP, and IBM Cloud.

- **S/4HANA Cloud**: S/4HANA Public Cloud (previously known as S/4HANA Cloud Essentials Edition) and S/4HANA **Private Cloud Edition** (**PCE**) are the only two S/4HANA cloud offerings that are applicable for RISE with SAP. PCE offers the broadest range of scope, industry solutions, LoB, and country versions compared to its Public Cloud offering.

> **Note**
> S/4HANA Cloud Extended Edition is not part of the RISE offering, but customers can still avail of this deployment option.

- **Tools and Services**: To help customers start the transformation journey from SAP ECC to S/4HANA, SAP offers a basic set of tools and services that may need to be augmented by additional services. The basic set includes the following:

  - SAP Readiness Checks

  - Custom Code Analysis

  - Access SAP Learning Hub

  - Cloud ALM

  - SAP Enable Now

- **SAP Business Technology Platform: SAP Business Transformation Platform (SAP BTP)** was previously known as SAP Cloud Platform Enterprise. As part of the Clean Core strategy, BTP offers integration and extensibility (development) with any other SAP partner or third-party solution. *Chapter 4* takes a deep dive into how BTP can provide access to exponential innovation.

- **SAP Business Process Intelligence**: Even though there is a focus on keeping the core clean and extending outside the core of S/4HANA, **SAP Business Process Intelligence (SAP BPI)** provides insight through discovery reports by identifying and recommending business process improvements. *Chapter 7* will provide a deep dive into how organizations can leverage the agility and faster adoption of new business processes when using BPI.

- **One Business Network**: To complete the offering, SAP is now providing access to the world's largest business network, including SAP's supplier, logistics, and asset intelligence networks, to foster cross-company connectivity and collaboration. As part of how business networks would be used as part of the transformation, *Chapters 9, 10*, and *11* look at this from an end-to-end perspective.

Summary

In this chapter, we provided more context to the challenges facing Spark4Life Ltd, but more importantly, discussed how to chart a course from a corporate strategy relating to top-line growth, bottom-line growth, and green-line growth.

We looked at how that corporate strategy translates to a business and technical strategy focusing on additional areas such as Customer First, Cloud First, Automation First, and Sustainability First, which provides additional value pools to focus on when determining the next transformation steps.

Finally, we mapped the transformation strategy to realization by looking at the value advisory, approach, and exponential technology.

As you proceed through the chapters, we hope that they will start to provide a clear view of the realization of the strategy of taking a corporate strategy and translating this into a business and technology transformation roadmap.

In the next chapter, we will explore RISE with SAP as a first step in the journey to digital transformation helping the organization to realize, adopt, and become an Intelligent Enterprise.

`

Eureka Moment – the Missing Link

In the previous chapters, we have gone through changes in approach to digital transformation and its impact on the maker–operator ecosystem. We also touched upon the importance of the transformation of products toward service and the convergence of conventional value chains, along with the transformation of operations. We explained how this was further accelerated by the pandemic and other global impacting scenarios and their impact on the supply chain, and we looked at how organizations need to adapt to these industry shifts and imperatives. Some of the key industry imperatives we spoke about included business model innovation, continuous engineering, digital offerings, return on assets, security, safety, and a focus on overall equipment effectiveness.

This has put every organization under extreme pressure to be able to provide disruption-free services while allowing for dynamic scaling up and down, as per market demands. Organizations are also expected to maintain innovation at pace while providing a reduction in TCO and improved time to market. CXOs have been under extreme pressure to handle the economic, industrial, environmental and operational impact on both business and IT spending while focusing on simplification and value-added services.

In the previous chapter, we have gone through the pain points "Spark4life" as an organization has been going through and some of the challenges the different personas had to address. We will focus on the requirement around having a scalable, agile and a flexible yet sustainable hosting model to support the nimbleness when it comes to business agility. This is key to make sure the organization can adopt the industry best practices from a hosting point of view having SLAs at the application level and not just at the infrastructure level.

CXOs from Spark4life were talking to some of their counterparts and attended a few conferences where they heard about RISE with SAP and also the pros and cons that come with it. They are not sure about the applicability of RISE with SAP for their organization.

In this chapter, you will be able to understand how RISE with SAP and S/4HANA can support you to address the requirements of being sustainable, scalable, flexible, and agile, while providing a simplified ecosystem of one vendor to provide technical managed services. We will also walk you through the different myths and misunderstandings within the market about RISE with SAP, helping you to achieve the full potential of the solutions and be aligned with future cloud strategies. You will also understand the different options available today under RISE with SAP and the known restrictions/limitations of these options.

In this chapter, we will be covering the following topics:

- Understanding RISE with SAP

- Demystifying myths about RISE with SAP

- Exploring options available with RISE with SAP, including Standard, Tailored, Customer data center, Critical Data Cloud, and Partner-Managed Cloud

- Understanding an approach for use case traceability with RISE with SAP

Let's get started!

Understanding RISE with SAP

In this section, before we start explaining what RISE with SAP is and how it can address the industry shifts and trends discussed in the earlier chapters, let's focus on typical industry challenges around the move to the cloud. Organizations are still figuring out a plan of action for an opportune business case to support their move to the cloud while leveraging the benefits of SAP Business Technology Platform to the fullest extent possible. At the same time, organizations are also looking for simplification of the vendor ecosystem to move away from a separate contract with a technical managed services vendor and SAP when it comes to end-to-end product SLAs. The following diagram provides a summary of what the reality is when it comes to the importance of a hybrid cloud and how it overlays with the move toward S/4HANA for clients:

Figure 3.1: What organizations are struggling with when it comes to moving to the cloud

In January 2021, to address these concerns and to provide a strategic direction for a cloud strategy, SAP announced RISE with SAP, a milestone offering to support customers' transformation to an intelligent enterprise. RISE with SAP provides customers a faster time to value and flexibility to adapt to changes without having an upfront investment. RISE with SAP provides both a platform for unified technical managed services and product-related support, along with access to the **Business Technology Platform** (**BTP**) to transform the IT, business, and end user experience. RISE with SAP allows customers to extend and integrate their S/4HANA instance with any other SAP, partner, or third-party solution, both in the cloud and on-premises, and enables them to turn their data into value. Let's now deep-dive into what RISE with SAP is all about and how it can help organizations achieve business transformation.

What is RISE with SAP?

In this section, we will focus on what RISE with SAP can offer, along with what is available as part of the overall offering and its impact on an organization's transformational journey. RISE with SAP is an offering with a single contract and single vendor concept for both your infrastructure, technical managed services, and SAP solutions (SAP S/4HANA Public and Private, BW/4HANA **Private Cloud Edition** (**PCE**), along with BOBJ/BI PCE and many other SAP products). RISE with SAP provides organizations with a journey with multiple patterns to move toward intelligent enterprise-based solutions, irrespective of where the organizations are within their journey. RISE with SAP provides one responsible vendor for pre-defined service level agreements, along with established operations and support processes. The move to RISE with SAP will support organizations in focusing less on maintenance or vendor management and more on transforming business models, leveraging the full potential of the cloud and SAP's BTP to induce innovation embedded with artificial intelligence/machine learning and automation. This is possible by being able to leverage the features of business process analysis (SAP Signavio), custom code analysis with the approach of a clean core, and side-by-side extensibility to keep the digital core clean while being able to leverage 2,200+ APIs, readily made available for the organizations.

RISE with SAP is offered on a subscription basis and delivered by SAP, along with other implementation partners and leading infrastructure providers to maximize customer choice. The following figure provides an overview of multiple entry points and the components involved in order to support clients on their journey toward an intelligent enterprise:

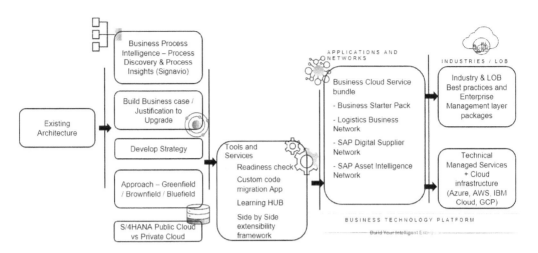

Figure 3.2: Different blocks within RISE with SAP

As shown in the previous diagram, there are different points to be considered when it comes to RISE with SAP. The following is an overview of the key items:

- **Business process redesign**: For every client, the deciding factor of moving to the cloud typically is more than just technical and would involve a strong reassessment of their existing business processes. This also provides an opportunity to simplify complex scenarios they have built within the organization, either due to urgency or due to no strong design authority in place to govern the central template. Business process intelligence as part of RISE with SAP is built on SAP's business-centric data model along with expertise from multiple global implementations, across 400,000 customers and 25 different industries. Products such as Celonis/Signavio (depending on the client's licensing options) can be leveraged to analyze the existing variants around how the business processes are used currently and benchmark them against industry standards. This will ensure the redundancies are optimized before moving the same into the new S/4HANA landscape on RISE with SAP. Based on this analysis, clients can leverage embedded intelligence within business processes by leveraging SAP's workflows, **robotic process automation (RPA)**, and other AI business scenarios.

- **Business case/strategy**: Based on how simple or complex your existing architecture is, you need to identify the business value that would be added by moving onto S/4HANA rather than making the move an IT-driven initiative. Hence, it is important to define a strong business case and strategy on what will change for the business and what value the move offers it. In *Chapter 5*, we will consider in detail the approach and different dimensions to define a strong business case.

- **Approach (Greenfield/Brownfield/Bluefield)**: Depending on the level of process simplification involved and considering the investment made so far along with the reusability component, you need to decide on which approach best suits the scope. This is a key input into the business case to be built.

- **Technical migration**: To assist with the migration, SAP has gradually released multiple tools along with service offerings to assist the journey to the cloud with RISE with SAP, with fast time to value and well-mitigated risk. Clients can choose from their preferred choice of hyperscaler to benefit from infrastructure and platform as a service model. It also provides an opportunity to merge systems instead of moving as-is onto the cloud. In some cases, client(s) might have multiple instances within the landscape of their current model but do not need to retain them as-is, given the transformation SAP offers in the newer versions.

- **Building an intelligent enterprise**: SAP, along with RISE with SAP, offers multiple industries and **line of business** (**LOB**) solutions that can simplify existing investments that you might have in your current landscape. To modernize and simplify the innovation layer along with the user experience layer, SAP has come up with one common platform called SAP **Business Technology Platform** (**BTP**). You can use the BTP for multiple use cases such as enabling multiple networks in a Digital Supplier Network, Logistics Business Network, or Asset Intelligence Network, and also for process intelligence with Signavio while keeping the core clean. The platform provides access to more than 2,200+ APIs to establish connectivity between on-premises, cloud, and non-SAP systems. This platform also has iRPA-based use cases for automation along with SAP workflows made available to support end-to-end business processes.

Let's now go through in more detail the points mentioned earlier around what points are addressed by RISE with SAP. The following diagram summarizes the various aspects of *"what is in the box?"* with RISE with SAP:

Figure 3.3: What's in the box with RISE with SAP?

As shown in the previous diagram, it is important to understand more about the software included versus the tools/scope around business process intelligence, BTP, and the business network-based functionality with built-in CPEA credits to help with the business part:

- **S/4HANA along with BW/4HANA PCE**: SAP S/4HANA along with BW/4HANA is SAP's flagship enterprise resource planning and analytics suite-based solution adoption, avoiding having to run these solutions on-premises. The solution(s) runs on SAP HANA, which provides real-time business statistics and analytics. Later in this chapter, you will see what is included for each of the solutions within private edition compared to other options available for clients:

  - **System hosting options**: RISE with SAP provides multiple options when it comes to hosting SAP on the cloud, such as SAP S/4HANA (public versus private), BW/4HANA, along with other BO, GRC and MDG services as needed by clients. SAP does provide clients with an option to choose from your own option available and if not comfortable can ask SAP to propose one of the hyperscaler solutions. Some of the latest cloud solutions have included IBM Cloud, AWS, Azure, and GCP. The following are different points to consider before finalizing the hosting provided:

    - Industry and regulatory standards

    - Cloud economics: running costs/pricing (Opex), plus the TCO, covering adoption, support, and innovation along with Egress

    - Uptime and availability SLAs

    - Data residency

    - Integration APIs

    - Security, privacy, and compliance

    - Time to value for LOBs and IT

  - **Licensing**: You need to consider the existing sizing along with the future sizing and the different type of users who would be using the functionality, either developers or core users, to determine the Full User Equivalent (**FUE**) and, subsequently, the sizing and licensing of the different components involved.

  - **Scope of services**: You need to finalize the scope of technical managed services as defined in the roles and responsibilities of SAP for RISE, with SAP categorized into Standard, Optional, and Additional to identify both the pricing impact and the scope coverage.

- **Business process intelligence**: As mentioned earlier, business process intelligence using the generated event log can evaluate your existing processes continuously and help you to understand, evaluate, and baseline the processes against industry standards. This, in turn, helps you both simplify and identify automation opportunities within the process being evaluated. You can use the process discovery option available as part of RISE with SAP to perform a one-time analysis of your existing process and to get recommendations and insights from SAP. In addition to the one-time report, you can consume either Celonis or Signavio (bundle cloud service), depending on the tools deployed within the client landscape for generating further insights. The following are some of the insights you can generate using the process mining approach:

- Analyze your processes, look at conformance versus multiple variants involved within business functions, and benchmark them against what other peers have been performing toward.

- Receive inputs and suggested use cases about how we will be able to optimize day-to-day activities across process areas within S/4HANA. The optimization can be achieved by leveraging features such as automation and workflows along with embedded AI/ML scenarios, which are readily available for consumption by business processes.

- **Technology cloud credits**: Being able to seamlessly integrate with other solution(s) within the landscape above and beyond the core S/4HANA is a reality with RISE with SAP, allowing you to use the existing model, along with services available on SAP BTP, to bring it all together. The architecture and possible services within SAP BTP will be shown later in the chapter. As part of the RISE with SAP offering, you can drive your innovation faster with SAP BTP CEPA credits made available. The following are some of the features to consider with SAP BTP:

  - You have access to 2,200+ pre-built API integrations for SAP and other third-party applications

  - You can leverage SAP iRPA bots, made available as part of the best practice package for S/4HANA to optimize the effort involved in the implementation of automation use cases to help reduce the costs

  - You can use native reporting capabilities within S/4HANA (FIORI applications, built-in SAP Analytics Cloud applications, and others) to deliver real-time, actionable insights

  - You can leverage SAP Analytics Cloud, both for reporting and planning purposes along with other embedded AI/ML use cases, to enable data-driven decisions

- **SAP Business Network Starter Pack**: SAP Business Network Starter Pack provides you with the functionality to establish dynamic digital connections with your trading partners and assets. As part of the RISE with SAP offering, you can apply network-wide intelligence based on generated real-time data and insights. The following list provides some of the key features of SAP Business Network Starter Pack:

  - It allows you to establish connectivity between the vendors to increase reliability when it comes to addressing disruptions for streamlined freight collaboration. It also provides access to a global network of carriers and reaches into wider third-party networks.

  - It allows you to collaborate with other suppliers to manage inventory better, confirm the availability of supply, and avoid disruptions. This is made possible by providing real-time sharing of information between your business and suppliers.

- It allows you to connect and share asset usage information to increase customer support and satisfaction. This is done by enabling real-time condition monitoring and predictive, collaborative maintenance activities.

- It allows you to optimize asset performance by merging asset management and maintenance processes along with the related data.

- **Embedded tools and services**: Gradually, SAP has come up with multiple services and tools for inclusion in the RISE with SAP offering. Some of the major ones include the custom code migration app, which performs checks on your existing custom code in the landscape. This analysis provides you insights into usage, comparison to the published simplification list, and future product roadmap mapping.

> **Note**
> While the custom code migration tool focuses on custom code analysis, it is important to consider the performance and ongoing usage of these custom code bits as well, given that it is an opportunity to do more than just move on to the cloud.

In this subsection, we have gone through the details of different components, such as the evaluation of existing architecture, along with putting together a business case and strategy to finalize process simplification and the approach to move to the cloud as part of RISE with SAP. We have also touched upon details of how business process intelligence along with SAP Business Network Starter Pack can help you to implement a streamlined supplier/carrier process. In the following subsection, we will be going through the tools and services available as part of BTP.

Exploring tools and services available within BTP as part of RISE with SAP

To be successful with S/4HANA implementation/migration as part of the move toward the cloud with RISE with SAP, it is important to have a complete understanding of the different tools and services that are available. You can leverage tools such as the custom code migration app and a readiness check to identify possible hotspots and redacted code components. The following is the approach you can adopt when using the custom code migration application:

- The application collects usage data, either with ABAP Monitor or from SAP Solution Manager

- You can then use the Custom Code Migration app to assess the custom code impact and reinforce the clean core principle, during SAP S/4HANA conversions and migration to SAP BTP

- The application will create transport to hold the recommended deletion of the objects to be executed during the system conversion to SAP S/4HANA

Some of the benefits achieved by using this tool are as follows:

- You can have a well-defined estimation of possible hotspots and performance problems prior to the execution of the move to S/4HANA

- You are able to identify and automate the deletion of the custom code not being used in the landscape to save costs during operations

- You can automate the remediation required for custom code adjustments to be made

- Supports clean core principles (returning to the standard approach for ABAP Objects)

In addition to the custom code migration application, there are also other tools that you can consider, such as a simplification list and a readiness check, to make sure your system is ready for the move to S/4HANA. Also, it is important to understand the key services within BTP to plan for the same during deployment. The following diagram provides key services on BTP:

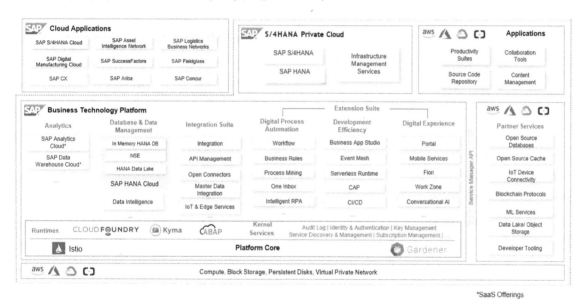

Figure 3.4: Different services to consider within SAP BTP

Along with the tools and services mentioned previously, once you have finalized the cloud-based hosting option, including the scope of services, it is also important to understand how to pick SAP S/4HANA public or private cloud edition. The following diagram provides a quick overview of the different options available within RISE with SAP:

Figure 3.5: Public versus private versus on-premises within RISE with SAP

Let's now do a deep dive into the selection criteria for each of the aforementioned versions to see why customers would choose them:

- **SAP S/4HANA public cloud**: This is a completely modern and native SaaS ERP solution with the full benefits of a proper SaaS solution. It has the fastest path to innovation with the lowest TCO. You would choose this option if you do not want to continue with your existing ERP solutions and want a completely clean core solution, with limited possibility of additional customization.

- **SAP S/4HANA private cloud**: This option is more suitable for customers who want to gradually move toward a SaaS type of landscape but require a well-defined technical managed services model. You would have a single vendor contract to manage the product, infrastructure, and technical managed services. The solution supports 25 industries and 64 countries, with the benefit of being a subscription-based model.

- **SAP S/4HANA on-premise**: You have complete control of the hosting landscape. You can custom-define the support SLAs and design them for high availability and disaster recovery, along with other non-functional requirements.

Along with the aforementioned points, let's look at other dimensions that can further support the decision criteria. The following diagram provides a breakdown of the three versions, based on the license, implementation, content ownership, application management services, content life cycle management, product support, technical operations, and infrastructure.

	SAP S/4HANA Public Cloud	SAP S/4HANA Private Cloud	SAP S/4HANA On-Premise
License Model	Software Subscription *		Perpetual Software
Implementation	Partner / SAP / Customer		
Content Ownership	**SAP** / Partner / Customer	**Partner** / SAP / Customer	
Application Management Services	SAP *	**Partner** / Customer / SAP ECS	
Content Lifecycle Management	SAP *	**Partner** / Customer / SAP ECS	
Product Support	SAP *	SAP *	SAP / Resell Partner
Technical Operations	SAP *	SAP *	Partner / Customer / SAP ECS
Infrastructure	Hyperscaler / SAP *	Hyperscaler / SAP*	Customer DC / Hyperscaler / SAP / Premium Supplier / Partner

Figure 3.6: Comparison across key commercial dimensions for RISE with SAP software selection

In continuation to the previously highlighted dimensions to compare which version would be suitable, the following diagram provides a breakdown based on deployment type, extensibility, modifications, release upgrades, upgrade entitlement, minimum upgrade frequency, model company, third-party add-ons, and partner templates.

	SAP S/4HANA Public Cloud	SAP S/4HANA Private Cloud	SAP S/4HANA On-Premise
Deployment Type	New Implementation	Conversion, Selective Data Transition, (New Implementation)	
Extensibility	Within S/4Extensibility Framework, embedded custom code and SAP Cloud Platform	Customize & Extend	
Modifications	Not allowed	not recommended, but allowed	
Release Upgrades	included and mandatory (limited flexibility option)	Customer owned, installation on request included	not included
Upgrade entitlement	2 times per year	yearly	yearly
Minimum Upgrade frequency	2 times per year	5 years (stay in mainstream maintenance)	not limited (maintenance to be considered)
Model Company	Enterprise Mgmt Layer Included and optional	Best Practice activation included and optional	not included
3rd Party Add-ons	Certified Public Cloud add-ons allowed	Defined list of S/4HANA qualified add-ons allowed*	allowed
Partner Templates	Dedicated Public Cloud templates planned	allowed	

* still under evaluation

Figure 3.7: Comparison across upgrade and other add-on scopes for RISE with SAP product versions

In this section, so far, we have reviewed and compared the product types in S/4HANA. Let's do a similar review for the scope of BW/4HANA along with what to expect from RISE with SAP. Similar to S/4HANA, you need to evaluate and agree upon the BW/4HANA-based version or type of data warehouse solution that you want to deploy (public cloud, private cloud, or on-premise) to ensure you have the right functionality available, as per your business requirements.

Let's do a deep dive to understand the selection criteria for each of the aforementioned versions and the reasons customers choose what they do:

- **SAP Data Warehouse Cloud**: A SaaS solution where the application, the upgrades, the performance, and availability are taken care of by SAP, like any other SaaS solution. This is also a product to adopt when you need to have a more business-driven solution that allows users to generate their own reports, with the technical layer exposed as a semantic layer. In the true sense of a cloud solution, you only pay for what you use when it comes to sizing. You can also leverage the SAP BW Bridge functionality to have a hybrid between traditional BW-based and business-based semantic functionality.

- **SAP BW/4HANA private cloud**: You can use this to either convert your existing BW or BW on HANA investment toward a cloud-based BW/4HANA PCE, or to implement a new instance of BW/4HANA from a greenfield implementation point of view. You can gradually move toward a pure SaaS solution in your own time.

- **SAP BW/4HANA on-premise/BYOL**: This version is more suitable for customers who have compliance or regulatory requirements from an organization's point of view. It is also more appropriate for government/defense organizations. It allows you to have your own custom SLAs and non-functional requirement architectural patterns.

Along with the aforementioned points, let's look at other dimensions that can further support the decision criteria. The following diagram provides a breakdown of the three versions, based on the license, implementation, application management services, content life cycle management, product support, technical operations, and infrastructure.

SAP BW/4HANA, private cloud edition – License,
Delivery & Operations View

SAP Data Warehouse Cloud

SAP BW/4HANA Private Cloud

SAP BW/4HANA On-Premise

	SAP Data Warehouse Cloud	SAP BW/4HANA Private Cloud	SAP BW/4HANA On-Premise
License Model	Software Subscription		Perpetual Software
Implementation (configuration after deployment)	Partner / SAP / Customer		
Application Management Services	SAP *	Partner / Customer / SAP ECS (as chosen by customer)	
Content Lifecycle Management	SAP *	Partner / Customer / SAP ECS (as chosen by customer)	
Product Support	SAP *	SAP *	SAP / Resell Partner
Technical Operations	SAP *	SAP *	Partner / Customer / SAP ECS
Infrastructure	Hyperscaler*	Hyperscaler*	Customer DC / Hyperscaler / SAP / Premium Supplier / Partner

* Included in SAP Subscription

Figure 3.8: Comparison across key commercial dimensions for RISE with SAP software selection

In addition to the aforementioned dimensions to compare which version would be suitable, the following diagram provides a breakdown based on deployment type, modifications, release upgrades, upgrade entitlement, minimum upgrade frequency, and business content.

SAP BW/4HANA, private cloud edition – Characteristics

SAP Data Warehouse Cloud

SAP BW/4HANA Private Cloud

SAP BW/4HANA On-Premise

	SAP Data Warehouse Cloud	SAP BW/4HANA Private Cloud	SAP BW/4HANA On-Premise
Deployment Type	New Implementation	Conversion (Remote, Shell), (New Implementation)	
Modifications	Not allowed	not recommended, but allowed	
Release Upgrades	Included and mandatory (limited flexibility option)	Customer owned, installation on request included	not included
Upgrade entitlement	Per wave	At customers request	yearly
Minimum Upgrade frequency	Per wave	5 years (stay in mainstream maintenance)	not limited (maintenance to be considered)
Business Content	SAP-lead and partner-lead content	SAP-lead content	

Figure 3.9: Impact on upgrade and other modifications with different versions of RISE with SAP product

In this section, we have explained what RISE with SAP is and the various components that are made available to customers, to facilitate and optimize their experience and effort while moving to S/4HANA along with RISE with SAP. We have also gone through the different versions and selection criteria available with S/4HANA, including the assessment across different dimensions.

In the next section, we will explore the known myths that customers currently face. We will also provide details on how you can demystify these myths.

Demystifying myths around the adoption of RISE with SAP

So far in this chapter, we have discussed what RISE with SAP is, what it has in the box, and what sorts of decisions or dimensions you need to consider before finalizing the type of version of SAP S/4HANA or BW/4HANA you would like to deploy. Along with these, it is also equally important to bust some myths about the adoption of RISE with SAP to ensure you have all the details required to make an informed decision.

Before we go through some of the myths and provide more clarity on how RISE with SAP can support a client's journey, the following graph shows some of the key responses of a survey performed by SAPinsider about the awareness of RISE with SAP:

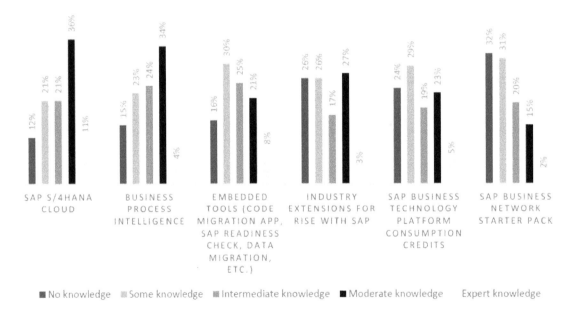

Figure 3:10: Survey results about awareness of RISE with SAP and the connected services

(Source: SAPinsider report – survey done in 2021)

The previous figure shows the understanding of the different stakeholders interviewed about their awareness of the RISE with SAP offering. Let's have a look at the different drivers that stakeholders expect from RISE with SAP based on the features provided. The following diagram provides an overview of the SAPinsider survey to showcase what drivers are expected from RISE with SAP:

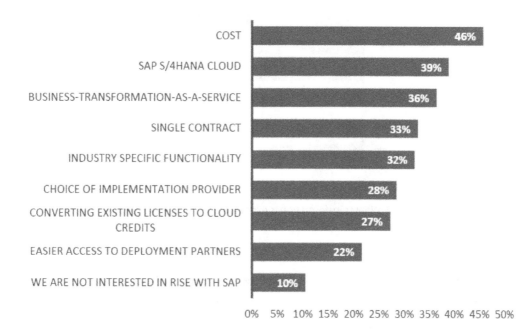

Figure 3.11: Drivers expected from RISE with SAP

(Source: SAPInsider report – survey done in 2021)

Along with the awareness and features of RISE with SAP that clients are looking for, it is equally important to understand what transformations clients expect RISE with SAP to drive within an organization. The following diagram provides a summary of this breakdown:

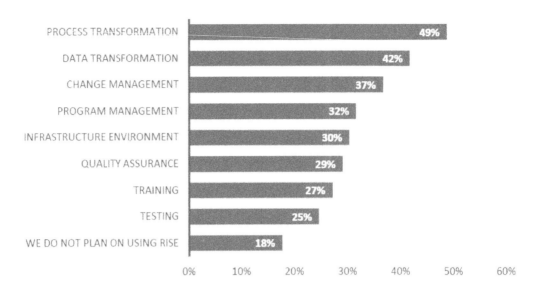

Figure 3.12: What transformation is expected from RISE with SAP

(Source: SAPinsider report – survey done in 2021)

Let's now have a look at some of the other myths and bust them to make sure you are well-informed when handling clients' questions or your business stakeholders' concerns regarding RISE with SAP:

- **Myth 1 – RISE with SAP is a product**: As mentioned earlier, RISE with SAP is not a product but actually an offering that combines multiple products from SAP under one umbrella, with the right business model structure. The products in question are SAP S/4HANA PCE, SAP BTP, SAP Business Process Intelligence, SAP Business Network Starter Package, and, last but not the least, the technical managed services of the SAP S/4HANA component of the offering.

- **Myth 2 – RISE with SAP is the same as HANA Enterprise Cloud (HEC) and known as HEC 2.0 / 3.0**: RISE with SAP is way beyond what HEC-based services or scope could offer, and SAP is not rebranding HEC as RISE with SAP with the same services. RISE with SAP, as explained so far, is a different variant with a new design, architecture, and type of SLAs being committed, along with an SAP BTP-based framework made available.

- **Myth 3 – you no longer need a Basis skill set, given that all of the technical managed services are now offered by SAP**: RISE with SAP only takes care of the under-the-hood technical managed services related to Basis activities. You are still expected to implement functional Basis activities to be able to configure the SSO, the source system connection setup, the transport setup for gitCTS or CTS+, along with ChaRM/Rev-Trac usage, if any. You can obviously opt for the **Cloud Application Services (CAS)** package on top of the standard services to support these activities if you don't have an application management vendor in your landscape providing such services.

- **Myth 4 – RISE with SAP includes only SAP S/4HANA implementation or migration to the hyperscaler of choice, and you don't have any additional use cases around AI/machine learning or other non-functional requirements being adapted**: The following diagram provides output from the survey carried out, highlighting the different tools and technologies that clients are adapting along with RISE with SAP:

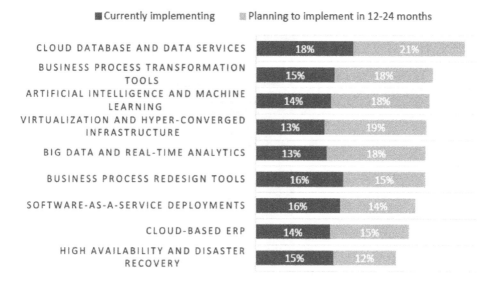

Figure 3.13: Tools being adapted as part of RISE with SAP

(Source: SAPinsider report – survey done in 2021)

In addition to these myths, here are some further considerations:

- Even if you are an organization that already had a relationship with one of the hyperscalers, remember that RISE with SAP deployment will be hosted in SAP's environment with that provider and not your own. This would mean you would still need to configure the connectivity if you want to use data from your RISE with SAP deployment in your other cloud-based or on-premise applications and environments.

- Given the data egress limitation, please plan your architecture accordingly.

- Even though the hosting provider may seem like the biggest partner role in the offering, a partner must also be selected in advisory, implementation, and application management roles. Determining which partner will assist with your deployment can also potentially impact migration costs if the implementation partner you choose already works closely with your selected hosting company.

In summary, let's look at the different concerns the stakeholders listed when it comes to the deployment/adoption of RISE with SAP:

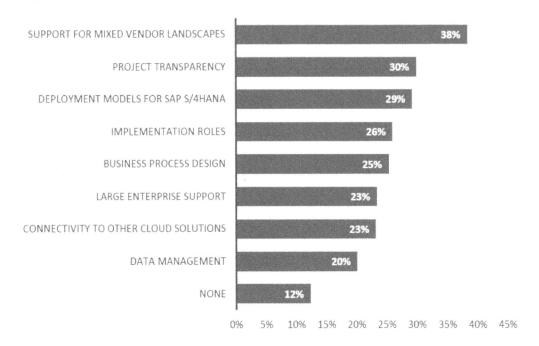

Figure 3.14: Concerns from stakeholders about RISE with SAP

(Source: SAPinsider report – survey done in 2021)

Hence, it is very important to clearly articulate and understand, by reading this book, what RISE with SAP offers, from the initial onboarding to the deployment, and from an ongoing business value add a point of view. In this section so far, we have explained the different myths and what you need to know to plan for the same. We also provided insights generated from a global study of awareness of RISE with SAP as a solution.

In the next section, we will go through the different options made available by SAP with RISE with SAP and how S/4HANA and other SAP products can be delivered through similar SLA-driven metrics. We will also explain why you should consider a given model for deployment.

Understanding options available with RISE with SAP

SAP provides RISE with SAP in multiple options to suit your needs and to provide the level of flexibility needed, while still being governed by the design principles set by SAP. The following options are available:

- Standard
- Tailored
- Customer Data Center
- Critical Data Cloud
- Partner-Managed Cloud

Let's go through each of the options in detail.

Option 1 – Standard Edition

In this option, SAP, based on different FUE models, has come up with different T-shirt size packages. As of today, there are well-defined t-shirt sizes ranging from XXS to 4XL, defined based on the FUE of your existing requirement and the sizing requirement of the HANA DB and application servers required to address the end-to-end requirement. These are non-customizable.

Option 2 – Tailored Edition

In this option, you get to choose the different parameters: from the sizing to the count of application servers to the number of landscapes required, along with the type of services you would need for each of the systems. This option typically tends to be more costly compared to Standard Edition due to the different sizing and services adopted.

Note that in *Chapter 5*, The *Cloud with a Silver Lining: Busting the Myth – Part 1*, and *Chapter 6*, *Cloud with Silver Lining – Part 2*, we will explain the roles and responsibilities for each of these options in detail, going through what are termed as Standard, Optional, Additional, and CAS packages.

Option 3 – Customer Data Center

This option is more suitable for clients who are not willing to move their workload to one of the hyperscalers (IBM Cloud, AWS, Azure, Google Cloud) but plan to bring the cloud to the customers' data center through SAP HANA Enterprise Cloud-based deployment. At the time of writing, this option is only supported by Dell, Lenovo, and HP. This is a turnkey cloud offering that is fully compliant with SAP private cloud standards of architecture, services, and security components being delivered to the customer data center, and it is backed by the same SLAs that RISE with SAP offers.

How does it work?

The hardware components along with the infrastructure maintenance are supported at the customer data center by Dell, Lenovo, and HP. On top of these services, SAP provides managed services for the operating system, SAP HANA DB management, and application Basis-related support. Support for functional application services, application evolution, and change management will be provided by either the customer or a partner selected by the customer. You can also request these services from SAP through CAS packages. The following diagram provides an overview of the split of services between Dell/HP/Lenovo, SAP, and the customer/partner:

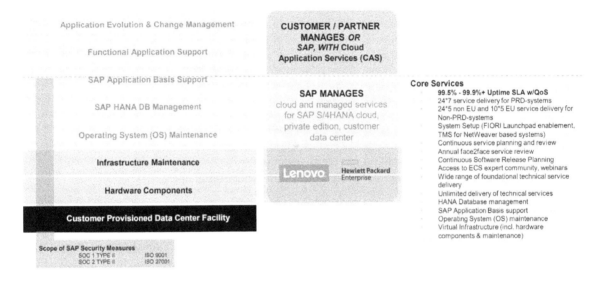

Figure 3.15: The split of activities between hardware provider, SAP, and customer

Why do customers really opt for this option?

The customers do not want to move their solutions or investment to the cloud but would still like to have the technical managed services option from RISE with SAP. For those customers, the Customer data center option is less disruptive to their operations and offers the merits of an OPEX model, while providing the same computing and technical managed services from SAP under the Tailored option.

It's the choice for customers that want to keep the landscape along with the data on-premises, while gaining the benefits of a subscription-based, agile, and consistent cloud experience.

Option 4 – Critical Data Cloud

The option of Critical Data Cloud is country-specific and is currently limited to Australia, with plans to expand it to the US – NS2-based services for now. This is a good option for clients where there are strict regulations and defense-type requirements to be supported, especially with end-to-end support that needs to be provided by in-country personnel with a 0% offshore delivery model. The pricing for this model would be on the higher side compared to other options, given the localized nature of the support handling. You would need to think through the entire support model in a much more comprehensive manner.

How does it work?

The following diagram provides a breakdown of how the different public cloud components from a customer usage point of view will interact with the SaaS products to be deployed within the Critical Data Cloud, as per the client's ask:

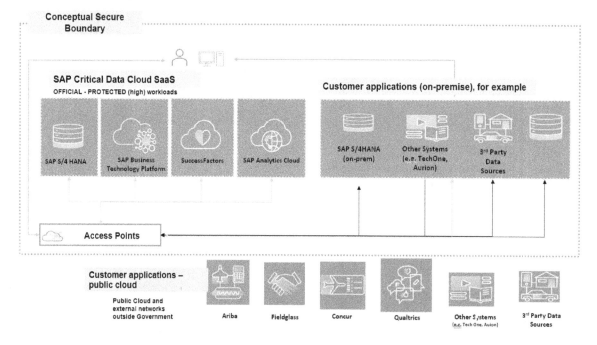

Figure 3.16: Critical Data Cloud integration with SaaS products

What services are offered by whom within the Critical Data Cloud scenario?

The following technical managed services will be supported by SAP and NS2:

- High availability supporting business continuity
- In-country disaster recovery
- Technical system operations
- Technical landscape deployment
- Technical upgrade installation
- 24/7 service delivery for production and 24/5 for a non-production landscape
- Setup of the RFC connections

Along with the technical managed services, SAP and NS2 are also responsible for supporting the following functional and infrastructure management scope:

- Consumption-based services for S/4HANA, BTP, SAC, and SuccessFactors (others can be added)
- Packages and partner-based add-ons for LOB-based solutions
- Highest flexibility on the infrastructure components with the best scalability options

Apart from the preceding, customer/SAP services/SI partners need to account for the following list of activities:

- Advisory and implementation services:
  - Value discovery and business case
  - Application implementation
  - Industry/LOB practices and business process
  - System conversion and selective data transition
  - Data harmonization and analytics
- Application management services:
  - SAP FIORI operations
  - Regression testing
  - Data volume optimization
  - Data quality optimization
  - System health monitoring

- Functional application management
- Technical AMS

• Innovation and extension services:

- SAP FIORI operations
- Regression testing
- Data volume optimization
- Data quality optimization
- System health monitoring
- Functional application management
- Technical AMS

These services can only be performed by AU or US citizens (at the time of writing, depending on which instance you select) for instances when it comes to technical managed services.

Option 5 – Partner-Managed Cloud

This option allows a partner to own third-party use rights from SAP for one or multiple cloud solutions. The partner then enriches the SAP solution by adding the provider's industry IP, services, and solution scope. The following diagram provides a summary of what is provided by SAP versus what is provided by the partner and what can be expected by the customer:

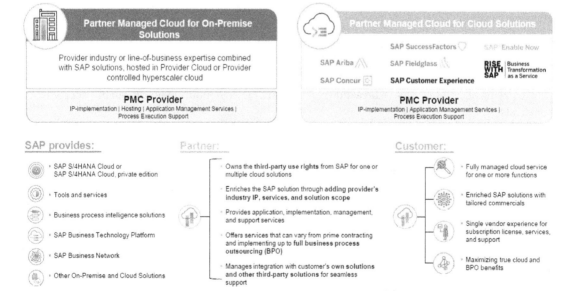

Figure 3.17: An overview of Partner-Managed Cloud for RISE with SAP

As shown in the previous diagram, SAP still provides the software components along with their licensing for SAP S/4HANA Cloud (public or private edition) along with the business process intelligence, BTP, and Business Network-based solutions. The partner is also responsible for providing the application, implementation, management, and support services.

Customers from this option get a fully managed cloud service for one or more functions with enriched SAP solutions, with tailored commercials and a "true" single vendor experience for a subscription license, services, and support, maximizing the true cloud and BPO benefits.

Why PMC?

Partner-Managed Cloud (PMC) allows for a completely tailored offering by the partner involved to fulfill customer requirements that are not addressed by an out-of-the-box RISE with SAP solution (Standard or Tailored), especially with multiple non-SAP solutions also included in the mix.

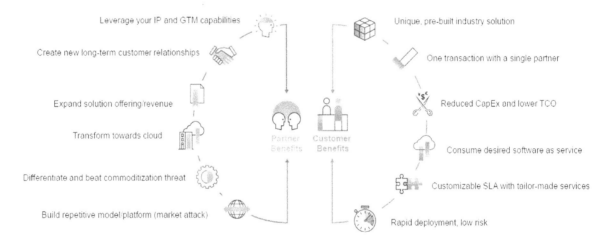

Figure 3.18: What to expect from PMC

The following diagram provides a breakdown of the PMC-based option and how it can be packaged for clients:

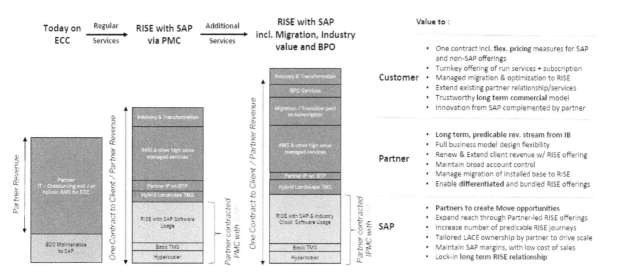

Figure 3.19: Packaging options with PMC

Based on the options discussed so far, it is important to have a good understanding of the commercial model and how you can bundle these options through either reselling or CCFlex/Direct for the customers. The following table provides a clear summary of the commercial model available for the partner with different RISE options available:

	PMC	Resell	CCFlex / Direct
SAP Software is...	Bundled or wrapped with partner's managed services, support and Implementation	Resold by partner to end customer and supported by SAP	Direct from SAP to end customer and supported by SAP
License granted is...	Subscription based allowing partner use rights for the delivery to end-customer	Subscription based allowing end customer use rights	License granted direct to end customer
SAP Support...	Is given to partner who manages the SAP Cloud system for customer.	To the Customer	To the Customer
Key Condition(s)	1. Partner has the use rights 2. Partner wraps and provide a service(s) together with subscription software 3. Partner Provides 1st and 2nd line support to end-customer	1. End customer has the use rights 2. Services offered independently of SAP cloud services 3. Standard SAP Enterprise Support + optional enhanced support services	1. End customer has the use rights 2. Services not included; partner may offer services independetly 3. Standard SAP Enterprise Support + optional enhanced support services
Partner Value	• Long term, predicable rev. stream from IB • Full business model design flexibility • Renew & Extend client revenue w/ RISE offering • Maintain broad account control • Manage migration of installed base to RISE • Enable differentiated and bundled RISE offerings	• Full ownership of customer engagement model • Top line recurring revenue from installed base • Unlock partner owned install-base • Manage migration of install-base to RISE • Additional cross/upsell services and support offerings including developing IP extensions	(CCFlex) • Reward to penetrate installed base • Maintain ongoing Operate relationship • Drive holistic Client offering with RISE • Targeted approach to migrate installed base • Leverage existing operate resources
Customer Value	• One contract incl. flex. pricing measures for SAP and non-SAP offerings • Turnkey offering of run services + subscription • Managed migration & optimization to RISE • Extend existing partner relationship/services • Trustworthy long term commercial model • Innovation from SAP complemented by partner	• Direct relationship with selected partner • Partner expertise to align to customer localization, regulations and industry specialization • Additional partner offerings to accelerate transformation to RISE • High customer satisfaction and ultimately renewal by SAP enabling the partner	(CCFlex) • Build on existing trusted Partner relationship • Integrated RISE migration offer • Accelerate RISE migration w/ existing Partner • Renegotiate operate agreements

Figure 3.20: PMC versus Resell versus CCFlex/Direct commercial options for RISE with SAP sales

> **Note**
>
> To become competent in position, and sell and deploy the solution of RISE with SAP, it is important to cover various roles, such as sales executives, presales consultants, customer engagement executives, solution consultants, and partner cloud architects in the context of RISE with SAP functions/topics, such as RISE SAP S/4HANA Cloud central components:
>
> - Business networks
>
> - BTP
>
> - AMS and transition services
>
> - Cloud economics
>
> - Intelligent enterprise
>
> - Introduction for partner cloud architect tasks

You can access the learning paths for these roles at the following links:

- Sales executives: `https://learning-journeys-prod.cfapps.eu10.hana.ondemand.com/#/learning-journeys/learningJourney/1410bdd988b9494b898fea8bc9209ec4`

- Presales consultants: `https://learning-journeys-prod.cfapps.eu10.hana.ondemand.com/#/learning-journeys/learningJourney/3d56dc978b5743f697bd414a31463525`

- Customer engagement executives: `https://learning-journeys-prod.cfapps.eu10.hana.ondemand.com/#/learning-journeys/learningJourney/cafc0ae9c07d4bf494fabd8dc0a2853b`

- Solution consultants: `https://learning-journeys-prod.cfapps.eu10.hana.ondemand.com/#/learning-journeys/learningJourney/6187736ceda94805a50278e67c174610`

- Cloud architects: `https://learning-journeys-prod.cfapps.eu10.hana.ondemand.com/#/learning-journeys/learningJourney/1b98b92104584bb89cab9d05cc18aa83`

In this section so far, we have gone through different deployment options available within RISE with SAP, such as standard, tailored, customer data center, critical data cloud, and partner-managed cloud. We also explored which option should be selected for what scenario to ensure you have the right model in place when deploying S/4HANA with RISE with SAP.

In the next section, we will be providing inputs on how you can plan for use cases and their traceability when it comes to deploying them on RISE with SAP. We also touch upon different non-functional requirements that you need to be considering prior to deploying a solution with RISE with SAP.

Use case traceability and what to plan for with RISE with SAP

In this section, we will provide insight into the use cases for S/4HANA implementation and the relevant non-functional requirements to be validated. The purpose of implementation or migration toward S/4HANA on RISE with SAP is to modernize the ERP components within a client's landscape and to simplify the processes where applicable. A typical implementation or S/4HANA landscape can consist of multiple SaaS and on-premise products, depending on the scope of the client, with different integration modules to support day-to-day operations. The following diagram provides an overview of the conceptual architecture of a typical client:

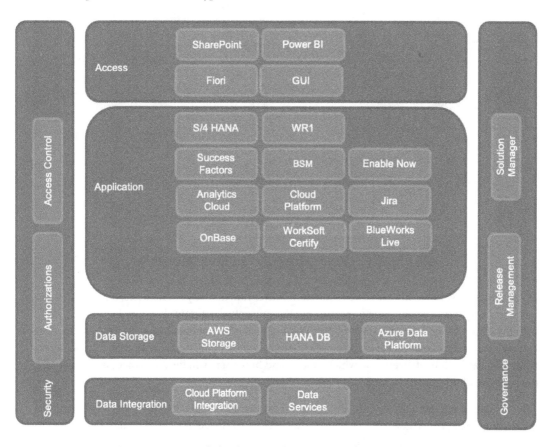

Figure 3.21: A sample landscape with S/4HANA within RISE with SAP

Before we deep-dive into the checklist of items to be considered for each of the use cases that you might choose to implement, it is advisable to understand how connectivity would happen between your current user network and the hyperscaler on which your S/4HANA or other components would be hosted, compared to other SAP BTP and SAP Cloud applications (SaaS solutions). The following diagram provides an overview of the different networks you might be accessing data across, along with the type of connectivity established, to ensure you plan your requirements accordingly:

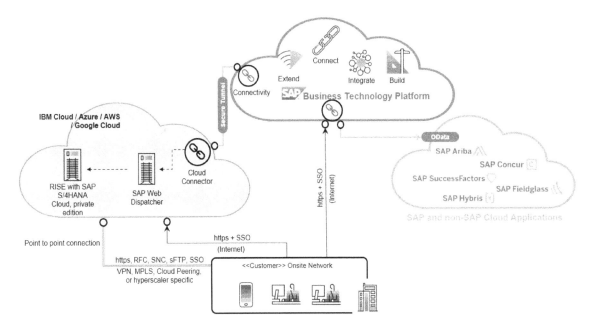

Figure 3.22: A multi-cloud connectivity pattern with RISE with SAP

Once you have identified the use cases required to deliver functionality to end users, it is important to map them out to the various components, as per the conceptual diagram shown in *Figure 3.22*, along with the connectivity diagram to ensure that all functional requirements adhere to the best practices and architectural patterns, as suggested by SAP. This helps you maintain from day one traceability on which use case will be delivered by which system and how users will be able to access them during the life cycle of the landscape made available to them.

After validating the use cases functionally, it is also important to clearly document the non-functional requirements that play a key role in ensuring that users not only get the functionality they want but also how they want it with respect to the following:

- Latency
- Performance of the transaction
- Availability of the system

- Accessibility of the system

- Business continuity requirement

- SLAs for support

Before we deep-dive into the checklist to address these requirements, let's have a quick drilldown of how the interconnectivity between the partners (SAP and associated Technical Managed Services vendor) and the client's systems would work to ensure your requirements are well wrapped around that design.

The following diagram provides the key components RISE with SAP would have and how each of these would connect with each other to provide the required services for the client/user:

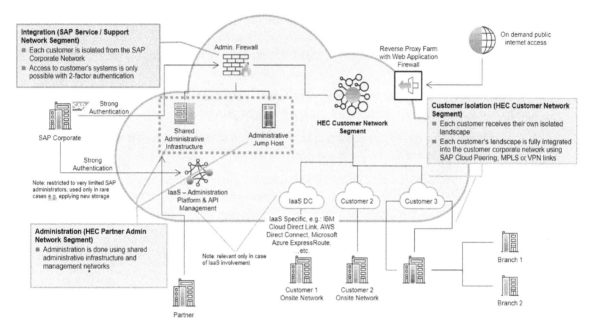

Figure 3.23: SAP, Customer, and Partner connectivity within RISE with SAP

Based on the points mentioned in this section, let's go through some of the checklist items that you need to consider when planning to go with RISE with SAP:

- The scope to be finalized:

  - Need to finalize the scope with regard to S/4HANA, BW/4HANA, GRC, SolMan, BOBI, and many other components that can possibly be supported by RISE with SAP

  - For each of the components, you need to agree upon the type of implementation as either Greenfield, Brownfield, or as-is lift and shift

- Need to consider the integration component to be used based on various other ecosystem components in scope

- Plan out the different data centers from which your systems would be interconnecting with each other

- Non-functional requirements:

  - Review the sizing along with the future growth to ensure you can avoid downtimes at a later date

  - Need to finalize requirements around the pairing of your primary and secondary data centers

  - Need to finalize requirements around high availability and disaster recovery (short distance versus long distance) along with active-active versus active-passive, and ensure you ask the same prior, depending on which hyperscaler you choose, as not all hyperscalers deliver these solutions in the same way

  - Finalize the IP range as per the number of systems deployed, as typical SAP RISE deployment would need a /22 to be provided for the systems to be provisioned

  - Plan the network-related remediation to be applied based on different firewalls to be updated, depending on where all your source systems are currently located

  - Plan the Direct Link/Direct Connect/ExpressRoute, depending on the hyperscaler selected, to get the process initiated, as this would be the responsibility of the client team and not SAP to get the connectivity established up to the endpoint provided by SAP

  - Need to plan around the ingress/egress packages provided to ensure you do not end up incurring additional costs due to data movement across various solutions not planned for within the same account setup

- Functional requirements:

  - If needed, finalize the best practice package from SAP or an industry package that any of the partners can provide, along with the EML diagram that SAP offers with preinstalled configuration for industry solutions. This can incur additional costs and, hence, needs to be validated prior to being communicated to SAP.

- Effort above and beyond RISE with SAP scope:

  - There are multiple activities that you (the client) still need to plan for, even after choosing RISE with SAP, as a lot of functional Basis services are not included as part of the technical managed services scope provided by RISE with SAP.

- For instance, the following activities need to be performed by the client:

    - Source system connectivity

    - Housekeeping jobs from a functional system scope point of view

    - SSO configuration

    - ChaRM/Rev-Trac setup

    - Job management tool/job scheduling for functional jobs at the configuration level

    - Application-level security

    - Functional configuration

    - Technical and functional testing

    - Project management effort to engage and request services from SAP, including internal services with other stakeholders to execute upgrades or follow-up system refresh activities

In addition to these points, it is critical to thoroughly understand the roles and responsibilities within RISE with SAP to have a clear view of what is included and what is not included. You also need to consider adding optional or additional services to avoid additional costs at a later date.

In this section, we have gone through different non-functional scenarios and an approach to address these with the project life cycle when it comes to different stakeholders. We also have gone through inputs when it comes to connectivity and other possible restrictions that need to be addressed proactively.

In the next section, we will walk you through a client case study and how they were able to transform being an intelligent enterprise based on the value levers mentioned previously in this chapter.

Exploring a case study for transformation with RISE with SAP

We will now walk you through a client example and what to consider when evaluating RISE with SAP as an option across different entry points. It is important to understand the stage at which you are to evaluate whether RISE with SAP is the way forward. At some point, eventually, while you would merge the adoption of RISE with SAP, it is critical to understand what to expect.

For instance, every client journey can be categorized into the following:

- Optimize the core

- Unlock legacy

- Unleash digital

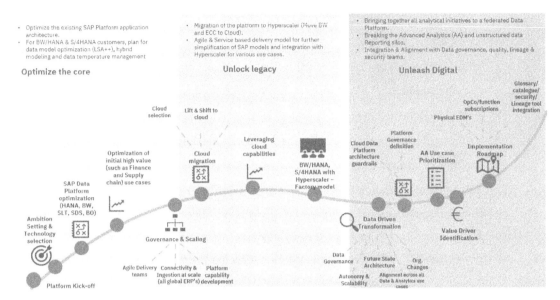

Figure 3.24: A sample journey map for a client with RISE with SAP

The clients who are already at the stage of **Unleash Digital** might not immediately move on to RISE with SAP, as they already are using one of the hyperscaler-based solutions optimized for their business processes, along with the likes of Intelligent Robotic Process Automation bots, business process mining with the likes of Celonis and Signavio, and embedded AI/ML use cases for process optimization, leveraging the likes of AI Business Services where appropriate. These clients would like for either the next contract refresh, new storage models, or new data fabric models, at which point RISE with SAP addresses their requirements.

Clients either at the stage of **Optimizing the core** or **Unlocking legacy** to adapt new solutions and scenarios are more prone toward adopting RISE with SAP, along with one of their choice of hyperscalers. This is to take advantage of the best of both worlds in terms of hyperscaler functionality (moving on to the cloud) and a single vendor support model.

Based on the understanding of RISE with SAP, Spark4Life has been able to demystify some of the myths the CXOs had and were able to lay out a clear plan of action. The plan includes moving to hosted services with an end-to-end SLA and transformation built into the solution.

> **Note**
>
> Moving to RISE with SAP is not the answer for everything, and hence, while it is best to have a single contract or single vendor-related scenario, you would still need to plan the rest of the components, depending on where you are on the journey to cover all the possible patterns, similar to the journey shown here.

Based on the journey map shown previously, the following are the key points to look out for:

- Think about your functional and non-functional requirements upfront in order to make sure the design put forward by SAP has these addressed, such as high availability, disaster recovery, and frequency of updates

- Networking along with site-to-site VPN versus other connectivity is still the client's responsibility

- Sizing is the client's responsibility

- SSO along with Charm and other key components would need to be managed by the client/service integrator

- Any OS-level activity cannot be performed by the client and needs to have a dependency on SAP to perform the same

- Be aware of all other optional requests and have a calendar schedule in place to make sure you request for the same spread with proper planning, as the collaboration, technical ownership, and testing are still the client's responsibility, as are upgrade activities

Source system connectivity after the VPN or other connectivity configuration has been addressed by the client/SI should be handled by the client/SI itself. The following diagram shows what benefits RISE with SAP offers:

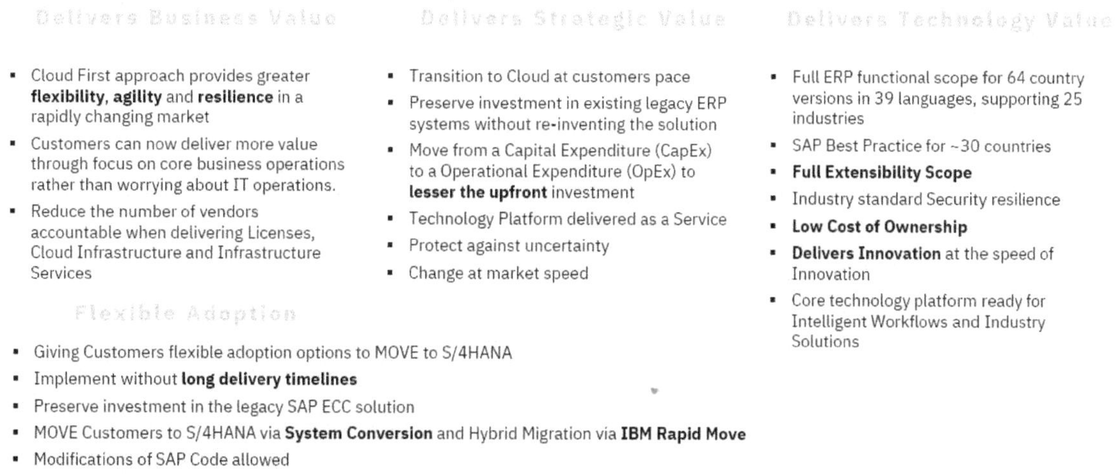

Delivers Business Value

- Cloud First approach provides greater **flexibility, agility** and **resilience** in a rapidly changing market
- Customers can now deliver more value through focus on core business operations rather than worrying about IT operations.
- Reduce the number of vendors accountable when delivering Licenses, Cloud Infrastructure and Infrastructure Services

Delivers Strategic Value

- Transition to Cloud at customers pace
- Preserve investment in existing legacy ERP systems without re-inventing the solution
- Move from a Capital Expenditure (CapEx) to a Operational Expenditure (OpEx) to **lesser the upfront** investment
- Technology Platform delivered as a Service
- Protect against uncertainty
- Change at market speed

Delivers Technology Value

- Full ERP functional scope for 64 country versions in 39 languages, supporting 25 industries
- SAP Best Practice for ~30 countries
- **Full Extensibility Scope**
- Industry standard Security resilience
- **Low Cost of Ownership**
- **Delivers Innovation** at the speed of Innovation
- Core technology platform ready for Intelligent Workflows and Industry Solutions

Flexible Adoption

- Giving Customers flexible adoption options to MOVE to S/4HANA
- Implement without **long delivery timelines**
- Preserve investment in the legacy SAP ECC solution
- MOVE Customers to S/4HANA via **System Conversion** and Hybrid Migration via **IBM Rapid Move**
- Modifications of SAP Code allowed

Figure 3.25: The benefits of RISE with SAP

In this section, you have how seen a journey toward S/4HANA with RISE with SAP can provide you both transformational and operational benefits. We also explained how the journey can be phased out at different stages, including "optimize the core," "unlock the legacy," and "unleash digital," based on your existing adoption and business maturity. There are multiple entry and exit points that you can plan to address business requirements.

Summary

In summary, we have started this chapter by explaining what RISE with SAP is as well as the different components involved with RISE with SAP. We then went through the details related to business process intelligence, SAP Business Network Starter Pack, and other tools and services available with RISE with SAP. We also got an overview of the different product versions available with RISE with SAP and what they mean to our landscape. We then shared the results of a recent study of what people know about RISE with SAP and what they expect from it. This helped to demystify some of the gaps you might have in your landscape by comparing it to an existing landscape.

We also walked you through the different options available for S/4HANA and BW/4HANA and compared options across different dimensions. You also got a good understanding of deployment options, such as standard, tailored, customer data center, critical data center, and partner-managed cloud. Finally, we concluded the chapter by talking about what non-functional requirements need to be considered when moving onto RISE with SAP, along with a client case study to showcase the journey experience.

In the next chapter, you will learn how process mining can be used to optimize the landscape support model while helping to design an automation solution.

Further reading

Beyond the details shared, you can use SAP Learning Hub if you would like to do a further deep dive into the different courses available. The following figure provides an overview of the different learning paths available:

SAP Learning Hub – Over 50+ education course contents available for RISE with SAP

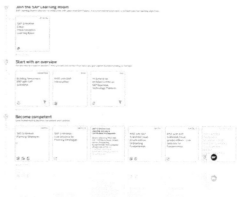

New SAP Certifications and Learning Paths Example:

Recommended Learning Journey:
RISE with SAP S/4HANA Cloud, private edition Onboarding Fundamentals

Part 2:
The Journey with RISE with SAP

In this part, we will explain how process mining and intelligent workflows will form the crux of your virtual enterprise solution – what you as an organization are looking for in order to achieve the objectives that you have set out. This part will then go into the details of what RISE with SAP entails, its roles and responsibilities, service scopes, SLAs, and various other details you need to know about RISE with SAP. Furthermore, it sets the context for why data migration, along with data governance and data quality from day one, are key components of the RISE with SAP journey.

This part has the following chapters:

4

Intelligent Enterprise and Sustainable Design

Current events have been taxing—excruciatingly agonizing at times—as industries and enterprises adapt to customer demand and market dynamics. As the COVID-19 pandemic continues to impact many industries across the globe significantly, organizations realize that to operate in these unprecedented times of crisis, they need to be agile, robust, and secure. The CxOs of these already strained organizations are under immense pressure to make difficult choices so that their businesses and IT are resilient. This resiliency is being tested across industries by the ability of organizations to proactively respond, anticipate, and scale according to supply and demand. Competing in this volatile and unpredictable environment necessitates evolution toward being driven by automated business processes and intelligent decision support systems to optimize the scale of operations. It involves applying advanced technologies to transform static, siloed processes and data consistently to stay coordinated with customers and employees alike in both physical and digital worlds.

In this chapter, we will take the first steps toward understanding how CxOs can use the tools and services offered under RISE with SAP to help pave a roadmap for their teams to move ahead—unlocking the value hidden in their enterprise data siloes. This marks a move toward standardization, and yet being flexible and nimble enough to accommodate industry trends, enabling new revenue streams and opportunities to create exceptional experiences for their customers and employees, with much-needed acceleration for a faster time-to-value. Essentially, we will lay down the foundations to enable enterprises to capture new markets and offer new business models with RISE with SAP.

Spark4life has just set sail on the journey of their transformation and has now got an appreciation of the fact that the 'Rise with SAP' offering by itself is not an elixir to all their problems. After busting some of the myths on Rise with SAP, the Spark4life CxOs have asked their organizational teams to take stock of the ground realities uncover the hidden challenges in people, processes, and underpinning technologies. Though there are some key tools and services which the IT and Business leads of 'Spark4life' are keen on discovering and are doing their due diligence within the organization and getting insights in several global conferences from the industry players. They are evaluating these tools for adoption, which will help accelerate discovering their transformation goals and putting together a roadmap to achieve the business outcomes which they envisage will help turn the tide for their organization.

In the next section, let us cover the market trends and technologies within this wave of transformation across several industries, including the various lenses through which organizations have to apply the why, what, and how of the market forces and technologies that will shape the future of their organizations. Let's understand how recent upheavals in the market dynamics are forcing organizations to bring forward their transformation initiatives.

This chapter covers the following main topics:

- Holistic transformation
- Assessing capabilities
- **Business Process Intelligence** (**BPI**)
- Keeping the core clean

Crisis presents opportunities for change and innovation, with much-needed focus and investment. 60% of executives surveyed by the **IBM Institute for Business Value** (**IBV**) say they recognize the current need and opportunity for transformation and are using this time to dramatically accelerate their company's digital transformation. Two-thirds also said that the pandemic had enabled them to advance specific transformational initiatives that had previously been met with resistance. Moreover, the technologies that enabled these companies to start their transformation have also changed, with the hybrid cloud and the adoption of AI seeing a dramatic rise during the pre- and post-covid standing. The significant adoption of a hybrid cloud model seen across the retail, energy and utilities, insurance, and travel sectors allows them to extend their services via new channels directly to the customer securely and resiliently for their e-commerce and supply chain processes, while AI provides the foundations to create engaging experiences, improving their **Net Promoter Score** (**NPS**) and desperately needed customer retention initiatives.

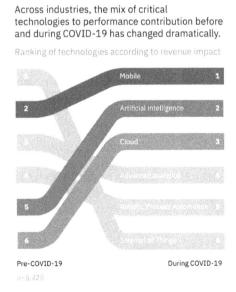

Fig. 4.1: Top technologies driving growth in a time of crisis

According to **IDC** (`https://www.idc.com/getdoc.jsp?containerId=prMETA47037520`), global spending on digital transformation is expected to reach 6.8 trillion by 2023. The myriad business challenges presented by the COVID-19 pandemic have ensured that the global economy remains firmly on course for its digital destiny, with 65% of the world's GDP set to be digitalized by 2022 EOY, and direct **digital transformation** investments to total $6.8 trillion between 2020 and 2023.

Various industry leaders are at different stages of their digital transformation journeys: some of them are exercising their due diligence in terms of a technical evaluation of the business challenges identified, and some have been through one iteration of the transformation and have found the rhythm and direction of what it takes for a successful outcome. On the other hand, those who have set sail on their digital journeys to tame this unprecedented crisis are now facing the challenge of what to make of their recent investments. The excitement and furor of new ideas and the use of advanced technologies with the hybrid cloud model at their disposal for building next-gen solutions are losing traction due to a lack of market relevancy or, at worst, have created solutions and now are looking for a problem to solve or altogether solving a wrong problem. Having said that, let's look at how we identify the business case or **end-to-end** (E2E) process that needs to change, along with the more holistic approach to people and technology required to ensure the smooth adoption of change, the transition from old to new ways of working, and the transformation of our business domains.

Holistic transformation

In the SAP world, digital transformation is perceived to be the technical conversion of your ERP core into a new digital core – or throwing a few technology components in to digitize some of your processes. Alternatively, on a broader scale, it may seem to involve procuring a few GSIs to perform brownfield, selective, or greenfield migrations to adopt the industry's best practices and then training your employees to embrace these changes within your enterprise. Digital transformation must be much more profound and broader with its business goals, spanning ecosystems of stakeholders, employee participation, and technology choices, providing a north star for future business and operating models with a clear roadmap. It can no longer be left to the CIO office or IT teams to initiate and lead transformation. Instead, the role they take on going forward should be the role of enabler, democratizing the technology involved to support the process. This warrants a paradigm shift in how we have traditionally thought of transformations. Fundamental baselines such as cost optimization, simplifying the landscape, or process improvements can no longer be the only goals of digital transformation. You're after mission-critical processes, customer touchpoints, and untapped markets – those places where value is created, lost, or derived. These are your targets. If you are not aiming at where the value is, then ultimately, it seems like a tech project. The CxO office and the leadership across your organization need to empower and inspire the entire workforce to reimagine their enterprise, toward the most up-to-date forms of intelligence. New ways of working go hand in hand with being resilient enough to meet customer needs and seek out new products and services. This is how you cater to evolving demands and become a brand identity that customers, employees, and leaders can identify with and feel motivated and passionate about. Sustainability should be incorporated as a critical imperative throughout the themes, outcomes, and strategies that the transformation teams push and should be embedded into the organizational culture.

A culture of innovation

It takes more than a single idea and the appropriate budget to get it to the top rungs of the company to convert it into reality. The critical element here is *people* – and that does not just mean employees, but also your customers and partners. All of the levers of the mammoth ecosystem should work together to move in the same direction. The company's passion and culture are reflected in its products and services. This, in turn, rubs off on your customers, consumers, and partners, with optimal engagement turning them into fans and followers, and creating a community that supports and critiques changes to your products.

An excellent example is Tesla, which garnered significant attention early in the decade by building up the momentum and market to prepare for the next wave of change and releasing a product that redefined the automotive industry. Mind you, the timing (and therefore the planning) couldn't have been more perfect given that sustainability has moved up the priority list of the major players in the industry. The product reflects the company culture and innovatively disrupts the market. However, more importantly, innovation continues after sales; continuous improvements and updates that are pushed add value by the day and exceed customer expectations. They now passionately voice their opinions and the ideas that may shape their next generation of products over social media. This dynamic boosts the acquisition, retention, and customer lifetime value of Tesla's clients.

To instigate a culture of continuous innovation and improvement in this way, the leadership within an organization can start by identifying, for instance, E2E business processes or organizational units that are ripe with ideas or involve protagonists who are open to change, as resistance will lead to low adoption and thereby significantly set back the vision that was put forward. There will always be inertia and bias toward what was developed in the past as being the best way to operate the business. Maybe it is, but could it be improved or bolstered with new technology to transform the business entirely? This bias continues to be prevalent within many organizations contemplating the move to S/4 HANA, where the perceived value created in ECC systems over the years seems to surpass the benefits of moving to the new digital core. Instead, the question could be, could we derive the same value by standardizing and automating the same processes? The business units or the process owners open to these kinds of ideas are the people you can start with.

As ideation can happen at various levels of the organization, it is important to keep the vision in sight, which could be derived from an outside-in view of your organization – for instance, improving the customer experience across channels, or bringing in new **lines of business** (**LoBs**) that offer connected products. Alternatively, it can happen inside-out with LoB owners clearly outlining process improvements to make on Days Sales Outstanding, insights from on-field staff, and business operations owners advising on ways to reduce asset management costs or improve the customer onboarding turnaround times. Let's briefly understand these two perspectives, to which an organization can allocate some time and resources before embarking on its transformation agenda.

An inside-out/bottom-up perspective

The leadership within an organization and the management can focus on two to three business domains that create the most value for the company – so, what is the best customer service or product that your company can offer, and how is the value from the value chains of a particular LoB process propagated to customers, partners, or whoever your value beneficiaries are? Are there channels there to allow that to happen? What changes can you make to your process that will make it more consumer-friendly? Is there an opportunity to introduce automation to reduce the process turnaround times? Which process performance indicators are calling out for help? Could employee productivity be boosted with an intelligent digital assistant to close out complaints and open cases to improve the NPS? Could customer experience be improved by redefining how the market segment engages with customers, changing how customers, partners, and suppliers have historically perceived the company?

An outside-in/top-down perspective

Another façade that can help determine what the organization should focus on is to improve its understanding of the implications of technology trends and their digital impacts on the business and its sources of revenue. Take AI, for instance – when thoughtfully applied, it can enable a massive leap beyond standard approaches in terms of delivery speed, cost, and quality. This allows companies to test new markets, business models, and products at a much greater speed and lower costs. Several opportunities lie untapped within other technology trends at varying degrees of maturity and applicability – such as quantum computing, cloud computing, process automation, and virtualization. With the right mindset and business acumen, any organization can create new markets and have a first-mover advantage. Any analysis must consider how shifts in the adoption of digital operations and engagements bring about changes in the supply and demand of industries and their evolving ecosystems.

Keeping track of competitive threats poses similar challenges. On the one hand, boutique tech-driven companies emerge on the horizon in swathes as new ventures or start-ups, with the coefficient of exponential technologies. On the other hand, some incumbents disrupt new services and business models. Therefore, a keen CxO's eye should watch out for enterprises that can compete in terms of what their organization is good at, differentiate themselves, and create more attractive offerings for a customer base. This is more of an outside view that boards can take to essentially frame questions for the internal management and employees to ask, ponder, and reflect upon when strategizing for the next best technology-driven business case.

Mentioned next are some of the other eminent threats that can take an organization by surprise, like a blind spot to watch out for when ideating or considering the next strategic moves your enterprise can make:

- **Geopolitical environment**: This can reshape borders; disrupt global supply chains; change legislation, tax, and tariffs; and complicate existing standards. Brexit is an example of this.

- **Environmental, Social, and Corporate Governance (ESG) change**: This forces companies to pivot from traditional resources to more finite and sustainable ones within continuously expanding markets. This needs to be adapted to the gas and automotive industries.

- **Regulatory and compliance requirements**: Every country, state, or city within global markets may have to deal with continuously changing complex national or international regulations such as the **General Data Protection Regulation** (**GDPR**), sustainability measures and the associated compliance risks for underlying supporting systems, and fluctuations in currencies in the regions in which companies sell their goods and services. Being global yet hyper-local with agility is the need of the hour.

- **Cybersecurity and data privacy**: There has been a rise in cyber attacks on corporate networks. The use of ransomware and finding flaws in open source libraries have become commonplace. Having watertight security checks and policies in place to ensure the security of data and the core systems is now top of the agenda for CISOs.

The other perspective is the pace at which new emerging players on the market are technology-native companies that may outsmart the incumbents in a couple of years. They are technology-savvy and have the best-in-class e-commerce sites, social media channels, mobile apps, or even virtual stores on Metaverse. These highly competitive new market entrants are pushing the operating trends toward "virtual reality" within the organization in terms of how they engage with the customers. The proliferation of technologies such as the IoT, 5G, **Robotic Process Automation** (**RPA**), AI, **Machine Learning** (**ML**), robotics, and quantum computing are already knocking on the doors of big players, leaving CxO offices flummoxed and lost in all the possibilities and the choices that must be made and made relatively quickly. Companies need to respond to these challenges. Doing nothing is not an option. Tech startups seek new opportunities and invent market segments that necessitate adapting and changing quickly, or else incumbents have to play catch up. Big companies can start small, adapt fast, and innovate iteratively to deliver market-making platforms underpinned by technology. Technology will be pivotal to changing ways of working, accelerating your time-to-market, and introducing new services and products to your customers. Therefore, once you have identified your customer-centric value pools using the assessments we have previously discussed, your transformation teams need to operationalize the technologies to deliver the changes required for the desired outcomes. It takes discipline, governance, and the right control to allow your bright minds to unleash their ideas on a level playing field within your organization. Next, we will discuss some aspects to consider when utilizing technology as an enabler of your digital transformation.

Technology as a service

Today, the need to innovate and transform at speed is a given. Changing and overhauling all the existing systems in the landscape to modernize and completely digitize them is an unwieldy challenge. Moreover, agility and speed need frameworks to innovate at scale, and the tools to do so need overarching governance and architectural models. Your enterprise should consider market-standard architectural practices that could be adopted (TOGAF 9.2 or Open Business Architecture) to put some sense and methods behind the challenges that this plethora of technologies can bring to the landscape and help you navigate the choices. Guidelines and architectural principles for design domains, such as API-first, microservices, and event-driven, will make design choices and patterns more predictable. This will make them greater assets and prepare them to be reused for repeatable success – for example, prescribing how to build, publish, and discover ready-to-consume microservices with the required controls and maintenance, which are centrally supported by the core IT teams. Every new microservice will go through quality controls and checks to standardize and make them available to all developer communities, internal or external. Once these platforms and practices have been established, think of how they can be synchronized with DevSecOps practices. The perfect resonance between these can propel your organization with agility toward the right IT mindset to take on new innovative ideas at full speed. The application life cycle will have prescribed methods and tools for quality checks, automated unit-to-regression tests, and release pipelines to production environments –enabling continuous development and improvement from an idea to its execution in a holistic sense. This approach would provide an overarching framework and apply the rules of the game, boundaries in which teams can create and extend their systems and data following the recommended standards for hybrid and multi-cloud environments.

The culmination of all these themes will result in your enterprise being ready for the reinvention that is required to handle well-assessed business challenges and opportunities—transforming how people, processes, and technologies are organized to operate efficiently and tap into new markets with innovative sustainable, engaging services and products.

In the next section, you will get a good grasp of how to assess the gaps in your organization's maturity that need to be addressed to attain the outcomes it set out to achieve through its transformation.

Assessing capabilities

The market forces discussed previously exert a lot of pressure on organizations. For many companies, the challenge of technical change and changes to processes needs to be considered upfront even before they look at resolving external challenges. Being innovative is an early decision an enterprise can take to thrive in this environment. They need to create capabilities that can respond to these forces. However, the larger and more mature the organization is, the more challenging it is to change systems and processes and retrain people.

Nevertheless, many organizations are biting the bullet and starting their transformation journeys with the RISE with SAP offering. It's a crucial first step but shouldn't be mistaken as a panacea to take on all the challenges an organization faces – it is more of an enabler to reaching a strategic business outcome. It can also be a foundational core part of the transformation roadmap that a company needs to build upon to reconsider its priorities and direction of travel. It helps accelerate and create an enduring "strategic vision" to differentiate your enterprise within the marketplace and reimagine its brand and purpose. The assessment of your enterprise's capabilities outlines the organizational and operating model changes that will help put the organization on the right path. An assessment also helps lay down the blueprint for an enterprise to get started with the digital transformation that will shape the business—giving it clarity on developing ways to respond to competition and operational challenges in order to tap into opportunities in new markets. A journey of continuous innovation and improvement begins and keeps on iterating itself to adapt and respond to customer expectations, at times increasing or even maintaining that market share. Your transformation continually evolves with a series of disruptive steps, and RISE with SAP is the first step that will help kickstart this journey.

Developing an enterprise strategy is challenging. Each element is complex, and the big picture is difficult to visualize. Identifying the critical aspects of digital transformation is crucial and translating them into a tangible value impact requires assessing an enterprise's capabilities and appropriate business models. To compete in a world of flexible, open-value networks, companies must focus on the few activities where they have a differentiating advantage in the value they provide or the cost they deliver compared to the competition. The **Component Business Model** (**CBM**) points the way forward by giving executives leverage to drive flexibility, scalability, efficiency, and openness throughout their enterprise. The CBM helps enterprises assess and understand the capabilities it has today and the gaps that need attention in terms of the systems, processes, and abilities required to reach a strategic goal or vision with a detailed roadmap.

CBM for SAP (CBM4SAP)

A CBM is a framework for modeling and analyzing a business for organizing and grouping business activities into the basic building blocks of a company, called business components. A CBM helps break down your business into its competencies and the capabilities required to operate it. Then, identify the missing parts and optimization required within your competencies to reach your business outcomes by asking simple questions and benchmarking them as you go along by following industry standards. The following illustration, *Fig. 4.2*, shows an example of assessments across various dimensions of the components; when the assessments of these components are aggregated together, they provide a complete view of where an organization needs to focus its attention to build its capabilities in line with its vision.

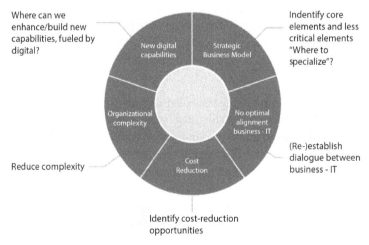

Fig. 4.2: CBM assessments reveal insights to develop new or improve existing capabilities

- A CBM can help examine organizational competencies, capabilities, and strategic priorities, identify gaps and opportunities, and develop a transformation roadmap for "where to take action and why"

- A CBM allows you to make customer issues and experiences the primary evaluation criteria for modeling future capabilities

- With a CBM, digital transformation can be "modularized" – broken down into a set of more minor activities, allowing you to determine the pace and timing of change

- A CBM clarifies how you run the business – all the capabilities, processes, and performance indicators you need to run your business

A CBM is not simply a way to reimagine the future of the organization. It accelerates its evolution toward an intelligent enterprise, both inside and outside, by enabling insights that can be actioned.

Aggregating activities by business competency leads to a view of an enterprise that is broken down into components, and these components can be characterized according to the business value they provide. Although different enterprises and industries may categorize business competencies differently, every piece should be accounted for under a business competency. Therefore, this business model allows your organization to expand and evolve without increasing complexity while reducing risk, driving business performance, boosting productivity, controlling costs, and improving capital efficiency and financial predictability.

This CBM assessment process involves three phases:

- **Model**: How do you run your business? Distill the complexity of your business into an enterprise-on-a-page. Capture details such as underlying processes and KPIs.

- **Analyze**: Where do you stand now? Assess each component of your CBM map using multiple lenses, such as strategic criticality, technological impact, and performance maturity.

- **Strategize:** Where should you take action? Bring your assessments together to generate a heat map illustrating where to act. Your heat map is the basis of your roadmap for change.

The following snapshot depicts the CBM SAP map in a CBM.AI tool with its components and the competencies of how it can be used to represent an enterprise on a page.

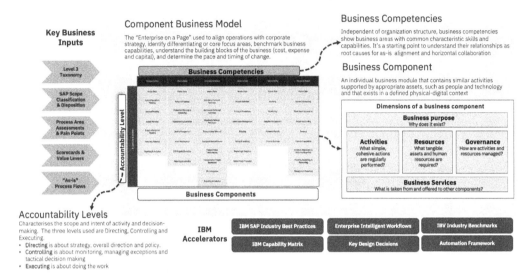

ENABLING TRANSFORMATION WITH CBM
Build the foundation to accelerate the Transformation Roadmap

Fig. 4.3: A CBM.AI tool with an enterprise-on-a-page view

Each component definition includes its governance, business services, the resources (including data and systems) involved, and the activities (processes) that are carried out to deliver the capabilities of that business component. Let's look at them in detail.

CBM.AI: This cloud-based tool has elevated the experience of SAP S/4 HANA discovery discussions by being digital and engaging for any organization using CBM SAP maps to assess their enterprise capabilities and operating models and uncover the gaps in qualifications for the realization of the strategy. The traditional **Business Process Hierarchy** (**BPH**) capability matrix has been transposed into the CBM.AI tool as an SAP CBM map, enabling deeper dives into scope and capabilities. The business owners and leadership can then validate capabilities and tie them to requirements, enablers, organizational impacts, and business value.

Anyone performing these assessments can dynamically generate heat maps (for the differentiation they have in the market); reflect global or local variations of processes; and **Adopt, Add, Abstain, and Adjust** (the **Quad "A" methodology**) the SAP business processes, processes that need to be outsourced, and automation opportunities or opportunities to infuse advanced technologies such as AI into processes.

With a CBM4SAP engagement (and any other CBM engagement), any organization can leverage benchmarking data for over 900 performance metrics, access innovation assets and offerings to drive incremental value, and link CBM components to Blueworks Live (an industry best practices process repository) process maps for deeper process discussions.

A CBM SAP map: It demonstrates how you run your business using your current SAP landscape – the collective set of components, processes, and metrics that form the core of your business. At the surface, a component looks simple, but underneath, it captures complexity—SAP processes, architecture, benchmarks, metrics for processes, connected applications, the knowledge base, and more.

Successful transformation programs begin with a solid foundation built on an accepted and aligned understanding of the why, what, and how. CBM4SAP helps uncover some of the crucial questions that an enterprise needs to answer before embarking on its transformation journey, such as what the scope of transformation is, what the capabilities required for the change are, and how the organization is going to get there.

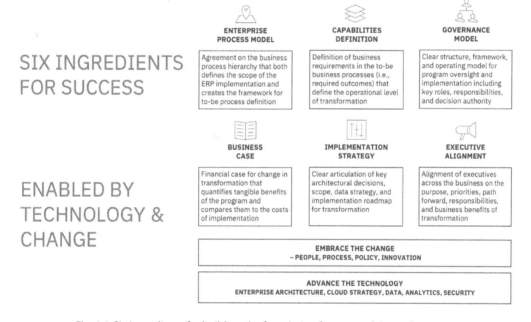

Fig. 4.4: Six ingredients for building the foundation for successful transformation

There are six ingredients: the enterprise model, the architecture, the implementation roadmap, the governance model, the business value, and the executive alignment. Supported by enablers such as data, analytics, change management, and security, the project teams not only look at the S/4 HANA scope or the encompassing processes but can also go beyond the scope to see what other options are available for the enterprise to consider for its transformation journey and its ideal outcome.

CBM4SAP involves three different phases for the transformation teams in your organization. Each phase has a unique output that is input to the next phase, and each phase enables you to define the strategy toward the outcomes that you set out to achieve.

These three phases are outlined here:

CBM4SAP model phase:

- We use the CBM SAP map to classify the in-scope processes in the core as competitive and differentiating. This is an essential first step to driving the adoption of standards for core processes and focusing valuable detailed design time on competitive and differentiating strategies.

  Before client engagement begins, we use a CBM to align IBM's pre-configured IMPACT industry solution with the in-scope processes. This mapping drives a "why not standard" approach and links the underlying IMPACT accelerators.

CBM4SAP analyze phase:

- By mapping IMPACT to the client's in-scope processes, we layer in the associated Level-3 business process models, which demonstrate the best-practice E2E processes for SAP S/4HANA. These examples drive "fit-to-standard" workshops and include business roles, Fiori apps, data elements, and so on.

Industry-specific IBV benchmark data is automatically linked to the in-scope processes to support a quantitative assessment of a client's performance against its industry peers and identify key improvement areas or measures to take.

CBM4SAP strategize phase:

- The output of each fit-to-standard workshop is a clear designation of the Quad A methodology for each in-scope process. A CBM provides a visual heat map to designate where a client is starting to deviate from the standard.

- Capture change impacts during the fit-to-standard workshop for each in-scope process to understand and plan for the organizational change associated with the move to SAP S/4HANA.

- The heat maps derived become the critical inputs for your transformation roadmap. Business capabilities are linked to each in-scope process area to link current-state processes, future-state capabilities, and potential value pools to drive a business case for change:

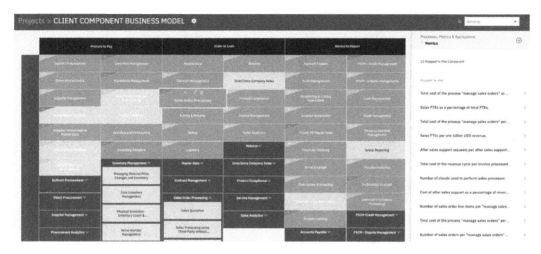

Fig. 4.5: The CBM4SAP heat map highlights components and capabilities that need focus

The component map of your organization provides a basis for developing strategic and operating insights for your business. By gauging the relative business value of different areas of the map, executives can determine which components demand immediate attention. This type of analysis yields a "heat map" that highlights the components with the most significant economic value.

This heat map and the underlying CBM become a key input for the next stage to derive the business and technology blueprint. A CBM is also a pretty popular way to look at the business architecture; it's a unifying mechanism, and at the top is the strategy that drives everything in the company. The second layer is the business architecture or the CBM. The business architecture can also feed into the strategy definition if this is laid out before the strategy is formulated, as it can help identify differentiating capabilities within a business. To define your system and architecture layers, you want to leverage your differentiating capabilities.

Furthermore, as depicted in the following illustration, within each CBM map, you will find a business process model layer, which can be combined with the "to-be" user journeys maps for a design-led approach to understanding the value-adding activities for customer experience – and how the underlying process models support it. This can help define the set of services, features, and functions required in the service and applications layer more granularly, supporting the journeys that need to be fulfilled. Depending on the requirements in terms of availability, performance, resiliency, and security, we can then understand the gaps and make choices within the technical architecture layer. Changes within these underlying layers of the CBM are recorded on a continuous calibration and integration mechanism throughout the transformation. You can detect issues; overlay them with different attribute assessments; use them to identify hot components (that need attention) in these different layers and the changes that are warranted in terms of people, processes, and technologies; and scope where changes need to be actioned.

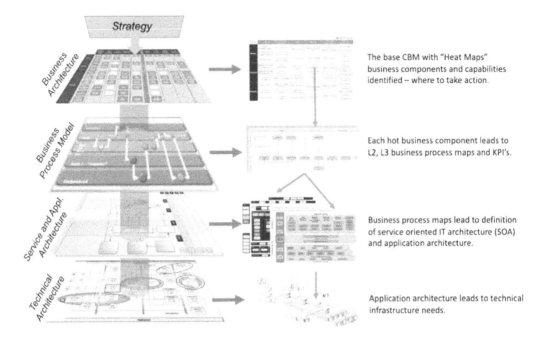

The base CBM with "Heat Maps" business components and capabilities identified – where to take action.

Each hot business component leads to L2, L3 business process maps and KPI's.

Business process maps lead to definition of service oriented IT architecture (SOA) and application architecture.

Application architecture leads to technical infrastructure needs.

Fig. 4.6: A CBM map with layered heat maps that links your business architecture top-down or bottom-up

From the inside out, the CBM lens enables organizations to improve how they manage people, processes, and technology. Centralizing redundant processes into modules can drive scale and efficiency gains and best practices across an organization. An outside-in view can help assess the ability to tap into industry networks, enables component-based firms to assemble best-in-class capabilities, and consolidate piecemeal offerings into solutions tailored for ever narrower market segments.

To define the application and technical architecture, the usage of a reference architecture for digital transformation in relevant industry sectors is recommended. This will help assess gaps in the current IT/SAP landscape and platforms and identify solutions and any new market-making platforms required to fill the gaps. Crucial "build vs. buy" decisions can be addressed at this stage for the necessary technical capabilities. The functional components can then be mapped back to the technical components to ensure there are no gaps within the to-be state-sustainable business design. Once the mapping is complete, the IT teams can identify data centers, make deployment choices for the technical architecture, and evaluate hyper-scalers and vendors to host these solutions and platforms. The creation of CBM components thus reduces the number of technology gaps, overextensions, and duplications, allowing the firm to cut inessential investments and identify opportunities to develop new services based on the excess capacity of existing technologies.

Lastly, the organization's business and IT teams must prepare a set of activities needed for the transformation. These include all the activities that will answer questions such as the following:

- How big a leap can the firm take?

- How much change can be absorbed?

- Which areas should the company focus on first?

- Where are the quick wins? (Good candidates include duplicated activities across processes and organizational units, especially those that would benefit from increased economies of scale, global sourcing options, and shared information)

This process results in a "transformation roadmap," a guide the firm uses to begin breaking an area of the business into components (say, a customer experience, service, new subscription-based product, or service) to potentially launch as a pilot, followed by a phased rollout. Compiling this set of activities should be done to ensure that the business and technical goals are achieved as part of the digital transformation journey and shared among the champions of this digital transformation. Initial success here will provide experience and proof points for further development of components for which value-adding opportunities were uncovered.

In the next section, we will dig deeper into the business process model layer to derive additional insights to bring your SAP S/4 HANA transformation to life.

Business Process Intelligence (BPI)

The quest of being an Intelligent Enterprise requires a strategy that clearly outlines the desired outcome, a granular evaluation of your business's capabilities, the supporting processes and technology that need to change, and a detailed roadmap (a set of activities and plans) for achieving your outcome. We covered this in previous sections with certain tools and accelerators that can expedite arriving at a robust strategy and detailing gaps in your existing capabilities.

The business process model heat maps and the activity set become the input for focusing on the processes that need work – and there could be many ways we could address the hotspots on the process map, with optimization, automation, or following industry best practices by adopting a new process. The implementation teams need a more granular set of activities to action in the systems landscape, architecture, and infrastructure.

An enterprise will require tools, accelerators, and services that provide maximum transparency by leveraging the production data to drive discovery workshop discussions and the generation of ideas, evaluate options, and collaborate across the organization to adapt and continuously evolve per customer and business needs. These tools will help convert the CBM assessments into an actionable list of to-dos to make process changes that will aim at a target operating model – and the related changes to process models.

The entire portfolio of tools under the SAP BPI offering (SAP Process Insights and SAP Signavio) has automated many laborious manual activities to automatically map diverse LoB processes based on actual data from existing production systems. This provides a detailed analysis of challenges and bottlenecks and simulates opportunities for improvement based on value. This becomes a value-based discussion that can help speed up the business case for the transformation. The organization can extend this and apply the same toolset to existing processes to benchmark sustainability and ESG initiatives. Best practices and recommendations for zero emissions at the corporate or product level, reducing to zero waste by engaging in circular business models, or tying in analyzing the sustainability of your processes can be baked into your S/4 HANA transformation. This may open up avenues for new services or products that would be unique in the marketplace, differentiating yourself as an "environmentally conscious" organization that customers are willing to buy into.

To ease the whole transformation journey and the choices to be made within it, RISE with SAP offers some exciting pricing for packaged services, including "full-time-equivalent" flexible user licenses and a contracted set of tools to help organizations focus on the maturity of their processes and any inefficiency, and benchmark this against the industry best practices, producing easy-to-follow reports and recommendations.

The BPI set of tools covered by this offering helps you jumpstart your S/4 HANA transformation without moving the needle on the cost of any additional new components. Still, should you wish to improve and monitor your enterprise processes continuously, you could consider investing in the SAP Signavio Process Transformation Suite. Alternatively, if your organization wants a wider array of options in terms of the tools for process transformation, it could consider Celonis Process Mining and the Celonis **Execution Management System** (**EMS**) platform, both of which can help with the automated journey of continuous process improvement.

We will discuss the scope and utility of each of these tools and services offered in the cloud in the following sections, including the phases or stages of the project in which you might want to consider investing in these tools. Before we get into the details of the value and the insights that each of the Process Transformation Suite components brings to an SAP implementation, let's understand why we require BPI in the first place following the CBM capability assessments, especially for an SAP S/4 HANA transformation.

Why BPI?

Traditionally, SAP ERP implementations have been one-off implementations. A project's technical implementation and customization used to extend over several years before emerging on the other side ready for business use – only for you to come to the realization that the process models implemented a few years back are now out of sync with the realities of evolving business needs and need to be changed to fit new industry standards. Incremental revisions to the core resulted in customization, which over several years, resulted in it becoming colluded with the amount of custom code, data, and customized processes. It became impossible to upgrade the system without another lengthy upgrade program. The latency of upgrade cycles and the adoption of new methods involved a lot of catching up, eventually ending up out of sync with what was required by a margin of at least 2 or 3 years, depending on the upgrade frequency, given the trade-offs in terms of the implementation costs of upgrades versus the benefits of these upgrades. In the meantime, organizations accumulated a lot of unwanted custom code and the SAP ECC modules became bloated with data beyond recognition.

Given the disruptions rampant in the past decade, retaining old processes and bloating systems with data does not help with agility and innovation. Moreover, there is an increasing perception that SAP systems are back-office and cannot evolve faster given the complexity of a highly customized ERP core. Instead, many enterprises have designed their customer- and partner-facing systems to comply with the amount of data and processes required by their ERP cores, which has also resulted in painful adoption stories. And has this led to fundamental improvements? Does it make sense from the standpoint of ROI? Most of the time, they are decommissioned within the first year. For an enterprise to move toward an intelligent enterprise vision and stay resilient, the back office, the middle office, and the front office systems must evolve continuously to stay in step with ever-evolving, dynamic supply and demand changes in the marketplace.

The *"keep the core clean"* messaging coming directly from SAP for S/4 HANA implementations couldn't be further from the reality given that organizations migrating their ERP cores have been inclined to bring unwanted baggage from their old systems to the new digital core because of the inherent bias of what has worked up to now is the best practice, which is not always true. It only makes sense to retain the differentiating business processes and assets that give an enterprise a competitive advantage by adapting them to the new digital footprint of S/4 HANA and adopting the net new and commodity processes that S/4 HANA offers with industry standards built into them. This leads to adopting the industry's best practices and the standardization of processes, the latest and best features that SAP has to offer, which helps innovate business processes more frequently with minimal challenges to upgrade cycles for the digital core. The digital core remains lean in terms of data and clean in terms of extensions.

So, how do we make choices on which processes to keep and what to leave behind when innovating with an S/4 HANA implementation? Its advanced, enterprise-level digital core technology is rendered useless without the continuous improvement of processes. The frequent innovations and simplifications released by SAP to stay in step with changes to industry practices warrant having some tool for process governance, monitoring, and insights to provide resilience and flexibility to adapt quickly to changing market dynamics. The RISE with SAP offering addresses this need by bringing together the strength and agility required by an enterprise to think holistically about its transformational goals. RISE with SAP is not positioned as part of a cloud or hyper-scaler discussion or a digital transformation discussion – it should be considered a tool within a "business transformation" discussion. It not only enables the back-office processes to evolve faster but also the middle- and front-office processes. It certainly realizes the "one contract, one partner" approach, as explained in *Chapter 3, Eureka Moment – The Missing Link*. It also adds critical supporting services and components to realize your business transformation. Whether BPI + Signavio or Celonis for process transformation and excellence or SAP **Business Technology Platform (BTP)** services for building and deploying hybrid-cloud-based value-adding extensions, these are all packaged under one contract as flexible credits that can be used for your transformation initiative. This provides a clear runway for an organization with the right tools to generate actionable insights and convert them into technology-driven processes helmed by people. In the following sections, let's take a brief, whistle-stop tour of the components covered under the RISE with SAP offering and their critical features.

BPI Starter Pack for RISE with SAP

To introduce SAP BPI + Signavio as part of RISE with SAP, this is not just an offering to simplify the license model. Instead, it provides all the tools and accelerators, along with best practices, to look at your S/4 HANA transformation efforts through a business transformation lens. The following figure provides a good overview of the tools and services, starter packs, and platform services included as part of the offering:

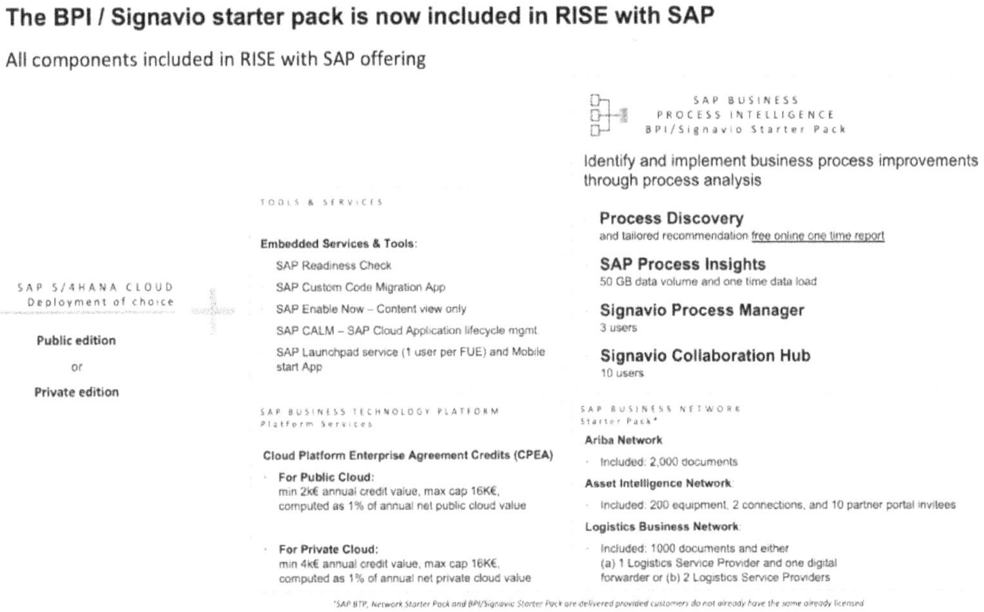

Fig. 4.7: Components and services included in the RISE with SAP offering

The following components are included in the SAP BPI + Signavio Process Transformation Suite:

SAP Process Discovery: This is a report generated by SAP based on the data you provide from your production systems to compare your current business process performance with industry benchmarks and derive unique insights for the SAP ECC landscape. The report consists of **process performance indicators** (**PPIs**) aligned with various LoBs and E2E solutions. The following data points are covered by these performance benchmarks:

- Unique insight into your current operational business process performance and functional usage based on data from your SAP ERP, including benchmarks with which to compare your operational business performance and use to your industry peers

- Specific recommendations for six LoBs and seven E2E processes, with SAP S/4HANA functionalities, automation, intelligent technologies, and SAP Fiori apps

- Your transformation teams can use this cloud-based interactive solution as a summary report to build your case for an SAP S/4HANA transformation and to secure buy-in

12 optimization goals for 6 lines of business across 7 end-to-end processes

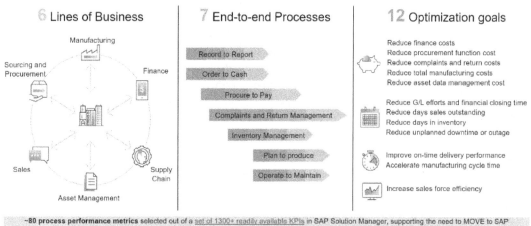

~80 process performance metrics selected out of a set of 1300+ readily available KPIs in SAP Solution Manager, supporting the need to MOVE to SAP S/4HANA, collected from the customer's SAP ERP systems and benchmarked against peers (3000+ data sets per January 2021).

Fig. 4.8: Process discovery scope for LoBs and business processes against industry benchmarks

Process Discovery is free of charge and is an interactive report on how your organization fairs against the industry standard PPI for processes across the LoB will help executives focus on the most critical process performance issues.

SAP Process Insights

If your organization wants to embark on the Process Excellence journey, your teams can get insights into process bottlenecks and inefficiencies in their production systems using the production data, by injecting it into yet another component covered by the RISE with SAP offering. They will then have a more insight-driven, data-based assessment of the performance or inefficiency of their processes, as made possible with SAP Process Insights. This analysis can be undertaken by providing a one-time extract of your production data, or by plugging it directly into SAP Process Insights using data extractors or connectors for continuous process improvement and Process Excellence. Essentially, this data and the information available on how processes have been implemented and historically executed is quite valuable in process discovery workshops. Conclusions are then based on actual data rather than what someone in the organization thinks a process is. This helps understand compliance issues and remediate them by continuously measuring any deviations as process changes are implemented. It sets up the foundations for Process Excellence initiatives within an organization. With Process Insights, you can get immediate recommendations for more than 100 configurations and master data fixes, with more than 300 additional, built-in innovation recommendations for S/4 HANA, such as SAP Fiori Apps, automation opportunities, or ML-based performance improvements, directly linked to the process under consideration. Get started here: `www.s4hana.com` or `www.sap.com/pathfinder`.

Process Excellence

Process Excellence is achieved by continuously monitoring business processes and improving their performance to support business objectives. Address frictions, inefficiencies, and non-compliance as they arise and track and monitor the remedial measures to see the efficacy of the changes made – the proliferation of technologies and the possibilities they can bring to an enterprise. Still, a realistic assessment of their use and applications to solve a business challenge is hardly ever made. We need to derive insights into our business operations based on data rather than building a hypothetical model based on subjective, qualitative, and manual methods, which is how some business experts understand it. This is not restricted to compliance, process standardization, or the KPIs associated with efficiency; it is also about agility – continuously evolving and adapting to change, and the automation that can be applied to processes. The other key aspect often overlooked is customer experience, which has also gathered a lot of attention in recent years, especially with the rise of e-commerce and the resilience of organizations that serve customer needs being tested. For excellence at scale along this horizontal, we need a proper handle on the operational model and process management.

With Process Excellence as a practice and its supporting toolsets, as we will discuss in the next section, users get a guided, automatic, data-driven assessment of the health and viability of a company's processes. This can identify the root causes of performance issues and built-in corrective recommendations. With the automated monitoring and visualization of processes in real time, an organization can benefit from rapid cost and time savings while improving efficiency and optimizing its processes.

SAP BPI – Signavio Process Transformation Suite

While SAP Process Insights is currently only for the SAP footprint on the landscape and is a lighter way to kickstart your understanding of where inefficiency is and what value could be derived if you were to go with the suggestions generated by the report, SAP Signavio Process Transformation Suite pushes the envelope further, allowing an enterprise to take control of its business operations by not only process mining and revealing hotspots in processes across the SAP and non-SAP landscape but also governing, modeling, and collaborating on processes centrally to digitize them further. With a business process repository built-in, you can adopt the industry best practices, process benchmarking, metrics, and KPIs.

Signavio Process Transformation Suite enables business process experts and owners to design the to-be process model while simulating new process alternatives by incorporating AI/automation or simplifying the process altogether. Collaboration between stakeholders or business process owners defines which processes are being worked on, where an upcoming change could affect their specific business, and whether to vote for or against an idea on how to change an operation or part of a process.

This establishes a culture of Process Excellence, with governance for ongoing, automated, and continuous improvement and insights you can use quickly. The same applies to the cybersecurity standards associated with processes and industry benchmarks and the best practices for implementing them. This could flag any existing processes and adopt some best practices to avoid inadvertent oversights during the process design, which may be detrimental to a business and its day-to-day operations.

SAP Signavio Process Transformation Suite consists of multiple cloud products and can be used to perform either a business transformation (designing new processes) or apply Process Excellence (post-implementation for improving existing processes). The focus of each initiative will be different. However, the capabilities required for completing each of these tasks across industries are similar. The following figure gives an overview of all the components available under the SAP BPI solution:

Fig. 4.9: SAP Signavio Process Transformation Suite and SAP BPI components

Let's briefly understand the capabilities and features of the components of the SAP Signavio Transformation Suite.

Journey Modeler: SAP Signavio Journey Modeler enables you to operationalize customer experiences by connecting journeys and processes, metrics, systems, and roles, allowing you to understand, improve and transform your journeys and processes. It enables experience widgets to be included in the journey model to understand what works well and where teams need to focus on improving customer or employee touchpoints. It provides a journey complexity score by analyzing the complexity of the journey offering indicators and the potential to enhance a journey. It's also worth referring to journey to process analytics if your organization wants to reduce the gap between Process Excellence and siloed user experiences.

SAP Journey to Process Analytics is a toolset under the SAP Signavio suite that helps solve the experience gap with combined process and experience reality by combining process and experience analysis to understand, improve, and transform the experience of customers and employees. This is what is called experience-driven process mining. This helps provide a clear picture of the feelings of your customers at every touchpoint of interaction with your company by leveraging the digital footprints left at each process step – your process data – and merging it with data from your experience management systems – such as customer survey data and customer satisfaction scores. You can also integrate experience data into SAP Signavio Process Intelligence with the new Qualtrics connector to SAP Signavio (beta at the time of writing). This still has a few roadmap items, but it is worth taking into account, as it is quite a powerful experience-driven value analysis tool for translating insights into action quickly.

Process Manager: A BPM solution that professional process modelers can use to collaboratively design, model, analyze and optimize current (as-is) or to-be target processes. You can use drag-and-drop process modeling to create BPMN 2.0 complaint process models. You can compare old and new process models to simulate process changes and contrast and compare how they impact cost, time, and resource allocation for decision-making. Process modelers/process owners can collaborate on process models by sharing and getting feedback, reviews, and comments across the suite. You can analyze the Business Process Hierarchy offline and store and retrieve business process models from your organization's process repositories or SAP's best practices process models. The risks and controls reports can be run on existing or newly created models to highlight risks and the controls identified for them.

SAP Signavio Process Intelligence: This solution offers advanced process mining algorithms to deliver real-time insights on process frictions and inefficiencies with data ingestion from SAP and non-SAP landscapes per the scope of the process. It also provides powerful data-based insights into ongoing improvement opportunities and risks as they arise. Your transformation teams can visualize the real operation of processes and start process analysis right from when data flows in to check for conformance or bottlenecks, with a collaborative approach to process improvement. These in-depth process analytics can be combined with experience mining (as explained for Journey to Process Analytics) for actionable improvement on process variants that impact your business the most. Your teams can run simulations to optimize processes with recommended RPA and ML improvements to see how they affect the process performance and run costs.

Collaboration Hub: Collaboration Hub allows for collaboration across the entire suite of products. Your teams can collaborate within workspaces to comment, receive automatic notifications, and use presentation mode directly within the tool to communicate changes across geographies. It helps streamline coordination across stakeholders during process mining, design, and execution and allows you to be notified of any new proposals for changes to processes you are associated with. Teams can curate and add content relevant to a process and control what is being published per the agreed changes. With broader collaboration across teams and crowd brainstorming, developer communities and business users alike can co-innovate, contribute to more ideas, optimize processes, and increase buy-in for digital changes.

Process Governance: With this solution, your organization can automate the approval and publishing of your process changes. This will help change your methods of working from being Excel-based to being entirely digitized and automated methods of capturing, connecting collaboratively, and communicating between teams to provide key stakeholders with the right level of attention for process governance, such as risk controllers, process owners, and quality management teams. This will help improve the process change turnaround times by co-ordinating tasks, keeping track of outstanding tasks, and, thereby, swift accountability. You connect the workflows to process mining discoveries and deviations for further investigations to provide Root Cause analysis to create jobs for required process changes.

Process Improvements: SAP BTP helps democratize innovation, enabling business people to improve processes using the latest low-code and no-code environments, including user-friendly RPA. The resulting extensions become part of the process, which extends the functionality of the process while keeping the core clean. SAP Workflow Management allows you to design process workflows across the LoBs of the organization or ones external to the organization, orchestrating process execution using **SAP Intelligent Robotic Process Automation** (**SAP iRPA**), and democratizing data and processes via the API Hub using the APIs. SAP Data Intelligence derives insights from data across heterogeneous landscapes to make processes more autonomous. The scenarios and usage of **Cloud Platform Enterprise Agreement** (**CPEA**) credits for SAP BTP under the RISE with SAP offering will be discussed in the upcoming sections.

The following figure provides a good overview of these tools that could be used in different stages of implementation. Whether you have embarked on a business transformation, IT transformation, and/or Process Excellence initiative, all the tools are applicable with varying degrees of usage for your processes:

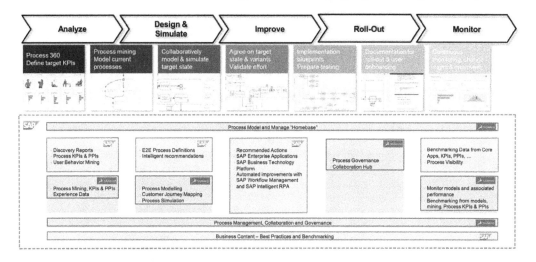

Fig. 4.10: SAP BPI component view by project implementation phase

SAP BPI helps make business process improvement a continuous endeavor, with several improvements being pushed to the production environment. Once your organization has the SAP BPI components on the landscape, your teams can drive holistic, E2E process transformations to optimize their operations, improve customer excellence, and control operational risks. It enables business owners and operations teams to make learning, adapting, and innovating a core competency within the organization, flagging the deviations and inefficiencies that need to be resolved with execution engines such as SAP Workflow or SAP iRPA. That's where SAP BTP comes in as the foundation for an intelligent enterprise. All applications and innovations that augment business processes can be built with the prebuilt integrations suite, ready-to-go extensions suite, and analytics so that you can quickly solve business problems. Any organization can integrate data from multiple systems and create new UIs or extend its business processes through new experiences for customer-facing applications, such as e-commerce, partner portals, or supplier relationship systems. Providing E2E visibility and transparency in the process and generating a slew of data that, when analyzed, can help derive insights and intelligence to optimize your operations further closes in on the vision of an Intelligent Enterprise. Let's dive into what makes an Intelligent Enterprise and how BTP helps realize this vision of an Intelligent Enterprise.

An Intelligent Enterprise

Any enterprise can become intelligent by applying emerging technologies and industry best practices to agile, integrated business processes to increase resilience, profitability, and sustainability. Intelligent Enterprises are organizations that can learn and adapt faster than their competition. Once you have implemented SAP S/4 HANA, you have leveled up in your digital maturity – your standardized E2E processes run seamlessly and have been enriched with intelligent technologies across the board. Doing so brings you to the next level of automation and transparency that can be realized by the platform services and technologies offered by SAP BTP. The following figure shows how all the elements of an Intelligent Enterprise are offered by the SAP cloud solutions with some critical layers of an Intelligent Enterprise strategy:

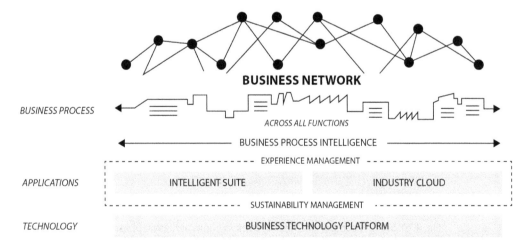

Fig. 4.11: Intelligent Enterprise – critical layers of the strategy by SAP

Let's parse through the layers to understand how they work hand in hand to realize the vision of Intelligent Enterprise laid out by SAP.

INTELLIGENT SUITE: At the heart of the strategy is S/4 HANA cloud/on-premises, running all the core enterprise processes. It supports E2E business processes and best practices; this is the ERP layer in which SAP has been a world leader for many decades, keeping up with the complex reality of a modern economy. It offers cloud applications that are modular and integrated, with a unified user experience and a standard data model.

INDUSTRY CLOUD: The cloud delivers highly verticalized and innovative applications for your specific industry and verticals. With its industry cloud, SAP has unmatched capabilities across more than 25 different industries with best practices that you can access on the cloud. It's an open marketplace that carries an array of modular industry-specific apps developed by SAP and its partners worldwide for industry-specific needs and is built for interoperability. These applications built on SAP BTP extend S/4 HANA processes, LoB cloud solutions, and SAP Business Network using open APIs, standard business processes, and data models.

BUSINESS PROCESS INTELLIGENCE: BPI is seamlessly embedded into the Intelligent Enterprise to support value-driven transformation and process improvements. In the previous section, we delved extensively into this layer by covering how SAP BPI helps an organization transform its operations in iterative increments.

BUSINESS NETWORK: The business network takes the strategy beyond your four walls. Your organization can collaborate seamlessly with trading partners to drive connected processes and experiences. Business networks help with interconnections between businesses, creating the world's largest and most comprehensive business network. Business communities can connect with every company across the organization's supply chain using the world's largest supplier network through SAP Business Network, for example, with more than 5.5 million connected enterprises, and combining it with other networks, such as SAP's Asset Intelligence Network and SAP Fieldglass for contingent workers. This will help you get a single view of your carbon footprint and react faster to supply chain disruptions.

EXPERIENCE MANAGEMENT: This offering is for optimizing E2E customer experiences, and it's not just about point-of-sale or customer-facing systems; rather, the moments that matter – customer and employee touchpoints. When it comes to customer satisfaction, the NPS, the logistics of production, and the delivery process can matter just as much as purchasing. Experience management solutions such as Qualtrics provide insight into the sentiments and feelings of everyone involved in your business, customers, employees, and other critical stakeholders. This lets you fully leverage the power of human insight and intelligence, which helps you understand your business faster so that you can adapt and innovate faster.

SUSTAINABILITY MANAGEMENT: Climate change is an existential threat, and we owe a habitable planet to future generations, but it's not just about doing what's right. Business customers are ready to pay premiums to buy from organizations with purpose, and employees are more loyal, productive, and engaged in purpose-driven organizations. Investors also now include sustainability in their company valuations, so it's time to bake sustainability into how your organization does business and make sustainability a standard dimension of corporate management, just like productivity or revenue growth. However, you can't act on what you can't measure, so to help drive sustainability practices, a new sustainability portfolio has been launched by SAP to help you inside your organization and across the entire value chain.

SAP BTP: SAP customers choose RISE with SAP to implement SAP S/4HANA Cloud and transition their company into an Intelligent Enterprise. However, to realize the full benefits of SAP S/4HANA Cloud, companies such as yours must embrace SAP BTP. Using SAP BTP and SAP S/4HANA Cloud as part of RISE with SAP, you can integrate, enrich, and extend live data from SAP S/4HANA Cloud and improve decision-making with ML and analytical capabilities. SAP BTP is a one-stop shop for all your database needs, analytics, application development and integration, and intelligent technologies to support connected experiences and confident decision-making. SAP BTP provides prebuilt integration, a unified data model, proven tools to simplify extensions, prebuilt bots, and workflows for accelerated automation. Simplify and accelerate your business transformation, wherever you are in your digitalization journey, with SAP S/4HANA and SAP BTP as part of the RISE with SAP package.

To sum up, we started with BPI by showing how SAP Signavio and Celonis are used to understand process gaps and inefficiencies using business-critical process value maps, with costs, resources, and ROI all accounted for. Now, the SAP BTP platform and the technologies you have at your disposal allow you to reimagine work in a way that changes the whole cost structure associated with that workflow. Next, we will understand how we integrate intelligence to make processes self-driving, self-healing, and self-governing.

Autonomous processes

The key to understanding intelligent processes and workflow is to study the distinction between them. Both sound similar, but there are a few notable differences. A process is a series of steps or an operating procedure within a single function or application that is key to running an organization's core functions. While a workflow centers on these core functions and the decision criteria that come along the way, you're examining business rules, listening to events, and flexibly routing the job while ensuring the critical path of the work is progressing to completion.

A workflow is an elevated concept when compared with a process. Workflows can have different levels of complexity depending on the span of tasks and work being covered, either internally or externally for the organization. Workflows can span across siloed, single-function processes such as accounts (AP/AR), requisition generation, lead management, hiring, or even virtual cyber-threat analysis within an LoB. Workflows can also span across interconnected processes that make up one horizontal process across LoBs or industry functions – for example, lead to cash, customer acquisition, talent acquisition, integrated planning, outage detection, or KYC. They can span across an organization or beyond, with customers, partners, and even consumers orchestrating E2E business processes, LoBs, and horizontals extending beyond an organization's boundaries. One workflow can contain many sub-processes and may have a single critical path it traverses that stitches them together to move toward an outcome.

Interconnected multi-function workflows are integrated across an organization's processes, systems, and data – and connect people. While a workflow is carried out, we can start to apply insights inferred from ML models derived from data to decide the next course of action. Intelligent workflows are dynamic in nature and can reroute by sensing changes in the states of processes and incoming data from the physical world using **Operational Technology (OT)** or the connected digital world via **Information Technology (IT)**. They execute tasks and actions through automation and surface the outcomes and outputs through intuitive UX features such as SAP Fiori or SAP **Conversational AI (CAI)**. The combination of exponential technologies and human/machine collaboration and integration makes these mission-critical workflows intelligent. That's where value is created, lost, or derived, and that's where our focus should be.

Meanwhile, process automation focuses on tasks or transactions that need to be executed in a particular sequence that is predictable and repeatable. These commodity tasks can easily be automated to accommodate certain variations based on business rules. When we choose to automate a few tasks or all tasks, we make processes either semi- or fully autonomous as far as they are triggered with the right data to move through a sequence of automated tasks. These autonomous processes or sub-processes can then be invoked by intelligent workflows, cutting across LoBs and managing an E2E process.

Your transformation team's primary focus should be addressing business problems by identifying mission-critical workflows and processes, determining where and how we can make them intelligent. We apply exponential technologies to make workflows smart enough so that they begin to learn and inform both those working within the workflow and broadly within an Intelligent Enterprise on how best to address problems and then improve performance. Intelligent workflows learn from day-to-day operations and transactions and help people (customers, partners, and employees) to perform more efficiently and intelligently.

Once we have the fabric of intelligent workflows running across our organization, the organization moves closer to being an Intelligent Enterprise in which the processes are autonomous, self-healing, and self-driven, supporting people to complete their operational tasks. This augmentation for your employees and organization has far-reaching benefits regarding technology adoption, cultural evolution, and enabling expertise within the organization.

Intelligent workflows are critical to an Intelligent Enterprise and change the way the enterprise does the following:

- Get work done to deliver their promises to their customers through their products and services
- Break silos of process and data for a more integrated, agile environment that enables real-time, transformational data insights when combined with SAP BPI
- Take the organization from base automation to E2E, automated, and intelligent business process execution that makes life easier for employees
- Lets employees shift focus from repetitive and mundane tasks to more high-value jobs to use their potential to the fullest

In addition, intelligent workflows enable companies to gain a competitive advantage by orchestrating data up and down their value chain, uncovering new revenue streams, and creating engaging experiences in moments that matter for customers and employees, with faster time-to-market. We will deal with intelligent workflows in depth in the next chapter. In this section, we will focus on the process automation capabilities that SAP can offer.

SAP BTP makes consuming these advanced technologies simpler and more efficient and makes it quicker to integrate them into the digital core while keeping it clean. SAP Process Automation Suite, available as part of SAP BTP, helps build and model critical business workflows. Prebuilt content available from SAP and its partners i- imported into your environments to accelerate the time-to-value. In the next section, we will briefly discuss how your teams can go about identifying the processes to fully automate them using SAP Process Automation Suite or using Celonis BPI components, combined with SAP BTP, to unlock the value of your processes and data.

1 – the discovery of processes

The idea is to discover good candidate processes for intelligent workflows. You can start with SAP Process Insights + SAP Signavio Process Intelligence to mine, process, and task the data from production environments. Analyze processes based on system usage and user interactions to uncover inefficiencies and identify gaps and stay in step with industry best practices and the target customer experience. This is also made possible with Celonis's prebuilt accelerators for SAP S/4 HANA's findings on E2E processes – with preconfigured KPIs, dashboards, and analytical and RCA widgets, more process and task mining functions are available at the click of a button. Celonis utilizes process analytics, while Variant Explorer paints a factual picture of the process performance with KPIs. With either of these tools, it can be as simple as starting with low-hanging fruits in process areas where there are good opportunities to improve significantly with quick wins by extending a process. Your project teams can select the right processes based on value, volumes, process maturity, the system landscape, and business priorities out of identified process backlogs that have the maximum business benefit with the least amount of effort to improve it.

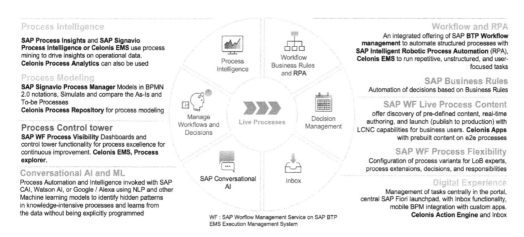

Process Intelligence

SAP Process Insights and SAP Signavio Process Intelligence or Celonis EMS use process mining to drive insights on operational data. Celonis Process Analytics can also be used

Process Modeling

SAP Signavio Process Manager Models in BPMN 2.0 notations, Simulate and compare the As-Is and To-be Processes
Celonis Process Repository for process modeling

Process Control tower

SAP WF Process Visibility Dashboards and control tower functionality for process excellence for continuous improvement. Celonis EMS, Process explorer.

Conversational AI and ML

Process Automation and Intelligence invoked with SAP CAI, Watson AI, or Google / Alexa using NLP and other Machine learning models to identify hidden patterns in knowledge-intensive processes and learns from the data without being explicitly programmed

Workflow and RPA

An integrated offering of SAP BTP Workflow management to automate structured processes with SAP Intelligent Robotic Process Automation (RPA), Celonis EMS to run repetitive, unstructured, and user-focused tasks

SAP Business Rules

Automation of decisions based on Business Rules

SAP WF Live Process Content

offer discovery of pre-defined content, real-time authoring, and launch (publish to production) with LCNC capabilities for business users. Celonis Apps with prebuilt content on e2e processes

SAP WF Process Flexibility

Configuration of process variants for LoB experts, process extensions, decisions, and responsibilities

Digital Experience

Management of tasks centrally in the portal, central SAP Fiori launchpad, with Inbox functionality, mobile BPM integration with custom apps. Celonis Action Engine and Inbox

Process Intelligence · Workflow Business Rules and RPA · Manage Workflows and Decisions · Live Processes · Decision Management · SAP Conversational AI · Inbox

WF : SAP Worflow Management Service on SAP BTP
EMS Execution Management System

Fig. 4.12: Comprehensive view of the components required for intelligent process automation using SAP Signavio Process Transformation Suite and/or Celonis process mining and EMS

2 – business process modeling

Once you have identified the candidate process for an intelligent workflow, you can model the to-be process with the innovations and automation that you have in mind. You can accelerate the design using SAP Signavio Process Manager, Collaboration Hub, and Process Governance to take voters and approve the target process. You can go through the what-if and simulations, substituting rote sub-processes with automation, ML, or advanced technologies to see the impacts on costs, resources, and process turnaround times. The idea is not to have the perfect target process but rather to have a good MVP for a process that can be deployed without much disruption to your operations. This is an iterative process, so there will be many more opportunities to improve in the future. Start with what you think is possible, given your team size and skill sets. Similarly, Celonis offers process modeling and collaboration tools to project teams.

3 – Workflows, RPA, and business rules

Once the target process model is ready, you can use SAP Workflow Management to build and modify workflow by importing the target process model (BPMN 2.0). The developers can build an approval UI within the workflow tasks to connect user experiences. Moreover, to execute transactions on S/4 HANA, such as creating a sales order or purchase order, you can enable SAP iRPA or other RPA bots (UI Path, Automation Anywhere, or Blue Prism) that your organization may have already developed to automate repetitive tasks. Celonis offers EMS for automation with the action engine, which can be further integrated with these other RPA bots mentioned. Furthermore, suppose that certain complex decisions and conditions must be evaluated before your intelligent workflow executes a task or invokes automation. You can maintain these complex business rules in the Business Rules Framework service available under the SAP Workflow management service. These rules can be invoked independently via APIs published on the API Hub for BRF with security protocols you have configured when activating the service on SAP BTP.

4 – process visibility and inboxes

The SAP Workflow Process Visibility cockpit allows you to consume partner content, capture events as they happen during the workflow execution, and create process variants without any changes to the workflow code using a visual, no-code UI. Process Visibility also offers prebuilt dashboards, which your teams can bring up swiftly to visualize the number of transactions and processes in flight. You can also plug in SAP Process Intelligence to monitor any deviations within processes. This enables Process Excellence, transparency, and transformation by providing one view of a process no matter where it runs (in an SAP or non-SAP cloud or in on-premises applications).

5 – continuous improvement and process mining

SAP BPI, if enabled, can continuously monitor newly automated processes and/or intelligent workflows using the target process model as the baseline. Using the data mining algorithms will check conformance levels and suggest any improvements. Your teams can quickly analyze process deviations, do root cause analysis, and detect areas where optimization and automation can be applied.

Before now in this chapter, we have looked at several tools, platform services, and cloud solutions used to identify, improve, automate, and monitor processes and extend them beyond the core. In the next section, we will look at a few other SAP BTP services used for extending the digital core and other services peripheral to SAP BTP included as part of the RISE with SAP offering and the free tier, which your teams can explore and assess whether they want to use for any value-adding extensions or to create reusable assets and IP that will differentiate your processes.

Keeping the core clean

Every aspect of global business today seems to move significantly faster than 10 years ago. For on-premises enterprise systems, a clean digital core is the only way to cope with that speed. SAP's rationale behind the "clean digital core" paradigm is simple: allow customers to extend their SAP S/4HANA software while eventually making software updates non-events. A clean core facilitates faster software deployment, as well as the easier adoption of SAP innovations, process improvements, and regulatory changes. This reduces the **Total Cost of Ownership** (**TCO**) without jeopardizing flexibility. In practical terms, keeping the core clean means the following:

- Applying a zero-modification policy from the project's first day
- Eliminating enhancements that are redundant to standard code and functionality, as well as "clones" of standard code
- Using released APIs, only leveraging the key user (in-app) extensibility of SAP S/4HANA to its full extent
- Employing the capabilities and services offered by SAP BTP to build larger extension applications
- Utilizing SAP Integration Suite

In the following section, we will discuss extension scenarios and the extensibility options that allow us to keep the core clean while meeting our business requirements.

Extension Scenarios

Any organization should have a set of processes and extensions that offers it a competitive advantage and presumably, they would like to carry it over into the new world of S/4 HANA. SAP provides several extension mechanisms through UI adaptations, personalizations, and KUT across the development stack, classified under In-App Extensibility. Side-by-Side Extensibility mechanisms offer loosely coupled extensions, allowing for complete flexibility and extensibility for custom UIs to connect to the S/4 HANA backend through standard OData APIs or be integrated into custom application logic written as a service connected to a database on SAP BTP. Both these extensibility options (In-App and Side-by-Side) have a clean core agenda at heart to create upgrade-stable extensions for cloud and on-premises deployments. However, not all custom extensions fit into these patterns and extension mechanisms and required modifying the SAP codebase for on-premises deployments of S/4 HANA, which resulted in painful and prolonged upgrade cycles. Now, recently, SAP has come up with Embedded Steampunk (within the S/4 HANA stack), which changes how extensions can run within the core, closer to the data within the same context, calling local APIs without the need for data replication and invoking a stable ABAP interface. We will look at this latest extension mechanism and the other two that we have discussed.

The recommendation is to avoid extensions where possible and use adaptations through the standard configuration to follow best practices and prevent dependence on custom extensions. However, if there is a need, we don't have to avoid it altogether and can consider the following extension scenarios.

1. **Key User Extensions: In-App Extensibility**:

   The following figure depicts all the In-App Extensibility options, cutting across the layers of the UI to the database available as part of the S/4 HANA extensibility:

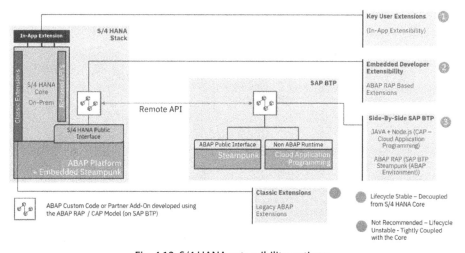

Fig. 4.13: S/4 HANA extensibility options

In-App Extensibility builds on the insight that most ERP application extensions are similar and require a limited set of technologies. The critical user (In-App) extensibility mechanisms in SAP S/4HANA have been designed to enable key users to configure such extensions in a self-service fashion. They offer a powerful toolset for extending the data model, business logic, and UIs of SAP S/4HANA, which can be leveraged so that key users or business users can develop and publish these extensions.

2. **The Embedded Steampunk (on-stack) developer's extensibility**

This option empowers ABAP developers to extend standard SAP processes with custom extensions that require tighter integration (tightly coupled) with the SAP S/4HANA codebase and data while keeping the digital core isolated from the custom code. This will help minimize the efforts of regression testing during SAP S/4HANA upgrades. Technically, this will allow you to develop custom extensions on the same ABAP platform that the SAP S/4HANA on-premises instance or SAP S/4HANA Cloud tenant uses. The clear separation between custom and standard code is achieved by adopting the ABAP RESTful application programming model based on CDS views and optimized ABAP, along with released DDIC objects and local APIs to future-proof your extensions. You can use the Developer (on-stack) Extensibility option to extend standard processes, create custom OData services to be consumed by locally deployed SAP Fiori apps, or build custom APIs for integration. All these options are based on stable extension points and public APIs. Extensibility that does not block SAP software updates is allowed and continues to work after an update without manual steps. This reduces the effort of custom extension maintenance significantly. More extensibility is possible for SAP S/4HANA Cloud, private, and on-premises editions. You have full customization and extension options. Even the modification of the SAP standard code is possible, although you should strictly avoid it to keep the core clean and stable. However, the custom ABAP development hardens the maintenance of the custom code over a period as the corpus of extension increases. Dependencies between your custom code and the SAP standard code need to be kept in check to avoid the same challenges you faced with ECC cores. Custom code management becomes more critical here.

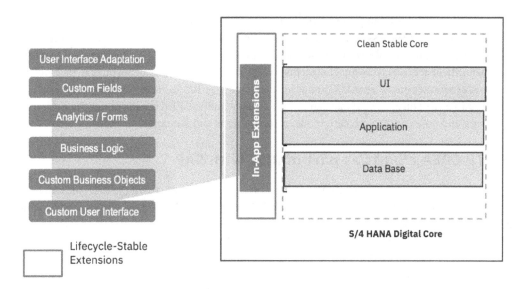

Fig 4.14: S/4 HANA extensibility options

3. **Side-by-Side Extensibility**:

SAP BTP has been designed to make building and integrating side-by-side extensions that are loosely coupled for SAP products much easier compared to other generic platforms. A key extensibility option in the Side-By-Side toolkit is the SAP BTP ABAP Environment (Embedded Steampunk, aka ABAP Cloud), which provides a dedicated, stable ABAP interface between the platform and the custom solutions and supports multi-tenancy, allowing partners to offer multitenant SaaS solutions. Your development teams could also use the **Cloud Application Programming (CAP)** model alongside the ABAP **RESTful Application Programming (RAP)** model for extensions that are cloud-ready and upgrade-stable. We have briefly touched upon several benefits of SAP BTP for SAP landscapes in terms of integration, security, and open APIs. Consider these traits of SAP BTP as a side-by-side extension platform:

- It is one platform for extending both cloud and on-premises solutions from SAP

- It provides integration for your extensions at the UX, process, and data levels

- It offers comprehensive security from the UI to the backend

- It enables smooth connectivity to SAP solutions and easier discovery and consumption of APIs and events across applications

- It is integrated into the life cycle management of hybrid landscapes

Along with the extension mechanisms discussed, SAP BTP also offers a wide range of capabilities and services tailored to the needs of enterprise applications. As part of the SAP Connectivity service, SAP provides a cloud connector as a simple and secure way to connect your on-premises, cloud, or hybrid landscape to SAP BTP. The connection between your SAP BTP account and your cloud solutions from SAP (for example, SAP SuccessFactors® solutions or SAP Integration Suite) goes directly through a secure internet channel. Establishing these connections has been dramatically simplified through the extensibility of services to connect systems to SAP BTP. The number of manual steps (such as exchanging certificates or entering URLs) has been massively reduced. Next, we will discuss some of the key cloud services on SAP BTP that can be consumed with the CPEA credits under the RISE with SAP offering and how they fit with certain extension patterns and scenarios.

SAP BTP CPEA credits as part of RISE with SAP

RISE with SAP covers limited SAP BTP CPEA credits (based on the actual cost of the RISE subscription) as highlighted in the *BPI Starter Pack for RISE with SAP* section. CPEA cloud credits cover a few basic scenarios and use cases, for use by a limited number of business users. SAP BTP services are calculated based on metrics, so it is advised to use the SAP BTP Estimator to see the subscription costs for the services and whether the CPEA credits will cover all or some of the services you want to use in your first use case. Some of these use cases are discussed here to help you understand what a prudent use of these credits for SAP BTP platform service might be and to derive the benefits that your organization seeks for scaling its innovations or extensions.

To help reimagine some extension and innovation scenarios, SAP Discovery Center is a good resource. It can help point to GitHub repos and the supporting resources to help you understand how SAP services can be applied to certain use cases. You can explore and estimate the benefits of using the missions with a deep dive into deploying and running these services.

Use case 1 – creating a unified experience using the SAP Launchpad service (SAP Workzone)

The SAP Launchpad service (now bundled into SAP Workzone) offers a central entry point for accessing various SAP solutions on the cloud and on-premises. This enhances the productivity and efficiency of business users by seamlessly allowing them to access relevant apps and content centrally in one place. It provides consistency through a harmonized UX and smooth integrations for different UI technologies and third-party web apps. Many solutions such as SuccessFactors, IBP, and S/4HANA are tightly integrated and can be accessed within the SAP Launchpad shell. Customers can also configure access to third-party systems and launch them from a tile on SAP Launchpad. SAP Mobile Start is provisioned automatically with the SAP Launchpad service, which means all SAP Launchpad service customers can get a mobile experience with SAP Mobile Start with minimal setup. Rolling these out to targeted business users and owners will help increase the adoption of new UXes and, more importantly, create ambassadors for change within an organization.

Use case 2 – process automation

SAP Workflow Management and SAP iRPA are part of the Process Automation suite: a few processes will differentiate an enterprise from its competition, and it should carry them over. Differentiating processes and value-adding assets could also be reimagined with automation and intelligent workflows, as explained previously. This could also mean weaving intelligence with ML and AI engines into the

E2E process to make it more intelligent and autonomous. Opportunities for process automation can be explored in their initial phases to improve your technology, ROI, and competitive advantage, and then democratized at scale via other identified candidates for process automation. Moreover, suppose an organization has already ventured into RPA with SAP. In that case, how well SAP Workflow Management has been integrated and works with third-party RPA can be tested using APIs. Thereby, you can see the longevity of the investment made by your organization well before embarking on a digital transformation.

Use case 3 – SAP Event Mesh and SAP Kyma for cloud-native extensions

SAP S/4 HANA Cloud comes with business processes and transaction events that can be critical to an event-driven architecture and extensions such as sending out notifications to customers or external third-party systems to act on certain activities or triggering a specific workflow or automation. Essentially, Event Mesh could also be configured for IoT scenarios to perform predictive maintenance activities based on outliers from streaming data – for example, triggering a service order for the technician to perform a health check on an asset to pre-empt any downtime. All of the orchestration required can be built using the events, microservices, and serverless functions in Kyma and combined with Event Mesh, which supports Cloud Event v1.0 and is an open standard for events.

Use case 4 – the Custom Code Migration app

Traditionally, the Custom Code Migration app was set up on an SAP S/4HANA sandbox system in the customer environment, although this may not be the case with some customers who don't have access to the SAP S/4HANA sandbox. Alternatively, they can use the Custom Code Migration app on the SAP BTP ABAP Environment, which they must be separately entitled to. With RISE with SAP, you have the option to use your included CPEA credits for this.

Use case 5 – ABAP Steampunk (ABAP PaaS on BTP)

Based on the suggestions from the Custom Code Migration app, developers can decide to move some of the legacy ABAP code to the cloud using the ABAP PaaS and an RAP model based on CDS views and validate the requirements and see how it fits with the whole Side-by-Side Extensibility concept.

Use case 6 – SAP CAI

SAP CAI offers a single intuitive interface for training, building, testing, connecting, and monitoring chatbots embedded into SAP and third-party solutions, a high-performing **Natural Language Processing** (**NLP**) technology, and low-code features to ensure faster development. Many use cases in terms of employee experience and customer experience that use NLP and trigger automation via simple commands make a good case for further optimization and high adoption.

Free tier plan

Beyond the SAP CPEA credits available with a RISE with SAP offering, SAP BTP has over 50 services offered for free with the pay-as-you-go plan. There is no upfront commitment with the pay-as-you-go plan, and the user pays only for what they use beyond the free limits. It can be used for experimentation and trying out the free services, which often can cover your essential exploration and proof-of-value scenarios. Combine this with SAP developer missions and SAP Discovery Center. The best part of the free tier is its boosters, which automate spinning up services and the associated user accesses in an automated fashion, with a developer able to jumpstart their development with the use of SAP Business Application Studio. The idea of deploying your application within hours is made possible. All of the work from your free tier/trial accounts is carried over to the development systems once the organization decides to go ahead with the services on SAP BTP. You can move your developments to production, with a few more environments such as staging and production, depending on your SAP landscape, and with cloud subaccounts on BTP connected to their respective S/4 HANA cores. Combined with the CPEA credits offered under RISE with SAP, this is good enough to try out the scenarios mentioned. Should there be a requirement to upgrade the plan, the user can subscribe to a pay-as-you-go tier.

Other embedded tools and services

SAP Readiness Check for SAP S/4HANA Upgrades helps with ongoing S/4 HANA upgrades and maintenance to assess the readiness of S/4 HANA systems in preparation for an upgrade to a selected target SAP S/4HANA release (including the chosen feature package stack or support package stack) and give you an indication of the required efforts. It's a self-service tool to identify the mandatory prerequisites and preparations well before an upgrade project starts and enables implementation teams to understand its implications. This early insight means you can scope and plan your upgrade project with a higher degree of accuracy.

The following checks are available in SAP Readiness Check for SAP S/4HANA Upgrades:

- Simplification items
- Recommended SAP Fiori apps
- Integration
- Custom code analysis
- SAP innovative business solutions
- Add-on compatibility

The **SAP Enable Now** solution provides advanced in-application help and training capabilities, helping organizations improve productivity and user adoption and increase the end user's satisfaction. Change management and support teams can efficiently create, maintain, and deliver in-application help, learning materials, and documentation. A RISE with SAP license now covers prebuilt embedded content for S/4 HANA (view-only). Your organization can provide a new workforce with continuous learning support with SAP Enable Now and, with additional licenses, can now create and publish new training content on processes to transfer knowledge to the new workforce.

SAP Cloud Application Lifecycle Management (**SAP CALM**)): SAP CALM for S/4 HANA Cloud is equivalent to the solution manager for on-premises S/4 HANA. It complements SAP cloud implementations with SAP Activate Methodology across all phases. A dashboard provides an overview of the status of the activities and covers process management, requirement gathering, project tasks, and test and deployment management. The post-go-live stages help with running and maintenance. You can plug in your S/4 HANA cloud landscape to start monitoring your processes and the integrations with predefined KPIs for BPMON and define the integration services and scenarios to be monitored. Any failures or defects are detected instantaneously and alert management generates notifications for them. They can be followed up with the Root Call Analysis feature and corrections can be applied automatically by built-in workflows.

Spark4life has now started its transformation journey with the CBM.ai tool to get quick insights on the business architecture through the CBM heatmaps, to understand the capabilities their organization needs to build upon and the ones they can capitalize on. Further they have embraced the business process insight tools to understand which processes are candidates for improvements and how they can leverage the services offered by SAP BTP under Rise with SAP offering or by offloading the legacy custom extension and code by adopting the new extension mechanisms on SAP BTP to make their ECC systems leaner. Further, the IT organization is already planning to run a few ideation hackathons to understand what could be next business innovation that could catapult them ahead of the competition. And to help this ideation and provide their tech and business teams alike some tools and platform services, IT organization is encouraging their teams to sign up for the free tier services on BTP and asking them to follow tutorials from the https://developers.sap.com/tutorial-navigator. html to earn badges and bring forward some proof-of-values through their innovation use cases discovered in ideation sessions.

Summary

In this chapter, we understood the external and internal drivers of change an organization should look out for when assessing its capabilities, how tools such as CBM.ai can be used to define the business architecture and roadmap to realize the desired outcomes, and how SAP BPI + Signavio Process Transformation Suite helps zoom in on process heat maps from CBM assessments to identify process improvements. Furthermore, we understood how several platform services such as SAP Workflow management and SAP BPI can be combined to configure autonomous processes. Toward the tail end of the chapter, we considered extension mechanisms for S/4 HANA processes and discussed the platform services on SAP BTP to which the CPEA credits offered under RISE with SAP could be applied, with examples. These platform services could be instrumental for your extension and innovation agenda, differentiating you and offering a faster time-to-market.

In the next chapter, we will learn about the details of all the different packages available within RISE with SAP, making it clear what is included and what is not. The reader will also understand how to build the business case for the adoption of RISE with SAP while providing alternate options for deployments with hyperscalers and covering some crucial decisions that will impact your RISE with SAP journey both short-term and long-term.

Further reading

- *The specialized enterprise*: https://ibm.co/specialized-enterprise
- *Component business models: making specialization real*: https://ibm.co/cbm-specialization
- *Four steps to implement Component Business Modeling*: https://ibm.co/cbm-four-steps
- *Accelerating Digital Reinvention with component business modeling*: https://ibm.co/cbm-reinvention
- Get started here: www.s4hana.com or www.sap.com/pathfinder
- IDC report on digital transformation investments reaching $3.4 trillion by 2026: https://www.idc.com/getdoc.jsp?containerId=prUS49797222

5

Cloud with Silver Lining: Busting the Myth – Part 1

In previous chapters, we have gone through different technology trends and the problem statements faced by CXO profiles, and how RISE with SAP can be a potential approach to address the demands from both a business and IT point of view. Some of the key challenges every organization faces around business transformation are the **total cost of ownership** (**TCO**), enterprise agility, scalability, and flexibility to adapt to a new business operating model. It is important to how SAP optimizes product strategy and functionality and other solutions built around this to avoid re-work or potential cost overrun.

Spark4life as an organization has now been able to understand the importance of RISE with SAP and how it can help their requirements. But in order to be able to convince the executives within the organization, they need to build a strong business case in order to be able to justify how the investment will be self-paid.

In this chapter, you will be able to understand how you can build a business case within your organization to adopt RISE with SAP and the different points you need to consider before finalizing your architecture with RISE with SAP. By the time you are done with this chapter, you will be in a good position to define the different dimensions involved, along with their impact and the associated options when considering RISE with SAP.

In this chapter, we will be covering the following topics:

- Putting together a business case for RISE with SAP
- Industry trends influencing S/4HANA adoption with RISE with SAP
- Understanding the architectural patterns within RISE with SAP
- Exploring what is possible and what is not possible within RISE with SAP
- Looking into alternate options for RISE with SAP

Putting together a business case for RISE with SAP

In this section, we will start by outlining the different use cases that other organizations have been thinking through and when RISE with SAP would also be the right option. Since an announcement from SAP asking organizations to move to S/4HANA by 2027, there have been questions raised around whether this is a technical move or whether there is also a business-driven approach to how new features and functionalities can justify the move to S/4HANA. Some of the key use cases or drivers to consider are as follows:

- **Journey to the cloud with reduced dependency on multi-vendor maintenance:**

  - Most organizations have different vendors providing the implementation or application management services, along with the hosting and maintenance services through IaaS and PaaS models.

  - Organizations also deal with SAP separately when it comes to product support.

  - The aspiration would be to have a single vendor who can be both responsible for the product- and the infrastructure-related services. This will help in obtaining a business-driven outcome based on system usability rather than system availability alone.

- **Multiple systems consolidated into a core ERP solution:**

  - Most organizations have built different instances over time and segregated them either based on business unit-specific requirements or geographic location, causing multiple silos of information

  - Organizations lack a single source of truth to quickly respond to business requirements

  - The aspiration would be to have a single source of truth across an organization, which is both easy to maintain and puts a harmonized data model in place

- **Process simplification:**

  - Every organization at the time of implementation has a global template in place, which is then either extended as per the localization requirements or due to new business models coming into play

  - Organizations also go ahead and extend the process with custom flows that are not in alignment with the global template, causing more deviations from the agreed-upon process

  - Users also end up leveraging different workarounds given the system has the option due to other dependencies (if any)

  - The aspiration would be to get a real-time view of the process along with the usage and identify any compliance issues pro-actively rather than reactively

- **Mergers and acquisitions:**

  - Over time, most organizations see mergers and acquisitions happening, which either involve a non-SAP solution or another version of SAP solution with different flows

  - The aspiration would be to quickly provision to merge one landscape with the other by ramping up on the infrastructure piece, along with the right design in place

- **Sustainability ambitions and compliance:**

  - Most organizations either have a hard target or a soft target around achieving net zero from a sustainability point of view when it comes to carbon footprint based on various socioeconomic factors

  - The aspiration would be to have a solution in place that can extend the existing data to facilitate tracking and reporting

- **Regulatory adherence:**

  - Organizations need to be able to quickly ramp up for any regulatory changes around the GDPR and financial requirements, among other things

- **Digital business model and enhanced user experience:**

  - Organizations are looking for solutions that are consistent across applications when it comes to the user interface and in compliance with the accessibility guidelines to support a diversified workforce

- **Automated processes embedded with Artificial Intelligence (AI)/Machine Learning (ML):**

  - Organizations are looking for processes that are both simplified and automated for configuration and development-related activities.

  - Along with being automated, it is also important to have AI- and ML-based use cases embedded into day-to-day activities to reduce manual intervention. Examples include invoice paper scanning or GR/IR reconciliation.

- **Keeping the digital core clean for any customizations to be done for more frequent upgrades/ maintenance activities to be performed:**

  - Organizations are looking for solutions that can be upgraded and maintained with much less effort compared to typical ERP solutions where every upgrade or maintenance needs a very long downtime and testing effort

  - The aspiration is to be able to perform upgrades more often without impacting the core functionality offered by SAP

The following figure provides a snapshot of how many customers have gone live and how many of them are in progress compared to the actual licenses sold. It summarizes what the actual opportunity is in terms of the number of ECC customers. Hence, for each of these customers or organizations still on ECC and planning on moving to S/4HANA, it is important to consider the use cases and drivers mentioned previously (and depicted in the following figure) to plan accordingly.

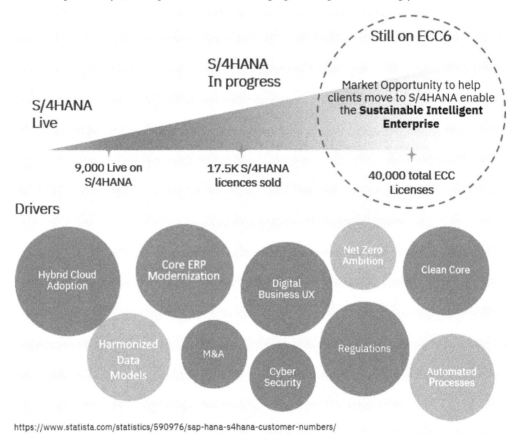

https://www.statista.com/statistics/590976/sap-hana-s4hana-customer-numbers/

Figure 5.1: Use cases to be considered when moving onto S/4HANA

The preceding diagram summarizes the different stages of client landscapes and the various aspirations or value-adding scenarios that clients/CXOs want to address with the adoption of S/4HANA. These dimensions, factors, drivers, and use cases are going to be critical for you to put together the business case for the move to S/4HANA while adopting the RISE with SAP cloud offering made available by SAP.

To achieve the right business case, it is important to have enterprise-wide adoption of a set of tools and checkpoints to manage opportunities, objectively identify the next steps, and forecast the business value accurately. This is critical to ensure we can improve the chance of putting together a validated business case. It also needs a standardized approach, along with the right action plan to close the funding approval process. The business case "build and approval/purchase cycle" goes through three key stages:

1. **Need**: This stage is about recognizing and considering what the organization has been looking for in terms of its mindset and the goals, desired experience, and tasks to be accomplished. Key questions to consider would be as follows:

   - Can we identify the challenge(s) the organization is having today?

   - Can the organization continue with what it is doing and help build a compelling case around adding business value and a self-service model?

   - Does the organization have a valid driver identified based on what has been mentioned earlier in this section?

2. **Evaluation**: This stage is about evaluating and selecting the approach or solution based on the need identified in the earlier stage. The outcome would help with a well-defined action plan to agree upon the solution to be adopted. Key questions to consider would be as follows:

   - What is the offering or the right tool that can address the business problem at hand?

   - What outcomes can we expect, and which vendor can help us achieve these?

   - Can we have a demo around the business problem we have before agreeing to the implementation?

3. **Commitment**: This stage is about negotiating and purchasing the solution and services required to address the business problem organizations might be having. Key questions to consider would be as follows:

   - Have all the options been considered? If yes, is the option at hand the best option to move forward with?

   - Has risk analysis been done around the solution and the service provider?

   - How committed are we as an organization to the solution?

Let's go through each of the stages in detail.

The need stage of the business case proposal

As part of the *need* stage, we would need to review and validate the existing documentation, along with the assessment criteria and other non-functional requirements. The following figure provides a summary of the approach to kickstart the decision process and to facilitate fast results for building a strong business case for the move to RISE with SAP:

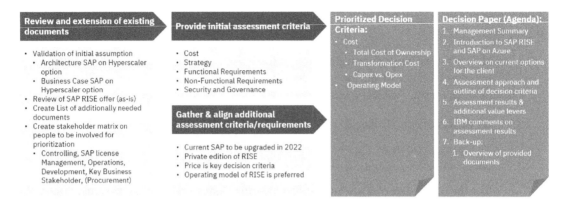

Figure 5.2: Approach to finalizing the assessment criteria in the "need" stage

As shown in the previous figure, it is recommended to always consider two alternatives based on a best practice approach in five assessment dimensions across hyper-scalers and with or without RISE with SAP. In this case, as an example, the assessment was performed between SAP on Azure without RISE and SAP on Azure with RISE with SAP. The five dimensions mentioned as part of the assessment criteria are as follows:

- Cost

- Strategy

- Functional requirements

- Non-functional requirements

- Security and governance

The following figure provides the details for each of the dimensions listed here, along with the decision criteria and the sample questions you should be considering when putting together the business case for both S/4HANA and RISE with SAP. The sample questions provided are only illustrative and do not mention all the possible questions you need to consider.

Examples of typical decision criteria and corresponding questions

Assessment Dimension	Decision criteria	Sample Questions
Cost	• Implementation/Migration Cost • Total cost of ownership	• How do the options compare in terms of implementation cost/effort model? • How do the options compare in the total cost of ownership? • ...
Strategy	• Suitability to Cloud-Driven Application Development • Compliance to IT strategy	• How well does the option support your IT strategy? • Does the option contain strategically restrictive components? (exit strategy) • ...
Non-Functional Requirements	• Innovation Cycles • Operating Model • Speed to implement • Adaptability to Non-Functional Requirements • Ability to segregate business units • Change Management Effort to adapt to standard	• Does the option allow of S/W Release upgrade flexibility for S/4HANA? • Does the option support Hybrid Migration or Transformation? • Does the option support iRPA (Intelligent Robotic Process Automation) or DevOps? • ...
Functional Req.	• Software Maturity • Functional Scope • Customization Flexibility • Integration & Testing • Upcoming Business Requirements • Interconnectivity	• How much does the option cover all scope and functionality requirements relevant to you? • Is the option flexible for enhancing the S/4HANA Solution to meet your non-standard requirements? • To what extent does the option allow integration of tools or methods? • ...
Security & Governance	• Governance Model • Compliance with external regulations • Security	• How well does the option comply with governance Model of your company? • How well does the option comply with your external regulations? • ...

Figure 5.3: Assessment criteria and sample questions

The evaluation stage of the business case proposal

Once you have completed the review of each of the dimensions and their associated criteria, you need to ensure all personas and business requirements, along with IT standards, have been addressed. After the initial data gathering and review, as part of the *evaluation* stage, you can further evaluate the dimensions and the compliance in iterations to refine the approach and close all gaps before moving on to the next phase. The following figure provides an overview of the different phases or iterations to achieve the objective of a finalized evaluation based on the dimensions of cost, strategy, non-functional requirements, functional requirements, and security/governance:

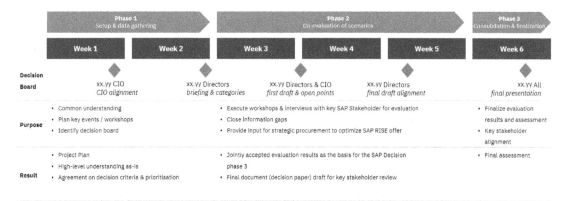

Figure 5.4: Phases to finalize the evaluation results for the adoption of SAP with RISE

As shown in the previous figure, each phase of the assessment as part of the evaluation stage will help achieve the final assessment outcome, along with the business case-related inputs to drive the approval of the business case. Let's quickly review the purpose and result of each of the phases mentioned in the previous figure:

- **Phase 1: Setup & data gathering:**
  - The purpose of this phase is to establish a common understanding while planning for key events and workshops to be conducted to further review the solution and the product being considered
  - The result would be an agreed-upon project plan and a high-level understanding of the as-is landscape and solution, along with prioritized decision criteria

- **Phase 2: Co-evaluation of scenarios:**
  - The purpose of this phase is to execute the workshops and interviews with the SAP stakeholders to close the information gaps. This phase will also provide input for optimizing the solution.
  - The result would be jointly agreed-upon decision criteria on the part of the organization and SAP, along with other vendors.

- **Phase 3: Consolidation & finalization:**
  - The purpose of this phase is to finalize the evaluation results and the assessment findings, along with the stakeholder alignment
  - The result is the final published evaluation assessment to be executed

In addition to the phases and their purposes provided, in each of the phases mentioned here, it is important to understand and document the following points to make sure the evaluation can be objective and have actionable insights:

- What does the business or client want?
- The mindset
- The goals
- The desired experience
- The tasks to be fulfilled
- A **mutual action plan** (**MAP**) based on the ask
- Validation of the opportunity through documenting
- Customer stakeholder strategy
- Competitors, if any

- Ecosystem

- Funding

- Solution differentiators

- Business value drivers

- C-level executive drivers or line-of-business drivers

- Customer challenges

- Compelling events

- Organization pain points

- Disparate systems

- No real-time information is available for decisions to be made

- Insights are more static than dynamic as per changes in the business model

- Complex technical debt built over a period of time around the landscape

- Lack of agility when it comes to adopting new ways of working

- Offline processes for day-to-day activities with reduced adoption of the system functionality

It is also important to understand and provide answers to the following questions:

- What are the key technical and functional requirements that will help you lay out the transition path from the current state to the future state of vision?

- What are the ongoing and future projects with respect to mergers and acquisitions or other prerequisites around ecosystem-related components that need to be addressed to adopt S/4HANA?

- What is going to be the set of criteria, along with the various strategic, business-related, operational-related, and technical-based benefits, to be considered?

- What deployment option are you going to consider based on your current investment in the process and adherence to the standards?

- What tools are you going to leverage to help identify the TCO and **return on investment (ROI)**?

- Take into consideration the lessons learned from other global engagements with other clients through your partner ecosystem

Once you have completed the *need* and *evaluation* stages of the framework that have been discussed previously, it is vital to document the score for the opportunity or business problem around the following criteria listed in the *evaluation* stage before the *commitment* stage is followed through. This will help put together an opportunity map that helps validate the business case. The following is a sample representation of what those criteria would mean, with a breakdown in terms of weak, moderate, and strong categorizations based on the landscape and requirements of the business or clients:

- Compelling event:

  - Weak – No compelling event/we don't know

  - Moderate – Compelling event exists, but the impact or delay is not significant to the customer

  - Strong – Compelling event exists, and the impact or delay is significant to the customer

- Funding:

  - Weak – No funding/we don't know

  - Moderate – Budget exists but is not yet approved or secured

  - Strong – Budget exists and is approved and secured

- Solution and differentiators:

  - Weak – No SAP solution fits or the differentiators are unclear

  - Moderate – Partial fit and/or little differentiation from the competition

  - Strong – Good fit and/or strong differentiation from the competition

- Customer stakeholder strategy:

  - Weak – Limited engagement with IT only. No C-level access, weak SAP relationship.

  - Moderate - Engaging at the business and C level. Customer champions advocating SAP internally.

  - Strong – Trusted reliable relationships with business owners/decision makers. SAP is the preferred vendor.

- Customer challenges:

  - Weak – Customer challenges not understood or identified

  - Moderate – Customer challenges understood but impact not quantified

  - Strong – Customer challenges understood, impact quantified, and root cause(s) are clear

- Customer business drivers:

  - Weak – Business value not identified and/or business case not validated or agreed upon by the customer

- Moderate – Business value and/or business case is complete but not validated or agreed upon by the customer

- Strong – Business value and/or business case is complete and validated or agreed upon by the customer

- Competitors:

  - Weak – Competition unknown or strong competitor in place

  - Moderate – No competition or a weaker competitor has been identified and a strategy is in place to address this

  - Strong – Competitive advantage of SAP in terms of price, product, relationship, and brand

- Partners and ecosystem:

  - Weak – Partner strategy unknown. Partner not identified or has conflicting interests.

  - Moderate – Partner options evaluated, strategy agreed upon, and engagement plan in place.

  - Strong – Strong SAP/partner presence with alignment on deal closure.

The commitment stage of the business case proposal

Post-completion of the *need* and *evaluation* stages, we will now walk you through the *commitment* stage to ensure the solution agreed upon can be negotiated and purchased. Organizations during this stage should typically look out for ways to risk assess both the solution and the service provider involved. The key objectives are to achieve the following:

- The right financial and contractual terms

- Risk analysis for the solution and service provider

- A go or no-go decision

The outcome of this stage is to have a detailed deployment plan both from a system and resource point of view, with clear dependencies on both the service provider and other vendors called out, as well as the internal business users to be involved. Once the plan is agreed upon, the organizations during this stage will commit to the change execution with both internal and external stakeholders.

As a sample representation of the criteria and score options provided for the dimensions mentioned previously across each of the stages, the qualitative assessment shows that both options that we evaluated, one with Hyperscaler 1 and the other with Hyperscaler 2, are very close to each other in all categories – they are designed to be comparable. The following figure provides a summary of the dimensions and the scoring across each:

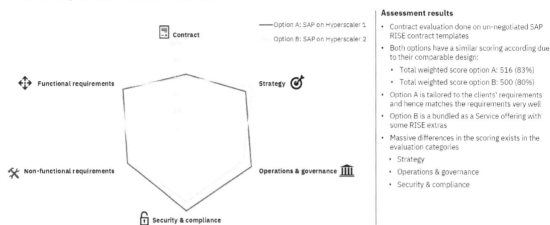

Overview on qualitative assessment results*

— Option A: SAP on Hyperscaler 1
.... Option B: SAP on Hyperscaler 2

Contract

Functional requirements

Strategy

Non-functional requirements

Operations & governance

Security & compliance

* Shown values in % of max fulfilment

Assessment results

- Contract evaluation done on un-negotiated SAP RISE contract templates
- Both options have a similar scoring according due to their comparable design:
  - Total weighted score option A: 516 (83%)
  - Total weighted score option B: 500 (80%)
- Option A is tailored to the clients' requirements and hence matches the requirements very well
- Option B is a bundled as a Service offering with some RISE extras
- Massive differences in the scoring exists in the evaluation categories
  - Strategy
  - Operations & governance
  - Security & compliance

Figure 5.5: Representative maturity assessment of the model

Based on the maturity assessment, along with weightings across the dimensions of **Contract**, **Strategy**, **Operations & governance**, **Security & compliance**, **Non-functional requirements**, and **Functional requirements**, we have been able to showcase the differentiated scores between RISE with SAP and non-RISE with SAP and the costs and benefits involved as a sample.

Overview on assessment results

Criteria	Weighting	Option A: SAP on Hyperscaler 1		Comment
Contract	1/6	63%	60%	• Contract evaluation based on RISE contract templates • No blockers identified, optimization in negotiations expected • Both options low on cost transparency and business flexibility
Strategy	1/6	85%	95%	• The licensing of RISE (as a Service) meets the client's strategic requirements better
Operations & governance	1/6	93%	81%	• Option B is a bit more complicated due to the client to manage SAP for RISE systems
Security & compliance	1/6	99%	88%	• SAP on Hyperscaler 1 address all security and compliance requirements • SIEM can be integrated (planned feature Q1 2021)
Non-functional requirements	1/6	85%	82%	• Option A matches the non-functional requirements more because the flexibility is better • RISE plans ServiceNow and considering client integration
Functional requirements	1/6	91%	94%	• RISE is offering some extra functionalities as Business Process Intelligence, Technology Platform and Business Network, which are not relevant now but can be used with credits
Overall scoring	100%	83%	80%	

Figure 5.6: Business criteria and sample cost-benefit analysis

Industry trends influencing S/4HANA adoption with RISE with SAP

We have walked you through the different stages of creating the business case and the importance of an iterative approach with both the internal and external stakeholders. One of the key ingredients that we touched upon was to have a clear view of the industry trends and best practices. To be able to support this requirement, it is important to understand the key industry trends and the impact they have on the market. In this regard, the **Institute of Business Value (IBV)** as part of a study performed in 2022 predicted businesses struggling when it came to the adoption of S/4HANA around various use cases, along with their impact on the business. The following figure summarizes the top five industry trends highlighted by the IBV study for clients globally:

Figure 5.7: Key industry trends that influence the adoption of
S/4HANA with RISE with SAP (source: IBV study, 2021)

Let's review each of the trends before going into the details of each of these trends:

- **Digital transformation has become a way of life…**: Organizations and companies in this context need to re-evaluate how they manage their assets, infrastructure, and talent. Cloud is a key focus area to enable faster and more effective collaboration.

- **Human capital is precious and scarce…**: Prioritize employees' financial, mental, and physical well-being by providing flexibility and encouraging authenticity.

- **Sustainability and transparency are urgent priorities…**: Organizations and companies need to provide more transparency around their initiatives and production methods to connect with purpose-driven consumers.

- **Tech adoption should reshape business operations…**: Building integrated systems that revolutionize business models across the entire landscape.

- **Trust and security underpin sustained innovation…**: Integration of cloud security practices in overall security strategy is essential.

Based on these five trends mentioned previously, let's do a deep dive by further splitting these trends into nine different scenarios:

- **Shift to S/4HANA with discovery assessment**: Describes how you can ensure key business stakeholders are aligned with the business, process, data, and system insights gathered through detailed analysis of the as-is and to-be operating models to best articulate the business case for the modernization of SAP, along with an action plan for implementation.

- **Getting back to the standard with a clean core approach**: Describes how you can ensure that you design adaptive systems, optimizing the technical build through code, data, and processes. This means returning to the mindset of keeping the core clean by adopting industry standard best practices while allowing for innovation through extensibility.

- **Safeguarding the effort to migrate to S/4HANA**: Describes how you can ensure key business stakeholders are aligned with the business, process, data, and system insights gathered through detailed analysis of the as-is and to-be operating models in order to best articulate the business case for modernization of SAP along with an action plan for implementation.

- **Data first**: Describes how you can ensure you use the right data migration methods, tools, and best practices to accelerate the move to S/4HANA by up to 30%. The usage of the right tools and techniques will provide a safe and predictable path to go-live. You can leverage tools such as SAP DI, SDI, and BODS, along with built-in options such as Migration Cockpit to migrate clean data into the target S/4HANA system.

- **Empower the move to the cloud**: Describes how you can ensure cloud platforms and services can increase scalability, flexibility, and business agility while reducing the TCO and operational complexity through containerized extensions and innovations. Enterprises are released from large CAPEX for on-premises infrastructure into an OPEX-driven cloud model that maximizes business value.

- **The intelligent sustainable enterprise**: Describes how you can use SAP and partner innovations to help achieve your sustainability ambitions across finance, supply chain, and logistics to enable net zero business operations. This is possible with responsible sourcing and circularity in supply chains along with a single pane of visibility across analytics requirements.

- **Connected enterprise**: Describes how you can use the power of Industry 4.0 solutions that define how the target data model enables the future adoption of AI/ML, automation, the IoT, and streaming analytics with edge computing. You can also use a well-defined data fabric that weaves together the transactional and analytical data to provide hidden meaning from key insights.

- **Continuous improvement/ongoing improvement**: Describes how you can drive continuous innovation through operations not only with application lifecycle management best practices but also by increasing operational efficiencies, reducing points of failure, and de-risking the solution used by the business through proactive CI/CD initiatives.

- **Security**: Describes how you can ensure safe and compliant operations with a trusted application estate by carrying out security hardening, ensuring the compliance of SAP systems and landscapes, and bringing a historic and overarching view of all the security aspects that affect SAP technology.

In the following sections of this chapter, we will be focusing on the first three scenarios mentioned here around the shift to S/4HANA, getting back to the standard with a clean core approach, and safeguarding the effort to migrate to S/4HANA. We will cover the remaining scenarios in the upcoming chapters.

Shifting to S/4HANA and the relevance of outcome path and sizing

Based on the nine different scenarios mentioned previously, we will focus mainly in this section on the shift to S/4HANA-related scenarios. Within this scenario, the discovery assessment is for the client or you to decide how you can identify which scenario is the right approach. There are different scenarios to be considered, such as greenfield, brownfield, hybrid migration, or to continue staying on ECC until you get further clarity around the adoption of S/4HANA within your landscape. The following figure provides you with the different business objectives, along with their purposes and what your outcome path would be, which will be a key driver toward building the right business case for S/4HANA and RISE with SAP as an approach:

Figure 5.8: Different migration paths to S/4HANA based on business objectives

In addition to the outcome paths mentioned in the preceding figure, another key contributing factor toward building the business case for RISE with SAP would be to have the right understanding of the impact of licensing costs and the type of users your organization currently has, and how you are planning to consume these services going forward. Once you have decided which migration path is appropriate, you need to understand the following four key dimensions of PCE licensing as part of RISE with SAP:

- Core access
- Digital access
- Infrastructure add-ons
- LOB and industry solutions

The following figure summarizes these four dimensions and the related components contributing toward the derivation of the **full usage equivalent** (**FUE**) concept, which then, in turn, drives the infrastructure requirements as part of RISE with SAP:

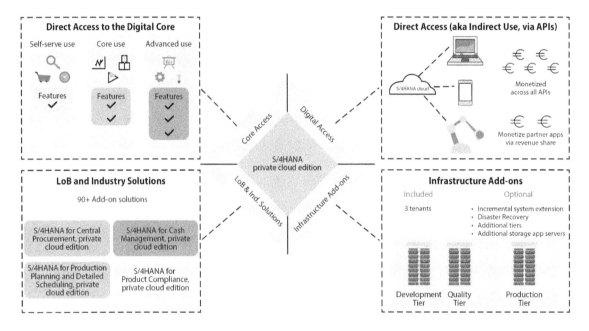

Figure 5.9: Four dimensions to derive the sizing of S/4HANA system

In the preceding figure, within *Core Access*, you would need to consider the S/4HANA usage for advanced, core, and self-serve use cases. These will also cover display user rights and approval user rights for all solution capabilities of RISE with SAP S/4HANA Cloud, private edition. The following figure provides a clear demarcation between Developer, Advanced, Core, and Self-Service users so that you can evaluate which type of licenses you will need and by what count:

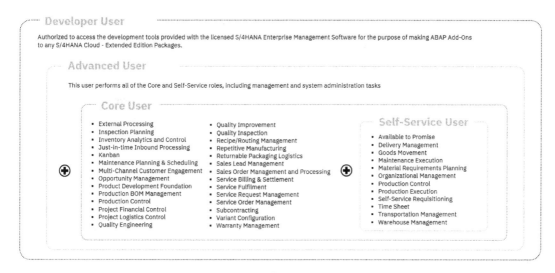

Figure 5.10: Segregation of activities performed by Core, Self-
Serve, and Advanced user groups within S/4HANA

Based on the type of access required and the different add-ons to be considered, you can come up with the FUE calculation using the information provided in the following figure to decide on which T-shirt size is the closest to that which addresses your business asks. You can also tailor the requirements beyond what are provided as part of the T-shirt sizes but to get going with the business case, this is a very good starting point for your organization.

Figure 5.11: FUE to T-shirt size mapping

> **Note**
>
> SAP has also released a 4XL T-shirt size in certain scenarios to address requirements of 9 TB+ scenarios for the HANA DB.

Along with the type of licenses based on the FUEs and the sizing, you would also need to have a clear view of the SLAs provided by RISE with SAP to be able to decide on whether you would need **high availability** (**HA**) and **disaster recovery** (**DR**), along with what backup category would best suit your organization. The following figure summarizes the value delivered by RISE with SAP and the core features of RISE with SAP and how they contribute to operational efficiency, along with the reduction of the TCO:

Features of RISE with SAP S/4HANA Cloud, private edition

- Enhanced Service Delivery SLAs
  - 24*7 service delivery for PRD-systems
  - 24*5 service delivery for Non-PRD-systems
- System Setup Activities
  - FIORI Launchpad enablement
  - TMS for NetWeaver based systems
- Continuous Service Planning and Review
- Annual face2face Service Review
- Continuous Software Release Planning
- Access to ECS expert community, webinars
- Wide range of **unlimited** Advanced Technical Operations services w/o restrictions on consumption

Value delivered

- **No surpRISEs due to unexpected costs** from over-consumption of additional advanced technical operations services. True predictability of costs.
- **No delays from lengthy commercial processes** to contract additional technical operations services
- **Best practice service plan** executes services proactively without customer triggers and ensures optimal system health and performance
- **Continuous reviews** ensure high agility and optimal alignment with business requirements
- **Continuous Software Release Planning** keeps systems well-maintained and healthy, allowing business continuity

Figure 5.12: SLAs provided by RISE with SAP along with value delivered

In the preceding figure, we have provided information about the basic features and the value delivered through those features, especially around no unexpected costs, no delays from lengthy commercial processes, built-in continuous reviews, and continuous software release planning. In addition to the features mentioned earlier, you also would need to be aware of the different categories delivered as part of RISE with SAP, along with the service level you can consider for each of the systems to be requested. The following figure provides an overview of these categories around availability, DR, data storage/backup, planned maintenance, service request management, and change request management, along with the associated service levels available:

Category	Service Description	Service Level
Availability (uptime level)	Calculated on a monthly basis; excluding planned maintenance Technical availability of the individual SAP system measured by a logon check within the network boundaries of the SAP HANA Enterprise Cloud, thus excluding WAN and application availability and any planned downtimes.	99.7% uptime for PRD 95% uptime for Non-PRD
Disaster Recovery (optional) - for production systems only	SAP Declared Disaster Recovery of a data center and movement to the alternate DR Data Center. Recovery Point Objective (RPO) and Recovery Time Objective (RTO).	12 Hr RTO with 30 Min RPO * 12 Hr RTO with 0 Min RPO **
Data Storage & Data Backup	Backup retention period	1 month for PRD, 14 days for Non-PRD
	Data backed up in accordance with frequency and data retention policy	100% of data backed up
	Data replicated to a secondary location	100% of backups are copied from primary location to secondary location
Planned Maintenance	Monthly maintenance window to perform maintenance activities triggered by SAP; customer requested activities requiring downtime not included	4 hours per month
Service Request Management	Office hours in which Service requests are processed. In the Service Request Management all requests according to a service will be processed. Office hours to be mutually agreed between SAP and the customer	24*7 service delivery for PRD-systems 24*5 service delivery for Non-PRD-systems
Change Request Management	Office hours in which change requests are processed. Office hours to be mutually agreed between SAP and the customer	24*7 service delivery for PRD-systems 24*5 service delivery for Non-PRD-systems

Figure 5.13: Different service categories and their associated service levels

You also need to be aware of the different priorities and their associated **incident reaction times** (IRTs), which play a key role in the response from SAP to potential system- or product-related issues. The following table provides an overview of the different SLAs for the IRT as per the priority to be assigned:

Priority	Incident Reaction Time (IRT)	SLA for IRT
1 – Very High		20 minutes (7*24h) (problem determination action plan within 4 hours – as agreed in the contract
2 – High	The amount of time between SAP Support Level 1 is notified of the incident and the first action taken by an SAP support person to repair the incident.	2 hours
3 – Medium		4 hours
4 – Low		1 Business Day

* Azure, IBM Cloud, GCP, SAP DC ** AWS.

Figure 5.14: SLAs for IRT

Along with the support model provided by RISE with SAP, it is key to have an understanding of the different deployment options and other dimensions that are supported by the RISE with SAP compared to on-premises in order to make the right decision. The following figure summarizes the different dimensions and the effort included in the as-a-service model of what we refer to as RISE with SAP:

	SAP S/4HANA Public Cloud	SAP S/4HANA Private Cloud	SAP S/4HANA On-Premise
Deployment Type	New Implementation	Conversion, Selective Data Transition, (New Implementation)	
Extensibility	Within S/4Extensibility Framework, embedded custom code and SAP Cloud Platform	Customize & Extend	
Modifications	Not allowed	not recommended, but allowed	
Release Upgrades	included and mandatory (limited flexibility option)	Customer owned, installation on request included	not included
Upgrade entitlement	2 times per year	yearly	yearly
Minimum Upgrade frequency	2 times per year	5 years (stay in mainstream maintenance)	not limited (maintenance to be considered)
Model Company	Enterprise Mgmt Layer Included and optional	Best Practice activation included and optional	not included
3rd Party Add-ons	Certified Public Cloud add-ons allowed	Defined list of S/4HANA qualified add-ons allowed*	allowed
Partner Templates	Dedicated Public Cloud templates planned	allowed	

* still under evaluation

Figure 5.15: Deployment options comparison across scope dimensions

In addition to the dimensions shown previously, the other dimensions you should be considering are the license model, implementation team, content ownership, application management services, content lifecycle management, product support, technical operations, and infrastructure. The following figure provides insight into who is responsible for each of the dimensions mentioned earlier across public cloud, private cloud, and on-premises deployments:

	SAP S/4HANA Public Cloud	SAP S/4HANA Private Cloud	SAP S/4HANA On-Premise
License Model	Software Subscription *		Perpetual Software
Implementation	Partner / SAP / Customer		
Content Ownership	**SAP** / Partner / Customer	**Partner** SAP / Customer	
Application Management Services	SAP *	**Partner** / Customer / SAP ECS	
Content Lifecycle Management	SAP *	**Partner** / Customer / SAP ECS	
Product Support	SAP *	SAP *	SAP / Resell Partner
Technical Operations	SAP *	SAP *	Partner / Customer / SAP ECS
Infrastructure	Hyperscaler / SAP *	Hyperscaler / SAP*	Customer DC / Hyperscaler / SAP / Premium Supplier / Partner

* Included in SAP Subscription

As a Service   As a Product

Figure 5.16: Ownership across different dimensions for different deployments

Upon validating the different dimensions mentioned earlier, you would need to select the right choice when it came to the deployment model and the infrastructure to support, along with the components within the bundle that SAP offers as part of RISE with SAP. The following figure summarizes the components discussed so far and what you need to consider when coming up with a cost for RISE with SAP around S/4HANA:

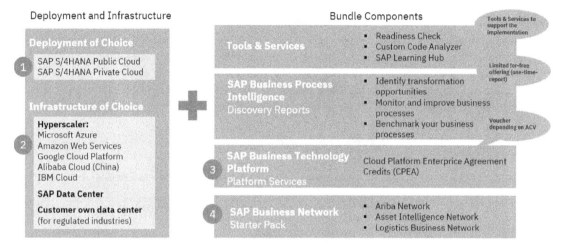

Figure 5.17: Deployment choice along with component bundle as part of RISE with SAP

Based on the details discussed before now, it is important to have the understanding and also the split of material number-based approach to identify the right selection when discussing with SAP. The following figure provides a sample SKU number for different offerings that can be selected as part of RISE with SAP.

	Public Cloud			**Private Cloud**		
Offering	Rise with SAP S/4HANA Cloud	Rise with SAP S/4HANA Cloud + XM*	SAP S/4HANA Cloud (China, NS2)	Rise with SAP S/4HANA Cloud, private edition	SAP S/4HANA Cloud, private edition (China, NS2)	SAP ERP, private cloud edition
SKU	8010836	8010840	8010837	8010833	8010834	8009438 (exceptions only**)
Bundle Components	**Fixed entitlements** Ariba Supplier Network AIN: 200 equipment, 2 connections, and 10 partner portal invitees LBN: freight collab option **Variable entitlement** CPEA (2K min, 16K max, 1% of RISE Ent Mgmt net ACV value)	**Fixed entitlements** Ariba Suppl. Network AIN: prem. membership LBN: freight collab option **Variable entitlement** CPEA (2K min, 16K max, 1% of RISE Ent Mgmt net ACV value) **XM Entitlement** 25 XM for IT for every 1 FUE	N	**Fixed entitlements** Ariba Suppl. Network AIN:200 equipment, 2 connections, and 10 partner portal invitees LBN: freight collab option **Variable entitlement** CPEA (4K min, 16K max, 1% of RISE Ent Mgmt net ACV value)	N	N
Tier	Y – Tier 1 and 2	Y – Tier 1 and 2 collapsed, Min of 500 FUE	Y – Tier 1 and 2	N	N	N
Minumim FUE	35	500	35	40	40	40
Region	All (excl. China, NS2)	All (excl. China, NS2)	China/NS2	All (excl. China, NS2)	China/NS2	All
Channel	Dir, Resell, CCP (PMC with exceptional approval)	Dir only (no Resell, no CCP and no PMC)	Dir, Resell (No CCP) (PMC with except. approval)	Dir, Resell, CCP (PMC with exceptional approval)	Dir, Resell (no CCP) (PMC with except. approval)	Dir

Source: SAP

*Qualtrics/Experience Management

** Exceptional option for selected, complex customers who want to move to the cloud, but are not yet ready for S/4HANA

Figure 5.18: Offering and related SKU for products within RISE with SAP

Before you finalize the scope of services with RISE with SAP based on sizing, the SLAs, the system configuration, and other key parameters as described previously, it is also important to have a good understanding of the roles and responsibilities matrix, specifying who is responsible for carrying out related activities – SAP or the customer/organization. Customer activities can be done by the customer's SAP team or the customer-engaged SI. For instance, overall project management and coordination with different stakeholders for a release version upgrade still would be the responsibility of the customer, as RISE with SAP only takes care of technical upgrade activities. These services can also be filled in with the **cloud application services (CAS)** packages offered by SAP or by SI partners. Another example is the transport setup of CTS+, along with transport deployment itself, which would be outside the RISE with SAP standard scope. Having a thorough understanding of the following categories mentioned in the figure will enable you to plan the scope and set the right expectations upfront with both the IT and business stakeholders to avoid any surprise costs as part of the engagement at a later point in time.

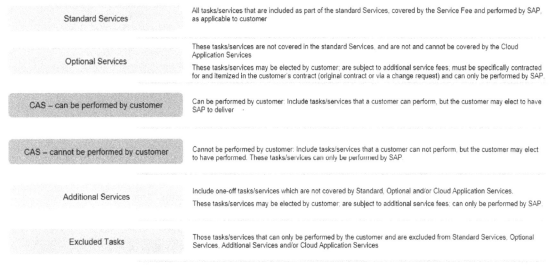

Figure 5.19: Categories of tasks within RISE with SAP

The following figure provides some examples of each of the task categories mentioned previously when delivering or planning to sign up for RISE with SAP:

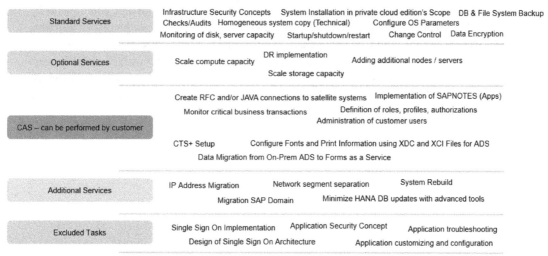

Standard Services	Infrastructure Security Concepts System Installation in private cloud edition's Scope DB & File System Backup Checks/Audits Homogeneous system copy (Technical) Configure OS Parameters Monitoring of disk, server capacity Startup/shutdown/restart Change Control Data Encryption
Optional Services	Scale compute capacity DR implementation Adding additional nodes / servers Scale storage capacity
CAS – can be performed by customer	Create RFC and/or JAVA connections to satellite systems Implementation of SAPNOTES (Apps) Monitor critical business transactions Definition of roles, profiles, authorizations Administration of customer users CTS+ Setup Configure Fonts and Print Information using XDC and XCI Files for ADS Data Migration from On-Prem ADS to Forms as a Service
Additional Services	IP Address Migration Network segment separation System Rebuild Migration SAP Domain Minimize HANA DB updates with advanced tools
Excluded Tasks	Single Sign On Implementation Application Security Concept Application troubleshooting Design of Single Sign On Architecture Application customizing and configuration

→ The complete list can be found in the R&R Document

Figure 5.20: Sample tasks included in each category as part of RISE with SAP

You can find more information about the roles and responsibilities as per the variant you have chosen around Standard or Tailored PCE by referring to the following link:

```
https://www.sap.com/about/agreements/policies/hec-services.
html?sort=latest_desc&tag=agreements:product-policy/hec/roles-resp
onsibilities&tag=language:english
```

In the next section, let's focus on the importance of a clean core-driven approach and how that can help towards a strong business case and ease of adoption of S/4HANA.

Getting back to the standard with a clean core approach

In this section, we will focus on the clean core approach when it comes to optimizing the core within ECC and then applying this when migrating to S/4HANA to avoid obsolete code and duplicate functionality being moved to the new S/4HANA instance. Over time, it is usual to have WRICEFs (customizations performed by organizations) left in the system that are not being used anymore. It is also possible to have potential performance issues and customizations that are no longer required when moving to S/4HANA.

In the clean core approach, you would be using different SAP and partner tools to identify the hot spots and validation with the simplification list to identify what customizations are still needed and which can be deleted. The customization objects to be retained are evaluated as per the side-by-side extensibility design rules to transfer the changes onto **Business Technology Platform** (BTP). This will help keep the digital core clean and lean, allowing for more frequent upgrades.

You also need to be able to clearly articulate your innovation and future landscape components by mapping the digital core to your base requirements, along with the usage of products such as Ariba, Fieldglass, Success Factors, and Concur to ensure you get the full advantage of the features made available by SAP. With RISE with SAP, you can leverage the one-time report with Business Process Intelligence – Process Insights to get insights around what current bottlenecks you have, and which areas are mapped to which components within S/4HANA, including the custom code mapping to the standard functionality made available by SAP.

The following figure provides an overview of the different components to be considered:

- Data cleansing and profiling
- Code analysis
- System usage analysis
- Data scanning and assessment
- Code usage analysis
- Complexity assessment
- Data quality
- Code remediation
- End-to-end process documentation
- Data harmonization
- Code simplification
- Efficiency assessment
- Data temperature/archiving
- Code modernization
- Process harmonization:

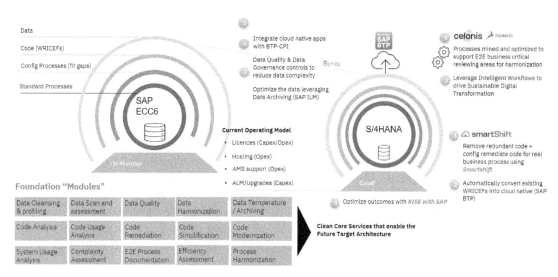

Figure 5.21: Clean core approach and the designated foundation modules

You would need to evaluate each of the points mentioned in the previous figure and ensure there is a source on which to target the transformation. The seven steps shown are as follows:

- Optimize outcomes with RISE with SAP by moving workloads onto the cloud provider of your choice (part of RISE with SAP)

- Automatically convert existing customizations into cloud-native extensions using SAP BTP (additional SI partner-based engagement)

- Remove any redundant code within the landscape, along with configuration remediation for business processes using smartShift as a tooling option (an additional purchase to support the journey)

- Simplify the business process and optimize end-to-end support using products such as Celonis or Signavio (included with Signavio licenses but need to be enhanced by other modules within Signavio if used to full potential)

- Leverage intelligent workflows in order to drive sustainable digital transformation use case adoption (additional SI partner-based engagement)

- Integrate cloud-native apps with BTP-CPI (additional SI partner-based engagement)

- Optimize the data by leveraging Data Archiving where applicable to optimize the cloud spend (additional SI partner-based engagement)

If you do not already have products such as Celonis or Signavio in use currently in the landscape for ongoing product cycle optimization, this is the right time to invest. They will help generate insights beyond typical L3 process documentation. They will also help you identify automation opportunities as well. In the next section, we will discuss how to safeguard the investment being made by the organizations when it comes to efforts around migration to S/4HANA.

Safeguarding the effort to migrate to S/4HANA

We earlier reviewed the different sizing factors, along with other scenarios that need to be validated prior to pricing the solution. It is important to review the overall TCO-based components and their influence on supporting organizations to make the right decisions thereafter. This is important to ensure you are prepared not only for the shift to S/4HANA but also covered in terms of the support cycle needed for the next 3 to 5 years and beyond. You will have to plan out different expense heads for the components involved and clearly outline the outcomes for them. The TCO calculation involves multiple components such as the following:

- **Hardware/software investment**: This component covers the license cost for the products, along with the infrastructure that you will need to procure to support your requirements, both functional and non-functional. The different expense heads to be considered within this component are as follows:

  - Technical architecture and infrastructure

  - System software

  - Application software

- **Implementation costs**: In addition to the hardware and software investment, you also need to factor in the implementation costs and derive the ROI to validate the cycle time. It is important to validate how much of the work being done as part of this cost is reusable in support mode post-implementation to ensure you have a sustainable model in place. The following are some of the breakdowns to be considered as part of the overall implementation costs (the costs for people, process, and technology towers need to be included):

  - Project management

  - Organizational change management

  - Process design or simplification

  - Technical setup

  - Testing

  - Training

  - Business setup

- **Application management and ongoing continuous improvement**: Post-implementation, you also need to account for ongoing application management and continuous innovation activities to keep the solution up to date both from the point of view of technical debt and functionality. The following are the different expense heads to be considered for making sure you can maintain and improve the solution over time:

  - Hardware/software ongoing maintenance

  - Operational activities

  - Continuous improvement initiatives

RISE with SAP provides models across each of the aforementioned categories providing end-to-end technical managed services along with BTP integration. This will help you to achieve more than just migration to S/4HANA to address the approach towards a clean core and sustainability, among many other features and use cases possible with BTP. The following image summarizes the TCO being reduced by about 30% compared to the same services being executed either using existing ECC or S/4HANA being on-premises or on another hyperscaler outside RISE with SAP as a solution.

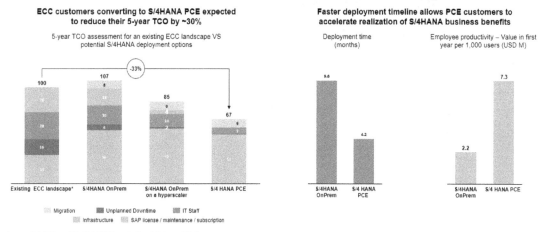

Source: IDC ECC and S/4HANA TCO study (Nov. 2020) and IDC S/4HANA Business Value Study (March 2020).

Notes: Model company used for the study: $10.7B in annual revenue, 42.4k employees, 2.2k IT staff, 4.6k ERP users. The TCO model is calculated on the forward looking cash flow basis; existing ECC landscape costs do not take into account past investments (ECC licenses, infrastructure, etc.). S/4HANA landscape includes S/4HANA Professional Use, SAP HANA, runtime edition for applications & SAP BW

Figure 5.22: TCO comparison across different deployment options

As shown in the previous figure, the TCO reduction with S/4HANA PCE (RISE with SAP) is mainly driven due to the committed SLAs from the following components:

- The infrastructure components

- The technical managed services

- The software component at the application level

The scope of these committed services and the SLAs help the clients with a platform to focus on innovation rather than the maintenance and regular housekeeping of the instances between multiple entities. Along with the TCO reduction, it is also important for you to understand the business drivers and the business benefits possible through S/4HANA PCE, which, in turn, will result in improved productivity for your business users. *Figure 5.23* provides an overview of the top seven business drivers, along with the possible business benefits. Let's summarize the top three business drivers:

- Faster access to analytics/reporting
- Improved customer experience
- Lower operational costs

These drivers can help achieve a 30% shorter delivery lead time along with a 40% reduction in days sales outstanding and a 60% increase in operational efficiency.

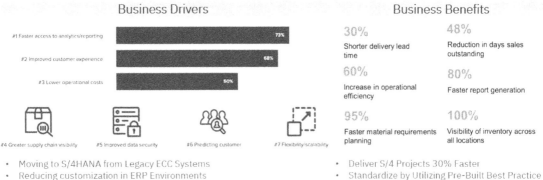

Figure 5.23: Benefits of a RISE with SAP-driven transformation approach

You can categorize these benefits into different categories, such as business, strategic, technical, and operational benefits. This will help modularize the business case to be built and presented across different audiences. The following figure provides a categorical breakdown of each of these sections to provide you with the information required to position S/4HANA as the NextGen transformation product, along with the need for technical managed services around it with RISE with SAP.

   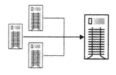

Business Benefits

- **Full scope** of SAP S/4HANA scope incl. LOB and industry processes, supporting 25 industries
- Wide range of defined **partner add-ons**
- **64 Country/Region versions** in 39 languages
- Your **SAP concierge service** to move to the cloud

Strategic Benefits

- **System conversions** and brownfield migrations into the cloud
- Application and technical operations out of **ONE hand**
- **Safeguarding** prior investments into SAP systems

Technical Benefits

- Access to S/4HANA **Extensibility Framework**
- Side-by-side and **In-App** extensions
- Code enhancement & **code modifications**
- **Expert configuration** (full IMG access)
- **Scalable** platform

Operational Benefits

- **Resilience and TCO** of hyperscaler infrastructure
- **Technical operations** done by SAP
- **Upgrade installation** on customer request

Figure 5.24: Business, strategic, technical, and operational benefits of RISE with SAP

So far in this section, we have discussed where clients are struggling, and we have gone through details around the importance of the following:

- Having a clear strategy of move to S/4HANA (greenfield, brownfield, or hybrid)
- Having a view of what licensing models you would like to adopt
- Having a view of innovation and unique business models with process re-design
- Having a view of technical managed services for both product and hardware compared to just hardware, with other options such as partner-managed cloud or hosting services offered by hyperscalers

Let's now go through the different services and tools you can leverage to perform the required analysis in order to derive the costs for both the implementation/migration and support points of view. These services need to provide support for both technical and functional components. An example is that you need to consider not just technically moving the ECC onto S/4HANA but also how you can simplify and transform the process while reducing maintenance costs with automation embedded by AI/ML.

To optimize the time taken to prepare the business case, there are well-defined automated solutions in place to perform an assessment on the aforementioned points and come up with a streamlined output to consume. We also recommend evaluating the findings based on SAP standard tools, along with the partner output provided, to get an additional drill-down where applicable. Let's now go through some of these tools made available by SAP that can help you in the process of business case creation to assist with the items mentioned previously:

- **SAP S/4HANA Readiness Check**: Validates the readiness of the existing ECC system(s) that you might be currently using to migrate to SAP S/4HANA in terms of custom code and the functionality used, along with the system sizing, and the type of modules activated currently.

- **Process Insights Report**: SAP as part of the acquisition of Signavio offers a one-time report along with RISE with SAP which provides specific insights into the lines of business along with potential bottlenecks and automation opportunities to be able to simplify your business process before moving onto S/4HANA including recommendations around the FIORI apps and the path to move to S/4HANA.

- **FIORI Apps recommendation report**: Provides a list of FIORI apps from the library available that can be considered depending on the type of transactions your business has been frequently accessing to perform its day-to-day operations.

- **SAP S/4HANA benchmarking assessment/value lifecycle manager (VLM)**: This is an SAP toolset made available to customers. With this option, you are able to track, monitor, and optimize the expected value of the S/4HANA initiative with other external benchmarking surveys, comparing it with industry peers.

- **Transformation Navigator**: This tool analyzes the goals of your project and builds a technical business case, including a roadmap of what to consider with S/4HANA. It uses the existing landscape information to create a technical recommendation of the to-be landscape.

- **SAP Roadmap Explorer**: Provides a list of innovations on the roadmap to be achieved within the quarter. It provides a breakdown either based on product, process, or industry.

- **SAP Innovation and Optimization Pathfinder**: This tool provides a list of innovations based on KPIs related to business.

- **SAP Best Practices Explorer**: This is a repository of all the best practice packages available both from SAP and from relevant partners. The explorer also provides the setup details not just for configuration or analytics but also for master data-related configuration as well, including the process flow diagrams and the required test scripts for the scenarios mentioned.

- **SAP Quick Sizer**: This helps you size the SAP HANA database and application layer, especially in cases where you do not want to go with the precedent of historical data.

- **SAP Sizing Report**: This tool runs within your existing ECC systems that you are planning to migrate to SAP S/4HANA. It provides complete configuration details from a hardware sizing point of view – more useful in brownfield-type projects.

- **Spotlight by SAP & S/4HANA Customer Story Finder**: Two tools that focus on providing insights into the transformation journey for a client by identifying what needs to be prioritized and also examples/success stories from other customers who already have moved to SAP S/4HANA.

- **SAP S/4HANA Value Advisor**: Provides a quick way to measure the potential value of S/4HANA for your business.

To conclude on the business case approach, you need the business case to consider all the aspects mentioned so far, along with the calculation of the TCO and ROI. This will help you commit to the adoption of RISE with SAP and the S/4HANA component, along with other SaaS components as applicable. If done right, the business case exercise will help you with the cost identification of the license and hardware for the next 3 to 5 years, helping convert the infrastructure cost from CapEx to OpEx. It will also provide detailed insights into the staffing costs for the transformation effort while transitioning to S/4HANA, and the very important aspect of an enhanced user experience, made possible with simplified processes and insights driven by automation and AI.

In the next section, we will walk you through the architectural patterns and the different points to consider prior to finalizing your scope with RISE with SAP to avoid any surprises at a later point in time.

Understanding architectural patterns within RISE with SAP

In *Chapter 3*, we provided a high-level overview of the different points to be considered when planning to move to RISE with SAP. In this section, we will focus on a deep dive into the architectural patterns around these connectivity options and how they impact your adoption of RISE with SAP.

Firstly, it is important to understand the multi-cloud connectivity pattern, which provides an insight into how your other SaaS- or BTP-based extensibility or BPI-based components will integrate with your S/4HANA or other RISE with SAP-related components deployed on your choice of hyperscaler. As you can see in the following figure, SaaS products such as Ariba, Concur, and others are connected to BTP through an OData connection and then using the cloud connector, the SAP BTP landscape establishes connectivity to the SAP S/4HANA-based solution in question on RISE with SAP.

You can directly connect to the RISE with SAP landscape to access the FIORI launchpad and other system GUI-based components. You can also connect to the SAP BTP landscape to work on extensions through the established extensibility platform when accessing the SaaS products as needed depending on your use case.

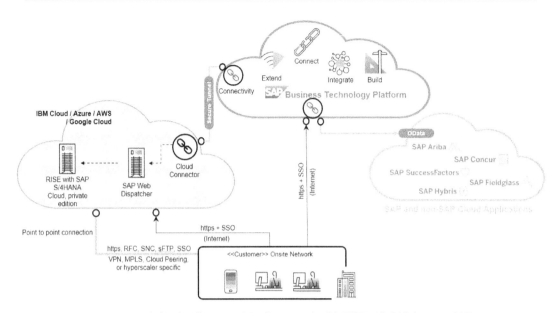

Figure 5.25: Multi-cloud connectivity framework with RISE with SAP (source: SAP)

In addition to customer network connectivity expanding on the connectivity of SAP and the support vendor, the following figure provides insight into how SAP, for instance, will be using the jump server or Bastion host to connect to the SAP systems of the client to provide product-related support. While SAP will have a common platform through which the different client networks will be monitored and managed, the client networks themselves will be physically segregated to avoid any overlap between the client deployments. This is made possible with different networks and connectivity types such as site-to-site VPN or Direct Link/Direct Connect/ExpressRoute, which will be used to establish the connectivity between the client's network to the RISE with SAP systems. Any other users trying to access will have to log in to their respective VPN or customer networks first before trying to connect to the RISE with SAP systems. The following figure provides an overview of different entry points into the infrastructure for each of the stakeholders of the support team, the client users, and SAP themselves:

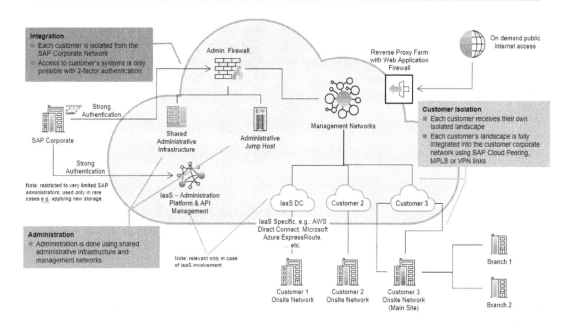

Figure 5.26: SAP, client, and user connectivity overview (source: SAP)

In continuation to the connectivity diagrams shown previously, it is also important to understand the approach being used when it comes to **Domain Name Server (DNS)** connectivity for supporting the incoming domain name being exchanged with the network's internal component. This is critical for making sure any external-facing website or domain is properly translated. The following figure provides a brief overview of how the information is exchanged:

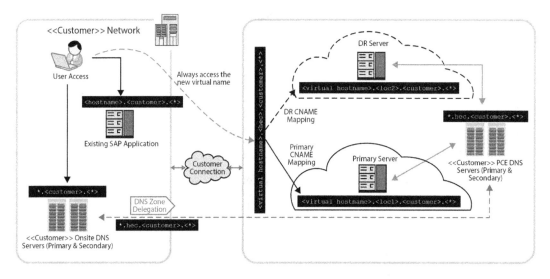

Figure 5.27: DNS workflow with RISE with SAP (source: SAP)

Doing a deep dive to validate what information is to be planned by the clients or customers, you will need to provide the DNS IP for the required domain along with the wildcard certificate from your internal CA and the associated external internet-facing URL for the target domain. The following figure provides the details of the different activities involved and how the translation happens between you and the RISE with SAP network.

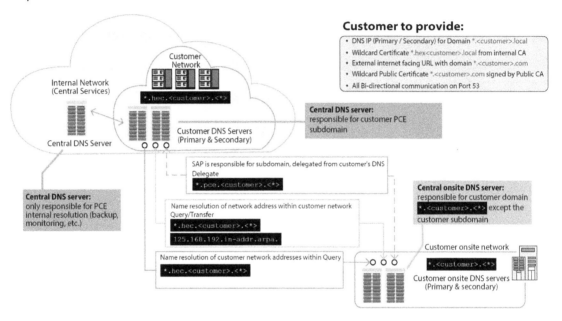

Figure 5.28: DNS resolution workflow (source: SAP)

In addition to the connectivity and DNS setup, security plays an integral part in setting up the whole landscape within RISE with SAP as well and is not an afterthought to support the use cases. A few of the components addressed by RISE have been listed here:

- Security measures are audited and confirmed through various certifications and attestations
- ISO certificates
- ISO 9001 – quality management system
- ISO 27001 – information security management system
- ISO 27017 – implementation of cloud-specific information security controls
- ISO 27018 – protection of personal data in the cloud
- ISO 22301 – business continuity
- SOC1 (ISAE3402/SSAE18) type II
- SOC2 type II

- C5*
- Advanced IT security architecture
- Dedicated account, subscription, project
- Separate VNET/VPC for each customer
- Security-hardened systems
- Backup and DR
- Long-distance DR/short-distance DR
- Threat and vulnerability management
- Security patch management
- Regular penetration testing
- Regular vulnerability scanning
- 24/7 security monitoring center (cyber SOC)
- Customer-performed penetration testing
- Customer data flow control
- Regional data storage (e.g., the EU or US)
- European data protection and privacy policy
- Network security
- Dedicated account/subscription/project
- **Network security group** (**NSG**)/security group/firewall
- Azure Security Center/AWS Security Hub/IBM Manage services
- Azure Monitoring/CloudWatch/Cloud Monitoring/IBM AIOps or Instana
- Azure Logging/CloudTrail/Cloud Logging/LogDNA
- Web application firewall
- Dedicated connectivity – ExpressRoute/AWS Direct Connect/IBM Direct Link
- Load balancers/subnet
- Subnets
- Network filtering
- Intrusion prevention systems
- Two-factor authentication

- Proxies with content filtering
- Secure product development lifecycles
- Secure operations
- Asset management
- Change management
- Security incident management
- Anti-virus and malware management
- Backup/restore management
- Identity and access management
- Security awareness training
- Physical security
- Video and sensor surveillance
- Access logging
- Security guards
- Fire detection and extinguishing system
- Uninterruptible power supply
- Biometric access control in certain locations

For additional details, please refer to these links:

- "Defense in Depth" security architecture with SAP S/4HANA public cloud: `https://blogs.sap.com/2021/12/12/rise-with-sap-defence-in-depth-security-architecture-with-sap-s-4hana-cloud-public-cloud/`
- "Multi-layer Defense in Depth" architecture of SAP S/4HANA Cloud, Private Edition: `https://blogs.sap.com/2021/10/04/rise-with-sap-multi-layer-defense-in-depth-architecture-of-sap-s-4hana-cloud-private-edition/`

The following figure provides a summary of multiple protections at various levels and which validation is performed at which stage of the security provided.

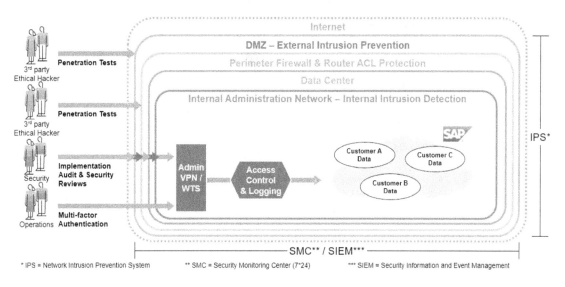

Figure 5.29: RISE with SAP security layers and related entry points (source: SAP)

There are other architectural patterns which RISE with SAP provides around HA and DR that are unique to each hyperscaler as per the choice of service and scope identified for the client's requirements. The following figure provides a summary of how after the design has been finalized, the different interfaces will connect with the S/4HANA instance as an illustrative example.

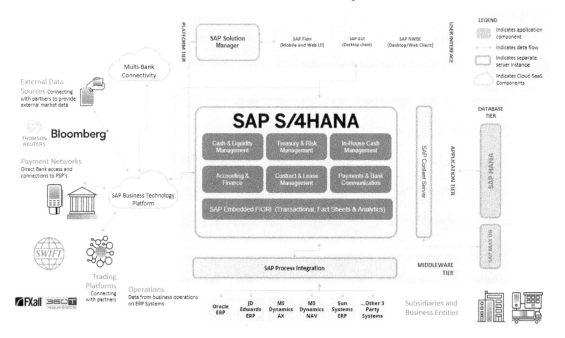

Figure 5.30: Sample S/4HANA landscape with integration in the context of RISE with SAP

Based on the patterns discussed so far, let's discuss the onboarding process and what would be the level of detail you would need to provide to align with these architectural patterns. Once the design is finalized and the requirements are agreed upon, you need to provide the following information:

- User details provided by SAP once the agreement is in place.

- SID details for the systems and the other relevant components in the landscape, along with the planned downtime windows for SAP to plan the required updates through the lifecycle, as shown in the following figure:

SAP Solution	Tier	SAP SID/ SID for HANA System DB	Clients*	Planned Downtime Window	Financially Relevant
S/4HANA	DEV	DS4/HD4	100 110 050**	<e.g. First Tuesday each month 06:00 – 10:00 CET>	(Y/N)
	QAS	QS4/HQ4	100		(Y/N)
	PRD	PS4/HP4	100		(Y/N)
Webdispatcher	DEV	WS1	n/a		(Y/N)
	PRD	WS3/WS4	n/a		(Y/N)
Cloud Connector	DEV	DCL	n/a		(Y/N)
	PRD	PCL	n/a		(Y/N)

Figure 5.31: SID details template for the systems to be installed

> **Note**
>
> The list can change depending on what your scope is, along with which components have been agreed upon.

As an extension to the SID template shown previously, you need to think through all the required components not only for the primary services but also for the associated cloud connectors and add-ons. This is to ensure you can validate them beforehand on the usability within RISE with SAP – the following table is a representative list you can use as a reference point:

PCE Template	Product	DEV App SID	DEV DB SID	QAS App SID	QAS DB SID	PRD App SID	PRD DB SID
Additional Tenant	S/4HANA	SSx (1-9)	HSx (1-9)	n/a	n/a	n/a	n/a
Additional Tenant	Web Dispatcher	Wxx (01-99)	n/a	n/a	n/a	n/a	n/a
Analytics	BOBJ	DBD	n/a	n/a	n/a	PBO	n/a
Analytics	Lumira	DLU	n/a	n/a	n/a	PLU	n/a
BW/4HANA	BW/4HANA	DBW	HDB	n/a	n/a	PBW	HPB
BW/4HANA	Web Dispatcher	WB1	n/a	n/a	n/a	WB2 / WB3	n/a
CAR	CAR	DCA	HDC	QCA	HQC	PCA	HPC
Cloud Connector	Cloud Connector	DCL	n/a	n/a	n/a	PCL	n/a
Convergent Charging	Convergent Charging	DCC	HCD	QCC	HCQ	PCC	HCP
DS-Agent	CPI-DS Agent	DSD	n/a	n/a	n/a	PDS / PDD	n/a
EIM DP Agent	EIM DP Agent	DDP	n/a	n/a	n/a	PDP/PDQ	n/a
EWM	EWM	DEW	HDW	QEW	HQW	PEW	HPW
EWM	Web Dispatcher	WW1	n/a	WW2	n/a	WW3 / WW4	n/a
Fiori Hub	Fiori	DFH	n/a	QFH	n/a	PFH	n/a
Fiori Hub	Web Dispatcher	FW1	n/a	FW2	n/a	FW3 / FW4	n/a
GTS	GTS	DGT	HDG	QGT	HQG	PGT	HPG
Optimizer for S/4HANA Embedded TM	Optimizer	DOS	n/a	n/a	n/a	POS	n/a
PO	PO	DOP	n/a	QOP	n/a	POP	n/a
S/4HANA	S/4HANA	DS4	HD4	QS4	HQ4	PS4	HP4
S/4HANA	Web Dispatcher	WS1	n/a	n/a	n/a	WS3 / WS4	n/a
SAC Agent	SAC Agent	DSA	n/a	n/a	n/a	PSA	n/a
SLT	SLT	DSL	n/a	QSL	n/a	PSL	n/a
Solution Manager Documentation	Solman ABAP	NSD	HDS	n/a	n/a	n/a	n/a
Solution Manager Documentation	Solman JAVA	DSJ	n/a	n/a	n/a	n/a	n/a
Solution Manager Full	Solman ABAP	DFS	HFD	n/a	n/a	PFS	HFP
Solution Manager Full	Solman JAVA	DFJ	n/a	n/a	n/a	PFJ	n/a
Transportation Management	TM	DPM	HDP	n/a	n/a	PTM	HPP
Transportation Management	Web Dispatcher	n/a	n/a	n/a	n/a	n/a	n/a
Transportation Management	Optimizer	DOE	n/a	n/a	n/a	POE	n/a
Trade Management	BW/4HANA	DBW	HDB	QBW	HQB	PBW	HPB

Figure 5.32: Sample landscape components

- Provide the language(s) to be configured.

- Highlight whether any best practices need to be installed and provided when setting up the landscape from the packages made available by SAP.

- SAP also has the option of an **Enterprise Management Layer** (**EML**) image if you are planning on starting the assessment beyond best practices.

For more information about EML, refer to `https://blogs.sap.com/2020/05/25/ introducing-enterprise-management-layer-for-s-4hana-cloud-extended-edition/`.

- In addition to best practices, RISE with SAP also has SAP Business Network Starter Pack, which extends transformation beyond the core S/4HANA implementation by allowing the creation of connections with the different suppliers, vendors, and related assets of an organization (the cope of enabling these for the S/4HANA needs to be evaluated as per the agreed effort, along with the overall design to be adopted in the landscape).

- Other information to be provided is based on the Data Centre IP range for the primary and the DR Centre IP range in case DR is included.

- Need to provide VPN-/direct link-related questionnaire information, along with the IP ranges for DNS configuration.

The following figure is the information about the primary data center and DR data center IP range to be provided:

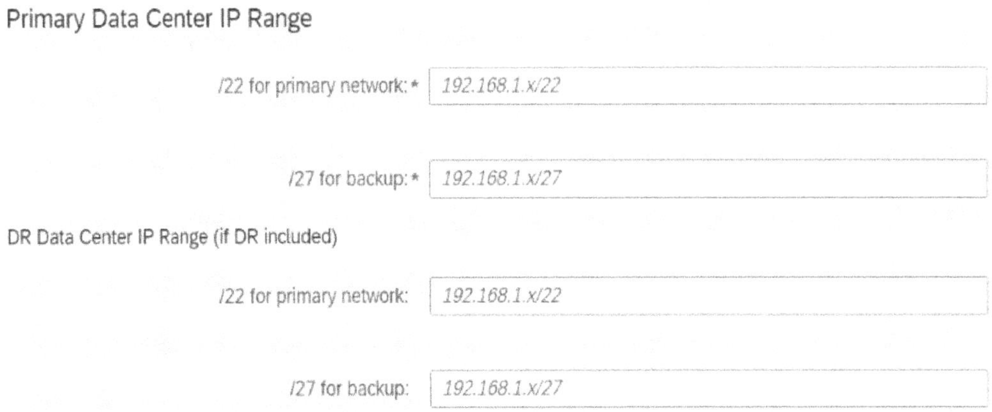

Primary Data Center IP Range

/22 for primary network: * 192.168.1.x/22

/27 for backup: * 192.168.1.x/27

DR Data Center IP Range (if DR included)

/22 for primary network: 192.168.1.x/22

/27 for backup: 192.168.1.x/27

Figure 5.33: Primary and DR data center IP range information template

Along with the IP range information, the following screenshot is for the information about the DNS configuration:

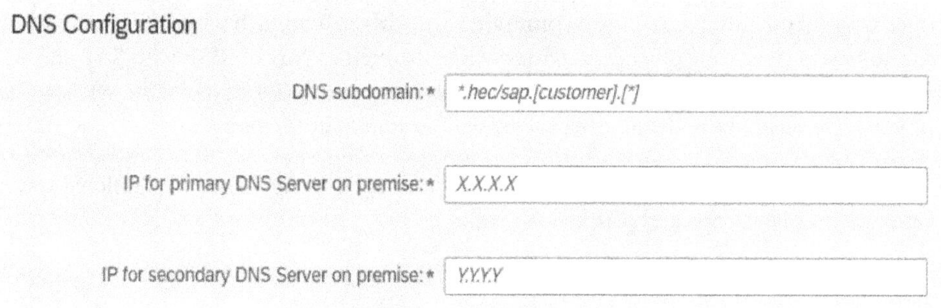

DNS Configuration

DNS subdomain: * | *.hec/sap.[customer].[*]

IP for primary DNS Server on premise: * | X.X.X.X

IP for secondary DNS Server on premise: * | Y.Y.Y.Y

Figure 5.34: DNS configuration template

Finally, we need to provide the contact information for different skills to have them included or reached out to for the onboarding process. The following screenshot provides the different roles to be provided:

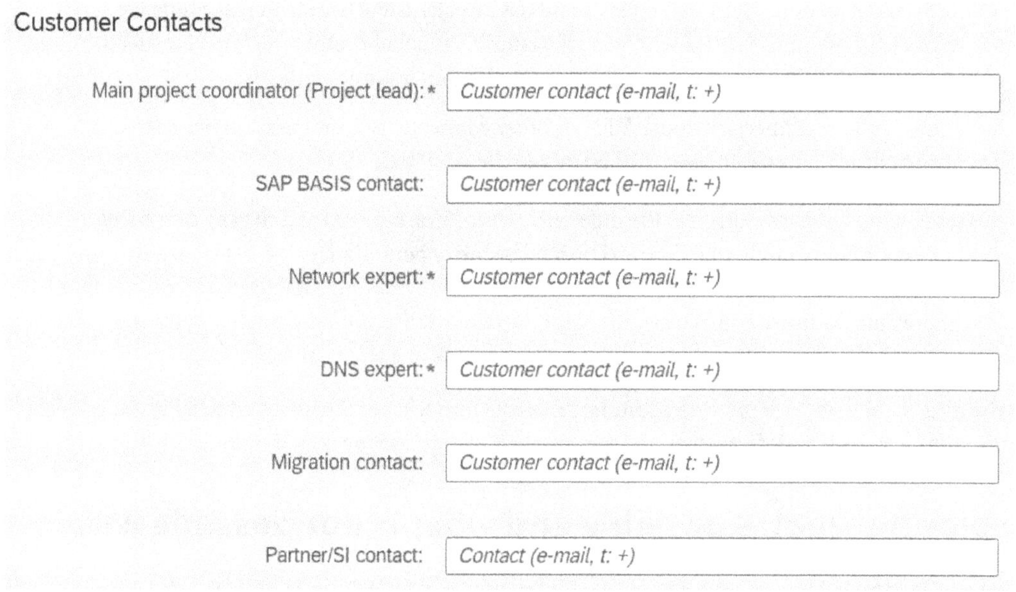

Customer Contacts

Main project coordinator (Project lead): * | Customer contact (e-mail, t: +)

SAP BASIS contact: | Customer contact (e-mail, t: +)

Network expert: * | Customer contact (e-mail, t: +)

DNS expert: * | Customer contact (e-mail, t: +)

Migration contact: | Customer contact (e-mail, t: +)

Partner/SI contact: | Contact (e-mail, t: +)

Figure 5.35: Contact information template for onboarding

In addition to architectural patterns and connectivity, along with the inputs to be provided to the SAP team to initiate the onboarding process for RISE with SAP, it is also important to clearly understand the internal organizational dependencies. For instance, you will need to have a full inventory of the interfaces and the concerned owners of the system and data to simplify the integration aspects post-move to the RISE with SAP landscape. You would also need to ensure the concerned network team is involved in the process from the beginning to make sure the required ports and firewall configuration are enabled.

Given the change in operating model and committed SLA-driven approach with RISE with SAP, it is important to have a clear view of what activities will be covered as part of RISE with SAP and what activities you would still need to plan for as part of maintenance activities. Some of the key points are listed for your reference (more details are covered with examples in *Chapter 6*):

- Have a clear understanding of what standard services, optional services, and additional services offer for your landscape and plan out accordingly

- Think about your cloud security and other regulatory requirements beforehand

- Sizing is your responsibility

- SSO, along with Charm and other key components, would need to be managed by the client/service integrator

- Any OS-level activity cannot be performed by the client and depends on SAP

- Be aware of all other optional requests and have a calendar schedule in place to make sure you request for the same spread with proper planning as collaboration, technical ownership, and testing are still the clients' responsibility, including upgrade activities

- Source system connectivity post-VPN or other connectivity configuration has been addressed by the client/SI, or should be handled by the client/SI itself

In this section, we have gone through the different architectural patterns and the key topics to consider around network connectivity, DNS, HA/DR, and security compliance. We also went through the onboarding checklist and what information needs to be provided to SAP to provision the system. This is important to ensure you can ask the right questions upfront before finalizing the deployment model within RISE with SAP and to avoid any hidden costs at a later point in time.

In the next section, we will provide additional insights into what is possible and what is not possible within the RISE with SAP framework so that you can plan the scope of activities accordingly.

Exploring what is possible and what is not possible within RISE with SAP

In *Chapter 3*, we discussed the different factors to be considered before deciding on the scope of RISE with SAP. In this section, we will mainly focus on the overall solution that you will need to deploy beyond technical, managed services and how RISE with SAP fares in terms of that expectation.

The following figure provides an overview of the different components as mentioned on the left-hand side of the figure, starting with **Run Infrastructure**, where you have the option to choose the choice of hyperscaler with which you would like to deploy the solution from an infrastructure point of view. You would also need to have the **Run Systems** component, which comprises your technical managed services that are provided by SAP, along with the committed SLAs as mentioned earlier in this chapter. This is also inclusive of the business continuity procedure, which would be needed with optional services such as HA and DR, which you can opt for at an additional price.

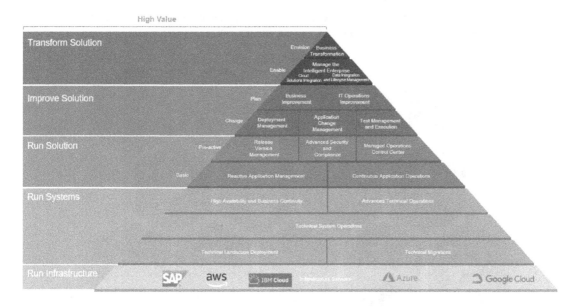

Figure 5.36: Different scope items to consider beyond RISE with SAP

Beyond that, there are services that you will need to plan out in terms of application management if AMS or implementation if a greenfield implementation to support you on the transformation journey, and these are not included in the package by default when it comes to RISE with SAP. Refer to the next chapter for more details on the CAS packages and the recommendations for when to choose one for your requirements.

In summary, so far, you have gone through the pyramid of scope in this section on what RISE with SAP can offer. The overall RISE with SAP offering has a well-defined scope in terms of the technical managed services and the associated SLAs. It is important to understand these activities and the scope before finalizing both commercial and other follow-up services scope to avoid surprises later.

Looking into alternate options for RISE with SAP

Many vendors offer either partner-managed cloud-based offerings or landscape-as-a-service offerings with outcome-based end-to-end services to enable the SAP clients to move, build, and manage their SAP environments in the public/private cloud as a part of their cloud value transformation journey. It is a Nextgen service offering powered by state-of-the-art automation, embedded with AI for flexible and on-demand provisioning and outcome-based management of the SAP landscape. It is powered by consistent tools, methods, and architecture from SAP, similar to what RISE with SAP can offer but minus the BTP and product support governance. You will have to plan for product governance through the partner that is providing the offering to make sure there are no dependencies on SAP in terms of product availability.

The context of these alternate option-driven use cases is that independent use cases align with traditional SAP-managed services providers to provide basic management services and no transformation services.

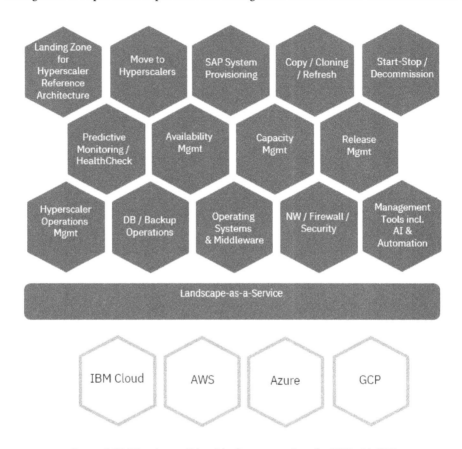

Figure 5.37: What is possible with alternate options for RISE with SAP

In summary, RISE with SAP has exciting BTP services and other foundation services for you to pick from, but it is critical to understand and plan for what you need in order to avoid any surprises later on. This is important when you are considering global expansion, along with your regulations and other points of architecture expectations in place. Therefore, ideally, if you would like to have the standard technical managed services with certain limitations but still a platform that provides you with better integration and a single vendor-based approach, you should be considering RISE with SAP rather than other customized services for planning your future scope.

Summary

To conclude, in this chapter, we have provided a walk-through of what all dimensions and criteria need to be considered for building a strong business case to move toward S/4HANA and RISE with SAP. We provided you with sample questions and a sample scoring mechanism, which you can customize to either increase or decrease the weightage of the dimensions concerned. We also highlighted the importance of always comparing RISE with the SAP-based option, along with another private cloud hosting option, to make sure you have a balanced point of view. You also got an overview of the industry trends and the different scenarios other clients or organizations are adapting to in order to stay relevant in the market to support dynamically changing operating models.

We also walked you through the architectural patterns to be considered for RISE with SAP and explained the key topics around DNS and security compliance, which would play a key role in confirming RISE with SAP is in alignment with your organization's expectations. We then concluded by exploring what is possible and what is not possible within RISE with SAP, along with possible alternate options in case the scope is not being met.

In the next chapter, we will dive deeper into the roles and responsibilities as part of RISE with SAP, along with the approach to handling multiple upgrades or rollouts within RISE with SAP, and a deep dive into the CAS packages for you to have a complete understanding of ways of working around RISE with SAP.

Further readings

The following are links for the CAS packages to get more details about each of the packages and the associated RACI around what SAP will do and what is expected of the customer or customer SI:

- *Functional Application Management*: `https://assets.cdn.sap.com/agreements/product-policy/hec/service-description/sap-cloud-application-services---functional-application-management-english-v3-2022.pdf`

- *Regression Testing*: `https://assets.cdn.sap.com/agreements/product-policy/hec/service-description/sap-cloud-application-services-for-regression-testing-english-v10-2021.pdf`

- *Data Volume Optimization*: `https://www.sap.com/india/docs/download/agreements/product-policy/hec/service-description/sap-cloud-application-services-for-data-volume-optimization-en;glish-v10-2021.pdf`

- *Data Quality Optimization*: `https://assets.cdn.sap.com/agreements/product-policy/hec/service-description/sap-cloud-application-services-for-data-quality-optimization-english-v10-2021.pdf`

- *Cloud Integration Testing*: https://assets.cdn.sap.com/agreements/product-policy/hec/service-description/sap-cloud-application-services-for-cloud-integration-testing-english-v10-2021.pdf

- *Application Security Updates*: https://assets.cdn.sap.com/agreements/product-policy/hec/service-description/sap-cloud-application-services-for-application-security-updates-english-v10-2021.pdf

- *Application Operations*: https://assets.cdn.sap.com/agreements/product-policy/hec/service-description/sap-cloud-application-services-for-application-operations-english-v10-2021.pdf

- *Application Monitoring*: https://assets.cdn.sap.com/agreements/product-policy/hec/service-description/sap-cloud-application-services-for-application-monitoring-english-v10-2021.pdf

- *Operations Improvement*: https://assets.cdn.sap.com/agreements/product-policy/hec/service-description/sap-cloud-application-services--operations-improvement-english-v10-2021.pdf

- *Managed Operations Control Centre*: https://assets.cdn.sap.com/agreements/product-policy/hec/service-description/sap-cloud-application-services---managed-operations-control-center-english-v10-2021.pdf

- *Deployment Management*: https://assets.cdn.sap.com/agreements/product-policy/hec/service-description/sap-cloud-application-services--deployment-management-english-v10-2021.pdf

- *Data Integration and Lifecycle Management*: https://assets.cdn.sap.com/agreements/product-policy/hec/service-description/sap-cloud-application-services---data-integration-and-lifecycle-management-english-v10-2021.pdf

- *Business Improvement*: https://assets.cdn.sap.com/agreements/product-policy/hec/service-description/sap-cloud-application-services--business-improvement-english-v10-2021.pdf

- *Advanced Security and Compliance*: https://assets.cdn.sap.com/agreements/product-policy/hec/service-description/sap-cloud-application-services---advanced-security-and-compliance-english-v10-2021.pdf

- *Release Version Upgrade*: https://assets.cdn.sap.com/agreements/product-policy/hec/service-description/sap-cloud-application-services-for-release-version-upgrade-english-v9-2021.pdf

6
Cloud with a Silver Lining: Busting the Myth – Part 2

In the previous chapter, we provided you with details about the different categories and scenarios you need to take into consideration for building a strong business case for the adoption of S/4HANA along with RISE with SAP as an offering. We discussed the *Need*, *Evaluation*, and *Commitment* stages involved in the process and their relevance, along with sample questions and the associated scoring. We also touched upon the different industry trends and their significance while moving to S/4HANA and RISE with SAP to ensure it doesn't become another IT-driven initiative. The details provided included insights into sizing, the onboarding checklist/items to be considered, and the approach to safeguard your investment toward migration to S/4HANA. Finally, we talked about the architectural patterns and an overview of what is possible and what is not possible to introduce high-level activities as part of RISE with SAP.

Spark4life now understands the importance of building the business case and what all dimensions are to be considered to do the same. They also are aware of the functional and non-functional requirements to be considered for supporting their vision of being agile, nimble, flexible and scalable as a business. They want to do a further deep dive into the roles and responsibilities to ensure there are no surprises at a later point in time.

In this chapter, you will be able to understand the different types of variants widely adopted by organizations when it comes to RISE with SAP, along with the roles and responsibilities. This is important to make sure you are well prepared in identifying both the right scope and the ongoing support model to be considered. By the time you are done with this chapter, you will be in a position to call out what is standard versus optional versus additional services and know how to handle the application-managed services within the RISE with SAP construct. You will also be able to understand how to handle/approach multiple roll-outs and upgrades within the RISE with SAP landscape.

We will be covering the following topics:

- Understanding the standard and tailored editions
- Understanding what the roles and responsibilities are – standard versus optional versus additional
- Looking into the approach for handling rollouts and upgrades as part of RISE with SAP
- Understanding changes to **application management services** (**AMS**) with RISE with SAP
- Exploring **cloud application services** (**CAS**) packages

Let's get started!

Understanding the standard and tailored editions

In this section, before we deep dive into what the standard and tailored editions are, let's do a quick recap of the T-shirt sizing approach explained in the previous chapters. The licensing or T-shirt sizing derivation can either be based on what you might already have in your current landscape plus the growth projection or based on the number of users with the earlier Quick Sizer approach. You need to consider the dimensions around "core access," "digital access," "infrastructure add-ons" or LOB, and related industry solutions to derive the **full usage equivalent** (**FUE**).

Based on the previous dimensions, you can map them to the available T-shirt sizes from SAP. The following figure provides an overview of the usage types along with the definition of what is referred to as FUE and how that translates into different user types:

Figure 6.1: FUE to T-shirt size mapping

> **Note**
>
> SAP has also released a 4XL T-shirt size in certain scenarios to address requirements of 9 TB+ scenarios for the HANA DB.

Once the T-shirt sizes for different applications along with the use cases as per the industry trends mentioned in the earlier chapter are identified, you would need to finalize the scope around the services you would expect as part of RISE with SAP. Based on the scope, you can decide whether a standard or tailored option would best suit your requirements. Let's go through what the standard and tailored options are to support your decision-making process.

The standard option for RISE with SAP

In this category, you, as an organization, have the option to select what is predefined from SAP as a package without any additional services included. This category applies to small- to medium-sized organizations that do not have large, customized requirements and have limited S/4HANA spread and related use cases.

You can choose this option across any hyperscaler and expect consistent service scope, as mentioned in the previous chapters both public or private cloud editions along with the other associated BTP-based services with Logistic Business Network, Business Starter pack, and Asset Intelligence Network. It doesn't give you flexibility in changing your configuration beyond what the predefined T-shirt sizes already offer in terms of the number of tiers and the related configuration.

The tailored option for RISE with SAP

In this category, you have the option to customize the configuration and the number of systems/landscapes you would need to support your functional and non-functional requirements. A few of the non-functional requirements you need to consider would be around a batch load, application/transaction response time, availability of the systems, business continuity, conformance to regulatory requirements, and many others. You can provide the configuration of additional application servers or custom storage, RAM, and SAP requirements compared to what is recommended by SAP to suit your requirements. In addition to the other scope items provided for the standard option, you need to also consider the following items as part of the tailored option (labeled as *bundled cloud services*):

- SAP Digital Supplier Network (Ariba Network) is limited to 2,000 documents and does not include supplier enablement or deployment

- SAP Logistics Business Network is limited to 1,000 documents and can either have one logistics service provider and access to one digital forwarder, or two logistics service providers

- SAP Asset Intelligence Network is limited to 200 devices, 2 connections, and 10 partner portal invitees

- SAP Business Process Intelligence is limited to 1 production tenant and a one-time data upload of a maximum of 50 GB of storage

- SAP Signavio Process Manager is limited to three users

- SAP Signavio Collaboration Hub is limited to 10 users

- Access to the SAP Custom Code Migration app, formerly known as Custom Code Analyzer, along with Process Discovery and SAP Readiness Check services

> **Note**
> Make sure you clearly evaluate the expiry date of the cloud service options just mentioned, as these will be discontinued after a certain year (at the time of writing this book, it was given as December 31st, 2030).

In this section so far, you have understood what the standard and tailored options are and how to choose between them based on additional bundled cloud services along with the flexibility in choosing your required profile parameters. You need to evaluate these based on pricing and maintenance aspects before deciding to choose the option. In the next section, irrespective of the standard or tailored options, let's focus on the roles and responsibilities of RISE with SAP and the associated standard, optional, or additional services.

Understanding the roles and responsibilities of standard, optional, and additional services

In this section, we will walk you through the roles and responsibilities of RISE with SAP, which have been categorized by SAP into standard, optional and additional services. Organizations need to understand which activities within the technical managed services are covered by default within the contract and what other activities need to be added either as optional or additional as required. While each of the activities contributes towards the well-defined SLAs and single accountability both from a product and an infrastructure point of view, there is an additional cost involved when it comes to these optional and additional services. The following figure shows, on the left-hand side, how multiple services being performed by different vendors or having different add-ons is only going to complicate the support model with committed SLAs, whereas the right-hand side of the figure shows how a well-integrated service model given a single vendor is responsible for both product and infrastructure services:

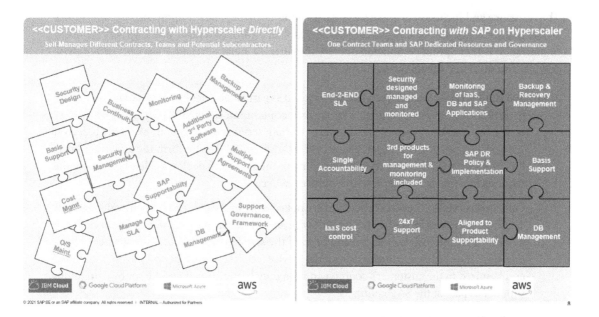

Figure 6.2: Typical roles performed by different vendors compared to the integrated model by SAP

In addition to the SLAs, add-on component allowance, and other architectural patterns (HA/DR and Backup), it is also important to have a comprehensive understanding of which of the services are included and what needs to be further added. This will help you build a strong business case along with other services/dimensions mentioned in the previous chapter. By adopting this approach, you would be able to avoid any hidden costs later. We recommend you evaluate each activity mentioned in the roles and responsibilities before getting into a contract around RISE with SAP. This will also help in understanding the governance and engagement model you would need to have in place to work with SAP and other potential system integrators in your landscape.

To help you analyze the different activities, SAP has provided well-documented *Roles and Responsibilities* documents spanning 11,300+ line items and 30+ different categories of products, databases, operating systems, service delivery, and upgrades where applicable. You can find more information about the roles and responsibilities at the following link as per the variant you have chosen around the standard or tailored PCE: `https://www.sap.com/about/agreements/policies/hec-services.html?sort=latest_desc&tag=agreements:product-policy/hec/roles-responsibilities&tag=language:english`.

The relevance and inclusion of these services are completely dependent upon each organization's scope, requirements, and type of products deployed. You cannot generalize every activity for every organization without proper evaluation of these activities. At a high level, SAP has categorized these services and tasks into the following:

- **Standard services**: All tasks/services are included as part of the default service fee and performed by SAP (or by a premium supplier in the case of premium supplier deployment) depending on the hyperscaler chosen by the customer. Certain services are only done explicitly based on the service request to be raised by the organization for SAP to perform the activity. Hence, it is important to have a good understanding of the same and deploy a calendar to raise the requests in a timely manner to avoid a last-minute rush.

- **Optional services**: These tasks/services are not covered in the default scope provided by SAP. These activities can be performed by SAP with an additional charge. These tasks/services can be elected by the customer above and beyond the standard services and are subject to both one-time and monthly recurring additional service fees. These must be specifically contracted and itemized in the customer's contract and can only be performed by SAP (or by a premium supplier as part of the SAP contract).

- **Additional services**: These tasks/services are not covered in the default scope provided by SAP. These are one-time tasks/services that can be requested from SAP and are subject to a one-time charge unless there is an impact on the underlying infrastructure, which might then incur recurring costs. These must be specifically contracted and itemized in the customer's contract and can only be performed by SAP (or by a premium supplier as part of the SAP contract).

- **CAS packages**: These tasks/services can be performed by the customer as a right of choice. However, if the customer does not have the required team or skills available, these tasks/services can be requested as an additional package from SAP to be delivered with additional fees. Later in the chapter, we will expand upon these CAS packages.

- **Excluded tasks**: These tasks/services are the ones that can only be performed by the customer and are excluded from standard, optional, additional, and CAS package points of view and will not be offered by SAP as part of RISE with SAP.

In line with the definition for each of the types of services mentioned, the following figure provides a quick summary of some of the critical activities/tasks that most customers would be performing, and shows which of them fall into which categories:

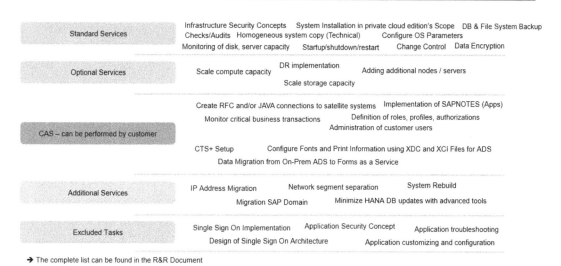

Standard Services	Infrastructure Security Concepts System Installation in private cloud edition's Scope DB & File System Backup Checks/Audits Homogeneous system copy (Technical) Configure OS Parameters Monitoring of disk, server capacity Startup/shutdown/restart Change Control Data Encryption
Optional Services	DR implementation Scale compute capacity Adding additional nodes / servers Scale storage capacity
CAS – can be performed by customer	Create RFC and/or JAVA connections to satellite systems Implementation of SAPNOTES (Apps) Monitor critical business transactions Definition of roles, profiles, authorizations Administration of customer users CTS+ Setup Configure Fonts and Print Information using XDC and XCI Files for ADS Data Migration from On-Prem ADS to Forms as a Service
Additional Services	IP Address Migration Network segment separation System Rebuild Migration SAP Domain Minimize HANA DB updates with advanced tools
Excluded Tasks	Single Sign On Implementation Application Security Concept Application troubleshooting Design of Single Sign On Architecture Application customizing and configuration

➔ The complete list can be found in the R&R Document

Figure 6.3: Different categories of activities and examples

As shown in the previous figure, let's review an example of Disaster Recovery. In a typical deployment, every client might not need Disaster Recovery for both production and non-production landscapes depending on the criticality from a business point of view. Hence, SAP does not offer Disaster Recovery as a standard service. This can be chosen by the customer to be included in the scope of RISE with SAP in both production and non-production systems. A certain one-time cost to do the initial setup and then an ongoing monthly recurring cost for maintaining and including one DR test per year will be added to the standard price.

Let's review some of the key groupings from the roles and responsibilities and the points you need to consider as part of the scope:

- **Service management**: This category focuses on account and service request management:

  - **Account management**: The responsibility is to address the delivery and operations kick-off, including the capacity management review, along with the planning. It also deals with system outages, escalation management, service performance review, and reporting periodically.

  - **Service request management** (technical support): The scope here is to receive and acknowledge the requests defined in the request tracking system and ensure the required collaboration is in place to process the request to closure. It is also needed to create a service plan for recurring and proactive services to avoid any execution delays while creating and maintaining the release plan for a managed landscape. What is not included is the definition of the tracking system to enter and update the technical requests regularly.

  - Both of these services are standard and included by default, whereas the services to support any specific industry regulations would be optional services, especially for industry standards such as GxP or HIPAA.

- **Managed infrastructure**: This category focuses on infrastructure services provided for components used as part of managed systems, including the ones required for IaaS deployment. Here are some of the key subcategories covered:

  - **Data center management**: This service provides support for data center facilities required to host the infrastructure and everything else associated with the virtual machines to be deployed. This is all covered under standard services by default.

  - **Network management**: This has a combination of standard, optional, and additional services, depending on the stage and the requirements provided. Some examples are splitting the systems into more than one network segment or adding additional VPN or Direct Link-based connectivity options. Depending on the non-functional requirements, you might have to choose all or limited services within this category.

  - **Hardware operations**: Most of the activities within this category are standard services provided as part of the scope. Some examples are monitoring disk capacity, monitoring server capacity, monitoring network utilization, and conducting managed service infrastructure maintenance. If there is a need to support the scaling up of the compute capacity, you can request it through an optional service.

  - **Storage management**: While management of the data files, filesystems, and disks per standard practices is included, the activities around scaling the storage capacity or enabling immutability capability for archiving use cases are optional services. On the other hand, reviewing and analyzing the impact of data volume/load on data environment performance along with the determination of hardware being able to meet the growth, including the planning around archiving, consolidation, and hardware upgrades, fall into CAS package scenarios.

  - **Operating system**: All the activities within this category are standard services and include activities such as the following:

    - Creating and maintaining OS users and groups

    - Informing customers regarding security incidents

    - Configuring OS parameters

    - Troubleshooting any OS-related problems

    - Working with OS vendors to resolve the problems

    - Monitoring of swap, page areas, and memory load

  - **System startup/shutdown**: All the activities within this category are standard services and include activities such as the following:

    - Performing scheduled startup/shutdown of the computing environment

    - Restarting the computing environment after failure

- **Backup/restore**: Predefined backup classes need to be selected when signing up for RISE with SAP. For any ad hoc backup requests, it would be handled as an additional service.

- **NFS DB Volume**: Pre-scheduled NFS DB or flat filesystem NFS volume snapshots or recovery are standard services. Any ad hoc request that needs to be performed will be categorized as an additional service.

- **Infrastructure integration**: Any services concerned with integrating customer Active Directory, Google IdP, and other identity management solutions are considered as excluded tasks from the scope. Customers, if interested, can engage SAP Consulting to support services around SSO setup.

- **File transfer capabilities (CIFS shares)**: This category provides support around activities related to mounting the remote customer SMB shares locally on the managed landscape along with the user and access management for those CIFS shares. Ensuring that the antivirus is up to date on the end user equipment connected to the provided shares, or the backup of data uploaded to shares to ensure data integrity is not in the scope of the service. The customer must ensure that data that gets uploaded to the CIFS shares is kept properly secured at the customer end, and the shares themselves are only backed up via standard filesystem backups, not allowing point-in-time recovery.

- **Managed SFTP server**: Basic management of the SFTP server is included in the standard services depending on the inclusion of the system into the scope.

- **Management of the wide area network**: Providing network infrastructure at the customer data center/site along with determining the appropriate size and purchase of the network connection between the customer and managed system (including the management of the telecommunication provider) are excluded tasks. If a customer would like to have cloud peering to establish the virtual connection to an SAP data center via the interconnection provided to access multiple clouds through one connection, then the same would need to be managed as an optional service. The option of cloud peering can only be used if SAP is connected to the same interconnection provider. A monthly subscription fee based on bandwidth consumption would be charged.

- **Database management around SAP HANA**: Within this category, SAP provides recommendations on database release management along with performing multiple monitoring-related activities. Certain requests for additional executions beyond the initial count would be considered additional services. It also contains a lot of other database activities around cleaning up and maintaining the right parameters, along with any schemas to be generated. Anything to do with performance fine-tuning with pattern identification or user role management would be the CAS package. Database options covered in this section are HANA, Sybase, MaxDB, SQL Server, HANA XS, HANA XSA, SDI, Streaming Analytics, and HANA MDC setup. There is a spread of standard, optional, and CAS package solutions in this category.

- **Core technical operations**: You have a spread of a different set of activities to be performed anywhere, from system installation to system refresh along with incident/release management and disaster recovery among key activities to be supported. Some of the key activities are as follows:

  - **System installation**: In this subcategory, the installation of the system as per the agreed configuration along with the setting up of the services is considered a standard service. Any other activities regarding the system rebuild or additional support during onboarding or for hyper care around project work are considered either an optional or additional service.

  - **Incident management**: End-to-end incident processing is covered as a standard service in this subcategory.

  - **Event detection and notification (monitoring)**: The monitoring and event detection of SAP system availability, along with any critical system states, is a standard service, whereas the monitoring of critical business transactions is a CAS package.

  - **General operations**: Any activity around the start and end of the managed systems along with technical troubleshooting of the technical issues is part of the standard services.

  - **SAP security management**: Defining and implementing the security concept/approach for the application level is an excluded task. Defining and implementing the security concept at the infrastructure level is a standard service. Implementing the OSS notes or patches relevant to security, either for OS or infrastructure, is also a standard service. Mainly, designing and implementing the SSO for systems is an excluded task.

  - **Homogeneous system copy/refresh**: Pre- and post-system refresh activities are out of scope as part of the RISE with SAP technical managed services scope. Core technical activities required to carry out the system refresh will be performed by SAP. Only two refreshes per year are included, and anything more than that would need to be an additional request.

  - **Release management**: Installing add-ons and other solution packages during the initial onboarding is part of the scope, along with any OSS notes to be implemented at the technical level. Anything functional is a CAS package when it comes to implementing OSS notes for application-related issues.

  - **System performance management**: The initial assessment of system performance issues along with troubleshooting of the same are standard services. Any analysis for application-related issues is considered a CAS package.

  - **Certificate handling**: Generating a **certificate signing request** (**CSR**) for load balancers, web dispatchers, data services, and BO systems is a standard service. Sending the generated CSR to the certificate authority is not in scope and is an excluded task.

  - **Disaster recovery**: Implementing DR as per the architecture is an optional service. It includes one test per year as part of the scope once the optional service is selected. Execution of any online disaster recovery tests for more than one execution is chargeable.

- **NetWeaver operations (ABAP and JAVA)**: Most of this section is CAS package driven delivered by the **Application Operations** package to be opted for if customers do not have internal support or another SI vendor providing the overall management services at the application level (for activities such as client operations, interface administration, and job scheduling, along with transport and output management).

- **Server provisioning (IaaS)**: This is for the provisioning of the unmanaged server with only IaaS provided to the customers.

- *Section 6.5* of the document covers the **CAS packages** around reactive, proactive, testing, and security services.

- There are also unique product-based sections around XSA, XI, PI, BOBI, BODS, Enterprise Portal, Sybase IQ, SAP Cloud Connector, Information Steward, Identify Management, Financial Consolidation, SAP Solution Manager, FRUN, Redwood, Test Data Migration Server, PowerDesigner, SAP Analytics Cloud, SAP Adobe, SAP FIORI, and SAP BTP-based services. It also has some technical components such as the Web dispatcher, LoadBalancer, OpenText solutions, SAP Enterprise Threat Detection, Zscaler, and other third-party interface applications regarding banking.

So far, given the multiple components and various patterns to be considered, it is important to evaluate the roles and responsibilities in detail to avoid any surprises and potential hidden costs from the solution. It is also important to ensure you can raise the service requests at the right time, as some of the standard services need to be requested through explicit service requests for the action to be performed, while some of the standard services are auto-delivered. The following figure provides an overview of the different types of services that a client implementation might require and highlights who would end up performing those activities:

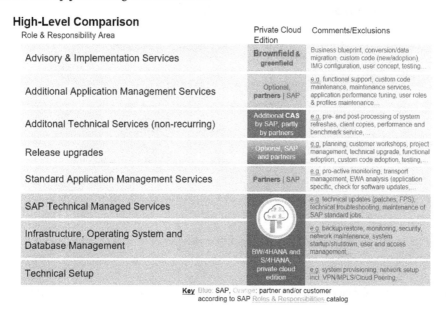

Figure 6.4: Services and type of scenario – who does what

For instance, advisory and implementation services would be required for Brownfield/Greenfield-based scenarios, and these would be delivered either by the client or by the **service integrator** (**SI**) involved. Some examples of these are business blueprints, conversion/data migration, and custom code adoption. In addition to these advisory services, in the case of application management services, it would be again either the client or SI for application-based scenarios. A few examples are functional support, custom code maintenance, maintenance services, application performance fine-tuning, and so on. Anything beyond these around SAP technical managed services will be delivered by SAP as part of RISE with SAP.

In the previous figure, the infrastructure, operating system, and database management-based services are delivered by SAP. The following figure provides a breakdown of these services to call out services around data center management, network management, hardware management, storage management, and operating system management, along with backup/restore and infrastructure integration. These are in the scope of RISE with SAP standard services, as mentioned in the previous listing.

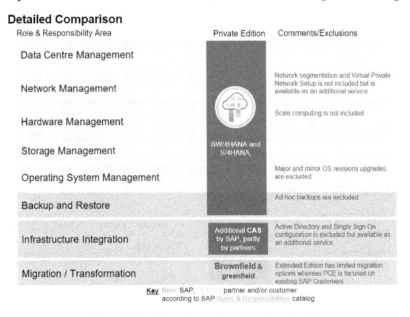

Figure 6.5: IaaS-based service responsibility split

You can find more information about the roles and responsibilities at the following link as per the variant you have chosen around standard or tailored PCE: https://www.sap.com/about/agreements/policies/hec-services.html?sort=latest_desc&tag=agreements:product-policy/hec/roles-responsibilities&tag=language:english.

In this section, so far, we have gone through the different types of services available with RISE with SAP (standard, optional, and additional) and their impact on pricing and things to look out for when finalizing the scope. We also provided a summary of various categories and the types of activities covered to ensure you plan the frequency along with the scope for system integration within your landscape.

In the next section, we will walk you through the approach to be considered when there are either multiple rollouts when deploying S/4HANA or when intending to upgrade your landscape through the tenure of the RISE with SAP deployment.

The approach for handling rollouts and upgrades on RISE with SAP

We have so far reviewed the definition of RISE with SAP, along with the different components involved such as the technical managed services, the business process intelligence component, the **Business Technology Platform** (**BTP**), and the business network starter pack. We have also gone through the roles and responsibilities across different tasks/services being provided as part of standard, optional, additional, and CAS packages.

In this section, let's go through what it means for an implementation project with either a single release or multiple releases or for an upgrade to be carried out within the RISE with SAP landscape for a given customer.

As mentioned in *Chapter 3, Eureka Moment – The Missing Link*, for every greenfield implementation, the customer now has the option to select from the available best practice packages available for S/4HANA or from the **enterprise management layer** (**EML**) image that can be imported into the S/4HANA system prior to the customer starting the implementation/customization effort. The options available for the customer would be as follows:

- **Option 1**: The decision is not yet clear to the customer on using the best practice packages as a starting point:

  - Before deciding on using the best practice packages, note that if you do not select these prior to the installation of the systems starting, then you would have to raise a change request, and with additional pricing to rebuild the systems as the best practice, activation happens during the initial system build and cannot be done as an add-on by SAP after the setup is complete.

  - You also need to consider the fact that most of the partners have an enhanced version of the best practices with solutions customized for the industries to further reduce your effort of customization along with add-ons required. So you would need to evaluate all possible options before deciding on getting the best practice packages activated. These industry solutions can be imported after the system handover from SAP as well.

- **Option 2**: The decision is clear to the customer to use the best practice packages during the initial system build.

  In this option, based on the different best practices selected as per the link mentioned (`https://rapid.sap.com/bp/#/BP_OP_ENTPR`), you also need to carefully choose the required business functions activation along with the client creations and the languages required to support the same. SAP during this period provides you with a comprehensive questionnaire to ensure all required components are captured upfront.

Once the systems are set up with or without the best practices, you might end up importing the industry solutions from other partners as appropriate. These will help you manage the show-and-tell approach when working with the business for validating the requirements and to agree upon the L3 process across different functional areas. The customer would still need to work with their functional BASIS and security teams to set up the required CTS+/gitCTS depending on the level of DevSecOps deployment you would like to plan along with source system connectivity to all the concerned systems in the customer landscape.

Upon getting this initial set of activities addressed, you would also need to focus on setting up the design authority model within your organization to ensure the global template to be set up can be governed both from a technical solution and from a functional integrity point of view. You can adopt the best practices from SAP Activate Methodology to achieve these goals/objectives during the implementation cycle and for handing over the same best practices to the application management team as well.

After the initial implementation, it is always important to keep evaluating the life cycle of features made available as part of the roadmap by SAP through each version, as more features and integration points are evolving, which you would need to keep a close eye on to both safeguard your current investment and to infuse continuous innovation into your overall solution.

The following figure provides an overview of the different components involved or to be considered when going through an implementation life cycle, along with the versions that are made available by SAP as part of the life cycle of S/4HANA:

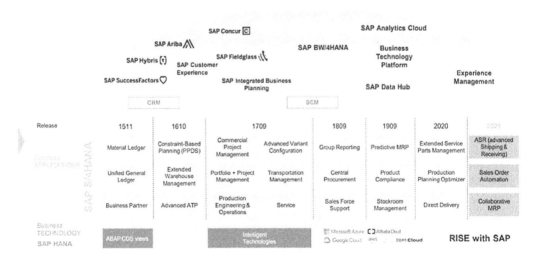

Figure 6.6: Complexity of the SAP landscape by version

Later in this book, in *Chapter 8*, *The Exodus – Data That Matters*, you will be reviewing multiple points around data migration, and the best practices to adopt along with analytics. This would play a critical role in the success of an implementation or rollout effort around the adoption of S/4HANA while leveraging the foundation offered by RISE with SAP.

It is also important to have the key drivers defined upfront, which will drive your organization toward an effective release and deployment strategy. Here are some of the different drivers to be considered:

- Upgrade strategy:

  - Overall landscape project plan

  - Technical versus functional

  - Business case with impact

  - On-premise versus SaaS-related

  - Deployment strategy

- Instance strategy:

  - N+1 Plus sandbox

- Testing strategy:

  - Testing automation COE setup

  - Testing coverage as per functional versus technical types of upgrade

  - Level of automation setup

  - User involvement

- Method definition:

  - Repeatable process

  - Assets and accelerators

After implementing S/4HANA through either the Greenfield or Brownfield approach, based on the N-1 version approach for release/support packs, there is a need to have a proper upgrade strategy in place, which can go hand-in-hand with the customer roll-out strategy. As mentioned previously in *Figure 6.6*, it is no longer about individual S/4HANA upgrades, and you need to consider the dependencies across the ecosystem both for SAP and non-SAP, along with other SaaS solutions. This is to ensure the target version being planned is compatible with the integration functionality.

Some of the key challenges that you can run into would be as follows:

- Multiple rollouts to different business units or locations based on the global template agreed upon either during the Greenfield approach or as per the existing template from a Brownfield point of view. This can cause an impact on the customization to be carried out either due to localization or due to other restrictions around the functionality itself.

- The ability to time the upgrades to SaaS products along with the on-premise solutions by checking the validation and dependencies as per the configuration used. This is to ensure the remediation activities are done in time and do not affect business-as-usual processes. Also, ensuring there is no impact on other parallel projects if any, or other rollouts if any are planned through the life cycle.

- As per the system adoption, the business would expect additional features and functionalities, which might be only possible with upgrades carried out to higher versions, and SAP might even reach out asking for upgrades to be done to resolve some of the critical product issues that the customer might encounter.

- Last but not least, you might still have to perform a technical upgrade due to the maintenance strategy and might not wait till the actual functional business case or features can be planned out.

To address these challenges, it is very important to have a proper alignment with the SAP release strategy and stay in line with the required version to ensure that standard maintenance support can be provided by SAP by proactively being able to address most of the issues at hand. A typical technical upgrade project to higher releases within S/4HANA takes an average of 2 to 6 months depending on the complexity and test scenarios within the customer landscape.

You can refer to the latest release and maintenance strategy at `https://support.sap.com/content/dam/support/en_us/library/ssp/release-upgrade-maintenance/maintenance-strategy/sap-release-and-maintenance-strategy-new.pdf`.

The document at this link provides details about the SAP product release and maintenance life cycle. This helps to come up with a customized landscape on a page plan for both existing and new products. This also needs to be integrated with the details for the maintenance strategy of on-premise products and other cloud-based products (especially due to the continuous delivery mechanism that SAP has with the SaaS offerings). The following figure provides an overview of the release cycle of the feature packages being released along with the support package stack from both features and maintenance points of view:

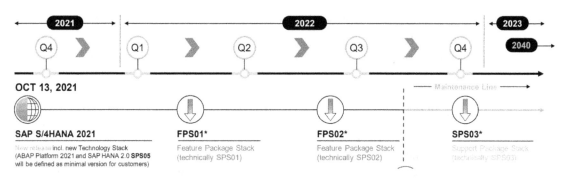

Figure 6.7: Release strategy from SAP for S/4HANA

In line with the product release and maintenance strategy mentioned previously, you also need to regularly evaluate the feature adoption roadmap within the customer landscape to ensure the scope can be properly validated to avoid any service disruptions at a later point in time. The following figure summarizes the various scenarios that a customer could face after the initial implementation to perform a technical upgrade to stay current or to support the innovation by enhanced feature packs. This also includes version upgrades to adopt automation and the adoption of AI with data-driven insights. There could also be a scenario where the customer might have to enable the integration of an embedded product into the S/4HANA digital core itself to provide additional LOB functionality to the business.

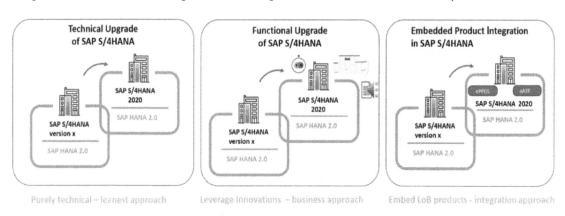

Figure 6.8: Different upgrade, enhancement, and integration scenarios

For each of these scenarios mentioned, it is crucial to think about the key points to be considered when handling multiple product integrations and rollouts based on the business application to-be states defined. Here are some of the key questions/points you need to think about when putting together the strategy for each scenario:

- Should I reshape the existing landscape when introducing the new functionality?
- Do I need "back to standard" steps before I can upgrade my S/4HANA?

- How can I migrate existing data to my embedded solution in case of new product integration as part of the rollouts?

- What are the dependencies and what is the ideal sequence in the context of the overall release plan?

- What is the strategy for the custom development of SAP FIORI UIs and other custom objects?

- Are there any updates required in the security strategy?

Based on your input, deploy a plan and prototype-based approach before applying the upgrade in alignment with the timeline to roll out the plan using the N+1 landscape, thus ensuring your current services to the business are not disrupted. The following figure provides an overview of the approach, starting with the evaluation of the goals being set with regard to the technical and functional features to be attained. It also provides insight into the timelines to achieve these features along with the setup of the prototyping system without disrupting the core S/4HANA landscape. This allows performing a dry run of the upgrade and simulating the downtime for fine-tuning the approach further.

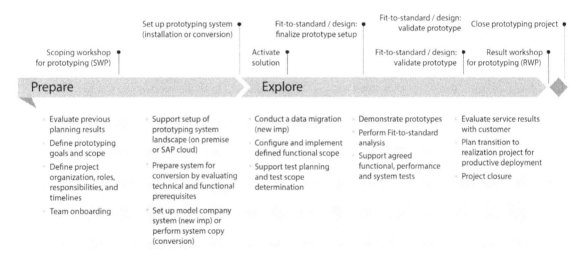

Figure 6.9: Plan for achieving the upgrade impact analysis with the N+1 landscape approach

RISE with SAP doesn't have an option by default for the N+1 landscape and would need to be planned accordingly to request for a temporary system to be set up along with the system copy to be performed. The next step to follow would be to start configuring the required functional scope or features on top of the upgraded system to validate the impact on existing functionality, if any, on the user experience or the business process. Finally, you get to validate and test the results with the business to get a sign-off before implementing the same in the actual landscape.

In summary, having the right deployment strategy would ensure that components such as best practice/industry-based solution usage, design authority setup, and the rollout approach, including the release schedule, are reviewed regularly. When defining a deployment strategy, it is crucial to identify the risks involved and have the right mitigation approach for each of the risks identified. Here is the list of risks to be considered:

- Application failure
- Infrastructure failure
- Capacity issue
- People failure
- Process failure
- Rollback issues

For each of these risks, there is a subsequent impact on the business due to an unplanned deployment strategy, which will impact the business not only from a business-as-usual activities point of view but also from a rollouts perspective. This can potentially end up impacting the system acceptance if you do not have the right deployment strategy in place. The impact can end up causing unplanned downtime, bad customer experience, lost revenue, burned-out staff, and wasted time/resources. To avoid such risks, having a defined method is the key, and SAP has well-defined scenarios in place around both functional and technical upgrades to be performed. But before we go through the method and the scenarios, let's have a look at various deployment strategies to be considered:

- **Parallel landscape approach**: You go ahead and have a parallel system upgraded that can be accessed by users along with the existing system for in-flight comparison of the functionality. In the case of discrepancies, you would have the option to back out and continue with existing systems.

- **Canary deployment**: You upgrade the existing systems but do not roll out the new features at the same time as the technical upgrade. You would slowly roll out prioritized features for super users, to begin with, and then, upon acceptance, roll it out to all the users.

- **A/B testing**: The enhanced functionality is exposed to only super users with enough details provided for validation. You have the option to back out in the case of issues being identified.

You can evaluate each of these deployment strategies for different scenarios such as technical versus functional, on-premise versus SaaS, SAP versus non-SAP, a direct user-facing portal type (FIORI launchpad), or more of a backend system, the possibility of parallel run with N+1 landscape or incremental versus full rollout of the features after the upgrade. One of the most frequently chosen deployment strategies for S/4HANA-based upgrade projects is the parallel landscape deployment strategy. It provides near-zero downtime release and rollback capabilities.

The fundamental idea behind parallel landscape deployment is to shift traffic between two identical environments that are running different versions of your application. The existing environment represents the current application version serving production traffic. In parallel, the new environment is staged running a different version of your application. After the new environment is ready and tested, the production traffic is redirected from the existing to the new system. By deploying this strategy, you can proactively identify the problems, and roll back by reverting the traffic to the existing environment if needed.

Coming back to the method adopted for the functional and technical scenarios, SAP has a well-defined Activate methodology both for functional and technical upgrades. The functional upgrade scenario has more touchpoints and scope to validate as compared to the technical upgrade scenario, mainly due to the integration and comprehensive functional testing to be carried out.

As an extension to the methodology and the different scenarios mentioned, it is also important to be aware of and use the right tools to support the preparation for the execution of the upgrade. You can use **Roadmap Viewer**, which is updated quarterly by SAP to understand the latest updates of the products in consideration and to evaluate which set of features are going to be part of the evaluation. The following figure provides an overview of the Roadmap Viewer product from SAP:

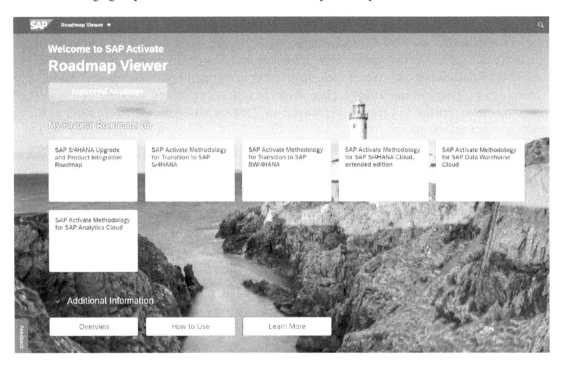

Figure 6.10: SAP Roadmap Viewer

You can also use the SAP S/4HANA What's New Viewer to document the functionality that is either new or has been updated since the last version or even removed due to new parallel functionality being provided. The comparison is done between your existing SAP S/4HANA version to the target version you are planning. Predefined upgrade templates are made available within the same tool to ensure all required scenarios are addressed.

The following figure provides an overview of the selections available in What's New Viewer:

Figure 6.11: Selection criteria for What's New Viewer

SAP also provides sample artifacts to ensure the best practices can be adopted. One such instance is a sample project plan made available as a template. The following figure provides an overview of different inputs the plan provides around the indicated task to be performed, the tentative timeline, the scenario selection to be customized, and the service components to be added as needed:

Figure 6.12: Sample project plan for an upgrade

You can access the "What's New Viewer" tool at `https://help.sap.com/doc/474a13c5e9964c849c3a14d6c04339b5/100/` `en-US/8880de6dbfb94ea3b0de1f26b40816dc.html`.

You can also leverage tools such as Solution Manager/FRUN and the maintenance planner feature to have a better view of the activities to be performed based on the method template published earlier in this section. It is also important to consider the simplification of list-based checks, which can be done using the process in OSS note 2502552 to validate the upgrade implications, if any, on the landscape.

In addition to these points, also consider the downtime option-related planning to ensure you can simulate the right timing for the landscape based on the source and target versions. You need to be well aware of the options available around **near-zero downtime maintenance (nZDM)** and the **zero downtime option (ZDO)** to ensure the impact on the business is well articulated and accounted for when carrying out the upgrade scenarios. The following figure summarizes the different options available:

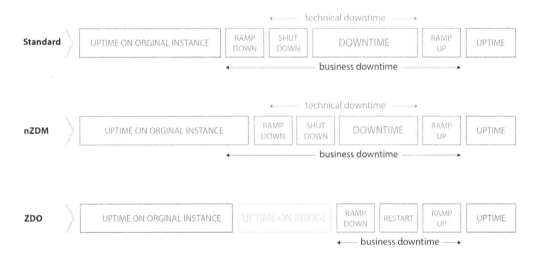

Figure 6.13: Different options to optimize the downtime during the upgrade

You can get additional details for the same at `https://assets.cdn.sap.com/sapcom/` `docs/2020/06/94ca0995-9d7d-0010-87a3-c30de2ffd8ff.pdf`.

Finally, it is crucial to be aware of the different services offered by SAP and plan them out as per the scope of the customer landscape to have the right product support where needed. The following figure summarizes the different services available from SAP that can be planned when performing the upgrade:

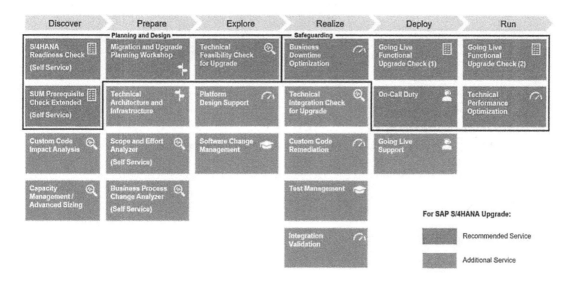

Figure 6.14: Different SAP tools and services you can consider during the upgrade

You can find additional details for similar services and inputs of converting different products into S/4HANA along the journey as the rollouts happen at https://go.support.sap.com/roadmapviewer/?sap-language=EN#group/AAE80671-5087-430B-9AA7-8FBE881CF548/roadmapOverviewPage/MATS4HANA.

In this section, we have gone through the scenarios possible when considering an upgrade to your S/4HANA landscape either for functional, technical, or new integration to be implemented. We also touched upon the relevance of scoping the upgrade and adopting the artifacts from the best practices published by SAP through the SAP Activate methodology. Finally, we talked about how we can leverage SAP tools such as What's New Viewer and associated artifacts.

In the next section, we will provide you with information about what to expect post-implementation of S/4HANA around AMS and the added value that RISE with SAP offers.

Understanding changes with AMS in RISE with SAP

In the earlier section, we reviewed the impact of RISE with SAP from implementation and multiple rollouts perspectives. In this section, let's now go through the AMS context and understand what has changed, and things to consider when planning for AMS within RISE with SAP. The following figure provides an overview of different types of services relevant to having an effective model of delivery to address different requirements from a typical customer landscape:

Figure 6.15: Services and flexibility possible with RISE with SAP

As you can see in the previous figure, there are different categories of certain services typically being **Always On** through the life cycle, some of them being **Scale Up/Down**, and the others being **On Demand**. These are recommended/suggested and can be customized as per the customer landscape/requirement and not delivered as part of RISE with SAP. You would have to either go with the CAS packages (even within CAS packages, not all the shown services will be performed, so you would need to go through the next section to understand the details of what is included in the CAS packages) or with in-house AMS support or with another SI vendor who you might be already working with for support. Let's have a quick look at some of the activities in each of these categories:

- Always On:

  - Business KPI benchmarking

  - Quarterly upgrade testing

  - Batch job monitoring

  - Garage for continuous innovation

  - COC set up with SAP

  - Interface optimization

  - User adoption support

  - Zero incident response

- Scale Up/Down:

  - Incident management

  - Customer success management

- Service requests

- Support business events

- Minor enhancements

- On Demand:

  - User training

  - Test library refresh

  - Cloud impact assessment

  - New features implementation

  - Knowledge base refresh

With RISE with SAP, key things to notice would be the following:

- You wouldn't have access to the operating system level or the infrastructure level to perform any fine-tuning or optimization by yourself. If any such task needs to be performed, you would need to coordinate with SAP to agree upon the impact. Depending on the support model and the best practices, it might or might not be accepted, as standardization is the key for the cloud model to work, especially with different compliance scenarios to be addressed from an SLA perspective.

- You are still in charge of the transport management with regard to moving the transport across the landscape manually, through ChaRM/Revtrack, or other available third-party transport movement tools.

- Any performance fine-tuning of the jobs or data SQL queries being triggered due to the user activity would need to be monitored by the non-RISE scope.

- Any recommendations from EarlyWatch Alerts generated, unless we have access issues to perform the same, would need to be taken care of by the customer.

- The responsibility to ensure all the right services are requested as part of the system maintenance for the category of not being auto-delivered should still be managed by the client.

- Source system connectivity configuration needs to be managed by the customer or SI vendor.

- The setup of additional housekeeping jobs needs to be managed by the customer or SI vendor.

- SSO configuration and setup need to be managed after the system handover as part of the **Committed Delivery Date (CDD)** by the customer or SI vendor.

- Job management tool setup and job scheduling, either through Redwood or other available tools, would be the customer's responsibility.

- Application-level security design and setup would be the customer's responsibility.

- Platform-level vulnerability and other penetration testing beyond what RISE with SAP offers.

- The functional configuration would be the customer's responsibility.

- Technical and functional testing in any of the patches or upgrades or for any implementation would need to be handled by the customer.

- Project management efforts to coordinate within your organization and to act as a liaison between SAP and other stakeholders would need to be handled by the customer.

Beyond these points, given that RISE with SAP will have its own FRUN instance to monitor the systems along with other secondary monitoring tools that each of the hyperscalers might be using to maintain the SLAs, you need to also plan whether you would need to have your own business process and technical monitoring KPIs. This would help ensure that additional monitoring of the KPIs with a single pane of visibility can be achieved. For this purpose, the customer can typically request an additional Solution Manager or FRUN instance to be set up along with the S/4HANA system to be able to configure the additional alerts beyond what RISE with SAP already has addressed for technical managed services-related monitoring. You would then be able to integrate this instance into your other systems in the landscape such as other SAP systems and with ServiceNow or Jira, depending on what ITSM-based tools you are using.

Let's now go through some of the activities within AMS and the frequency/scenarios when they will need to be performed by the client or SI teams. The following figure provides an overview from a system maintenance or upgrades strategy point of view:

Service	Remark
Check for SAP software updates (SAP Support Packages, SAP kernel updates)	On demand when requested by client if BASIS in scope or as part of EarlyWatch Alert analysis
Implement SAP Notes and other types of manual corrections in managed system to fix application related issues	Related to Fiori enablement, security notes & FPS/SPS implementation only.
Version upgrade of SAP Software: Upgrade planning and coordination	For version and support pack based upgrades as per scope agreed with client in the original AMS agreement
Version upgrade/update of SAP Software: Pre- and Post BASIS Tasks	Examples for this service include, run simplification check; unlock objects; remove inactive objects; implement upgrade related notes; run modification adjustment for technical issues.

Figure 6.16: System maintenance activities – what you need to know

In continuation to the previously shown set of activities, the following figure shows the service remarks around the post-upgrade activities, along with the version validation effort.

Service	Remark
Execute application related technical tasks as part of Release and Change Management (e.g. application testing, adjustments, content/functional activation)	For FPS/SPS implementation for SAP NetWeaver based systems only. Limited to execution of adjustment in SPDD/SPAU for SAP objects. Customer objects in SPDD/SPAU require customers decision during execution. Application, integration acceptance as well as regression testing, adjustments of implemented processes, UI's and integrations and release approval for transport remains customer responsibility or separate project tasks for the partner as per scope agreed within the AMS context.
Innovation workshop for software version validation	one (1) workshop per year on a remote delivery basis. The Innovation workshop assists with proper planning of an SAP S/4HANA, private cloud edition version upgrade.

Figure 6.17: SPDD and SPAU execution along with version validation – what is covered

The following figure provides an overview of the inputs around EarlyWatch Alerts and regular table growth validation efforts, including transport handling, which needs to be considered by the SI partner outside RISE with SAP:

Service	Remark
Analysis of EarlyWatch Alert reports for systems. Provide recommendations for changes related to SAP application (outside technical operations scope of standard service)	Performed only for productive systems, as part of EarlyWatch Analysis if BASIS in scope
Regularly check fastest growing tables in the SAP system and provide recommendations for archiving or reorganization	As part of EarlyWatch Alert analysis.
Create RFC connections within the SAP S/4HANA, private cloud edition solution landscape (Fiori, gateway server)	Related to SAP S/4HANA, private cloud edition solution landscape only.
Maintain SAP transport management system and configure transport routes and any further configuration (automatic import, scheduled import etc.)	Only for SAP NetWeaver ABAP systems if BASIS is in scope of AMS

Figure 6.18: Separation of responsibilities around EarlyWatch Alerts
and RFC connection/transport management

In continuation to the transport management just mentioned, the following figure provides an overview of the different activities to be performed for moving across transports in the RISE landscape by the SI partner/client team:

Service	Remark
Transfer and release of transport orders	
Execute transports to move objects between SAP systems	Related to Fiori enablement, security notes & FPS/SPS implementation only.
Adjustment of repository objects as part of software changes	
Configuration - On-premise resources (OData services) customer wants to use in SAP Cloud Platform (SCP)	SAP Forms by Adobe (Adobe Document Services/ADS) only: Create destination for ABAP backend system (Mapping virtual to internal system); Configure accessible resources /sap/bc/fp and /sap/bc/fpads
Configuration – HANA XS Engine Web dispatcher	Includes SSL configuration and certificate handling and is limited to technical Fiori Launchpad enablement only.

Figure 6.19: Transport-related activities

The following figure provides an overview of other activities that the SI partner/client team needs to consider around FIORI launchpad re-enablement or for establishing the trust relationships between SAP NW ABAP systems:

Service	Remark
Re-enable Fiori launchpad including all required connectivity setup	SAP Standard procedure includes Fiori launchpad enablement for one client per S/4HANA system. Fiori Launchpad will be made available over the load balancer, if it exists and has been configured
Establish trust relationships between SAP NW ABAP systems	Performed for Fiori launchpad enablement only.
Establish trusted connections from Web Dispatcher to Gateway, backend system (e.g. S/4HANA) and HANA XS engine of backend system	Related to Fiori enablement only.
SAP Forms by Adobe (Adobe Document Services/ADS): Testing	FP_PDF_TEST_00; FP_CHECK_DESTINATION_SERVICE; FP_TEST_03; FP_TEST_IA_01; FP_CHECK_HTTP_DATA_TRANSFER

Figure 6.20: FIORI and other application management

The preceding services, if required, can be requested by SAP as part of CAS packages in case you do not have the required skills available within your team. Beyond the proactive services, there is also a set of reactive services that you can request as an additional scope. The following figure provides an overview of the different types of services that the clients/customers can request from SAP to manage beyond technical managed services:

Service	Remark
Incident Management: Troubleshooting of functional incidents in SAP applications	Incidents reported by customer
Problem Management: root cause analysis and resolution of problems in SAP applications	In case of configuration/usage issues – in case of software bugs, re-route the issue to SAP support, if cannot be solved by you
Service Request Fulfillment: Perform Service Request Fulfillment for functional tasks in SAP applications	On customer request, e.g. adjusting tax keys
Event Management: Monitor functional event types in SAP applications	On customer request, e.g. during critical periods like quarter end closing
Change Management: Changes of functional configuration in SAP applications	e.g. for smaller customizing/configuration changes, custom code adjustments

Figure 6.21: Different SLDC scenarios around incidents, problems, and event/change management

Apart from the preceding services that you can request, the following figure provides an overview of the other reactive services that you can request from SAP for an additional charge:

Service	Remark
Continuous Operations	Performance benchmark, performance optimization
Extended Application Security Operations	To cover advanced and/or application-specific security tasks, e.g. security risk check, audit readiness check, interface security
Managed Operations Control Center	Central system health and customer application monitoring
Test Management and Execution	Application related e.g. after updates, upgrades, changes
Deployment Management	Release Strategy, Release Planning and Execution, Solution Manager - ChaRM
Operations Improvement	Continuous improvement of application operations, based also on customer's feedback
Business Improvement	Make suggestions to customer on how to improve business processes, business roadmap
Data Integration & Lifecycle Management	Data Lifecycle Management, Data Integration, Data Quality Management, Data Environment Health Check

Figure 6.22: Follow-up services around operations and business improvement scenarios

In summary, the day-in-the-life from the AMS perspective would be similar from a functional and security scope point of view with or without RISE. Whereas with BASIS, the technical managed services and the technical BASIS activities will be addressed as part of the RISE engagement, along with functional BASIS activities performed in addition to RISE with SAP by the customer. In the next section, we will go through the details of what the CAS packages offered by SAP are, and what the activities included as part of each of the CAS packages are.

Exploring CAS packages – what you need to know

In the previous chapter and earlier in this chapter, we reviewed the different tasks and services that are offered as part of RISE with SAP and how they are categorized within the *Roles and Responsibilities* document as standard, optional, and additional services. We also looked at a few examples of different tasks that have been categorized as CAS packages, which can be performed by the customer or SI. In case both options are not possible, then you can request SAP to perform these activities as part of RISE with SAP. Some of these CAS packages are either one-time or recurring services, depending on your contract. For instance, a one-time request package could be activities such as upgrade execution and data volume optimization.

Some other examples are as follows:

- Functional upgrade coordination and testing scope
- Security OSS notes and validation
- Application operations
- Data archiving and volume optimization
- Data quality validation
- System health monitoring (standard and advanced)
- Cloud integration testing

It is also possible to customize beyond the initial CAS packages made available by SAP by working closely with the SAP Cloud Advisory Architecture team. The following figure summarizes different CAS beyond the core package, which you can request or should be aware of to avoid any surprise cost at a later point in time. It will also help to plan your in-house or customer SI scope accordingly either for implementation or for the AMS:

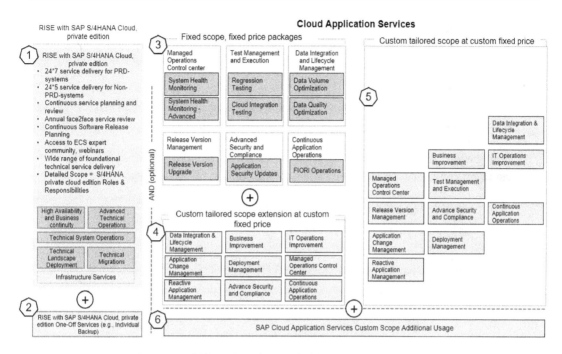

Figure 6.22: CAS services along with the custom-tailored scope

Let's go through each block shown in the previous figure:

1. This provides an overview of the commitments RISE with SAP default package offers around 24x7 service delivery for production and 24x5 service delivery for non-production systems. It also provides inputs around certain basic components such as technical migration, technical system operations, and HA/business continuity as part of the basic setup.

2. This provides the option to use additional services as a one-off request for certain activities such as additional backup/system refresh or DR testing and so forth.

3. This provides an overview of some of the fixed-scope CAS packages with a fixed price, such as system health monitoring, regression testing, cloud integration testing, and data volume optimization.

4. This provides an overview of the custom-tailored scope extension of CAS packages with the flexibility offered for activities such as application change management, business improvement, and IT operations improvement, among other activities.

5. This provides complete custom-tailored scope packages that can be chosen with SAP.

6. This provides an option for selecting some of the CAS services through custom scope additional usage.

Let's now go through some of the CAS packages and the associated tasks that are included as part of the package:

- **Release version upgrade**: Outside the CAS package, you would be responsible for planning and the functional validation and testing of the systems after the technical upgrade is performed by SAP. You also would be responsible for SPAU/SPDD activities for functional scenarios, including post-upgrade activities to be carried out. If you decide to go with SAP, it will provide a project manager to manage the program end-to-end. You would still be responsible for the testing effort. This package provides support for application BASIS-related tasks for the SAP cloud environment applications in scope. SAP will perform the following activities:

  - Upgrade planning, coordination, and execution of technical upgrade tasks

  - Release upgrade/update implementation

  - Execute application BASIS-related tasks limited to adjustments in the SAP namespace following the execution of SPDD, SPAU, and SPAU_ENH (only SAP namespace, SAP notes, no modifications)

  - Support transport management-related upgrade activities, including the following:

    - Inform customer about scope of transports needed to be released

    - Transport requests from the technical upgrade process are the responsibility of SAP

    - Provide general advice for issues related to transport problems

    - Provide general advice on creating transports to import in the upgrade process adjustments of repository objects as part of software changes (SPDD, SPAU, and SPAU_ENH of the customer namespace)

  - Reactivate the FIORI launchpad after the upgrade (one app per FIORI app type)

  - Exclusions are as follows:

    - Not provide any customer functional or business process analysis or validation related to any maintenance activities included in the scope of this agreement

    - Not provide any functional testing as part of this service

    - While the FIORI launchpad will be technically re-enabled, not all customer-used FIORI apps will be activated/configured as part of this service enablement or changed if required by a new release

  - Your responsibilities would be as follows:

    - Responsible to clear the transport queue from projects as part of pre-processing or prerequisite steps leading up to the version upgrade.

    - Impacted objects in SPDD/SPAU to be remediated at the application level.

- Application, integration, acceptance, and regression testing; adjustments of implemented processes, UI's, and integration; and transport management remain the customer's responsibility.

- This service does not apply to any other additional licensed software, in particular, not any type of third-party add-ons installed in the SAP cloud environment system. Such add-ons that are identified prior to or during the upgrade of an SAP cloud environment system will result in additional service charges.

- The customer is responsible for the coordination and retrofit of tiers beyond the defined package usage metric (four tiers) via additional upgrades or by methods such as requesting a system copy.

Note

For a detailed RACI on the tasks just mentioned, please refer to `https://assets.cdn.sap.com/agreements/product-policy/hec/service-description/sap-cloud-application-services-for-release-version-upgrade-english-v9-2021.pdf`.

- **Application operations**: This service helps you to get the complete applications managed by SAP with the pre-determined incident count. SAP will conduct the following tasks:

  - Provide continuous administrative support of systems in the cloud environment including investigation and resolution of technical application-related issues

  - Provide incident resolution and troubleshooting of technical incidents as detailed in the RACI matrix provided for this CAS package for items not included as standard services as per the *Roles and Responsibilities* document

  - Perform changes to technical system configuration as detailed in the RACI matrix for items not included as standard services as per the *Roles and Responsibilities* document

  - Perform service request fulfillment for application operations tasks as detailed in the RACI matrix for items not included as standard services as per the *Roles and Responsibilities* document

  - 24 incidents per year (could be a single or the same task with a count of 24 as max)

  - Exclusions:

    - Application implementation services are not in scope

  - Customer SLAs of service desk – 24x7 (English) and Mon-Fri (9 A.M. to 6 P.M. for Japanese)

  - Service delivery – Systems with production (English 24x7) and systems with non-production (English 24x5) excluding weekends

  - Initial reaction time (20 minutes for very high, 2 hours for high, 4 hours for medium, and 1 business day local time for low)

> **Note**
>
> For a detailed RACI on the tasks mentioned, please refer to `https://assets.cdn.sap.com/agreements/product-policy/hec/service-description/sap-cloud-application-services-for-application-operations-english-v10-2021.pdf`.

- **Data volume optimization**: This service is mainly focused on coming up with recommendations for archiving a strategy and its implementation in the landscape. Regular analysis of data volume and load will be performed, including a forecast of growth trends and initiating remediation proposals based on results. SAP will perform the following tasks:

  - Gather all the required statistics from your landscape and provide an overview of usage

  - Analyze data distribution among SAP systems and forecast the growth

  - Provide a dashboard that can help you keep track of the volume

  - Identify potential risks and provide required solutions to ensure you do not run into performance problems

> **Note**
>
> For more details on the RACI around the tasks mentioned, please go to `https://assets.cdn.sap.com/agreements/product-policy/hec/service-description/sap-cloud-application-services-for-data-volume-optimization-english-v10-2021.pdf`.
>
> For more details about the application monitoring related to CAS packages, refer to `https://assets.cdn.sap.com/agreements/product-policy/hec/service-description/sap-cloud-application-services-for-application-monitoring-english-v10-2021.pdf`.
>
> For more details about the managed operations control center-related CAS package, refer to `https://assets.cdn.sap.com/agreements/product-policy/hec/service-description/sap-cloud-application-services---managed-operations-control-center-english-v10-2021.pdf`.
>
> For data quality assessment around key master data objects such as Customer Master, Vendor Master, Material Master, Employee Master, Financials Master, and Supplier Master, you can refer to the RACI at `https://assets.cdn.sap.com/agreements/product-policy/hec/service-description/sap-cloud-application-services-for-data-quality-optimization-english-v10-2021.pdf`.
>
> Information Steward should be available in the customer landscape in order to opt for this CAS package.
>
> For full-fledged functional application management CAS package details, please refer to `https://assets.cdn.sap.com/agreements/product-policy/hec/service-description/sap-cloud-application-services---functional-application-management-english-v3-2022.pdf`.

There are other CAS packages as well if needed, and the links for these have been provided in the *Further reading* section of this chapter for your reference. In this section, we have so far provided a complete walkthrough of the CAS packages offered by SAP, and how you can either deliver these services by yourself or by working with SAP with additional customization possible on the scope for each of the packages.

Summary

To conclude, in this chapter, we have started off with understanding the options available when considering RISE with SAP around the standard and tailored options. We explained what you can expect from tailored options when it comes to the bundled cloud services that help you get more transformational abilities, especially with Signavio licenses included for Process Manager and Collaboration Hub. We then provided insight into the roles and responsibilities within RISE with SAP by summarizing the 1,300+ line document to categorize into main items that could impact the scope. We also highlighted the importance of having a clear understanding of standard versus optional versus additional services. You also got an overview of the approach you can consider when handling rollouts and upgrades in a RISE with SAP landscape.

We finally reviewed the approach when it comes to value-added scenarios possible with AMS and concluded with the possibility of choosing from CAS packages to deliver these services if needed.

In the next chapter, we will deep dive into the data-driven scenarios and how you can handle the data migration to avoid any disruption to the business and for a successful go-live. We will also cover the different options available with different products to provide an effective data migration outcome.

Further reading

Here are the links for the CAS packages to get more details about each of the packages and the associated RACI around what will SAP do and what is expected to be performed by the customer and SI:

- Functional application management – `https://assets.cdn.sap.com/agreements/product-policy/hec/service-description/sap-cloud-application-services---functional-application-management-english-v3-2022.pdf`

- Regression testing – `https://assets.cdn.sap.com/agreements/product-policy/hec/service-description/sap-cloud-application-services-for-regression-testing-english-v10-2021.pdf`

- Data volume optimization – `https://www.sap.com/india/docs/download/agreements/product-policy/hec/service-description/sap-cloud-application-services-for-data-volume-optimization-english-v10-2021.pdf`

- Data quality optimization – `https://assets.cdn.sap.com/agreements/product-policy/hec/service-description/sap-cloud-application-services-for-data-quality-optimization-english-v10-2021.pdf`

- Cloud integration testing – `https://assets.cdn.sap.com/agreements/product-policy/hec/service-description/sap-cloud-application-services-for-cloud-integration-testing-english-v10-2021.pdf`

- Application security updates – `https://assets.cdn.sap.com/agreements/product-policy/hec/service-description/sap-cloud-application-services-for-application-security-updates-english-v10-2021.pdf`

- Application operations – `https://assets.cdn.sap.com/agreements/product-policy/hec/service-description/sap-cloud-application-services-for-application-operations-english-v10-2021.pdf`

- Application monitoring – `https://assets.cdn.sap.com/agreements/product-policy/hec/service-description/sap-cloud-application-services-for-application-monitoring-english-v10-2021.pdf`

- Operations improvement – `https://assets.cdn.sap.com/agreements/product-policy/hec/service-description/sap-cloud-application-services--operations-improvement-english-v10-2021.pdf`

- Managed operations control center – `https://assets.cdn.sap.com/agreements/product-policy/hec/service-description/sap-cloud-application-services---managed-operations-control-center-english-v10-2021.pdf`

- Deployment management – `https://assets.cdn.sap.com/agreements/product-policy/hec/service-description/sap-cloud-application-services--deployment-management-english-v10-2021.pdf`

- Data integration and lifecycle management – `https://assets.cdn.sap.com/agreements/product-policy/hec/service-description/sap-cloud-application-services---data-integration-and-lifecycle-management-english-v10-2021.pdf`

- Business improvement – `https://assets.cdn.sap.com/agreements/product-policy/hec/service-description/sap-cloud-application-services--business-improvement-english-v10-2021.pdf`

- Advanced security and compliance – `https://assets.cdn.sap.com/agreements/product-policy/hec/service-description/sap-cloud-application-services---advanced-security-and-compliance-english-v10-2021.pdf`

- Release version upgrade – `https://assets.cdn.sap.com/agreements/product-policy/hec/service-description/sap-cloud-application-services-for-release-version-upgrade-english-v9-2021.pdf`

Back to the Drawing Board: Reimagined Processes

Let's continue with the journey Spark4Life has been set on. This chapter presumes that Spark4Life or a **Line of Business (LoB)** considering a transformation, or the business process owners of an end-to-end business process cutting across several LoBs, have been through the discovery stages. This will have given them much-needed clarity about the vision and appreciation of the required capabilities to reach the goal of broader business transformation/process transformation, as detailed in *Chapter 4, Intelligent Enterprise and Sustainable Design*. The inputs from this stage feed into the next stages of actual changes, derived from business process analysis. Then, you will design the business process for your **Target Operating Model (TOM)** based on your **Component Business Model (CBM)** heat maps, such as process capability heat maps. These are underpinned by service and architecture heat maps (platform components, applications, and infrastructure), the process insights of how **S/4HANA** can help fill the gaps, and the deltas that need to be assessed and solutioned, per the specific differentiations that the organization unit wants to achieve.

In this chapter, we'll see how we can take these critical inputs to design, simulate, and model the new processes for future customer and employee experiences, considering process changes or introducing new processes. Furthermore, we will look at the deltas in data to support the new processes and the technology that will help bridge the gaps identified.

We'll cover the following topics in this chapter:

- **Enterprise experience**: How to create experience-led process modeling future processes that drive enterprise and customer experience

- **Data to value transformation**: Explaining the fundamental components for data engineering in a landscape to derive insights and make sense of the data being collected across processes

- **Architecting intelligence**: The use of **intelligent processes** and how to put insights into action to extend business processes, using the amalgamation of automation and intelligent workflows for an intelligent enterprise

- **Going cloud-native with SAP**: How to marry the existing hybrid cloud and SAP BTP for extension and innovations with the S/4HANA components

Every era of business reinvention is essentially a dawning of technological, social, and regulatory forces. Nowadays, global leaders have a new challenge to help the planet with sustainability, ESG, and carbon emissions. We are at the inflection point to start a new chapter of the industrial revolution, with the convergence of technologies (**Industry 4.0**) and sustainability being key drivers. From the outside, the need to reinvent and transform businesses is being pushed onto enterprises, and now with Rise with SAP – S/4HANA transformations, enterprises are empowered to take on the challenge to push intelligent and sustainable transformation inside out.

In today's economy, it's often customers, employees, or suppliers' experience that differentiates you as an organization in the market. The experiences are created by harnessing the power of your data, enabling intelligent enterprise systems to run processes underpinning the customer journeys, and eventually driving the human experience. The value engineering built with these elements allows you to catapult a value proposition to your customers, helping you become a more profitable and successful business entity.

The enterprise experience

80% of CEOs believe they deliver exceptional customer experience, but only 8% of customers agree with that (refer to the *Further reading* section). This results in an experience gap. Failing to meet expectations is detrimental, and being aware that this is happening is crucial, as customers stop spending and employees start to disengage – all due to poor experiences.

The customer experience of any organization has an emotional impact on the moments that matter (customer touchpoints) for customers, which results in a strong brand recall if the experience is positive. Employees have an influencing behavior on customers, which can make or break these moments based on the employee experience. The enterprise experience reflects the values and culture of an enterprise in the trust and loyalty customers build up in the product or service they value. The best-run companies find ways to listen to the real voices of customers every day. It can be through **customer experience solutions** or data mining, sensing the experiences at the customer touchpoints across your customer-centric process. The insights from the experience data can then be converted into targeted value propositions to be delivered by employees/teams in a coordinated, seamless manner across the entire customer experience. Each touchpoint should tell a personalized story and deliver the same experience; storytelling starts at the core.

Your organization should develop enterprise capabilities to deliver experiences consistently with repeatable success, reducing the time-to-insight and time-to-adapt parameters as they evolve. To provide an exceptional operational and customer experience, the first step is understanding **operational** and

experience data. These data points are generated across several channels through a customer's interaction with your enterprise. The interactions could be physical, digital, or virtual, based on the customer channels and the value being offered. Several customer experience management platforms can help measure the customer experience through surveys on customer-facing sites, reviews, feedback, and social and/or direct contact with the company personnel through the contact center. The front office data can provide key insights into where the deficiencies are and what changes are required to provide a delightful experience.

Once you have insights into the customer experience, the relevant recommendations, best practices, and improvements needed in the enterprise core processes, such as HR, procure to pay, and lead to cash, can be implemented. Other considerations while these evaluations are happening could be how the organization turns insights into actions using cognitive process automation, underpinned by a low-code/no-code approach at the disposal of the business and IT teams. How do we deploy changes to the landscape, such as deploying the changes to contact center systems to enable employees to better serve a customer, with quick time to market to start measuring the PPIs/KPIs in real time as the changes take effect, moving back to an acceptable level? Companies need to be agile to deal with all the challenges that can be met to drive the change to stay relevant. *Agility is key here*, which means how fast your organization can adapt to a new situation. Agile companies need to know exactly how their organization runs, and what processes need to be managed, monitored, and measured for performance using a variety of data.

With **SAP Signavio Process Transformation Suite** or BPI, you can connect process data with people. By modeling, simulating, and doing a what-if analysis of your processes and journeys in one collaborative environment, you can easily see how others experience each step or interaction with business, by linking the journeys with underlying processes and assessing their complexity. With connected experience and process data, an organization can unleash the power of experience-driven process mining capabilities. You can see and experience the process reality and quickly discover relationships and anomalies, making people and experience count at every step of the analysis. With an inside-out and outside-in view of organizations, you can quickly identify what you need to do to improve immediately. You can work collaboratively across your organization by fostering your ability to execute and continuously innovate with a process-first, data-driven, and customer-centric mindset. In summary, time to insight and time to adapt together make an intelligent enterprise a reality, understand operations instantly, and holistically react and improve processes immediately. The following diagram depicts how customer touchpoints can be leveraged to drive insights and, in turn, a continuous process transformation for sustained competitive advantage.

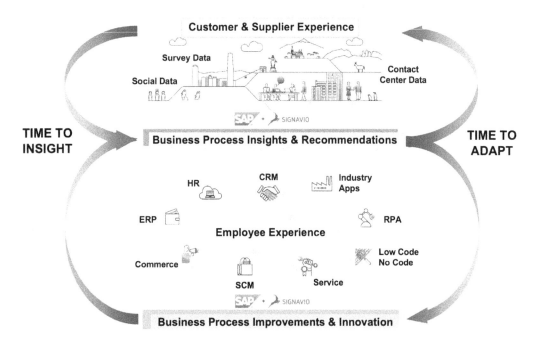

Figure 7.1 – Time to insight and time to adapt are key to an intelligent enterprise

So, besides organizational transformation that drives value inside-out, there are external factors such as competitors, technologies, and supply-demand dynamics that drive outside-in pressures for transformation, with customers at the center of these forces. Customer centricity is a crucial element of your strategy, and customer experience must be a top priority for your organization. Understanding how to drive customer experience and run a business to achieve high levels of customer satisfaction is imperative for its ongoing success.

In the following section, we will cover how you can go about addressing the customer experience right from the outset, with techniques of experience-led process design.

Experience-led process modeling

Experiences are deeply connected with your processes and how you operate as a company. The *process* is what happens in the systems, and the *experience*, conversely, is the value proposition delivered to the customer/consumer at the receiving end of the value chain of that process. So, a well-orchestrated process will provide a delightful experience. However, improving processes in silos will only help you improve the symptoms rather than fix the cause of inefficiency or a bad experience. With a customer-centric design approach, you will want to place the process experience at the heart of it. The design of the process needs to be coupled with the delivery of the experience from the beginning.

You can start the experience-led process design and modeling journey in many ways. You can start with design thinking workshops to understand the personas involved and their empathy maps. You can then map the challenges, what the employees enthuse about or want to refrain from doing, disdain in the whole interaction journey, and which of these systems or personal interactions can highlight the friction points or experience that needs to be improved. At times, a point solution may resolve an experience gap at that part of a process or subprocess, or it may reveal that the upstream or downstream of the process needs an overhaul. The same is true for the employee experience, the customer experience, and the agent experience.

It will be myopic if you don't have a centralized view of these experiences across a journey mapped against the process, which may have these different personas interacting with your processes and systems for "moments that matter." So, it is key to view the journey holistically rather than in silos by linking the underlying process and converting the insights gathered from the experience data. Thus, we should connect the dots between the process and journey and overlay the experience data with the help of journey mining and analytics, to understand and transform the business process with the insights derived, using the experience-driven process mining approach.

This mandates that the experience and process teams can no longer design new journeys in silos and necessitate process experts to be involved in the earlier stages of the process discovery and definition stages. The journey models thus developed have the journey pulse mapped to the process, its supporting roles/personas, and the supporting IT systems to operationalize your customer experience. **Data-driven journey modeling** is possible with the operational and experience data and can be realized through BI tools such as **Tableau** and **Google Studio** with the journey steps. Let's look at some of the tools and methods to convert insights to model and design processes to maximize the outcomes.

Experience and process design

Sentiment analysis combined with the customer journey gives the customer experience highs and lows at the customer touchpoints. This will draw out the personas and stakeholders to explain the challenges in non-process talk across the boundaries of the LoB or the system knowledge that limits experience. Focusing on a customer-centric approach, you would start de-risking innovations and transformations deviating from the intended outcomes. This could be based on data collected and insights derived from the NPS, sentiments from the social media feed, customer feedback, surveys collected, and process-mined data from business process intelligence. This approach has a positive outcome that employees can experience, showing the difference between just performing the job as per the training and providing a great customer experience while being delighted by the employee experience, delivered by the underlying systems and processes. In turn, this reduces the risks of adoption and acceptance by involving users or frontline teams, user interviews, and observations at the point of sale and other behaviors that customer interaction groups can bring to the journeys being designed. They will also have buy-in with the new journeys designed for customers as part of the process, and they will be the advocates within and externally for the organization on newly designed systems and processes for the new journey.

You can map the sentiments of the personas going through the journey in terms of the interaction by using the experience data captured through the **Qualtrics** or **Customer Experience Management** (**CXM**) systems your company may have. This 360° analysis helps to identify touchpoints, impact analysis, operational insights, underlying processes, and IT systems. So, the customer journey/experience can be an entry point for all the transformation discussions, which are easily captured in the customer journey maps. Then, you can drill down into the supporting systems and map these journeys into the processes that support them through the journey modeler.

Customer journey maps

Customer Journey Maps (**CJMs**) provide customer-centric entry points to your business process landscape. CJMs are high-level, intuitively readable diagrams that focus on the customer experience instead of internal processes. They help to understand how your customers perceive your products and services in their everyday lives and how their key decisions (for example, leading to a purchase or churn) are motivated.

The CJMs can be used in discussion with the CxO office, which understands the business in terms of CJMs, or the design teams, which understand the touchpoints and moments of truth, or to get to the details of the underlying process and the systems to start with.

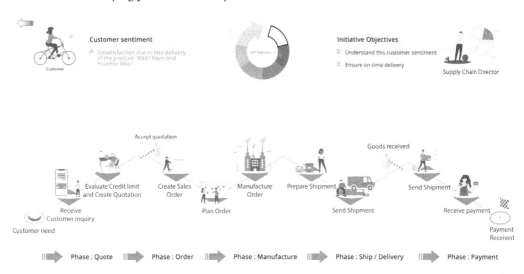

Figure 7.2 – Lead to cash customer journey map

The preceding CJM for the purchasing process depicts the to-be customer journey after process improvements. Customer sentiment has increased, and the company now has a better insight into the performance of the overall end-to-end process. The customer journey for the process provides insight into the steps the external and internal *customers* perform, with the sentiment and value they experience during the different process phases and the overall journey of buying goods.

Any CJM can then be connected with the underlying process model – that is, to a **BPMN 2.0** diagram, which is a digital representation of your actual work process and also captures decisions using the **Decision Modeling Notation (DMN)**. Furthermore, we move into the details using the journey modeler to connect systems to the process maps and the architectural capabilities of the enterprise. Customer journey maps and the journey modeler are essentially connecting the dots between the experience data and the operational data with systems, processes, and capabilities as the journeys evolve. This becomes quite powerful for E2E traceability.

Signavio Journey Modeler

The **SAP Signavio Journey Modeler** solution enables you to operationalize customer, employee, and supplier experiences by connecting journeys, processes, metrics, systems, functions, and roles, helping to transform your journeys in the context of processes into a journey map. A customer journey model combines a tabular industry-standard journey map and business process models, IT systems, and organizational units linked to each step in the customer journey. There are 12 different types of elements you can use in your journey models, including persona, journey stage, text, image, touchpoints, sentiment, external data widgets, linked journeys, linked processes, IT systems, organizational units, and embedded process intelligence widgets.

The journey complexity score connects journey models to the business process. You can see the correlation between the complexity of the journey model and the customer experience, and then drill down to the business process causing the complexity to reduce it. Alternatively, indicate whether you want to roll the same journey in another journey for an in-country variation to understand: how complex is that? How many decisions are to be made in the process? How many IT systems are involved? All of these questions can be answered with the journey complexity score. The journey modeler outputs a journey model, such as the one depicted in the following figure of a lead-to-cash process.

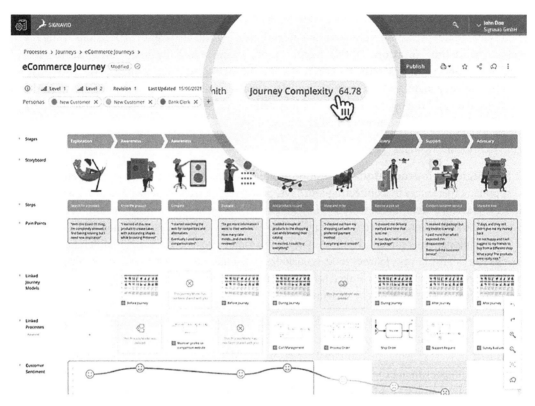

Source: https://www.signavio.com/post/introducing-journey-model-complexity-scoring/

Figure 7.3 – An example journey model (the lead-to-cash process), representing a customer experience and the underlying business process model supporting it

You can understand the "as-is" view of the current customer experience and the underlying process, and then design the "to-be" view to ensure that the complexity reduces and the experience score goes up. It's not only about the visual connection of the process but also quantifying what is in the process, the IT systems, the data objects, the handover between lanes, and the decision gateways. As well as this, it's about how you model your journey, and how you have linked it to your business process. The journey modeler gives level 5 and level 4 process views of the end-to-end process, and you can double-click on each of the verticals to get into the details with customer touch points with customer journey maps.

Discover your processes (measure and know)

With the use of BPI process mining for the E2E process in the discovery phases, we eliminate opinions, guesswork, or what you think a process is doing, depending on the data from production to analyze the process compliance, gaps, bypasses, and non-conformance and the ability to isolate all the issues.

During process mining, the process mining engines (such as **Celonis** or SAP Signavio) analyze processes based on event data to get a fact-based and objective view of what is happening – across all systems in a single environment, in most instances, it would be a source **SAP ECC** environment clubbed with other heterogeneous systems that help run the E2E process. The data extractors deployed on the source production environments operate in the background passively, collecting data to build metrics on the most frequently traced path by users to operate a process moving from one state to another, to complete transactions on the way. The simplistic login form is represented in the following figure. The process experts can add as many fields to the core data represented to capture insights as required.

CaseID	Activity	Timestamp
1	Open ticket	01.01.2013 08:23:45
1	Transfer ticket	01.01.2013 10:46:12
1	Problem resolved	01.02.2013 18:12:55
2	Transfer ticket	01.04.2013 07:12:34
2	Problem resolved	01.04.2013 07:23:59
2	Open ticket	01.07.2013 14:09:02
3	Problem resolved	01.07.2013 09:10:41
3	Open ticket	01.08.2013 11:30:07
3	Transfer ticket	01.09.2013 20:16:01
3	Close ticket	01.10.2013 07:12:16

Figure 7.4 – An example event log extracted from production environments

We can trace digital footprints by analyzing event logs:

- Every interaction in systems leaves digital footprints

- Process mining extracts and aggregates these records of event log data from key IT systems in the source landscape

- The technology then seamlessly reconstructs the actual end-to-end process flows, using the events and the semantic steps the process goes through

This creates an event log consisting of three fundamental values, as illustrated in *Figure 7.4*, consisting of the unique identifier of a process – for example, the case ID for the service ticket operations – the associated activity that has taken place to move it through the states of the process toward resolution, and most importantly, the timestamp for when the activity was processed. If required, this data can be combined with additional data for further mapping and analysis. However, this is the minimum necessary to understand the path traversed by users to complete the process.

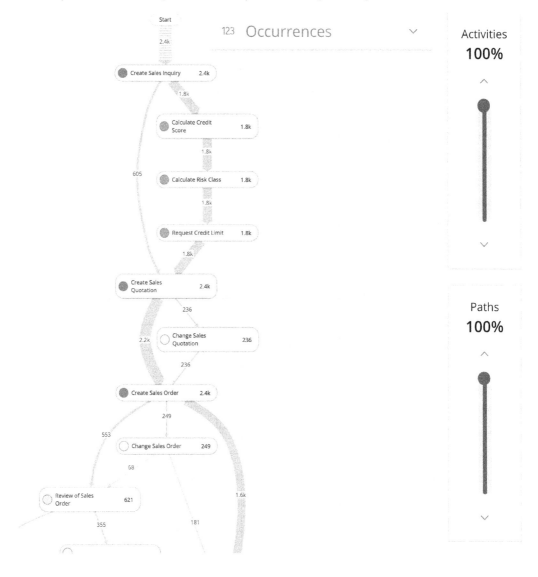

Figure 7.5 – Visualizing the process variants discovered by process mining

The data thus extracted will be used to visualize the process variants of the most minor and most frequently traversed paths by users of the systems. This data is then mapped to the semantic activities captured, indicating the key events the process goes through to draw the process maps. Once this is done, the heat maps (the most traversed paths), as shown in *Figure 7.6*, will help business process experts analyze the process variants, deviations, and non-conformance against the most traced variant and see how that affects the process turnaround times, by creating inefficiencies and bottlenecks in completing the processes.

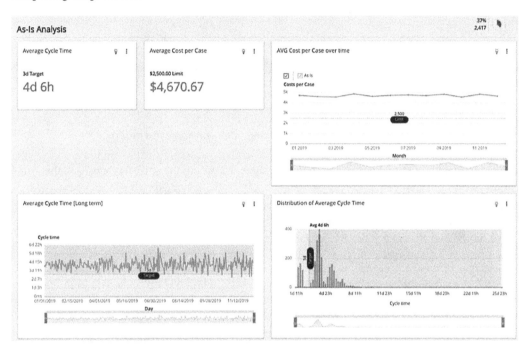

Figure 7.6 – Business KPIs for the process under evaluation

SAP Signavio Process Intelligence also gives a snapshot of the KPIs based on all the variants collected from the data in production environments. The widgets also provide levers to include and exclude specific variants to show how these impact the overall processes and highlight the most time spent – hot spot on the variant.

As depicted in *Figure 7.7*, the business analyst and process experts can use the visualization to identify opportunities to improve, automate, and optimize a process further. Visualization and the metrics derived can help in the areas such as customer satisfaction, compliance, quality, and process efficiencies, giving actionable insights to include in the "to-be" design.

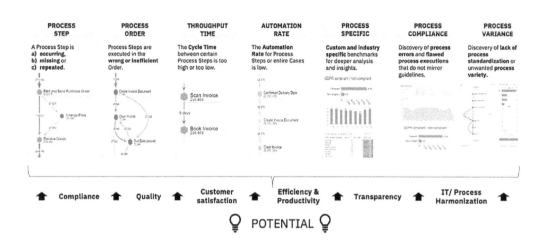

Figure 7.7 – Potential opportunities to optimize and improve a process

These are crucial insights at the start of a transformation and part of the **shift-left** approach that can be prioritized within a process discovery workshop. So, instead of relying on a business process owner to explain how a process is executed in a workshop, the data from your production environment makes transparent what is happening in a system. This is an immediate eye-opener so that efforts are focused on the high-frequency top five variants of the process; for example, rather than the outlier variants, the process traverses a couple of times from the thousands of transactions that were analyzed.

Furthermore, the data and the process semantics captured by the mining tools can help map this data to the BPMN notations of your business process. Some mapping is done manually to map the semantic activity to the process step at the L2/L3 level. This helps paint a picture of the process compliance that the organization defined when they did the implementation and shows where they are deviating. This can become a process excellence exercise for the "as-is" view, as depicted in *Figure 7.8*, and the project teams will have to decide whether they want to improve process compliance in the "as-is" world to avoid having a smoother transition of data and processes to S/4HANA. The activity also helps us understand the deviations, data gaps, and opportunities to improve upon the source in the first place.

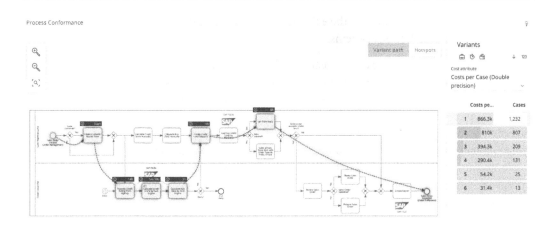

Figure 7.8 – How does your process-mined data conform to the defined "as-is" business process model?

Once you know where you are and where you want to be, you need to assess different ways to get there; this is a what-if analysis of a process. With BPI, you can simulate the value drivers, the overall value, and the cost to run the process. This will affect the processes and the decisions, so you can put together different scenarios, simulated by manipulating facts and building your business case. This business case is then submitted for validation of the "to-be" proposals. This business case can be further bolstered with opportunity assessments, areas to improve and bring in innovation and automation, and reflection on the cost versus benefit trade-offs of introducing them during the redesign. Your go or no-go decisions are thus supported by factual data and the complete cost and benefits case.

In the following section, we will run through the steps of converting discovered insights and opportunities to design a "to-be" process.

Insights to design

In this section, we will see how your teams can translate what you have discovered in process mining into a traditional process management discipline. So, once you know where you are today, you define the target. To do this, we can leverage best practice repositories, such as SAP Best Practices, IBM's Blueworks Live, or **Information Technology Infrastructure Library** (**ITIL**) for industry standards, to leverage these intellectual properties and define the "to-be" in the target state. This assessment of how much of the standard best practices, based on processes defined in S/4HANA, can be adapted to cater to the "to-be" processes and the CJMs happens early on in the exploration phases.

The analysis done in the previous section using the process mining techniques can help further accelerate and *shift left* certain aspects of the iterative design work, when combined with the recommendations that would have come out of the SAP Process Discovery reports and the SAP Process Insights reports. Recommended processes using pre-designed, standard/best practice processes, such as IBM Blueworks Live, SAP Best Practices process templates, or from the process repository within your organization. This will also indicate the best fit for the "to-be" processes and where an organization deviates from best practices. This analysis compares the existing and impacted business processes to the new and simplified processes of S/4HANA systems.

Similarly, the impact assessments of the custom codes in the source systems can be analyzed. With a *keep the core clean* strategy at the heart of the entire technical conversion to a new digital core, teams need to understand whether the code needs to adopt target custom development approaches, such as in-app or side-by-side, to continue complementing the standard best practices or needs to completely abstain, as the new processes cover the gaps that were previously supported by the custom enhancements, developments, and customization. A *fit-gap* analysis helps to combine the best of both worlds and comes with a holistically aligned target set of processes and systems that will support your target CJM, underpinned by the S/4HANA processes operating the best practices and recommendations on automation. The fit-gap exercise can be carried out for greenfield, brownfield, or selective transitions to S/4HANA to understand the gap between what S/4HANA offers and what your target "to-be" processes are. There will be more on this in the upcoming chapters. This can be further validated with the experience teams, the business process experts and stakeholders, and the CxO office by aligning with the target KPIs for the target operating model, which can be achieved by the transformation through the S/4HANA move.

Now that the "to-be" processes are strengthened by your teams, in the next section, we will see how they can simulate processes to evaluate how they perform against the cost, resources, and time parameters, striking a balance acceptable to your organization.

Simulating the "to-be" world

All the effort that has been put forward till this point by your organization is to ultimately drive changes, which, in turn, needs to evaluate the "as-is" situation and facts, with your key stakeholders making some firm decisions. As your teams get into the details of the processes, the BPMN diagrams that represent your level 3 process are either newly created or adopted from the standard best practices repository. The L2/L3 process levels within the process hierarchy can be used to understand the "as-is" cost, resources, and time factors, and also how introducing intelligent solutions such as RPA, process automation, and AI/ML-based decisions, or implementing standard processes will reduce process turnaround times or deploy a few more resources from one part of the process to the other. This is achieved by simulating and representing the facts and figures of the times, cost, and resourcing as attributes of a process task. This is done with the concept of the digital twins and representing the process in BPMN diagrams, with real-world representation through attributes.

By embracing the digital twins approach to designing a "to-be" future process, we can run several process simulations, visually presented through scenarios, to understand process performance, cost, and the opportunity to improve. *Figure 7.9* shows the process simulation feature within SAP Signavio Process Management.

[Simulation] Credit Management

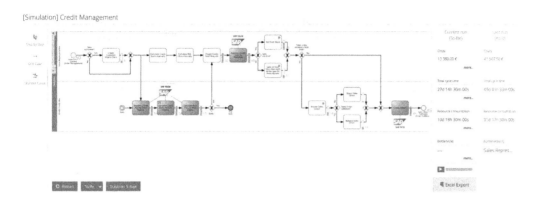

Figure 7.9 – Process simulations for desired outcomes, run against the
number of resources, costs, and time taken to run a process

This is, in a way, a "what-if" analysis, where your teams can check what would happen if they were to deploy two bots in a process task, what would happen if they were to eliminate a process step, or what would happen if they totally outsourced this process or one of its steps. This then highlights a cost-benefit analysis and helps create a business case for investments in systems and resources for that LoB process. Similarly, we can run a "what-if" analysis decision simulation based on decision modeling notations, or a decision tree, which can simulate business rules.

The new proposals on the target process design, the improvements with automation, side-by-side custom enhancements, or the use of AI or intelligent workflows design can be incorporated into simulations to see how the "as-is" and "to-be" costs of operating the process, the required human resources, or the process turnaround times are impacted. A vis-à-vis comparison, as depicted in *Figure 7.10*, can be issued for the "as-is" and "to-be" with the process owners, the process experts, and the design experts on the project to collaborate and vote on for final sign-offs.

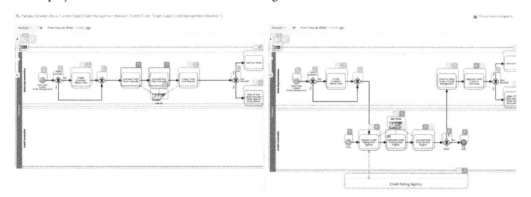

Figure 7.10 – An "as-is" and "to-be" vis-à-vis comparison in SAP Signavio Process Manager

Once you are on the other end of the spectrum, post-transformations, your teams can continue with the process excellence initiatives. In the next section, we will discuss how process excellence drives a culture of continuous improvement for existing and new processes. With SAP Signavio Process Transformation Suite, you can get a company on the page view and a leadership cockpit to govern, communicate, and collaborate across teams and prioritize the objectives that need major focus. This helps to measure the change you implemented and proactively monitor the processes you're your S/4HANA transformation.

Continuous improvement – the infinity loop

One-shot scans are great for auditors – a continuous end-to-end assessment feeding a scalable transformation engine enables an *infinite game*. The goal is not to migrate or improve as one shot but rather operate in an infinite loop of continuous discovery and improvements, monitoring the latest changes and moving from reactive to proactive. Don't be a victim of change but instead use the change as an opportunity to improve and implement a new practice. So, your organizations can have a **Center of Excellence** (**COE**) for automation or a CoE for process excellence, which collaborates for process changes, controls, and governs all the current and upcoming changes to processes. Once you embrace and leverage these tools (Celonis or SAP Signavio), which enable new practices within your organization, you are creating organizational capabilities to not only deliver on the promise you made to your customers/consumers about the customer experience but also guarantee the quality of the value proposition/product or services, to be delivered on time at the moments that matter most, enabling your frontline to be better equipped and enabled to deliver the experience. This activates this infinite loop of continuous process improvement and adaptation to changing market needs or operational excellence to support change, as your organization executes a strategy to move closer to your defined vision. People, technology, regulations, and processes are ever-evolving, and we must keep a vigilant eye to change direction if necessary. *Figure 7.11* gives an overview of the whole journey of process transformation.

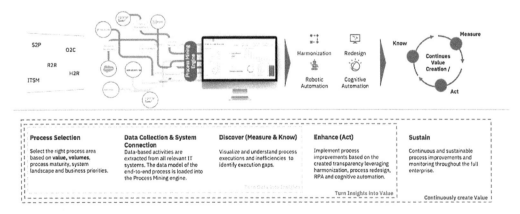

Figure 7.11 – From process selection to continuous improvement

In summary, every S/4HANA transformation is a business transformation. Business transformation is not a one-off but has to become a continuous improvement cycle. Business process insights help you to secure the success of enterprise transformation and also helps you shift left on time to value and time to market in the ongoing performance initiatives – whether they are enterprise transformation with conversion to S/4HANA, designing, modeling an end-to-end process, enabling process automation for identified process candidates, or helping to reach process excellence goals in a data-driven way, by identifying bottlenecks and gaps within your company, to reach best practices and industry standards on day-to-day operations. Organizations should encourage a shift from project-based use cases to continuous, lasting disciplines and transform at the core how it drives operational and customer experience.

In the next section, we will examine the required data engineering components to orchestrate data collected from the newly defined processes and connected systems to derive insights, to drive an organization closer to the goal of becoming an intelligent enterprise.

Data-to-value transformation

Traditionally, SAP has been perceived as a back-office company that provides systems to drive enterprise processes. The challenge has been with processes and data locked in siloed systems across LoBs. The value of these cannot be extended to the external world beyond the remits of LoB systems and processes. This results in a lack of visibility and transparency for all participating partners. To drive outcomes up and across the value chain requires data from all participating process systems, to drive action based on intelligent insights. Infuse automation to create further efficient and self-correcting intelligent process flows, transforming your data into something valuable for moments that matter.

When we talk about processes that go within and beyond organizational boundaries, involving partners, suppliers, or customers/consumers themselves, it's a requisite to have data pipelines and filtering mechanisms to sift through valuable data, which gets streamed in real time from connected systems and devices. This includes the telemetric data from IoT devices of connected operations, data originating from transactional systems internal and external to the organization, or master data generated at the core through governance channels. To drive the next corrective or pre-emptive action, we will need insights from this data, which, in turn, requires robust data engineering mechanisms within a landscape.

This will not only handle the extraction, transformation, and loading but rather cleanse, harmonize, enrich further with the context, and, more importantly, distribute the data to the systems that require it to make decisions. The movement of data is cost-intensive, so data pools and the related orchestration engines need to be flexible and agile enough to help reduce the cost of altering data ingestion and consumption patterns. This is true for all SAP and non-SAP systems as part of a transformation or post-transformation to drive continuous improvements. This is also essential for the intelligence fabric that we'll discuss in the following sections.

Managing data and the challenges it brings

Data sources conventionally have been focused on structured and managed corporate data sources. With data sources for intelligent workflows, we are moving much more toward big data in terms of velocity, veracity, variety, and data from disparate sources. So, it is immensely important to have capabilities to make it possible to collect data from business environments, such as manufacturing production lines with videos and pictures of the finished products, and real-time data pipelines pouring in sensor data from the field. All of this unstructured content then becomes one of the key drivers of insights for an organization. Social media platforms provide insights into the sentiments and feedback of customers or users of products. For example, to understand the sentiment of your customers on Twitter, you need to understand the concerns being expressed – for example, a water leak in a community causing inconvenience and a hazardous situation – and address them in real time by reacting to the information, by creating an automated ticket and assigning it to an engineer in proximity to the incident. If possible, sense, understand, and respond to preempt any unwanted events that impact your business. Much of this requires a much more sophisticated analysis of dynamic data and is not limited to fixed static mathematical models applied to conventional workflows and the analytics therein, as it was in the past.

These challenges are just scratching the surface of other considerations, such as security, ownership, and access control. Data architectures must be designed for security and support data policies and access controls directly on the raw data. The situation explained in the preceding example also brings in some interesting challenges regarding the ownership of data; the data may no longer be corporate-owned, is in the public domain, or needs to be collected anonymously without invading privacy and not violating any regulations, while still making sense of the social media feeds. Data may be owned, created, and distributed by a third party, your customers, communities, suppliers, partners, or shareholders that follow your organization for the latest news and updates. Some other critical aspects of data integrity and quality questions include how you would respond if there were changes in the format or structure of the data, the impact of the change on the downstream of systems, and how we mitigate this impact.

Managing the plethora of data sources and their challenges requires a vision or strategy for data-to-value transformation. Converting a risk to an opportunity on these strata of data types requires an information architecture that provides a solution to everyday business challenges, such as the following:

- The challenge in catching up with the fast-evolving technologies and capturing the value of the data generated
- Siloed data, thereby, applications and business capabilities, posing a further challenge in harmonizing processes and automating business operations
- Value-extracting mechanisms that can increase the utilization of data for modern cognitive or AI technologies

- The lack of a cloud migration strategy for data and non-scalable technologies underpinning the current state of the data landscape

- No clear path to a full realization of data-to-value for digital transformation

Data-to-Value (D2V) transformation capabilities

Organizations should strive to modernize their data architecture, lay foundational constructs to leverage AI, and democratize the use of intelligence to accelerate digital transformation. Data architectures must take into account semantic data, metadata, graphs, structures, and unstructured data by tapping into the full potential of emerging technologies, such as **Artificial Intelligence** (**AI**), automation, the **Internet of Things** (**IoT**), and **blockchain**, to leverage them as data sources and use them to action the insights discovered from the data collected. Some critical capabilities for realizing a data-driven intelligent enterprise are as follows:

- **Ingestion and integration mechanisms**: A data pipeline is a process in which data is collected, cleansed, transformed, harmonized, and refined. It includes data collection, refinement, storage, analysis, and delivery. Streaming pipelines allow connected IoT and telemetry devices to stream data through a set of algorithms and perform streaming analytics continuously from a source to a destination, for processing and analysis in real time or near real time. They enable you to plug in the IoT, blockchain, and robotics systems through core integration capabilities.

- **Data provisioning/orchestration**: A database triggers updates, delta calculations, and dissemination mechanisms using events and condition-based batch jobs or timers. To democratize the usage of data across organizational silos, modern data architectures must provide open standards interfaces that make them interoperable with market-standard cloud platforms and easy for users to consume data, using tools fit for their jobs. Data platforms should allow you to create and consume APIs to make it easy to expose and share data, but they also should offer bulk data transfers at high speeds wherever necessary, such as sharing blob and unstructured data on videos and images. They should also be optimized to share data across systems, geographies, and organizations.

- **Data modeling**: Common vocabularies and data models help define the semantics of data to be shared across a business. Shared data assets, such as product catalogs and common data models that cut across organizations, industries, and KPI definitions, require a common vocabulary to help prevent disputes during analysis. Invest in core functions that perform data curation, such as modeling meaningful relationships, data lineage, profiling and cleansing raw data, curating key dimensions, and measuring and defining business rules for data curation.

- **Data persistence and operational data stores**: These stores reduce the number of times data must be moved to reduce cost, increase data freshness, and optimize enterprise agility. This store consists of a central data layer/lake, which can accept structured and unstructured data from different data streams – that is, structured data from systems, unstructured data from IoT devices, and so on. High-frequency usage data should be stored on performant compute with hot storage using SAP HANA Cloud; low-usage or infrequent data should be stored in warm storage, such as extended storage in SAP HANA using dynamic tiering mechanisms. Archived or historical data will be stored in cold storage mechanisms using nearline storage, such as SAP IQ or HDFS storage. These data stores can be located on public, private, or hybrid clouds to provide agility based on data privacy and governance practices. At the edge, data requirements and persistence can also be served with a container orchestration system such as open source Kubernetes, and the OpenShift platform from Red Hat is often used.

- **AI and ML models**: AI and ML platforms are used to automate systems for data parsing, labeling, identifying outliers, gathering insights, and so on. At the same time, modern data architectures can help organizations unlock the ability to leverage AI and ML at scale on the cloud. The platforms used for leveraging data to create ML models should allow an entire life cycle, from modeling to training the data models, testing and validating them, visualized with ready-to-go algorithms and notebooks, to deploying them for inference in the cloud or on the edge. Examples include IBM Watson, Google TensorFlow, or the SAP Machine Learning platform on SAP BTP.

- **BI and analytics**: This is the ability to perform analytics on new data as it arrives in an environment. Process and analytics dashboards are a real-time reflection of process execution and bottlenecks along a process flow. Users can dig deeper from dashboards. We can utilize easy-to-use tools to build visualization, multi-dimensional datasets, and dashboards for business users and the computing required to deliver these on the fly. The intent is to maximize the value of data, unearth insights, and respond with agility in real time.

- **Data governance and security**: Data governance is the high-level planning and control of data management activities, enabling an organization to leverage data as a shared asset and *fit for purpose* by different personas for targeted scenarios. Although governance deals with decision-making and decision-makers, it does not specify decisions for decision-makers. Good governance allows management to execute corporate strategy and mitigate risks by doing the following:

  - Establishing guidelines for information management decision-making

  - Ensuring information is consistently defined and well understood

  - Increasing trust in data as a shared asset

  - Protecting data and complying with regulatory requirements

Data as a service

D2V capabilities accelerate value realization and help capture and target the right business opportunities as they evolve. They catapult an organization from data being a cost center to a profit center by turning it into **Data as a Service (DaaS)**. By creating a trusted data foundation, companies can support next-generation application extensions. They can innovate and apply the full potential of their data assets at a much faster pace to deliver immediate, targeted insights, act in the moment, and make complete, timely, and accurate decisions. A trusted data foundation can host operational data stores and data catalogs that help prevent access abuse and prevent draining S/4HANA performance by requesting the data readily available in an operational data layer, away from the core, in the cloud.

This data from the trusted data foundation layer and the insights created from it can further be democratized by allowing them to be consumed through a set of APIs, events, and change detection triggers that can notify the subscribing systems of the data changes. Also, ingestion mechanisms govern the data being fed into the single source of truth to harmonize the data, which is further fed into curated data layers or reusable data stores with common data models. Furthermore, the flexibility of open data protocols introduced by the enterprise-grade cloud data platforms allows the interoperability of the data between the cloud applications and databases used by your partners, suppliers, and B2B customers, allowing more frequent and transparent updates to the connected systems and processes. The trusted data foundation layer should have governance, access control, and data classification mechanisms based on the confidentiality and sensitivity of the data, such as the personal information of customers and employees, and organizational data separate from data that can be shared with customers and partners. Lastly, the visualization of the business insights derived from the analytical engine of the trusted data layer should be easy to build and consume across the processes and landscape, with appropriate security roles and authorizations. *Figure 7.12* shows different layers with capabilities that can be built and enabled based on the foundational data layer.

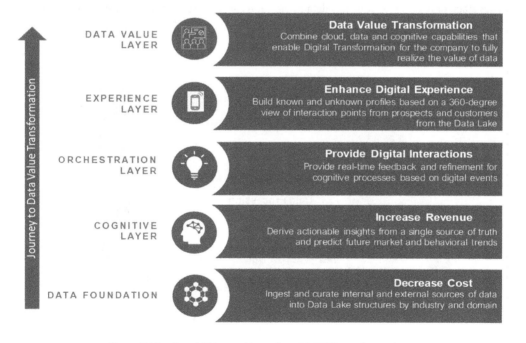

Figure 7.12 – Capabilities and benefits with D2V transformations

We will now delve into the SAP BTP data and analytics components in the cloud that can help you build these foundational and cognitive data layers by integrating them.

SAP BTP data and analytics

SAP BTP data and analytics services and products can handle the growing amounts of data stored in multiple locations, with controlled access for your entire organization to analyze and act on a single version of truth. The SAP BTP and analytic services consist of three key services:

- **SAP Data Intelligence**
- **SAP Data Warehouse Cloud**
- **SAP Analytics Cloud**

SAP Data Intelligence (SAP DI)

SAP DI is the data management pillar of the SAP BTP platform. It is the underlying data integration, orchestration, and data cataloging engine powering the SAP BTP. It is used consistently across the entire platform for integrating other data sources, integrating with third-party catalogs, and orchestrating data from the data processing engines within SAP DI. SAP DI has very tight integration with the data analytics stack of the BTP, as it brings data integration capabilities for SAP Data Warehouse Cloud. The following figure depicts the different capabilities offered by SAP DI and the integrations it offers out of the box to SAP and non-SAP systems.

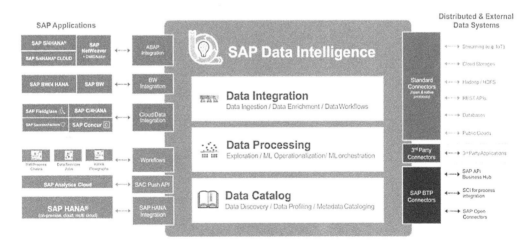

Figure 7.13 – SAP DI (SAP DI architecture)

SAP Date Warehouse Cloud (DWC)

SAP DWC comes with a built-in data integration capability of the data flow, based on a simplified version of SAP DI, which is used for ingesting data into the DWC. This tight integration with SAP DI brings in additional capabilities, such as data federation from DWC, ingesting data into other destinations, applying ML algorithms on top of the data, and building end-to-end data catalogs. All the artifacts built using the data flow created in DWC can seamlessly be used with SAP DI.

SAP Analytics Cloud (SAC)

Your organization needs to address two main concerns when migrating data to the cloud. First is data integration across hybrid multi-cloud environments, and second is making sense of the data with analytical engines. SAP Data Intelligence Cloud and the integration suite form the basis of this migration and are integrated out of the box. So, for example, you can compute analytical insights using SAP data intelligence and directly from the data intelligence pipelines, to trigger the execution of the inflow in the integration suite to take relevant actions on the transaction stack. You can't just do analytics for reporting; you also want to ensure that once you get valuable business insights, you act on them on the transactional stack, S/4HANA, or connected cloud applications. SAP SAC features a built-in intelligence to understand the business semantics of your SAP applications and your business processes. *Figure 7.14* gives an overview of the different components available under the SAP BTP data and analytics services.

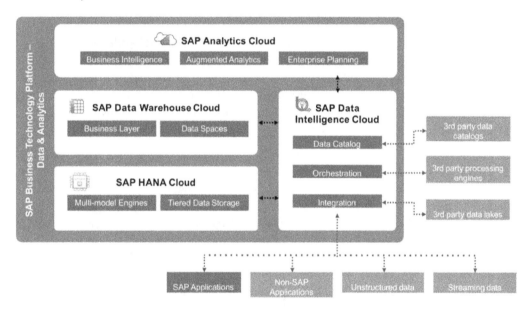

Figure 7.14 – SAP BTP Data and Analytics (DnA) services and products

SAP HANA Cloud

All of the other components in the SAP BTP DnA are made possible with a trusted data foundation for data, classified as data lakes, data platforms, and big data, built with SAP HANA Cloud at the core. The **SAP HANA Cloud** database is a cloud-native, in-memory database that provides real-time access to your data through a single virtualized access point, helping to reduce data redundancies and inconsistencies. SAP HANA Cloud provides replication of on-premise data sources that are managed centrally to discover, refine, and enrich data across your data landscape. The automated, embedded data lake component of SAP HANA Cloud provides data tiering as a single service to help reduce the total cost of ownership. Additionally, prebuilt connectors offer a comprehensive view of your data landscape, delivering data for analytics, planning, predictive modeling, and machine learning. SAP HANA Cloud supports security and high availability while integrating data from across an enterprise, including on-premise, third-party, and cloud sources, accelerating time to insight.

All the preceding components are packaged into a cloud data platform with a unified platform for data, which accelerates converting data into intelligence. Then, you can turn insight into intelligence. And the intelligence that the touchless automated process can consume is driven by the intelligent workflows. We will do a deeper dive in the upcoming section on how to design and architect these workflows using the intelligence fabric. Doing so energizes the rapid development of new business models or processes while keeping pace with steadily evolving core systems, thus maintaining stability and high-quality data management.

Architecting intelligence

Every company has key market-making platforms, which it uses to forward its offer or service to its customers. This, in turn, helps build a customer experience-based story at the core and outside the business. The data within and outside the organization driving an end-to-end process helps derive insights that can drive the **Customer Experience** (**CX**) intelligent moments, using ML and AI components. Let's call it an **Artificial Intelligent Experience** (**AI-X**). These moments can happen across the processes for suppliers or customers.

This would require a crucial collaboration within and across industries, where all process participants contribute via the data collected from the subprocesses they execute and derive value from it. This, in turn, requires a fabric of technology that weaves the experience, insights, and the people interacting with it, which not only helps the participants but also directs what could happen next and, at times, self-heals (corrective actions), based on the situation. This leads to autonomous self-healing and governing processes, with an intelligent workflow at the heart of it. Crucially, the human factor (people) will also have to step up to work faster and smarter with intelligent workflows. So, the human-machine interaction has to move up a level with other intelligent technologies at people's disposal, with the shallowest learning curve helping them level up their skills. With this, the leadership within your organization is also motivated to constantly search for new ways to work smarter to level up to the intelligent workflows.

As described in the previous sections, intelligence is derived from enterprise data collected from various sources, which is then put through targeted machine learning models and trained continuously. The journey doesn't stop here, as we need an AI fabric/intelligence fabric for scaling the adoption and execution of intelligent processes within an organization. In the next section, we will understand what the AI fabric is made of and how it works.

The AI fabric

Delivering intelligent workflows requires an AI strategy at the core and platforms that enable you to deliver it. AI should always complement humans so that the synergy delivers quick outcomes. This means augmented intelligence and leveraging human expertise to develop it further, helping a workforce to focus on the tasks that add the most value and delegating the commodity tasks to the automation factory as part of the intelligent workflow. And once the AI fabric is trained enough to automate itself, the experts will monitor these workflows as yet another arm of the workforce they manage as a supervisor.

The AI fabric can be loosely defined as it relates to orchestration, with *fabric* relating to things working together, and there are four key threads: engagement, learning, reasoning, and doing, as depicted in the following figure. The application of AI for the interaction of humans with machines. The use of AI to learn from the patterns and then reason with what has been learned and upgrade, based on new findings or feedback from users, and then apply the intelligence to make critical business decisions. Once a decision is made, RPA executes the tasks per the decisions and the steps dictated by the central intelligent workflow backbone.

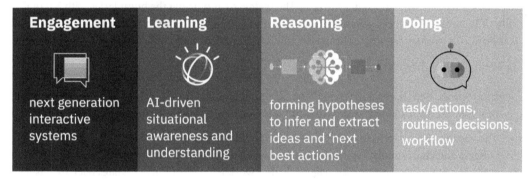

Engagement	Learning	Reasoning	Doing
next generation interactive systems	AI-driven situational awareness and understanding	forming hypotheses to infer and extract ideas and 'next best actions'	task/actions, routines, decisions, workflow

Figure 7.15 – The four threads that make up the AI fabric

The AI fabric helps to weave intelligence in processes and creates the intelligence plane required for an enterprise to execute the processes with an intelligence quotient. These are the systems tapping into the vast amounts of insights generated by the data plane, which we discussed in the last section, and making sense, decisions, and inferring using the ML models, which feed on data to self-correct, self-train, and improve on the accuracy of the outcomes-based – for example, using backpropagation for neural networks. These ML models are built on various algorithms using a mathematical model that can predict, classify, perform image classification or use computer vision to detect anomalies, or use **Natural Language Processing (NLP)** to ease interactions.

Let's start weaving the threads together, starting with interaction with systems – that is, AI-led engagement with people.

Engagement (AI-X thread – conversational AI and digital assistance)

We can make use of NLP and NLU to enable conversational AI. Changing and elevating employee and customer experience has been the fundamental goal of these technologies by removing the cognitive load as much as possible from human-machine interactions. Introducing conversational UI creates the least resistance to adopting and adapting to human interactions. You will have seen chatbots and digital assistants receiving considerable investments in recent years, which enables resource-stressed businesses to serve customers, and call deflections are required to be performed by bots. These bots understand the intent of commands and the conversation taking place and then extract the intent based on the entities identified in the conversational flow.

Those are all the classifiers that understand the intent of what a user is trying to do. In essence, it's a trigger for the work we request the machine to initiate or progress. It's a trained interaction system that uses NLP and NLU algorithms to decide where user interaction reduces human interaction, which is the key to creating a touchless interaction mechanism. This technology has found its way into retail stores, consumer-facing applications, customer service, and front-office processes – essentially, giving a face and voice to your digital workers. The *metaverse* is pushing the boundaries with **Virtual Reality (VR)**, where you are immersed in a virtual world, for instance, to interact, browse products, or collaborate in workspaces with colleagues while sitting in your home office.

Some examples and characteristics of AI-assisted interactions are highlighted as follows:

- Interactions with natural language with NLP and NLU engines on the cloud; no training is required for users to operate systems, and it is available in multiple languages.
- The use of voice and text for input and output for hands-free execution or, at times, the use of widgets and charts to display data in a meaningful, easy-to-understand way. These call for the skills of a digital worker and can trigger further workflow tasks or give updates back to a user.
- The ability to interact and orchestrate on several messaging and collaboration platforms, such as Slack, FB Messenger, CoPilot, or WhatsApp, that users prefer to use.
- They can trigger an assisted, unassisted, or step-by-step guided conversation based on conversational context and sentiment analysis.
- Mobile/desktop/tablet-enabled hands-free, textual, or voice-based conversations for digital assistants, such as Google Assistant and Amazon Alexa.

Learning (cognition thread – machine Learning)

There are two types of learning: the first one is **episodic learning**, where the same situation repeats itself for a decision to be made and the next best action to take place, and the second one is called **semantic learning**, which needs a bit of context to understand a larger pattern with enough confidence to make a decision. For example, a digital worker knows Joe is here to schedule a work order, so he will look up the weather, help decide the best weather condition to service an electricity grid transformer, and choose the soonest best day and time to get it scheduled.

On the other hand, semantic learning uses the context of a situation, such as threat detection – for example, an automated password reset being requested for John Smith. So, by executing specific steps, as we have been doing in the past, we can resolve this incident by automating the steps, resetting the password, and getting the service done. But just pause for a second and think, do you know who John Smith is? And why is he resetting his passwords seven times a week? Is he intruding on your system? Is it something like a user typo error that's getting him locked out? Things such as these identify a larger pattern of a repetitive process and how you make those things understood to at least trigger the proper action or investigation.

Some characteristics and examples of systems of learning are as follows:

- Continuous learning, based on positive or negative outcomes of previous decisions, using feedback mechanisms in the ML models for course-correcting different inference-based outcomes

- Contextual data, which helps conditions to be fed into an ML model to infer the following best actions on the probability of success

- A "what-if" analysis, based on varying contextual conditions, to help determine the best option to go within a given business condition

- Weather data, predictive forecasts based on historical data, image, pattern, voice, and text recognition AI algorithms, offered as ML models to be consumed by a workflow

- Systems of reasoning plus learning, such as **IBM Debater** (`https://research.ibm.com/interactive/project-debater/`), that sit in a cognition plane and continuously assess the user's decisions with alternative perspectives.

- For business applications, ML algorithms based on AI platforms, such as TensorFlow and IBM Watson, with prebuilt ML algorithms and tools for use in building and training ML models to be deployed for inference, to make decisions

Reasoning (the semantics thread)

A simple workflow with business rules can be a perfect reasoning engine when combined with ML that can deduct the semantics and provide its deductions for humans to help make decisions. IBM Debater is one such reasoning engine, but we don't need supercomputing power and gigabytes of data to solve common business problems, connect the dots, or reason with someone on the decisions being made. These are reasoning engines, and the logic in those algorithms will help us decide on a non-deterministic path when the answer is unclear. Refer to business rules and explore the alternative ways to get through the critical path of a process, or combine the context with a **K-Nearest Neighbor (KNN)** or **Density Clustering** ML algorithm to help decide on the best choice for a given situation.

These engines come back with confidence levels on each decision that is available for humans to make. An example would be a dynamic supply chain, where, based on the context of an inventory, the performance of alternative vendors is measured against delivery timelines, certain quality, and the targeted quantity. The ML would come back with a confidence level against the vendors, and then we combine them with other business rules on their ESG rating to come up with sourcing options. This would require a good context and data collection mechanism to provide all the data to the ML models to make the most of the data available at the decision-making fork. Dynamic workflows have intelligence built around it and are given contextual data to allow flow rerouting to the most critical tasks, to progress the workflow end to end.

Some characteristics of the cognitive reasoning workflow plane are as follows:

- These systems have the logic for reasoning and decision-making constructs with a semantic understanding of what is happening.

- Uses serverless/orchestration functions that can understand the intents/triggers from the UX/AIX and trigger the appropriate business process from the repository of digitally modeled business processes

- The workflow that represents the business process based on the intent recognized is instantiated and builds a working and business context at runtime, as the workflow is executed from start to end.

- The workflow tasks and next steps are based on the ML model, which understands the optimal paths (tasks) that can be taken, maintaining the critical path that needs to be traced in any given condition.

- The next best actions and flows are optimized with every single pass or instantiation of these workflows. In a way, ML is self-optimizing and self-learning, as with every pass, the ML algorithms are collecting data on the success of the decisions made and helping increase accuracy.

- It acts as a control tower for business process management, with analytics and process visualization widgets. It understands the efficiencies and performance aspects of the process being executed at any given time and point.

- Examples are SAP Workflow Management combined with the business rules engine on SAP BTP, and Kogito the workflow engine on the Red Hat OpenShift, which is a complete container-based workflow execution combined with the learning engines explained previously.

Doing (execution thread – automation engines)

The last thread in the AI fabric is the doing – that is, we put insight into action and get some work done, which has been directed by the central intelligent workflow and requested by the cloud-based automation agents to execute specific tasks on the participating systems in the landscape. This could be RPA, IoT device actuators, or people. These are either attended (assisted by humans) or unattended bots (self-driven) on process automation engines, which help to complete transactions, scan documents, derive key-value pairs, and respond to requests made by central workflows, which orchestrate activities, data, transactions, and processes. The automation bots communicate through APIs of the context data and data for execution, responding with a success or failure notification of the requested execution.

Some characteristics and examples of automation engines are as follows:

- Blue Prism, Automation Anywhere, UIPath, and SAP iRPA of the world reside on this plane

- They have their central cloud agent of automation working with the business/semantics plane, an army of bots with targeted business transaction execution, and are good at specific jobs

- The bot army can be instantiated and mobilized across multi-cloud, hybrid, and private public clouds in attended or unattended modes

- The army bots report a task's completion, status, and any errors that may have occurred

- The bots can work attended and unattended, reporting every single task to cloud agents, or can work uninterrupted until a task is complete and report the final status

- The bots are all enabled with API functions and can consist of code-based bots or screen-recorded bots, and they always have a data container that helps feed the underlying transaction execution

Next, we will understand some key considerations for intelligent workflows, which were partially addressed in the previous sections on data architecture, and there are a few more.

Design considerations for intelligent workflows

There are three areas when you think about designing and deploying intelligent workflows:

- **Data readiness (quality cleansed) for insights**: The quality of insights is determined by the quality of data, as is the decision accuracy of the ML based on the data. Bad data quality has a hidden cost to it, which impacts operations. Data is a currency in itself; it shapes the focus of a business platform and an intelligent workflow. So, data is quintessential when considering critical requirements associated with the qualified processes for an intelligent workflow. Also, you need to look at multiple internal and external data sources and see where they can enrich and embellish internal data, which has probably been lying dormant for some time. As Arvind Krishna, the IBM CEO, has rightly said, "You can't have AI without IA," which means that establishing an **Information Architecture (IA)** underpins the ability to drive AI. It also focuses on the notion of hunting for data that's meaningful and special to be able to maximize its value, versus just fishing for data in a lake on the go.

- **Applying exponential technologies**: When you start thinking about broader intelligent enterprise architecture and all that's involved, from data to integration and the experience along the way, it's not just about throwing a bunch of tech at it for tech's sake; it is about looking at where convergence makes sense. Scanning and identifying the different hand-offs and touchpoints of 3D printing, IoT, AI, and many other things can create value or reduce costs effectively. The right place is where the AI makes sense, and you want to apply data science to specific datasets. Or, the right place is where the manifestation of IoT can truly impact customer experience in connected appliances. So, the idea is to have the right combination of exponential technologies for optimal value.

- **Two-tier orchestration**: As we harmonize and adopt more end-to-end processes across an LoB, the need to standardize them becomes evident. This also gives us the opportunity to automate them using intelligent workflows, partially or completely. To achieve this process automation, we would require two-tier orchestration where we work across heterogeneous ecosystems (**TIER 1**), which is weaved into an E2E process orchestrated and managed by a workflow in the cloud, spanning across the landscape (**TIER 2**). Two-tier orchestration ensures the notion of a hybrid multi-cloud environment and the applications built off of it. Then, the infrastructure associated with it is essential in establishing intelligent workflows and business platforms in an intelligent enterprise. This enables us to deploy, secure, govern, and run with controls for data privacy and regulatory compliance and see how those shape potential use cases, which establish the value proposition associated with these business platforms.

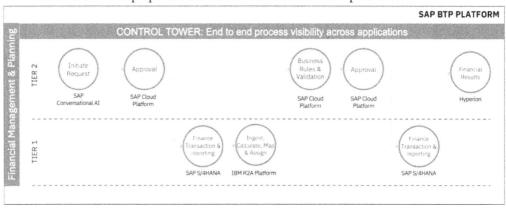

Figure 7.16 – Two-tier orchestration on SAP BTO for intelligent workflows

In summary, the intelligent workflows are infused with intelligence, provided by the ML models trained on the data collected from the siloed systems and collated in trusted data foundations. The intelligent workflow then drives the E2E processes (defined in the process model) using the RPA bots actioning on the activities, transactions, and tasks. While doing so, it can orchestrate data and events to connected IoT digital twins and systems, receiving responses on completing tasks and making operations more efficient and effective, from the inner core of the business to the outer edges of the global network. These intelligent workflows can then make the touchless process a reality. This means that we are taking costs out of the systems.

As highlighted in *Chapter 4, Intelligent Enterprise and Sustainable Design*, SAP BTP offers the SAP Process Automation suite, which has workflow management – consisting of process visualization, event collection, creating process variants, business rules, and tracking and monitoring of the workflows. We can also combine it with SAP CAI for the interaction with the users, SAP iRPA for the automation engine, and SAP AI Business Services, or we could use one of the powerful ML platforms, such as TensorFlow or Watson AI. All these components combine the ingredients explained previously to create an intelligent workflow. We will briefly run through how to put these components together to create an end-to-end intelligent workflow on the SAP BTP platform next.

Intelligent Workflows with SAP BTP

Orchestrate and extend Intelligent Workflows across people and organizations

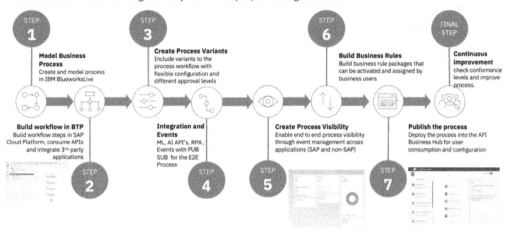

Figure 7.17 – The key steps in creating intelligent workflows on SAP BTP

Let's understand intelligent workflows with SAP BTP:

1. **Model Business Process**: As detailed in the first section of this chapter, we complete the fit-to-standard exercises or create a new "to-be" process design from the organization's best practices repository. The business processes are represented in the BPMN 2.0 notations, which can be easily pulled into the SAP BTP Business Application Studio low-code workflow development environment.

2. **Build a workflow in BTP**: The workflow can then be enhanced with the detailed business logic to execute tasks and consume data, using APIs from a third party or the OData Services from S/4HANA.

3. **Create Process Variants**: You can club the set of workflow tasks in a workflow variant block, which the citizen developers and business users can then use to alter the flow and create process variants in the process workflow console through the process variant file.

4. **Integration and Events**: While the execution of the tasks and the processes move from left to right, several events can be triggered for external systems to consume or can be consumed through the events and APIs offered by the external systems, such as the SAP BTP event mesh. The tasks can also consume the ML models through the APIs for inference, invoke an action on an automation bot (such as SAP iRPA, UIPath, or Automation Anywhere) to complete a transaction, or execute a real-world task through IoT devices.

5. **Create Process Visibility**: The process visibility dashboard has prebuilt SAP UI5 widgets that can help visualize several KPIs or PPIs, based on events and the number of transactions in flight. You can configure these, based on the requirements and KPIs you want to track.

6. **Build Business Rules**: As part of SAP Workflow Management, the business rules framework also offers easy-to-maintain and consume business rules to evaluate and make decisions, based on the available data during workflow execution and the context data.

7. **Publish the process**: Development teams can also publish packaged content on the SAP API Hub for other LoBs or monetize the content, if it is published, for the marketplace to discover and consume.

8. Users can access their inbox within the SAP Workflow Management console to action any tasks or pending activities, such as approving, rejecting, or delegating tasks to other team members.

9. The workflow instances applications provide detailed execution logs on each step and the tasks completed by the workflow, with a data snapshot of the context of the workflow.

10. The workflow cockpit, the inbox, and all the applications can be controlled with role-based access control on SAP BTP. This allows business and process owners to take corrective or preventive measures in a timely manner, as the need may be, to progress a process efficiently as it executes.

11. The whole workflow that represents the digital twin of the process can be instantiated or interacted by using APIs in runtime, which is also available on API Hub using OAuth 2.0.

12. The dashboard through process visibility helps pinpoint deviations, the users involved, and corrects a process, if needed, by introducing further checks (simple tasks) with a no-code workflow modeler to introduce new steps and deploying them at runtime.

Two-tier orchestration of the intelligent workflow in the cloud allows systems and processes to be connected across a heterogeneous landscape to exchange data in secure, governed, and controlled environments, unleashing the true value to be propagated further in the value chains with customers at the receiving end. So, it becomes essential to understand how tos leverage cloud environments to maximize and forward this potential value.

Next, we will look at some architectural patterns within a hybrid cloud landscape that your organization may want to adopt to accelerate the journey to an intelligent enterprise, and to align your technical capabilities to the business architecture that we defined in the previous section to innovate faster. We will see how we derive synergies out of the old and new landscapes that is in the making with SAP and non-SAP technologies and hyperscaler platforms.

Going cloud-native with SAP

Companies were pressed to innovate faster and bring new solutions to the landscape to respond to the recent unprecedented dynamics the market experienced, such as the rush to adopt hyperscalers. And for many companies, the best tactics included using the latest technologies to redefine business models, mitigate risks, comply with stricter and more punitive regulations, and take on opportunities in real time as they come.

These cloud-based tactical solutions may have helped, but the isolated approaches to acquiring and adopting technology only lead to significant delays (or, worse, failure) in realizing transformational outcomes. Instead, it requires a level of strategic alignment of the technical landscape to a business architecture and the capabilities needed to provide a resilient, robust, and secure architecture that is scalable and considers relevant areas of the business.

Conversely, you may find organizations that are already on their transformational journey and have acquired specific SaaS and PaaS hyperscalers per their strategic and tactical business needs, and they are just discovering the capabilities and benefits of the SAP business technology platform. These benefits range from native integration, openness for interoperability, a unified data model, integrity, and compliance resonating with their SAP S/4HANA and legacy landscape. They may end up having two cloud-native options for innovations and extensions.

This is quite normal, as many organizations have organically evolved into multi-cloud strategies, realizing that they can use the best of breed from each cloud, sharing the side-by-side extensibility space with BTP. Alternatively, it could be SaaS solutions in terms of functional applications (for example, Salesforce and Workday) and SAP BTP in extending or innovating in data, AI, automation, and process excellence with BPI solutions. Whether you combine SAP BTP with hyperscaler platform services for your innovations or use them for targeted capabilities such as iPaaS for integrations middleware, the goal is to deliver value quickly with faster time to market, given that multi-cloud environments can span a choice of application services, development services, integration platforms, or data services. Again, the direction is dependent on the vision of an organization or business regarding its products and services in the near and long-term future. The choice is further influenced by SAP's footprint on the landscape, where you are in the S/4HANA adoption journey, how open your organization is for open sources, dev communities and culture, internal and external to your organization, and cloud-native skill sets that your development and IT teams possess. So, we look at a few concepts of how to logically segregate and define some principles when navigating the multi-cloud hybrid landscape in subsequent sections.

Inner ring and outer ring

When we talk of the co-existence of pure-play cloud vendors with SAP BTP, you will need to consider and evaluate what extensions and net new solutions you want to develop and adopt that balance cloud infrastructure usage. The organization's digital maturity is further elevated when there are clear guiding principles on when to use certain cloud options and technology mixes in a landscape, to develop further capabilities and solutions.

Inner and outer ring-fencing of your landscape helps logically separate the process data and systems, based on the separation of concerns and functions. It provides an opportunity to focus on core operations, data, and essential business processes while simultaneously addressing the need to evolve quickly by providing agility to innovate at a pace on edge – for example, applications and systems closer to customers – while allowing critical enterprise systems to evolve at their life cycle speed. It separates the enterprise workloads from customer process workloads, yet propagates the value from the processes and data with native integration, which would have otherwise been locked out and taken advantage of a fast time to market.

Enterprise inner ring

Enterprise systems, processes, and data differentiate an organization and create a competitive advantage. At the same time, you need to exercise robust governance of data and processes for enterprise system integrity and ensure compliance. This goes hand in hand with applying the core clean principle to your S/4HANA transformation program, extended to include the SAP cloud portfolio of applications such as SAP Ariba, SAP SuccessFactors, and SAP BTP. If implemented correctly, this can provide modular, decoupled extensions to your core processes with integration and process automation suites, with native integrations, and yet offer cloud-native services such as serverless, microservices, eventing using SAP Kyma or SAP Event Mesh, and a unified data model (with SAP Graph), which is shared across the SAP products and LoB applications. Using the API gateway on API Hub on the periphery of the inner ring, including all the components, applications, data, and processes within the circle, you will be able to air-gap access to enterprise processes and data directly from peripheral systems on the edge or customer-facing enterprise landscape. Personas interacting with the inner ring can range from employees or partners to suppliers or customers (B2B).

Enterprise outer ring

Going with the logical separation, the outer ring includes customer/consumer-facing channels, supporting systems, and services for a front office, connected appliances, or operations that need frequent access to customer, order, or product data, or even the core processes and transactions. These systems and applications are deployed on hyperscalers such as IBM, Google, Amazon, and Azure. This allows capabilities such as quick response times, edge services, and content for the personalization of channels. They have a higher churn of new releases and updates to meet customer demand and changes.

These systems and applications could be e-commerce sites, self-service portals, IoT services for connected devices, telemetry data, and events from the edge applications. Data is then parsed and relayed through event mechanisms or data pipelines available on these peripheral cloud platforms to be then distributed within the inner circle, and consumed by enterprise systems (in the inner circle) to action or process it further. The outer ring can also share the data models and operational data stores from the inner ring, and tap into the eventing mechanisms or applications, with required security and access controls on applications that work closely with the consumer-facing applications from the inner circle. Some solutions may span the inner and outer circle boundaries, again having controlled access to data, and select what part of the process they can influence through SAP BTP, API Hub, or an enterprise iPaaS platform. A few examples of personas and systems that fall under the outer ring concept are customers (B2B2C), service providers, connected appliances, operational technology with manufacturing execution systems, consumers, open source communities, independent developers' ecosystems, and B2B/B2C scenarios.

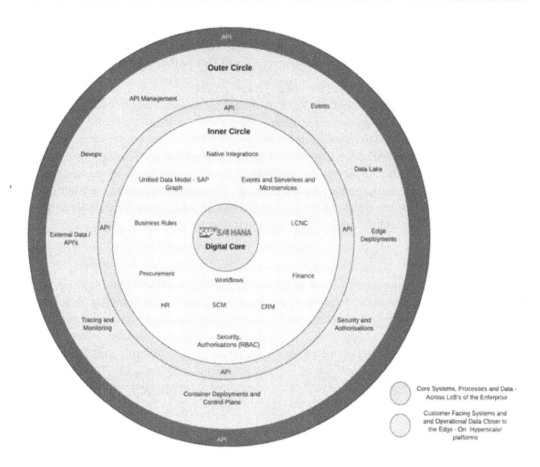

Figure 7.18 – Enterprise inner ring and outer ring concept

As depicted in *Figure 7.18*, the ring-fenced systems expose their processes and data as APIs/microservices for external applications to be consumed through hyperscaler API management or SAP API HUB. A loosely coupled API-first architecture, supporting a digital core or legacy SAP ERP system in the inner circle, balances the need for getting back to standard with the needs of a business for continuous innovation and differentiation with the outer core. This provides the opportunity for an independent life cycle of upgrades and changes for systems and processes within the inner and outer ring-fenced solutions.

Cloud-native options for side-by-side extensions

The way we deliver SAP is changing – from value locked into a rigid and inflexible ERP monolith to one with business agility while keeping the core clean. This SAP-modernized approach is also called a **lean ERP**. One of the core principles for this is to shift from traditional ABAP development and the reduction of non-value-adding code and data to cloud-native style approaches, while keeping the core lean and clean to drive continuous innovation necessary for a business to gain value and market differentiation. With cloud-native modernizations becoming commonplace due to the ease and simplicity of exploiting serverless and deployment services that don't need IT teams' intervention.

Any organization can start to embrace the shift to containerization for code modernization or landscape rationalization with the adoption of containerized applications, using **Red Hat OpenShift**, for instance. This provides E2E operations and application landscape management for Kubernetes with accelerators and operators to spin up cloud runtime loads. You can also choose from **Amazon Elastic Kubernetes Service** (**EKS**), **Azure Kubernetes Service** (**AKS**), and **Google Kubernetes Engine** (**GKE**) runtimes and the services offered by the cloud vendors based on the strategy. As explained in upcoming sections, there are some advantages to going down the Red Hat route. Next, we will run through some considerations of how Red Hat OpenShift gets you closer to accelerating and implementing the concept of the inner and outer rings in your landscape.

Red Hat OpenShift for SAP

Over the past few decades, we have moved through several phases of computing, and today, modern computing is more than the cloud; it is how we work and use cloud-native tooling to build assets and continuously improve them. The modularity of what we build has become simpler, moving from operating system footprints to application footprints, reducing the size of compute needed. The definition of how systems have been designed has shifted from external to internal and infrastructure as code, enabling faster deployment and scaling. Red Hat OpenShift containerization with modularized integration and eventing components, which can spin up to your requirements in a few clicks with prebuilt operators, precisely enables that, enabling your enterprise to be more nimble and agile to innovate with containers.

This line of thinking allows for organizational development and innovation teams to develop once and deploy anywhere, even on-premise. This is because Red Hat OpenShift allows for a hybrid cloud (multi-cloud or on-premises/pure cloud deployment) setup of your extensions, or any application, with cloud-native runtimes and development productivity tools, including automated cloud deployment pipelines spun up on demand. Abstracting your workloads from underlying infrastructure enables your enterprise to run on any cloud and safeguard the investments you are making today. Evolving regulatory, legal, and security requirements and changing hyperscaler strategies are challenging every business to evolve and transform at a rapid pace.

Figure 7.19 shows how SAP BTP and a hyperscaler strategy with Red Hat OpenShift can co-exist in harmony, making it possible to realize the inner and outer circle concepts we discussed previously.

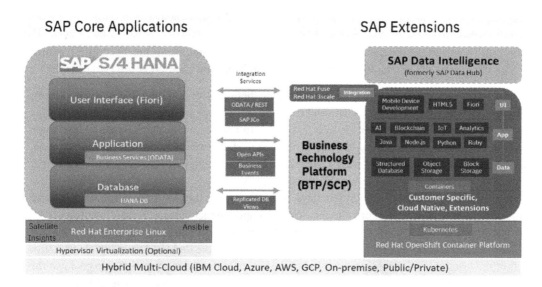

Figure 7.19 – Red Hat OpenShift for an SAP landscape

Illustrated on the left is the traditional approach to extensions with S/4HANA, and on the right is the new world of application modernization running on containers, allowing the freedom of development for side-by-side concepts with cloud-native development capabilities. Whether you go with SAP BTP and create the plethora of cloud-native extensions that utilize containers on the periphery or you opt for a pure Red Hat-based deployment for non-SAP or SAP applications, you can either have SAP BTP on the landscape or can be pure hyperscaler-based, which is a choice that you will have to make architecturally and base on the hyperscaler strategy that your organization has adopted. This drives us toward adopting containers for extensions or building new solutions, simplifying consuming cloud-native services for developers. This enables your enterprise to build production-grade solutions rapidly for user experience, mobility, integration, AI, or edge computing.

The evolved view in this approach is that the de facto choice is SAP BTP for the SAP components in the landscape. If you want to take a more abstract approach, you can use SAP BTP plus Red Hat OpenShift, as it gives you the full cloud-native experience from the outset. You use SAP BTP because it is suitable for the inner ring. Then, you start integrating a more comprehensive range of applications through OpenShift's broader ecosystems of event streaming, integration, and API management as an outer ring running on containers. This combination gives better synergy and flexibility in architecture, resulting in a richer experience and quicker time to market. SAP BTP is a natural choice to extend the process context and the data models beyond the core. If it is part of your licensing agreement as part of RISE with SAP, you may as well go for it.

The SAP clientele also has a choice to purchase more CPEA credits. A lot of innovations and prebuilt content by SAP and partners can be leveraged through SAP BTP every quarter, per the roadmap. If you want to do more open source development and not be worried about being locked in from a cloud development perspective, then consider Red Hat OpenShift. Your extension and innovation platform choice is further influenced by SAP's footprint in the landscape, where you are in the S/4HANA adoption journey, and how open your organization is to open source innovation. Development culture, platform services, cloud-native skill sets, and the hybrid cloud landscape are a few other facets to consider.

Alternatively, your organization may not want to make these choices upfront and abstract itself from all these changes, which may be overturned in the future as hyperscalers evolve. These strategies need some time and due diligence for an organization to decide how to shape its future landscape in line with business goals. So, the choices don't need to stall your digital transformation agenda, and you can continue accelerating with a cloud abstraction strategy. Red Hat OpenShift creates that abstraction layer and provides the scalability, interoperability, and control that organizations desire to continue on their transformation journeys, unperturbed by the cloud evolution. It creates an abstraction between the applications and their cloud computing that safeguards their investments. It's about getting from point A to B with the least number of changes in direction. The good part is that all SAP BTP extensions work in harmony and unison alongside the Red Hat OpenShift cloud-native applications/extensions – that is, you can choose the best of both worlds, even if you do go down the SAP BTP, iPaaS, PaaS, or IaaS routes. Speaking of these, we will look at some high-level architectural patterns to allow for loosely coupled or decoupled and modular architectural patterns to innovate at pace in the upcoming section.

Agile and resilient architectures

Organizations are beginning to realize that *cloud adoption* is not just the modernization of applications with lift and shift to the cloud. The true value is recognized by the change in the development and delivery practices, with continuous integration and deployment, and architectural and integration patterns.

From an enterprise architecture point of view, moving away from traditional integration in the core ERP toward a more agile integration becomes a challenge. This includes moving from a centralized enterprise service bus toward decentralized integration APIs, or even better, to microservices to have a smaller footprint on the underlying infrastructure, and fostering a reusable, scalable, and distributed architectural approach, as depicted here.

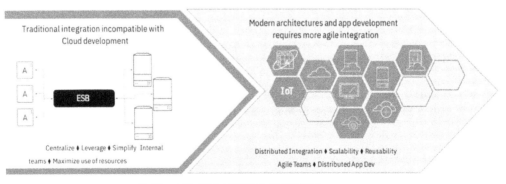

Figure 7.20 – Modern architectures and agile integrations

For example, you don't want applications hogging system resources 24x7 to serve a couple of requests. When you talk about event-driven architectures, you can have a serverless function invoked by an event, or a webhook call spinning up a serverless function briefly, serving the request just in time, and then spinning down. When you talk about headless architectures, which are more microservices driven for any frontend framework, you need only the required data that the user values. The Graph QL implementation for serving data is game-changing in these applications, although it needs to be supported by and adhere to the API first design approach, with the API contracts exposed by the underlying SaaS for the functional capabilities being delivered for both process and data. And when we look at edge devices, we are using data filtering, data pipelines, and deploying machine learning models on the edge, sifting out the most critical data points for further insights from what is being sensed.

Other architectural patterns such as pub-sub patterns allow subscribers to listen for events/messages and to react only if they are relevant to any action. Istio service mesh-based distributed microservices deployment leads to a failsafe, resilient, secure, and observable mesh network. So, we could almost end up with distributed architectural components with a capability matrix (of all things), applications, and digital entities that are part of that ecosystem, which drives the intelligent enterprise systems and processes. This is where we start seeing how we can design applications to become more modular, agile, and scalable across different clouds to be iterated more quickly and efficiently, leading to a composable enterprise. Now, let's deal with the question that might have been lingering in your mind for a while.

Is this possible with the ECC landscape? Yes, it is!

So, what if you are on ECC? The classic ECC, which has been extended over the years with layers of config, customizations, and process activation extensions, along with thick layers of code and data. This wrapping around ECC has sometimes made it unrecognizable from the original ECC. That's been done by design, as your organization wanted functionality that couldn't be delivered by standard SAP, which has led to technical debt piling up over time, making it cumbersome from an upgrade perspective and costly to maintain it. So, with the ECC on-premise landscapes, the idea is to simplify by shrinking these layers and moving customer code extensions to a more elastic cloud. It can be any of the hyperscalers mentioned in the previous section, cloud abstraction with Red Hat OpenShift, or a combination of SAP BTP and hyperscalers. And once you are on the hyperscalers, you are in a position to start introducing some of the platform services. So, you can already start the application or ABAP code modernization journeys to move some of your valued assets and extensions to the hybrid cloud, integrate them, and refactor them to consume cloud-native services.

Then, you can look at utilizing SAP DI and Syniti (discussed in detail in *Chapter 8, Exodus*) running on the cloud, which helps your organization to introduce data governance, harmonization, and cleansing in a staging area, with an E2E view of data quality. Then, you move on to data governance from a data perspective, see how you can authorize the master data, and then introduce an archiving strategy, which is not mandatory but is good for gauging what data is relevant to for day-to-day operations and shrinks the database footprint by archiving, making your ECC even more lean.

Once you have good data governance practices, you can move forward to start with a process-led view. This is where Celonis/SAP Signavio Process Transformation Suite come in to drive process insights, which give you an accurate picture of the process frictions based on the production data. You can initiate a process transformation journey to achieve process excellence and make the best of what SAP ECC can offer.

The next step would be to consider building intelligent apps and extensions using SAP BTP/hyperscaler platform services, as explained previously. Complement the processes with cloud-native extensions to adopt some of the best practices for candidate processes identified with process mining. Of course, it wouldn't be like for like with S/4HANA as your core, consuming some of the innovations and the efficiencies of the SAP HANA-based data model; nonetheless, you can transform how data and processes can be run to take your ECC process optimizations to the next level.

You don't have to be necessarily on S/4HANA to start innovations and optimizations. You can start optimizing the data, process, and extensions in ECC to make it leaner and cleaner to prepare for the next upgrade or move to S/4HANA in future. You can create a customer-facing app and connect to ECC via APIs to consume data and processes. You can containerize or refactor a crucial business logic or function module into a serverless function or microservice. The best part is that once it is containerized, you have safeguarded your investments to include it on your S/4 journey or adopt it per your hyperscaler strategy. You can run it on any hyperscaler and integrate and consume your SAP ECC data to create the same outcome. Essentially, you are abstracting your high-value extensions from the ever-evolving changes to the underlying cloud infrastructure.

Again, this can be a holding pattern for the ultimate goal of getting ready to move toward the S/4HANA digital core in the near or distant future, as the full potential of the enterprise processes is only realized when the enterprise core processes and the data are on the new digital core. While in the holding pattern, you reduce your cost and do some modernization. You can use a two-step approach – a tactical holding pattern, and keep optimizing and getting ready to then do a more planned and efficient S/4HANA transformation, which could take some time. The trade-off is to move today by addressing the bloated ECC or when you kick off your transformation and discover unwanted data, code, and processes as you go, which essentially prolongs the transformation timelines and efforts. The better approach could be to start the optimizations today to leverage what best could be offered by the hybrid cloud approaches discussed previously and then do a leaner and cleaner transition of your core to SAP S/4HANA. We will look at a couple of examples of the flexibility introduced by architectural choices, using a hybrid cloud, and some technology choices. There will be more on this in upcoming chapters, though the following section gives you a taste of things to come later on.

Composable enterprise

So, in summary, you are enabling each layer of your enterprise architecture to adopt the best-of-breed platform services, containerizing your extensions and your IP to safeguard your investments. From the experience layer to the enterprise applications layer, all the extensions and innovations can be underpinned by the choices made with SAP BTP and Red Hat OpenShift and its supporting products, based on how your inner ring and outer rings are defined.

For example, you can use the LCNC SAP AppGyver – rapid accelerators to develop React-based consumer-grade or SAP UI5/Fiori enterprise-grade user experiences at scale, running on the Red Hat OpenShift platform. Since the frontend is completely containerized, it can be deployed on any cloud closer to the users catering to their personalization. Edge-deployed applications have the benefits of high performance, tailored experiences, and content, and the best part is that they use the same data as you are using on SAP Fiori within your organization but with controls on data privacy. Combining the set of applications from SAP Fiori and the collection of React applications for B2B scenarios can be achieved easily with SAP Launchpad or via the SAP Work Zone or SAP Launchpad Service on SAP BTP, proving the maximum value for their investments.

One automotive industrial client has containerized the entire connected car applications, having more than 12 million cars on road. And then you have the Industrial 4.0 revolution, where technologies such as 5G and IoT open up opportunities to sense the environment to ensure health and safety, and sustainability aspects. An excellent example of this is how a mining giant in Europe is addressing the EHS for its employees. The dust levels on the mining sites or the tunnels are controlled by automated intelligent sprinklers that, when enabled, can bring down the dust levels within acceptable limits. This is using containerized edge applications to process data and apply ML insights to take remediating actions.

The best part is that all those innovations are being delivered at pace, enabled by agile, modular architecture, critical for developer productivity and velocity, faster time to market, and higher churn on these applications, managed by an automated deployment life cycle.

Figure 7.21 brings all the concepts and the architectural constructs together as layered enterprise architecture for an intelligent enterprise.

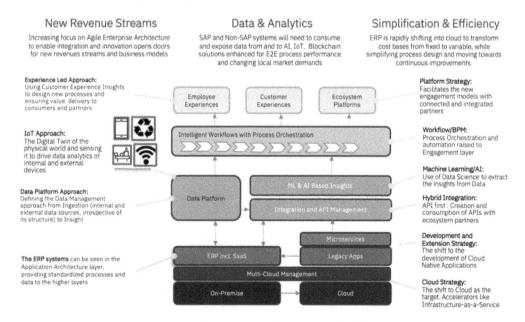

Figure 7.21 – Agile modular architectures with hybrid cloud

This agile and modular architectural approach can be realized with the platforms and hyperscalers of your choice, although it's recommended to have strong governance and architectural principles and patterns in place right from the outset. Your organization doesn't need to follow exactly the same approach, although it could be used as a target architecture to avoid technical debt and lock-in with particular vendors, allowing you to upgrade and innovate independently with decoupled modular architecture, underpinning the move to an intelligent enterprise.

Summary

In this chapter, we went from using the CBM heat maps uncovered during the discovery and analysis of your organizational capabilities to digging deeper into understanding what optimizations and improvements in processes and data are required for the TOM of an intelligent enterprise. Furthermore, we understood the data challenges and the platform characteristics to enable data democratization across your organization, and the constructs to build intelligent insights to drive outcomes per your transformation objectives. We then considered the architectural best practices for extending processes or data with intelligent workflows, how the AI fabric allows for processes to be self-driven, self-healing, and self-governing, and how the choices of cloud-native extensions on hyperscalers with your SAP landscape can be made as you transform your business. The whole approach requires small incremental changes to address the capabilities of a business and technical architecture.

In the upcoming chapter, we will invest some time in understanding how data is core to the success of the transformation and how toolsets from SAP and non-SAP vendors can help accelerate your data migration to a new core. This will lay down the foundation to then move into the implementation stages and key considerations before you do your first how pilot roll.

Further reading

```
https://medium.com/@CMcVoy/80-of-ceos-believe-they-deliver-superior-
customer-experience-661efabd16b0
```

The Exodus – Data That Matters

In the previous chapter, we provided you with input on the best practices to be considered when working with S/4HANA and RISE with SAP. One of the key aspects of the approach mentioned was how you can use the **component business model (CBM)** along with the to-be target operating model to achieve the business transformation you are considering. We also talked about the quad-A approach (adopt, adapt, add, and abstain) to support the fit-to-standard methodology while driving the simplification of the business process and different tools/accelerators that can be used to achieve this. Finally, we touched upon the importance of data in being able to generate insights beyond the traditional **extract, transform, load (ETL)** based approach, using different tools such as SAP **Data Intelligence (DI)**, SAP Data Warehouse Cloud, and SAP HANA Cloud, along with the usage of SAP **Business Technology Platform (BTP)**.

Spark4Life has made the decision to go ahead with RISE with SAP while transforming to S/4HANA as their digital core. They have a clear understanding of the best practices when it comes to pre-defined processes which SAP and other vendors offer along with the Fit to Standard approach they would like to adopt. One of the key questions which still needs to be addressed for them as an organization is around how the data will be migrated from their old systems to the new systems and what practices will be put into play to ensure the data is of highest quality.

In this chapter, we will be providing you with details about how important it is to plan your data migration to the target S/4HANA platform based on the type of migration activity in a proactive manner. For instance, depending on whether you choose Greenfield, Brownfield, or Bluefield (selective) migration, you might have to consider different approaches to address the data migration activities throughout the life cycle of the project. This is important to make sure your new S/4HANA-based solution has the right data for the business to be able to make well-informed decisions from day one instead of worrying about possible data quality or reconciliation-related issues. You will also be able to understand the approach to be taken when it comes to adopting the right framework when it comes to data governance, data quality, and data profiling.

We will be covering the following topics:

- Understanding different move/implementation scenarios and the relevance of data
- Looking into the importance of data migration – why, what, and how
- Understanding the importance of data governance and data quality

- Debunking myths around data migration
- Looking into the SAP Activate methodology and the adoption patterns related to data migration
- Looking into different options available for data migration

Understanding different move/implementation scenarios

In this section, before we deep dive into the details around the data migration strategy/approach to be adopted, let's go through an overview of different move/implementation scenarios possible when considering SAP S/4HANA along with RISE with SAP. We will then go through the type of data migration approach to be considered in each of the scenarios. The following are the three scenarios along with details of when to consider each of them.

Greenfield implementation

This scenario is applicable to customers who are either existing SAP (ECC) or non-SAP ERP-based customers. The main reason for considering Greenfield implementation is not being happy with the existing solution in place and wanting a completely new simplified design without carrying over the burden from the previous implementation(s). Customers also want to take the opportunity to re-design with a transformative approach along with new solution components (S/4HANA digital core along with other SaaS solutions).

For this scenario, you would need to identify all possible source systems along with the data selection to be considered to perform a comprehensive analysis of possible duplication and usability in the new solution. You also would need to work with the process owners to harmonize and cleanse the data between the enterprise applications before loading it into SAP S/4HANA. The following figure provides a summary of different capabilities you need to consider across different phases of a project along with possible tool usage:

Timeline	Prepare	Prototype	Build	Deploy	Run
Capabilities	Cleansing & Profiling		Master Data		Data Quality Monitoring
	Data Quality Assessment		Open Items		
	Source Identification		Historical Data		
		Data Harmonization			
		Data Standardization			
			Data Transformation		
			Data Validation/ Reconciliation		
Tools	DI / Syniti				

Figure 8.1: Capabilities by phase for Greenfield implementation

The key to success for this scenario is to have a "One Data model" established within the organization for the final solution followed by the mapping from the source systems. If there is no historical precedence available for the to-be data model, multiple dry runs of the data migration are the only way you can understand the required output for the business.

Brownfield migration

Unlike the earlier Greenfield implementation scenario, this scenario is applicable for customers who are either happy with their existing ECC instances or already have S/4HANA available on-premises or on another cloud provider and would like to consolidate the cloud strategy. One of the other reasons for customers to consider this scenario would be if they do not have an appetite for a multi-year or multi-region rollout. Rather, the customer is OK with optimizing after migrating the existing landscape onto the cloud, either both upgrading and migrating to S/4HANA or just migrating to the S/4HANA landscape.

For this scenario, while you might not have to plan data migration from different source systems, you would still need to consider business rule validation after the migration of the system onto the target landscape from a data validation point of view. You would also need to focus on a near-zero downtime-based approach to optimize the effort involved in migrating the systems along with the additional data updates to be made for the new scope if any are added. The following figure provides a summary of different capabilities you need to consider across different phases of a project along with possible tool usage:

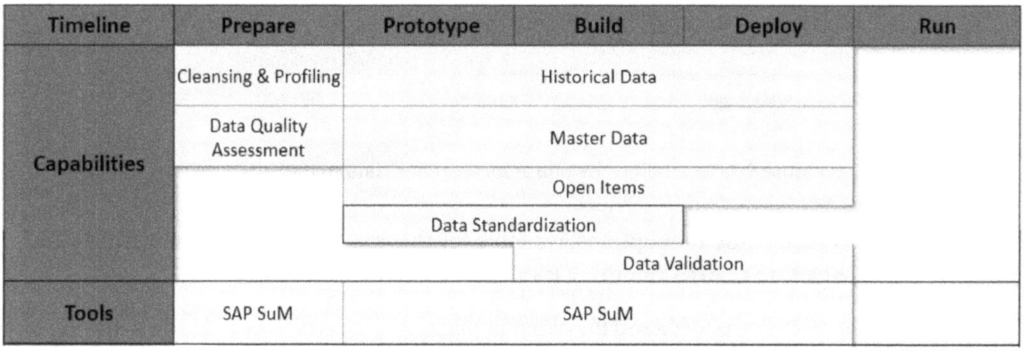

Timeline	Prepare	Prototype	Build	Deploy	Run
Capabilities	Cleansing & Profiling		Historical Data		
	Data Quality Assessment		Master Data		
			Open Items		
		Data Standardization			
				Data Validation	
Tools	SAP SuM		SAP SuM		

Figure 8.2: Capabilities across phases for Brownfield migration

Also, one of the key aspects that you need to be aware of is what a Brownfield-based approach with RISE with SAP means. The reason for this is you as a customer or **service integrator** (**SI**) partner won't have **operating system** (**OS**) level access to the S/4HANA target system within the RISE landscape. This would mean you would need to still perform the pre-migration and the actual move of the system itself from on-premises/another cloud onto the RISE landscape into an unmanaged server prior to getting that moved over into the actual RISE system. This is very important for you to plan the scope and effort/resources accordingly.

Selective data migration

Apart from the Greenfield- and Brownfield-based scenarios, you have another scenario termed selective data migration. By selective data migration, we mean you are able to copy over the structure of your existing system as is onto the target landscape without the configuration or the associated data in the system and later on decide on which section of the data needs to be moved into the target system. This approach is typically considered for mergers, acquisitions, and divestments or the consolidation of multiple ECC or S/4HANA systems into a single S/4HANA landscape.

For this scenario, you need to perform a comprehensive analysis of what your system of validation from which the configuration and the custom development will be retained will be. Once that system is identified, you also need to come up with a list of selective data, either by entities or by time series, that would need to be moved into the target system. There is custom mapping and development work involved while performing this type of data migration activity.

Timeline	Prepare	Prototype	Build	Deploy	Run
Capabilities	Cleansing & Profiling		Historical Data		Data Quality Monitoring
	Data Quality Assessment		Master Data		
	Source Identification		Open Items		
		Data Harmonization			
		Data Standardization			
		Data Transformation			
			Data Validation/Reconciliation		
Tools	SNP CrystalBridge	SNP T-Bone		SNP T-Bone	

Figure 8.3: Capabilities by phase for selective data migration

In the image shown earlier, the tool options available for this are SAP's **Data Management and Landscape Transformation** (**DMLT**) and/or CBS along with Natuvion/Datavard.

In this section, so far, you have understood the different migration scenarios possible when moving to S/4HANA with RISE with SAP, along with possible data migration approaches to be considered. We also mentioned the key points to consider when planning Brownfield migrations, especially around dependency with SAP when migrating an instance to the RISE landscape.

In the next section, we will start by walking through why data migration is important while explaining the why, what, and how parts to be considered.

Looking into the importance of data migration – why, what, and how

In this section, we will understand what it takes to establish a data migration strategy in terms of procedures and guidelines on how to identify, analyze, clean, convert/transfer, schedule, and load master data and transactional data identified as being in scope. The approach will also provide insights into and details of some of the tools and techniques you need to consider for loading data into the SAP S/4HANA system.

But before we talk about what the various stages or points to be considered for having a strong data migration strategy are, let's talk about why having a strong data migration strategy is important. Establishing S/4HANA is foundational to seeing data as a strategic asset, providing a dramatically improved user experience and serving as the raw material for intelligent processes executed through an intelligent workflow. Customers with the S/4HANA digital core in place can extend and reshape the business processes while removing friction along the value chain by adopting hybrid cloud and SaaS offerings such as SAP Ariba, SuccessFactors, SAP C4C e.g., Commerce Cloud. The following are some of the key points on why having a strong data migration approach is important for customers:

- Understanding the value of data to unlock the business case for S/4HANA:

  - Data has become the key to supporting the transformation of any organization along with S/4HANA

  - The growth in data-literate organizations has become influential when it comes to creating an ERP strategy for any customer

  - The types of data also consumed have increased substantially over the period of time

- Ensuring trust in data quality:

  - Data has become the foundation for the shift from transactional processing to intelligent workflows, which requires trust in data

  - Trust in data is all about ensuring the right quality by doing the following:

    - Identifying the right data sources

    - Ensuring data quality is engineered into the migration and continuous (master data) governance processes – quality is not a transient/one-off activity

    - Ensuring the right skills are embedded in the organization to drive continuous quality aligned with value and insight requirements (DataOps)

- Enabling intelligent workflows for translating data into actionable insights:

  - Data is the only raw material and it needs to have the context to translate into insights

Hence, it is important to tackle the critical success factors around the right data being available early in the project to avoid any rework or solution not addressing the known challenges. We suggest having a "data-first" thought process when it comes to the data migration approach for quick availability of data from legacy systems to SAP S/4HANA for use in process design and validation. The following figure provides an overview of the classical approach to typical data migration compared to the "data-first" approach:

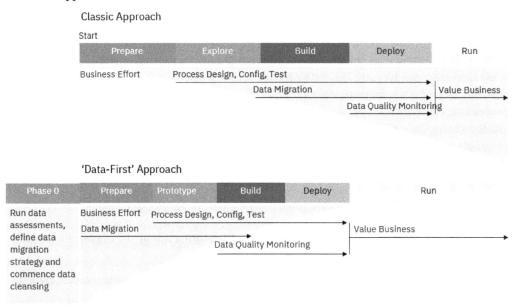

Figure 8.4: Data-first approach compared to classical approach

By using the data-first approach, you will be able to build confidence in the future state of the solution and data. Using cleansed data will also result in better system design and testing activities, ensuring the right value is delivered to the business. We have discussed so far the "why data migration?" part has given the significance of data and its value towards a well-orchestrated transformation plan for the customers. Moving on to what should be considered for putting together a strategy for data migration, it is important to understand the different stages prior to coming up with a comprehensive data migration strategy, such as the following:

- **Data assessment**: At this stage, you would need to identify the existing source systems along with other legacy systems that would support the design to be put into place. As part of this, you would list down the type of business process and the possible selection criteria, if any, to support the target model. Both a top-down and bottom-up analysis would be needed to lay out the business rule mapping along with filters as needed.

The output of this stage would be a comprehensive gap analysis to put together the entity-relationship model. One of the key deliverables of this stage would be a well-defined data dictionary or catalog to include details such as the name, description, source of the table, type, length, data type, validation rules, business rules, foreign key, and primary key.

- **Data quality and data cleansing**: This stage is about validating the correctness, consistency, and completeness of data. Maintaining data quality is an iterative process within your landscape and there are multiple factors impacting this. Some of the symptoms of poor data quality are as follows:

  - Inability to compare data from different source systems

  - Data incorrectly entered into the wrong fields

  - Lack of consistent data definition

  - Inability to consolidate data from different source systems

  - Inability to track data across time

  - Inability to comply with government regulations

  In order to improve upon the data quality within your landscape prior to the migration of data to the target S/4HANA solution, the following should be considered:

  - Quantifying the number and types of data quality-related defects

  - Assessing the nature and cause of the known data quality defects

  - Identifying and isolating data elements in data structures causing the possible quality issues

  - Standardizing and normalizing the data values, units of measure, and formats according to business rules to align toward the "one data model" approach

  - Verifying data values and reconciling where appropriate

  - Enhancing data via appending additional data to records in terms of both attributes to a given data record or creating more volume based on the different entities you might have

  - Matching records and identifying duplicate records (data de-duplication)

  - Consolidating multiple records into one master record where required

- **Extract, transform, load**: The ETL methodology is about different activities performed around the analysis, design, development, and implementation of data migration jobs. The approach typically comprises analyzing the data, extracting and transforming it, validating it, and loading it into targets with testing, and repeating the same process until the migration is successfully completed.

- **Gap analysis**: This stage is to ensure, based on the assessment and the other quality checks performed, you are able to identify the gaps between what is to be achieved versus what is available. This helps in creating the required business rules.

- **Migration testing methodologies**: Multiple people allocated should constantly be made responsible for the iterations of the data migration sprints to ensure there is enough coverage throughout the project life cycle. This also helps with a continuous improvement-based framework to be brought into the engagement model. In doing so, it is also important to ensure the work developed by a developer is tested by another team member. It is equally important to have well-established naming conventions and best practices for this.

- **Data export – SAP testing**: It is important to maintain different systems to allow the usage of enhanced business rules for testing purposes, rather than trying to overwrite the same test data generated during earlier dry runs.

- **Backup procedure**: Always plan for a proper backup at regular intervals to ensure you can retain an earlier-validated version in case any unforeseen data-related issues happen in the system.

- **Documentation and sign-off**: Finally, it is important to have an agreed-upon process for signing off on the data migration criteria and the results at various checkpoints throughout the duration of the project. These details would also be needed from an audit perspective.

So far, we have provided a walk-through of why having the right strategy for data migration is important, along with what needs to be considered to devise the strategy. It is also equally important to understand the big picture around how to handle data migration prior to finalizing the project plan when it comes to the execution of the migration activities. SAP has, over a period of time, added new functions and removed existing functions to keep the project experience consistent and optimized.

The following figure provides an overview of the data migration framework and how you can implement it with different components/options available to handle the data migration:

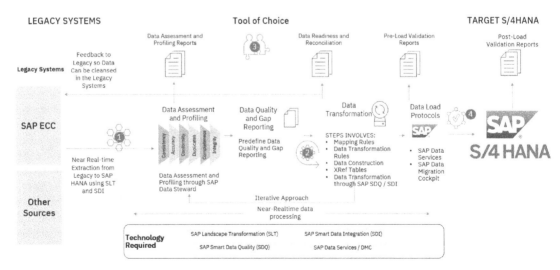

Figure 8.5: How to plan for data migration to S/4HANA

As shown in the preceding figure, starting from left to right, the journey kicks off with the identification of the source systems based on the data assessment to be carried out. Once the data selection and systems are identified, you would need to finalize the tool of choice, with either SAP BODS, SAP **Smart Data Integration** (**SDI**), SAP DI, SAP SLT, SAP **Data Migration Cockpit** (**DMC**) (made available within S/4HANA), or Syniti/SNP to extract the data and apply the business rules to be agreed upon prior to mapping the source data to the target data. Once done, you also need to have a proper data validation and reconciliation process in place to ensure the business has full confidence in the solution and the data being made available. Finally, you can go ahead and use the existing templates to directly upload into S/4HANA.

In addition to the points/stages mentioned earlier about what you need to consider when defining what the data migration strategy will comprise, you would also need to consider the relevant housekeeping activities to reduce the overhead when it comes to actual data migration activities themselves. Archiving historical data is one of those housekeeping activities to effectively manage data volumes.

The following figure provides a summary of different steps you need to consider after data migration to ensure as well as being compliant with any regulatory requirements, you are also reducing the footprint in the target system:

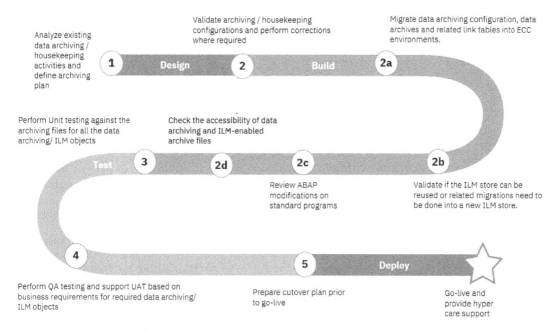

Figure 8.6: Data archiving journey as part of data migration

Along with the archiving approach, you also need to think about "data volume management" to control the creation or consumption of data in the landscape, which can end up causing more overhead when it comes to data migration. Typical data volume management-based activities are either deletion or data tiering-based maintenance. The following are some of the widely recognized client challenges with data that can be addressed with the approach mentioned so far:

- Generate data services that the business needs

- Seek innovation and use data as a basis for new growth

- Great business ideas but poor quality data is a big barrier

- Need to shape the data skills and knowledge

- Understand customers and trends

- Deliver smarter products and services

- Having lots of data but being unclear on how to get value

- The current data strategy is outdated or ineffective

- The data architecture is fragmented and the data platform is unscalable

- Exploit fully new technologies such as AI, **machine learning** (**ML**), and automation

- Focus data efforts where it matters most

- Business and IT transformation efforts are hampered by bad data

So far, we have gone through the details of why data migration is important along with what needs to be considered at different phases/stages to have a well-defined data migration strategy/approach. We also walked you through how you can plan for data migration activities. We then concluded the section by providing an insight into other housekeeping activities, which you also need to plan for, along with the data migration approach to make sure you do not have redundant data that is not adding any value. Some of the examples that we touched upon as part of these housekeeping activities are around data deletion and archival of the data. In the next section, we will go through the key ingredients of successful data migration and how you can adopt them (data governance and quality) in your strategy.

Understanding the importance of data governance and data quality

In this section, we focus on the importance of data governance and data quality. In order for any S/4HANA implementation to be successful, having data of the highest quality is very important. Maintenance of quality needs to be embedded both as part of the data migration as well as in pre- and post-data migration activities to avoid system usage issues. Data quality is defined by how effectively the data supports the transactions and decisions needed to meet an organization's strategic goals and objectives. In order to have a continuous data quality framework set up, you need to consider the following:

- **Data assessment**: Once we understand the data sources that are needed to drive the transformation, we need to profile the source, using the data-first approach mentioned earlier in this chapter to establish what data can be used and its quality to drive this analysis. This includes data re-duplication and assessing the impact on business processes at different layers.

- **Data migration**: Beyond just extracting, cleansing, transforming, and loading by moving data from the source of data into SAP solutions, applying well-defined business rules through a repeatable tool-based approach such as SAP DI or Syniti that complies with data security standards is a must.

- **Master data management including data synchronization**: Adopt a *single version of the truth* principle for master data – the master data is managed centrally and replicated/synchronized to all the required target sources to ensure consistent transactional processing and analytics using tools such as SAP MDG.

- **Continuous data governance and security**: It is important to define the source of data, whether from legacy or other external sources, to validate and define the required strategic rules and discipline to maintain the ongoing quality of data. It is also critical to establish a data quality management ownership model across the enterprise.

Along with the continuous data quality checks and validation, it is also key to have a proper framework in place around compliance toward well-architected data governance. Based on the points mentioned, you need to be able to identify clear data objects and the associated roles, as it is easy to mix up data governance and data management. Data governance establishes the framework, rules, and regulations required to govern data in a legal and lawful manner and to provide the designs for governance, including the relevant operating model components. On the other hand, data management is the monitoring and auditing of the way data is used within the organization to ensure it is aligned with the governance that has been put in place, including analyzing the quality and reviewing the content.

The data governance framework mentioned earlier is a cross-functional discipline allowing organizations to be comprehensive, consistent, and coherent in the way they can define, discuss, analyze, and use the data as information. It is the orchestration of people, processes, and technology that enables an organization to use data as an enterprise asset. The following are some of the key aspects of the framework:

- **Architecture**: It is important to understand how well an organization can design, develop, deploy, and manage data architecture.

- **Business rules management**: This is around how well the organization can define, develop, deploy, and manage the application of business rules across the enterprise.

- **Change management**: This is asking yourself are capabilities in place to adopt required organizational change and drive business value realization?

- **Data quality**: Is the organization able to consistently define and measure data quality and mitigate any data quality issues?

- **Metadata**: How well does the organization capture, manage, and access business, technology, and operational information on key corporate data?

- **Organization and stewardship**: Are there formal organizations and roles for supporting, managing, and improving governance processes and capabilities?

- **Policy**: How well does the organization define and manage organizational behavior using policy?

- **Privacy and security**: These are appropriate considerations in place for the protection of customer privacy and data security.

- **Regulation and compliance**: Is the organization correctly prioritizing activities to address people, process, and technology requirements for regulatory and compliance issues?

The following figure provides an overview of different layers to be considered to fulfill the points mentioned earlier:

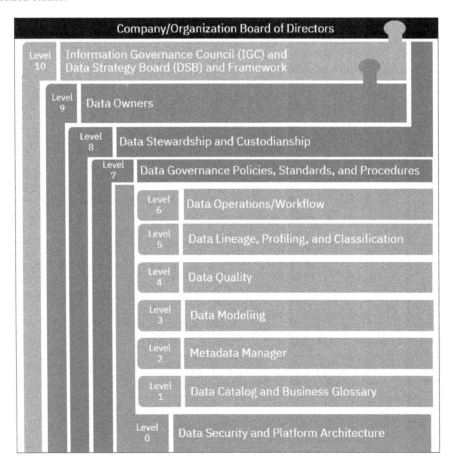

Figure 8.7: Different layers of the data governance framework

Let's review each of the layers mentioned in the previous diagram:

- **Level 0 (Data Security and Platform Architecture)**: Architecturally, this allows a variety of data sources, visualizations, data sinks, and transformational tasks to be performed to meet the business needs in a secure and performant manner. It addresses both at-rest and on-the-wire encryption along with end user authentication and authorization.

- **Level 1 (Data Catalog and Business Glossary)**: This ensures there is common business terminology cross-enterprise with the hierarchy of business information defined across subject areas. Building a business glossary and cross-functional data catalog will enable an organization to create, manage, and share an enterprise vocabulary and classification system.

- **Level 2 (Metadata Manager)**: This holds metadata in a form that can be viewed, searched, and accessed by development tooling.

- **Level 3 (Data Modeling)**: This creates logical and physical data models. Data models are created in ERDs or equivalent. Metadata Manager, in the previous layer, is used by developers to create new data models and drive the reuse of existing or newly created elements.

- **Level 4 (Data Quality)**: This is supported by the maintenance of quality rules to deliver consistent data quality.

- **Level 5 (Data Lineage, Profiling, and Classification)**: This accelerates faster and more accurate answering to regulatory entities or business needs.

- **Level 6 (Data Operations/Workflow)**: This helps you understand the data sources, data operations, and data flows that operate on the data.

- **Level 7 (Data Governance Policies, Standards, and Procedures)**: Having well-defined policies, standards, and procedures within a defined governance framework will ensure that the correct operations are followed when applying data governance.

- **Level 8 (Data Stewardship and Custodianship)**: The concept of governance lies in the day-to-day stewardship of information and data.

- **Level 9 (Data Owners)**: Collaborating across multiple lines of business to build information policies and standards.

- **Level 10 (Information Governance Council (IGC) and Data Strategy Board (DSB) and Framework)**: Information and data need to be governed cohesively and comprehensively, and support day-to-day operations at the same time.

Having a continuous data quality and data governance framework helps you ensure that the data migrated is of the highest value to your organization and avoid any usage-related issues after the initial data migration activities. More often than not, the systems end up with incorrect data after the initial migration due to no consistent methodology being followed on an ongoing basis.

In this section, we have gone through the definition of data quality and data governance in the context of data migration. We have also reviewed different components to be considered when it comes to having a continuous data ops-driven approach within your landscape. We strongly suggest adopting these frameworks into your organization, along with the data migration project and beyond, to ensure the right patterns are used.

In the next section, we will go through some of the common myths or misinformed pointers that customers have about data migration, along with the required checks and approaches to be taken to avoid following these without full knowledge.

Debunking myths around data migration

In this section, we will use the knowledge of the why, what, and how around data migration, along with the best practices mentioned when it comes to the adoption of data quality and data governance in the earlier sections, to help debunk some of the myths in the industry around the data migration approach. The general confusion around data migration always has been around how to decide what level of quality is enough for you to go through the life cycle of the project, as in some cases, the last stage of data migration from quality and governance might only be possible during the integration testing cycle.

Data migration to S/4HANA is also a time-consuming process and error-prone as well, if not planned appropriately from the initial stages of the project. There are different myths and issues that will create more delays in the adoption of the right solution. The following are some of the myths:

All data has to be migrated from the source systems: Many customers typically use the opportunity to move toward S/4HANA as an option to re-imagine process simplicity along with the data associated with that. In this context, all the data from the legacy system is not always needed when it comes to completing data migration.

Data migration is expensive: Depending on the complexity of the landscape and the timeline when new systems are going to be deployed, you can come up with a FinOps-based plan to highlight which system can be decommissioned along with the dependencies, if any. This helps with the overall cost and effort of data migration.

Data migration is a very lengthy process: While the more source systems, the higher the complexity, it is also important to be able to automate the process so that every time a dry run has to be done, you can simply do a proactive assessment along with any potential creation of both master and transactional data.

Let's also have a look at the different issues that occur while executing the data migration approach in the following table:

Sr. No.	Issue	Description	Check
1	Missing data	Data is not available/missing.	Verify respective tables and their fields in the target system are as per the source system.
2	Truncation of data	Data being lost by truncation of the data field.	Verify the field lengths of the source and target tables and ensure that data is neither garbled nor truncated.
3	Data type mismatch	Data types are not set up correctly on the target database.	Verify data type and format in the target system are as per the source system
4	Null translation	Null source values are not being transformed to correct target values.	Verify the translation logic for null values and ensure that null values are either not populated or get converted into correct values.
5	Wrong translation	The opposite of the null translation error. The field should be null but populated with a non-null value or the field should be populated but populated with the wrong value.	Verify the translation logic for values that need to be translated as null.
6	Misplaced data	Source data fields are not being transformed to the correct target data field.	Verify the data is populated correctly from the source to the target system as per the field mapping and mapping rules.
7	Sequence generator	Incorrect sequence number.	Verify the correctness of sequence generator logic/code.
8	Not enough records	Records are included/missing in the report.	Verify the correctness of the filter.
9	Duplicate records	Duplicate records are two or more records that contain the same data.	Verify the correctness of the filter and ensure that there is no duplicity of data in the target system.
10	Extra records	Extra records are included in the report.	Verify the correctness of the filter.
11	Numeric field precision	Numbers that are not formatted to the correct decimal point or not rounded per specifications.	Verify that the precision of data in the respective numeric field is accurate.
12	Rejected rows	Data rows that get rejected due to data issues.	Verify data conditions that might be braked the ETL for a particular row.

Table 8.1: Common issues related to data migration and possible checks to be performed

It is advised to review each of the myths and the issues mentioned earlier to avoid causing rework within your landscape. In this section so far, we reviewed some of the known myths around the data migration approach, along with the issues to be considered. In the next section, we will walk you through the role of data migration-related activities in each of the phases of the SAP Activate methodology.

Looking into the SAP Activate methodology and the adoption patterns related to data migration

In this section, we will go through different phases of the SAP Activate methodology and the relevance of data migration embedded within each phase. The following figure provides a high-level overview of the different phases to be considered:

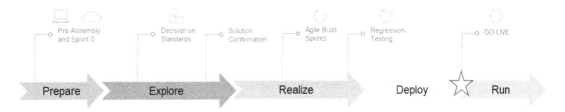

Figure 8.8: Phases within SAP Activate

Let's now go through each of the phases and the relevance of data migration and tasks to be planned within that phase. The **Prepare** phase sets the stage for the full life cycle of data migration. You need to work with your data governance and stewardship resources to understand your current data and the work required to prepare the data required for migration and to be used in the new solution being implemented. You will need to select the required data objects and adjust them accordingly based on the new design upon validation (for example, to add additional fields for the master data, which might need conversion prior to loading into S/4HANA). The data objects define the scope of the data that must be prepared as part of data migration. You need to then align your source data to these data objects, to provide the data that S/4HANA requires for a successful migration. These data objects help to enforce the validation and mapping of the data and the relationships between data.

In this phase, you will also need to assess the current environment, including the technology (applications and databases, spreadsheets, flat files, and web services), data volumes, data ownership, and data security used to support your existing environment. The prerequisite for this activity is that you have identified the data already required to be converted based on the data objects approach mentioned earlier. Ideally, you would need to define a staging area (temporary buffer place) to store the cleansed data in the intermediate stage between the legacy and target S/4HANA systems.

In the **Explore** phase, the identified data sources are extracted using different options, such as SAP DI, SAP BODS, SAP SDI, SAP DMC, or other third-party ETL tools available on the market. There are even some solutions available that have predefined solutions with products such as SNP, Syniti, and Enterprise Hub, which you can use out of the box to expedite the data migration process. More details about some of these options are available in a later section of this chapter. You need to use one of the tools as appropriate to complete the profiling of the data, after which you will be able to identify the data domains from the various input sources, holistically discovering which value in those cross-system domains is the most prevalent and enabling your resources to begin a cleansing activity within the staging environment.

Once the migration objects are associated with a migration project, file templates are provided for each migration object based on the templates published by SAP as part of S/4HANA DMC. You can then use these to populate them with the data from a legacy system(s) to be converted. Whether the data is static files (master data), dynamic open data/files (transaction data), or historical data (which can be limited), it will be mapped into these file templates provided for easy consumption in the staging area.

In the **Realize** phase, you will need to plan to perform a series of trial loads to ensure your solution is validated from end to end prior to final **user acceptance testing** (**UAT**) being carried out. One of the ways to validate data for each of the trial loads to be performed would be to have a reconciliation process in place that can compare the data before and after to make sure it is consistent. The data migration through S/4HANA DMC also compares the configuration of the targeted S/4HANA system against the input file to confirm that the data being loaded is always consistent with the "current" SAP environment.

The **Deploy** phase includes UAT. The data used to support this test is delivered via the same data migration approach utilized throughout the **Realize** phase with multiple trial runs. In addition to gaining user acceptance of the solution, UAT is the final assessment of the data's readiness for production.

In the **Run** phase, data is loaded into the production systems and your business validation team will validate all of the data in scope for cutover by reviewing the reconciliation reports created during the **Realize** phase of the project and confirming the validity of the load. This reconciliation procedure is typically documented by the business validation team in a predefined validation plan that is then used to quality assure the loads once completed.

In addition to the type of activities you need to perform from a data migration point of view across each of the phases within SAP Activate, as mentioned earlier, it is important to consider the support and inputs needed from many sources. The complexity of the data migration process and its fundamental contribution to the overall S/4HANA program requires clear ownership and accountability across all data migration activities. Therefore, each data migration activity will need to be assigned to a role within the data migration roles and responsibilities RACI to clearly define the roles and responsibilities involved in the data migration process. Before we go into the details of the activities along with the assigned stakeholder assignment, let us understand the benefits of this matrix:

- Clarity of ownership and accountability across all data migration activities. An individual may believe their responsibilities are obvious, but others may have made incorrect assumptions about what their role involves.

- Communication across your team and the business is enhanced.

- Delivery expectations are clear, and milestones can be planned and tracked.

The following table provides an overview of the different data migration roles and responsibilities:

Activity	Data Migration Core Team	IT	Business
Define data migration strategy	R		
Define data migration toolset	R	C	
Define data team structure and roles and responsibilities	R	C	
Define data team resource requirements	R, C	I	
Define the SAP data requirements (functional/technical)	R	C	C
Manage the definition of data standards	I	R	C
Define data standards	I	R	C
Define global coding	R	A	C
Identify the legacy data (functional and technical)	I	R	C
Legacy data discovery	I	R	C
Legacy data profiling	I	R	C
Identify data cleansing requirements	R	C	I
Physically cleanse legacy data	I	A	R
Legacy data cleansing – definition of business rules	C	R	I
Legacy data cleansing – implementation of business rules	C	A	I
Data cleansing status reporting	I	R	I
Managing data cleansing	C	A	R

Activity	Data Migration Core Team	IT	Business
Data mapping and transformation (source to target)	R	A	C
Manage the resolution of missing data	R	A	C
Identify missing data	A	I	C
Resolve missing data	I	A	R
Design legacy data extracts	C	R	C
Build legacy data extracts	R, C	C	C
Execute legacy data extracts	R	A	I
Design data transformations	R	A	IC
Build data transformations	R	C	I
Execute data transformations	R	C	II
Design automated data loads into SAP/target systems	R	C	I
Build automated data loads into SAP/target systems	R	C	
Execute automated data loads into SAP/target systems	R	I	
Design/document validation processes (business and technical)	R	C	I
Develop validation processes	R	C	I
Manual data entry	C	R	I
Trial data upload – execution	R, A	I	I
Trial data upload – validation and reconciliation – technical	R, A	I	
Trial data upload – validation and reconciliation – business	A	C	R
Dry run – planning	R	C	
Dry run – execution	R, A	C	
Dry run – validation and reconciliation – technical	R, A	I	
Dry run – validation and reconciliation – business	I	A	R
Data validation execution – technical	R, A	I	
Data validation execution – business	I	A	R

Activity	Data Migration Core Team	IT	Business
Data validation error exception reporting	R, A	C	I
Execution plan for final uploads	R	C	
Dual data maintenance (pre-cutover)	I	A	R
Data cutover planning	R, C	C	I
Data cutover management and execution	R, A	C	I
Cutover data validation execution – technical	R, A	I	
Cutover data validation execution – business	I	A	R
Cutover data sign-off	I	A	R

Table 8.2: Different activities within data migration and split of responsible teams (RACI)

Based on the previous table, the actual roles and responsibilities of your organization might differ. So, it is important to sit down with the process stakeholders and IT, along with the core team, to validate the role assignments, before kicking off the data migration approach. In this section so far, we have gone through the details of the data migration activities that you need to be aware of, along with the RACI split of the activities to be performed by different teams.

In the next section, we will focus on the different tools/options available to perform the activities covered so far.

Looking into the different options available for data migration

In this section, we will mainly be focusing on the use of different tools available to support data migration activities. This will help you streamline and automate the process compared to the traditional way of migrating data, which is mostly a manual approach. However, if not used in the right way, it can cause a lot of overhead for the migration team as part of the move to S/4HANA from RISE with SAP. The following are some of the key parameters to consider when deciding on the tool usage:

- **Direct table loads**: These tools upload data directly into tables. Customers are usually extra careful about this approach of loading data at the database level. This can be mitigated by demonstrating a few tests and proofs of concept.

- **Validation needs to be built out of SAP**: The inbuilt checks and validations that SAP has do not happen by these tools during the loading (these checks and validations happen when traditional loading methods such as LSMWs and bespoke development using recordings are used).

- **Load > clear > reload**: Flexibility of undoing the data loads and reloading the same data is possible with quick turnover times. This feature enables us to quickly fix and retest the loading processes if any data-related issues are encountered (for example, during testing).

- **Data mapping**: The tools work seamlessly depending on the quality of the mappings. Data mapping is critical to the success of the data loads and considerable time needs to be spent on this critical task. The effort involved in this is usually underestimated.

The following figure provides an overview of different tools that can be used to address the data migration approach:

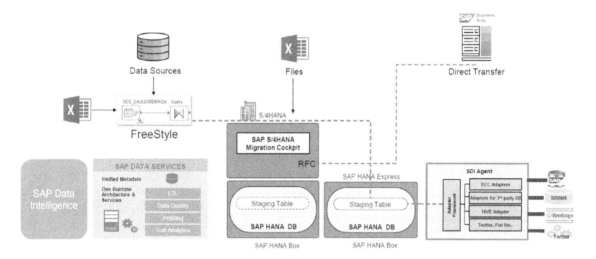

Figure 8.9: Different tools and how they can be used for data migration

Let's go through the different options/tools available followed by a comparison with the earlier-mentioned parameters:

- **SNP**: SNP as a third-party vendor offers a set of tools including CrystalBridge and T-Bone that provides built-in SAP data model content and complete transactional history for migrations, across multiple scenarios – all in one project. This enables near-zero downtime at cutover. These tools enable both ETL and process harmonization solutions for complex S/4HANA migrations, even with multiple SAP source systems.

- **Syniti**: **Syniti Knowledge Platform** (**SKP**) is a single tool that will be used for the analysis of source systems and the orchestration of data profiling, quality review, data cleansing, data extraction, data transformation, and cutover. The platform helps you solve complex data transformation challenges by bringing together industry knowledge driven by data along with the packaged solution and associated accelerators. The platform has built-in automation and workflow guidance driven by AI and ML to support data migration, data quality, and reporting on data migration handled. The platform also supports both the metadata and master data components involved in data migration-related activities, along with the data governance setup around the scope as required. A few of the key features available are as follows:

- A business user interface for de-duplication and construction of data
- Project-related data migration activities can be orchestrated across multiple business/project stakeholders via the tool
- Simulation and automation of data cleansing and data migration to S/4HANA
- All data and functional/technical documentation in one place – not across multiple documents (emails, Word documents, Excel spreadsheets, SharePoint locations, and so on)
- A post-project data quality capability that will use business rules implemented to keep S/4HANA clean

- **SAP Data Services**: SAP Data Services is a trademark ETL tool made available for connecting with both SAP and non-SAP systems. You have options to create custom workflows as needed by the business while being able to perform complex lookups or logic as needed. The tool has the potential to consume data from different sources and to either replace, merge, or create new fields where necessary. You can then write the data back to either the same system or the target system.

- **SAP HANA SDI/DI**: These provide tools to access source data and provision, replicate, and transform data in SAP S/4HANA. You can use them to load data in both batch or real time from different sources using pre-built and custom adapters.

- **SAP S/4HANA DMC**: SAP, as of S/4HANA, has provided the DMC tool option in order to streamline the direct data upload process for customers who might not have heavy transformation and would like to carry out a direct data upload. This cockpit can also be used by customers with complex transformations by using the modeler option prior to uploading the data into the cockpit tool.

   SAP S/4HANA DMC is used extensively by customers due to the following reasons:

   - It is the tool of choice because of the plug-and-play option
   - It has pre-configured migration content specific to SAP S/4HANA
   - It is integrated into the SAP Activate methodology
   - Easy and safe migration with defined step-by-step guidance through the migration process
   - It is flexible and extendable with migration object modeler functionality to handle customer-specific custom requirements

Based on the different tools listed, it is important to have a clear understanding of which tool is the right choice based on your requirements around S/4HANA data migration. The following figure provides the strengths and weaknesses of these tools against different parameters:

Use Cases / Capability Drivers	SAP SDI	SAP BODS	SAP DMC	SAP DI	SYNITI	SNP
SAP ERP (Source) – SOH | S/4 HANA (Target)	◕	●	◕	●	●	●
SAP ERP (Source) – SAP ERP (Target)	◕	●	◕	●	●	●
Non-SAP (Source) – SOH | S/4 HANA (Target)	◕	◑	◕	◑	●	○
Non-SAP (Source) – SAP ERP (Target)	◕	◑	◕	◑	●	○
Landscape Consolidation | M&AD | BU Restructure	○	◕	○	◕	◕	●
Complex Transformations	◕	●	◑	●	●	●
Scalability (High Volume)	◕	●	◕	●	●	●
Downtime Optimization	◕	◕	◕	◕	◕	●
Data Reconciliation Capability and Dashboard	◕	◑	◑	●	●	◕
Data Quality Assessment Capability	◕	◑	◕	◕	●	◕
Historical Data Migration (to SAP Target)	◕	◕	◕	◕	◕	●
Pre-Built Content	◕	◕	◕	◕	●	◕
ML/AI Features	◕	◕	○	◕	◕	◕
Cost of Implementation (Training, Licensing)	◑	◕	◕	◕	◑	◑

Figure 8.10: High-level comparison across tools for different features required for data migration

In this section, we reviewed the different options/tools available for consideration by the data migration team. We also went through the comparison of which tool has better coverage across different dimensions in order for you to plan the effort accordingly based on which tools you might already have in your landscape versus the final objective you would like to achieve.

Summary

To conclude, in this chapter, we started by describing the points to be considered based on the type of move being chosen around Greenfield versus Brownfield versus Bluefield migration to SAP S/4HANA on RISE with SAP. We then walked you through the why, what, and how of the data migration strategy/approach, along with debunking some industry myths and issues that customers face more often than not. With the why, what, and how defined, we also described the importance of data quality and governance in the end-to-end life cycle of loading data relevant to S/4HANA. We then went through how the activities mentioned earlier would align with the SAP Activate methodology and the associated RACI to be followed.

We finally reviewed the different options available in order to perform the data migration activity, along with the comparison across different tools available for performing the migration.

In the next chapter, we will deep dive into how you can handle the different levers around component business modeling, business process intelligence, predefined industry solutions, and other best practices for providing end-to-end implementation of S/4HANA. We will describe what the experience of doing an initial pilot rollout of S/4HANA is like versus when you do a big-bang rollout for all possible regions and users involved.

Further reading

The following are some additional links that you can go through to understand the ways of working and different deployment models when it comes to using SAP S/4HANA DMC:

- `https://blogs.sap.com/2021/03/10/part-1-migrate-your-data-migration-cockpit-from-sap-s-4hana-2020-sap-s-4hana-cloud-2008-migrate-data-using-staging-tables-and-methods-for-populating-the-staging-tables-with-data/`

- `https://blogs.sap.com/2019/11/29/sap-s-4hana-migration-cockpit-using-sap-data-services-to-load-data-to-the-staging-tables/`

- `https://blogs.sap.com/2019/12/02/part-3-sap-s-4hana-migration-cockpit-using-sap-hana-smart-data-integration-sdi-to-load-data-to-the-staging-tables/`

- `https://blogs.sap.com/2019/12/02/sap-s-4hana-migration-cockpit-using-sap-hana-studio-to-load-data-to-the-staging-tables/`

You can also read more about the deployment options in OSS note 2733253.

Part 3:
The Way Forward:
The Art of Possible

In this part, we will look at how the world you know today will be transformed through the enhanced ways of working made possible with RISE with SAP-based solutions and the ecosystem built around RISE with SAP. You will also get an overview of how pilots and future rollouts will bring in a flavor of innovation while ensuring that best practices are adhered to. You will then also be able to understand what the Art of Possible is, from an IT and business point of view, while perfectly aligning with your business outcomes.

This part has the following chapters:

9
The Pilot: High Stakes

In the previous chapter, we discussed the importance of clean data and the methods, tools, and critical activities performed to migrate data from your old systems to your target S/4HANA deployment. In this chapter, we will bring the practices and approaches explained in all the previous chapters together and understand how some of the accelerators help **Accelerate your Transition** – as in, how they can help you shift your implementation and migration timelines left using the ready-to-use content from SAP and its partners. We will also cover some key aspects of **UX strategy**, which will keep you true to your business outcomes and influence user adoption. Lastly, we will run through the crucial **change management** considerations to ensure the successful outcome of your S/4HANA transformation and how iterative release management with hybrid and cloud deployments supports your move to the digital core in a controlled fashion, exploring **continuous integration/continuous deployment (CI/CD)** mechanisms in the hybrid landscape. Toward the end, we will provide an example **pilot rollout** for a hypothetical company, which brings together all the knowledge you will have gained, applies it to different phases of a project, and helps your teams move cloud-native extensions with CI/CD.

Continuing with Spark4Llife as an organization which is on its transformation journey and is undergoing a transition from their old legacy ECC to S/4 HANA, its program teams have to consider several aspects during the execution phase which they uncovered in the discovery stages. They have learned about optimal way to get their data across to the new environment and have a clear architecture to implement it, and roadmap to execute on the process improvements with innovation. They still need to ponder how to shift-left their execution timelines, while being cognizant of how they will pilot and go-live in the regions planned for roll outs. Spark4Life will be considering these topics which have been discussed in the following sections:

- Accelerating your transition
- Iterative data loads
- UX strategy
- Change management
- Getting ready for the pilot

To reiterate, transformation is not a destination but a journey that allows you to adjust and adapt to the next steps as you discover new business challenges as your organization moves along. Many customers consider a phased approach to starting their journey and adopting S/4HANA and the innovations it brings along with it in digestible chunks. Quite often, the starting point for many organizations starting their RISE with SAP journey is an SAP ERP on-premises system. During the Discover phase (or even well before the Discover phase), the business goals and visions are understood by the transformation teams, as well as the capabilities required to achieve these goals and visions. The underlying processes that need to be adopted or transformed for the **Target Operating Model** (**TOM**) are uncovered with a series of Design and Discover workshops, which help you prepare for the new subscription economy in the hybrid cloud landscape.

Early involvement encourages buy-in on the part of the key business stakeholders, process owners, IT teams, and the operational support structures to create flexible business processes with embedded intelligence, downsize and rationalize IT infrastructure, and support and improve adoption while in the transformation phase. Whether you are starting with a highly customized SAP ERP on-premises or a legacy non-SAP ERP system and whether you opt for a brownfield or greenfield migration or a selective transition, the way you plan and execute the move to SAP S/4HANA and organizational change management is quite crucial for the outcome. Some pivotal choices are essential at the early stages, such as the one between the choice of a public cloud, private cloud, or on-prem S/4HANA deployment, and this is influenced by the point of departure or your current state of the ERP landscape.

For the public cloud, the points to ponder upon are as follows:

- Whether your organization has the readiness, the ability, and, critically, the mindset to embrace a complete paradigm shift with the transformation to move to cloud-based ERP with regular updates and innovations following standardized industry best practices

- Whether your current ERP systems and landscape have low complexity or customization

- Whether your organization has good governance for adopting fit-to-standard processes in the current ECC environment or is heavily customized and wants to simplify and start fresh with new business processes, leaving behind the old baggage of code and configuration

- It also could be a good choice if part of the organization or **line of business** (**LoB**) wants to adopt standard processes on the cloud and enter new markets with quick time-to-market, in which context the greenfield approach shows great promise

From a private cloud perspective, some key considerations would be as follows:

- Whether your organization is ready to start small, iterate frequently, and learn fast with an evolutionary journey to transformation, which is the case with large enterprises with a bigger SAP footprint.

- Whether you want to migrate from a highly complex and fragmented landscape and customized ERP to bring along your old processes while adopting the simplification and standardization that SAP S/4HANA offers for new processes – the best of both worlds. You have to be cognizant about the balance of what you want to carry over – for example, some of the old IP and code assets onto the new technology stacks, with modernization making the most of the existing data.

- Further, using that as the baseline, a private cloud is a good option if you want to customize per the business needs on the cloud while adopting what SAP innovation offers.

With on-premises, bear in mind the following:

- You can have complete control of your infrastructure and what you can bring along – for example, you can bring in all your code and data.

- Likewise, all the processes that have worked for you in the past can move onto the new technology framework and the code line offered by S/4HANA.

- Consider the balance you want to achieve to retain what is required from the old, improve in terms of what you can newly adopt, and move ahead fast. Remember, the best experiences happen when you travel light and are flexible to change to adopt the best that S/4HANA has to offer.

There is no right or wrong answer; it comes down to the direction of travel (what your North Star is), your point of departure, and how nimble you want to be when navigating the waters. You decide how much standard and custom code you want, impacting which part of the S/4HANA deployment you land in. The considerations outlined here will help you start conversations within your leadership and as you discover more, you can decide the best strategy for your transformation.

Likewise, the time-to-market is influenced by crucial technical steps and the scope of your transition; the other half of the equation is the readiness to change within your organization, so its agility in terms of people, process, and technology, and also the ability to manage these changes – these are the dominating factors that influence your choice of solution. Sometimes, the latter supersedes potential gains in terms of your technological capability, as there is an interplay between aspects of technical operation, such as the upgrade frequency your teams can handle. Consider that a cloud upgrade runs with significantly less support than in a classical on-premises setting, for example; the availability of extension mechanisms with SAP S/4HANA and SAP BTP for customization and code extensibility, if that's what your transition intends to exploit; the adaptability of best practice standardization; and whether the IT and development teams have the DevOps and cloud maturity, time, effort, and budget available during and post-transition.

Once you have ascertained the path and the speed of your transformation, many accelerator tools and methods can get you started and cover the ground quickly and efficiently following best practices. The next sections will discuss these in detail and indicate what to watch for when using them.

Accelerating your transition

In *Chapter 4*, you will have come across the one-time free SAP Process Discovery report (www.sap. com/process-discovery) offered by SAP to compare where you stand among your industry competitors regarding your process KPIs. Process Discovery is a PDF report based on the data collected from your productive environments (SAP ERP) that can get you started on the **Business**

Process Intelligence (**BPI**) journey or your S/4HANA journey (`https://demo.spotlight.cloud.sap/`). With Process Insights, you get a detailed report with process analytics based on a one-time snapshot of the actual live data from your production systems, covered by the RISE with SAP offering. This provides deep insights into process flows with PPIs and process variants, deviations from standards, best practices, and innovation recommendations.

These early insights can indicate your choice of S/4HANA deployment, either cloud or on-premises. Which S/HANA Cloud flavor is the right for you? Public or private cloud? And suppose you have already converted your system to S/4HANA (or are still on SAP ERP) – you can run SAP Innovation and Optimization Pathfinder on Spotlight, which provides details and additional content for S/4HANA to help identify opportunities for the innovation of your core system, business process improvements, and IT optimization.

The SAP **Value Lifecycle Manager** (**VLM**) is another accelerator that helps you discover, track, and realize the business value throughout your transformation. To jumpstart your move toward being an Intelligent Enterprise, you can start by creating a business case – it helps with benchmarking surveys and understanding your TCO and provides insights into your processes with KPIs. It's available at `https://valuemanagement.sap.com`. A few other value accelerators that can be leveraged in the early stages of the transition, such as the S/4HANA Business Value Advisor, are at your disposal, which provides an early view of the value that you can realize by moving to S/4HANA Cloud. Or you can also request an S/4HANA appliance trial system to prepare your teams to use SAP Fiori with some demo data to experiment with preconfigured processes. This also allows you to work with your business teams to establish a suitable configuration based on the SAP standard content and defines what to expect from the new digital core. All the tools and reports we discussed can help you decide on the value case for your Intelligent Enterprise vision and your choice of deployment and understand the possibilities. Once you have decided on your deployment approach, there are a few more accelerators that you can leverage, as briefly covered next.

S/4HANA public cloud/new implementations (greenfield)

This transition involves deploying a new instance of SAP S/4HANA by moving either from a non-SAP legacy system or an old SAP solution. The aim is to maximize innovation, adopt industry best practice business processes, and adopt new cloud solutions. You only want to keep the essential master data and transactional data from the existing solution.

The project teams can leverage the SAP standard processes wherever possible and deploy the solution incrementally with quick releases and sprints. You can perform a fit/gap analysis based on recommended best practices from the **Enterprise Management Layer** (**EML**) for SAP S/HANA or use the SAP best practices as preconfigured solutions with predefined **end-to-end** (**E2E**) business processes across all application areas using Fiori UX. This helps accelerate and simplify the adoption of SAP S/4HANA for a faster time-to-value. You can also use SAP Activate Methodology for RISE with SAP to get acceleration contents and recommendations available across different phases of SAP Activate Methodology with the SAP Activate Roadmap Viewer (`https://go.support.sap.com/roadmapviewer/#`).

The implementation teams can use different parts of the roadmap viewer for project management, technical architecture, and integration recommendations. Testing and operations and support best practices are also included. It provides content that will help you plan Discovery Workshops. Once the system has been installed, you need to utilize initial data that will be loaded into your new SAP S/HANA system using standard migration tools.

A new implementation approach is supported for all SAP S/HANA Cloud deployments. RISE with SAP offer several packages for industries and LoBs. With the most recent innovations and standardization, achieving the highest possible automation of business processes and UX based on Fiori design guidelines is made possible. Analytics for new data types and a new depth of insights can be generated. However, the deployment and adoption of S/4HANA on the cloud require a cloud mindset for embracing fundamental principles such as the following:

- Adhering to the fit-to-standard approach and Agile deployment using SAP Activate Methodology

- Using the preconfigured solutions to accelerate your implementation of processes

- Relying on modern integration technologies using the integration suite from SAP BTP and SAP API Business Hub for an API-led integration approach once complete

- Using extensibility mechanisms based on S/4HANA Cloud Extensibility and embracing Side-by-Side extensions on SAP BTP

- Crucially, keeping track of deviation from standard processes or extensions so that you can update them and adopt standard processes to replace them in the future, tracked and recorded using the **SAP Cloud Application and Lifecycle Management (SAP CALM)** tool

System conversions (brownfield)

Suppose you're leaning more toward keeping much of your existing ERP while moving to SAP S/4HANA. In that case, the SAP Readiness Check tool will provide you with all the information you need to decide on a proper transition roadmap by the end of the Discover phase. For system conversions, you will focus on the results of the readiness check, the technical preparation steps, and, crucially, several mock conversions during the transition phase.

Next, with a system conversion, you physically convert your existing ERP system into an SAP S/HANA system, also called **in-place system conversion**. The system conversion approach is a one-step procedure with a single period of downtime that comprises database migration to SAP HANA, a conversion of the data from the ERP data model to the new SAP S/HANA data model, and a software upgrade, which replaces the previous ERP application code with the latest S/HANA application code. A system conversion will scope your entire system, including your transactional and master data, configuration, and custom code, and bring it over to SAP S/4HANA. System conversions directly into the cloud are supported for SAP S/HANA Cloud, private edition:

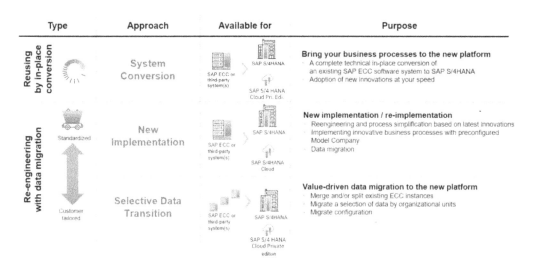

Figure 9.1: S/4HANA deployment options from your state of departure

For an SAP ECC to SAP S/4HANA system conversion, an SAP S/4HANA upgrade starts with a readiness check, maintenance planner, simplification item check, custom code migration, and use of the **database migration option** (**DMO**) of the **Software Update Manager** (**SUM**) tool for the conversion of each of the source databases – SAP HANA, IBM DB6, Oracle, and Microsoft SQL Server. We will briefly examine the usage of two essential tools, SAP Readiness Check and Custom Code Migration, which are recommended before or during the conversion. The following section provides a brief overview of the usage of these accelerators.

The Readiness Check tool

SAP provides Readiness Check, a self-service tool for evaluating the readiness of your existing system to be converted into the S/4HANA target release. It provides details on Simplification Items, recommended SAP Fiori apps, integration, custom code analyzers, SAP innovation business solutions, and add-on compatibility. The conversion can be carried out as a technical upgrade or functional upgrade.

Technical upgrades

Technical upgrades follow a critical path of the minimum required technical changes to skip through valuable upgrades to your business processes. Continuous improvement projects, which are functional upgrades, include a technical upgrade with added scope to take advantage of the latest business functionality immediately. SAP Readiness Check for an SAP S/HANA upgrade covers both areas.

When looking at a technical upgrade, you can focus on the analysis of the following checks for mandatory changes:

- **Simplification Items**: This selection reflects the relevant simplifications that can be brought in by comparing your source and target release. This check is mainly based on data table contents and user transactions. These are ranked based on SAP effort estimates for corresponding Simplification Items. Items can be filtered as mandatory and optional activities, including custom code analysis.

- **Add-on compatibility checks**: Any incompatibility of the add-ons installed in the source system will be shown to standard SAP S/HANA add-ons delivered as part of the SAP S/HANA release.

- **Technical integration**: Checks on BW extractors and blocked IDoc interfaces in the source or analyzed system are flagged.

Functional upgrades

The following checks are performed to provide some hints about which new business functionalities offer the greatest benefits to your business:

- Recommendations on relevant SAP Fiori apps account for the business process and transactions analyzed source system and the S/4HANA target version

- SAP Fiori lighthouse apps offer an immediate business benefit in terms of simplification and efficiency and increase the efficiency of tasks and processes for the user role specifically compared with classical **user interface** (**UI**) technologies

- Quick wins for the business's innovation potential are shown in business case story cards based on quantitative characteristics derived from the performance of your business processes in your analyzed source system

The Custom Code Migration app

The technical migration of the old code to the new code line on S/4HANA is a huge ask for S/4HANA projects. Customers typically use the unlimited extension capabilities of the ABAP Workbench, resulting in years of investment in their custom code. Since there are changes within the SAP S/HANA simplification and data models, some of the custom code from the SAP ERP system might need to be adopted within S/4HANA. The SAP Custom Code Migration Fiori app offers analytical capabilities that can help you understand the impact of your custom code and structure your work accordingly. The Custom Code Migration app is available in SAP BTP, ABAP Environment in case your project teams do not have access to the S/4HANA sandbox. This option allows you to perform SAP S/HANA custom code analyses for your on-premises ERP system remotely from the cloud.

This tool suggests the adoption of the custom code with a two-pronged approach:

- First, the compatibility of your existing custom code with your new target system is assessed for all the custom code objects in your source systems

- Secondly, an early assessment of how much of your code would be better to run decoupled on BTP rather than inside the core ERP solution is undertaken

Before your custom code remediation starts, the first step is to get an inventory of your custom code and transparency into what your custom code accomplishes. This involves getting data for the custom code used within your production environment using transactions such as SCMON and SUSG. The transaction SCMON monitors the usage of your custom code via the ABAP Call Monitor, and SUSG is used to aggregate the usage data in your existing system. Once you've identified your custom code usage, you can remove any custom code that is no longer relevant based on the data collected by the Customs Code Migration app, which helps remove unused custom code upon system conversion. To do this, it can load the code execution statistics directly from the ERP system and delete the custom code that has not been executed in the monitored period during conversion.

To ensure you have the correct usage analytics, run it long enough that it also recognizes the quarterly peak usage. Then, analyze the impact and create a plan. Finally, you need to perform the required custom code remediations. The final step to completing the custom code remediation is to make sure that your custom code performs at an optimal level using the SQL Monitor tool to fine-tune the performance of critical database queries. Optimize your code to ensure that it meets your own performance SLAs.

Selective Data Transition

If you want a more iterative transformation, then Selective Data Transition allows you to migrate by selected organizational units and datasets, bring your old configuration, and combine it with net new processes that never existed before. This allows you to bring in your unique assets from the old systems and add the best innovations and industry-standard processes. However, this is a more involved data and config migration, and requires more advanced data migration techniques, which were discussed in depth in *Chapter 8*, *Exodus*, and are also briefly discussed in the following sections. It is suggested to take this path if you need more control over the transition to support business scenarios such as the following:

- You want to phase your rollout across different countries, you want to go live per business/org unit, or you have a merger or acquisition in process

- You want to be selective to bring in application areas such as plant maintenance or logistics while adopting the best of what S/4HANA can offer for procurement or finance

- You want to spread the risk of pushing a big bang across several markets and improve the acceptance of change amongst different business units, employees, customers, partners, and suppliers

- You see the opportunity to rationalize the landscape, consolidate systems, or time-slice your data from the source to push the right amount required for operations and processes and archive the rest to keep your systems lean

Selective Data Transition can help move you from on-premises ERP to SAP S/4HANA on-premises or SAP S/4HANA Cloud, private edition:

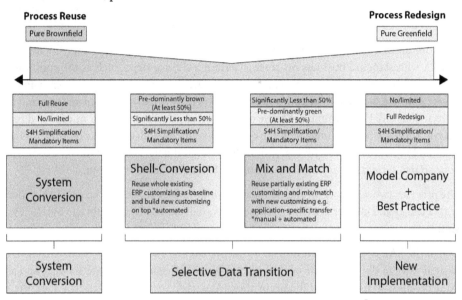

Figure 9.2: Spectrum of standardization for customization across S/4HANA deployments

There are two key flavors when it comes to Selective Data Transition:

- **Empty Shell Conversion**: In Empty Shell Conversion, a shell copy of a production system is taken, containing the configuration and processes without master and transaction data; this is converted into SAP S/4HANA first. If you choose to, you can customize the old processes and the ABAP code; this becomes the baseline. These are then harmonized with S/4HANA, and any required code is remediated to work with the S/4HANA code line.

- **Mix and Match**: With Mix and Match, you can adopt new processes; processes can be redesigned, harmonized, or eliminated in an empty S/4HANA shell and the customization of old processes can be pulled in as required to retain old processes.

The ABAP code repository is transported or manually transferred. Both scenarios require data migration for the adoption of processes, including the master and transaction data, and at the tail end of the migration, account balances and items open during the cutover. The Selective Data Transition approach allows enterprises to target the value and synergies of a consolidated project and leverage the investment that's already been made in existing systems.

Here are the key recommendations for your S/4HANA transitions:

- Make your SAP ECC systems lean before the transition! The best way to start this exercise is to reduce the custom code footprint in your SAP ECC systems – check the usage of custom **reports, interfaces, conversion, enhancements, and forms (RICEF)** based on the usage analysis explained previously. Only the value-adding code used in your production systems should be considered for remediation, if at all. This will also save time during the transition and map it close to the standard apps and reports available in the target S/4HANA version.

- Get your data clean before transition! The quality of master data is critical for the move to S/HANA with standard business processes. Certain technical steps, such as the conversion of customers and vendors into business partners as an SAP concept, may delay the conversion. Poor source system master and transaction data, inconsistencies across connected systems, and failed transactions still lying around are some of the most common reasons for unexpected project delays. They also have an impact on the quality of your embedded analytic reports. Moreover, start looking at the data archiving options for historical data to reduce the data footprint in your source system before you embark on your S/4HANA transformation.

- The previous two steps will set you up for future innovations and start your S/4HANA journey with a leaner and cleaner system and thereby also prepare you for the move to S/4HANA and shift the project timelines left from the Discover and Prepare phases.

- Use of the SAP S/4HANA sandbox or a trial system and having access to an SAP S/HANA system early in the project are critical success factors. This will help with scoping and allow your business to understand the innovations and gain first-hand experience with the new UI – SAP Fiori

- Go through a few rounds of mock conversions with your project teams. This means you make a complete conversion with all the required steps and changes in the sandbox environment. This first try can take anything between several days to several weeks. Still, it will provide insights, run an initial mock-up conversion to confirm your business case estimates, and help you understand the full impact. This process may uncover underestimated issues and therefore take time or it may be a rapid evaluation.

- Identify all opportunities as early as possible to use the content available (from SAP or developed by your organization) for automation, the use of **machine learning (ML)**, or the recommended intelligent quick wins in S/4HANA so that they are part of your process design and development decisions.

Iterative data loads

Chapter 8 covers the key technical steps of data migration in detail. In the following section, we will look at some critical activities and tasks that need to be performed in each SAP Activate phase to keep the data migration iterative and Agile to support any deployment approach, from new implementations to systems conversions. Before we go through the actual methods, let's understand some de facto SAP-provided tools for data migration:

- **The SAP S/HANA Migration cockpit** is suggested for the initial data loads into your new SAP S/HANA system from your source legacy systems. The Migration cockpit facilitates the transfer of master and transaction data from source systems to target systems using pre-built migration data objects to identify and transfer the relevant data. Besides the prebuilt data objects, it contains information about the relevant source and target data structure and models and the relationships between these structures.

  The mapping metadata and conversion rules are also part of the content that can be used for data transfer from source to target fields, which can be modified per your business needs. Changing the content in the migration objects triggers the automatic generation of migration programs. You can simulate a migration to verify the data quality and identify issues for error-free data loading. On top of this content, it also provides migration approach options. A unified data load into staging tables of the Migration cockpit from both SAP and third-party systems occurs via XML template files and you are guided throughout the data migration process. The other option is directly connecting to an ETL tool of your choice to populate data in staging tables. For S/HANA Cloud, private edition, you can also use the direct transfer option, which allows you to migrate data directly from your legacy SAP system into a new instance of SAP S/HANA without any intermediate storage. The data is extracted from the source SAP system through a remote function call in the case of a direct transfer. You will have to ensure the data quality in the source systems is good enough for the direct loads to commence.

- **Data quality** begins with a clear and detailed data integration strategy with a focus on immediately improving the data quality for the current initiative and maintaining this data quality at the enterprise level in the long term. Organizations (and their systems integrators) risk significant and costly consequences if they don't have a well-conceived enterprise data migration strategy that delivers a clean data pipeline to feed quality-checked, transformed, and enriched data into their target systems. In general, the following are the best practices any data migration project should consider to help significantly improve data quality and reporting; the earlier you start on these activities, the better:

  - **Data readiness**: Mitigating the risks by starting extraction earlier to find out more about data health.

- **Data migration**: Planning for iterative data feeds and tools that allow data-slicing techniques to target specific business processes and parts of the organization, leveraging common data quality, cleansing, harmonization, data conversion, and data synchronization techniques for dual maintenance if required.

- **Ongoing data quality and governance**: Continuous monitoring and improvement of the data produced in the source system and enabling business process-centered data governance. Keeping and cleansing what is required with controls on creating master data, applying GDPR policies, and anonymizing and pseudonymizing with authorization measures based on data sensitivity during the implementation phases.

With tools such as SAP **Data Intelligence** (**DI**), **Syniti Knowledge Platform** (**SKP**), and SNP, you can start assessing the data quality and improving it as you progress into subsequent phases of implementation. These tools accelerate importing of vast amounts of structured and unstructured data from ERP and disparate systems, which will be vital in supporting and driving your processes with insight and intelligence. Each tool can bring in migration objects, pre-built accelerators, data health assessments, and data migration dashboards. This is critical for the success and discovery of any deficiencies and the readiness of the data to adopt the industry's best practices. It is an iterative process in which the data is extracted upfront. These tools combine a staging area for heterogeneous data with near-real-time, incremental data migration, cleansing, and harmonization capabilities, enabling an Agile approach for non-disruptive implementation. Next, we will look at how to shift the migration left using the tools and accelerators we have discussed and thereby shift the project timelines for your S/4HANA transformation left too.

Mitigating the risks by starting earlier

One of the most significant risks in any digital transformation program is posed by its critical data track. Process teams are dependent on data for designing the process, and the data teams must deliver the data in whatever form they can for process design, testing, mock cycles, or the cutover, with critical loads happening at the tail end of the program when go/no-go decisions are made. More often than ever, things don't go as expected. The data quality, transformation, mapping, and other data cards and reports start turning red with hardly any time to turn them around, which results in either prolonged go-live dates or delayed program timelines. With a shift left, the "data-first" approach to data migration, we make risk reduction and risk aversion a common practice in our transformations:

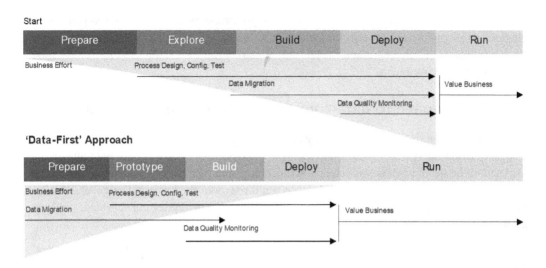

Figure 9.3: Shift-left or data-first approach to your transition

Tools such as SAP DI, SNP (T-Bone), SKP, IBM's **Enterprise HUB** (**eHUB**), and SAP **Data Migration and Landscape Transformation** (**DMLT**), available through SAP and its partners for data migration solutions, allow you to bring the data-first approach to life. This means shifting all the data extraction load and transformation activities left toward the start of the project by connecting to the production landscape. The option to enable near-real-time data and change captures results in zero downtime on the source production systems. Start spreading the data migration effort throughout the life cycle of the Explore phase and deliver production-quality data during that initial Explore phase and process testing.

Shifting heavy-lifting data migration activities to the start of the process allows your teams to review data profiles in an iterative mode with rigorous engagement with the business owners and key users when the business is not heavily tied up yet with the rest of the process design – it gives implementation teams and IT team members an opportunity to work with business counterparts hand in hand, emerge with relevant data of the right quality from production data sources, and make that data available for the design phase and also later for the mock cycle. The quick availability of data from legacy systems to SAP S/4HANA for process design and validation is the key to a successful agile implementation. Heightening the effort required from the business early in the program enables us to reduce the time necessary to complete our data-relevant activities and increase the time for which the solution adds value.

By the middle of the Explore phase, we will have all the data semi-ready and transformed, the quality of the data reviewed, and the relevant data records ready; from that point onward, the development and migration teams build, enhance, and enrich the existing mapping and configuration documents, while data continues to be updated by design in the target S/4HANA systems. This target-driven design approach is matched to the data migration solution, with updated source-to-target mappings if required. Next, you start to deliver production-quality data in the dev environment. The best part is that you can choose only a slice of data out of all the relevant information from the staging environments to be gradually pushed to the development, quality, or pre-production environments as your teams configure and adopt the new processes incrementally. All the data from various sources is harmonized in staging while the development and the business teams continue the design and implementation in the S/4HANA environments.

An Agile approach to data conversion and integration testing

With the flexibility of the data that loads at your disposal, you can use an Agile approach to iterate data quality, cleansing, synchronization, and testing in each sprint. The design, build, and unit tests are completed in the sprint process for each conversion object, and then they are added into the testing sprint cycles next. These sprint cycles continue to run throughout the Explore, Design, and Realize phases, allowing the accelerated delivery of conversion objects for test cycles and data loads until you start user acceptance testing:

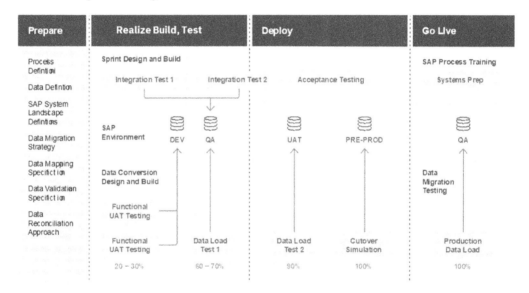

Figure 9.4: Data quality and data load stages with the percentage
of data extracted and cleansed at each stage

The data migration plan, based on this iterative approach, allows for three complete test data loads to confirm that the master data and relevant transaction data are exclusive, accurate, validated, and reconciled. Before the data is migrated, all conversion and load programs are fully, functionally, and technically tested E2E, alongside the integration tests so that the desired results are validated and signed off for the targeted processes. The initial load (20-30% of the data loaded and cleansed) from the source production system is made available for design and development validation, followed by the first wave of the test data load (60-70% of the cleansed data), the second wave (with 90+% of the cleansed data), and lastly the cutover simulation (100% of the data load, and cleansed). The final production data load can commence when previous steps are cleared, and the business and IT sign off the acceptance criteria of the project teams for the production load.

While data migration and the core conversion activities of process transformation, harmonization, and code migration are happening, part of your transformation teams needs to focus on the change management and the UX strategy as the project moves from left to right. To help you throughout your transformation, you will find an abundance of accelerators, best practices, recommendations, and so on. The content is available per each phase of the S/4HANA project through the SAP Roadmap Viewer. This helps accelerate your project implementation timeline and makes adopting the new systems into the enterprise seamless. Let's briefly discuss SAP Activate and the content it offers.

SAP Activate

As elaborated in *Chapter 7*, with any major ERP transformation comes significant challenges around missing E2E views for business processes, often executed in distributed systems across scattered landscapes and primarily based on highly modified and individualized business processes. This slows down the transformation, limits opportunities to use new technologies, and hinders laying the foundations for innovation.

And this is where using tools such as BPI and Process Insights to scan your system's data E2E provides transparency on the inefficiency and friction that the systems need to improve on to achieve the targeted KPI or process excellence goals defined by your organization. Once it is transparent where you need to improve, you need a roadmap that guides you to your destination with a clearly defined set of activities, tasks, and technological options and choices. This will help highlight the gaps in your to-be model and opportunities for innovation. This is where the SAP Activate innovation-as-a-service can help.

SAP Activate Methodology is a unique combination of SAP best practice pre-configuration, guided activities, tools for accelerated adoption, and extensibility that can help organizations implement SAP S/HANA solutions. It's designed for IT teams and business professionals involved in implementation and covers system setup, configuration, extensibility, and integration, resulting in an accelerated pace of innovation. Using the content and the prescribed methods and templates available, processes are quickly analyzed and adapted to SAP standards through fit-to-standard workshops.

SAP Activate Methodology is easy to use and is accessible in the SAP Roadmap Viewer. During your project life cycle, you will find the six phases of the SAP Activate Methodology: Discover, Prepare, Explore, Realize, Deploy, and Run. You will also find content for substantially different transition paths, whether system conversions or new implementations.

The content is split into deliverables and tasks that help project teams plan, execute, and manage their implementation projects better. Implementation roadmaps provide a thorough overview of related tasks, deliverables, and activities for your project teams, along with any connected acceleration assets in document and hyperlink form. Additionally, it allows you to download the project plan and activities to start the implementation process.

Some fundamental principles to abide by are a cloud mindset following the Solutions Standardization Board and SAP best practices. Some ready-to-consume E2E business processes across application areas and global standard templates are available in the EML (which we will briefly look at in the next section) and partner templates. It follows an agile implementation technique as part of the deployment approach. It comes with a structured quality approach, with clear sign-offs to ensure transparency and risk management during the life cycle of the implementation project.

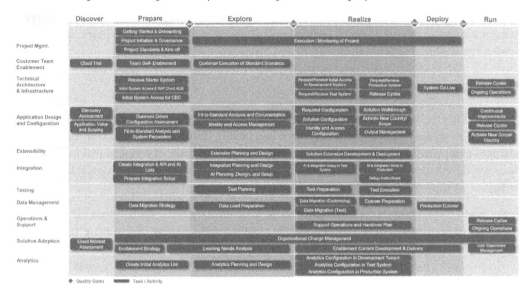

Figure 9.5: SAP Activate Methodology with implementation tasks in different phases

SAP's EML

Companies caught in the dilemma of whether to go down the conversion path or use selective transitions are forced to rethink their transformation strategy due to the complexities of highly customized systems, processes, and data – whether to first cleanse the data and move toward a greater level of standardization in their as-is state before they transform, or whether it's better to start from scratch, create a new implementation, and cleanse and bring along the minimum required master and transaction data to the to-be world.

However, if your organization does choose to go with the latter, the greenfield approach, your implementation teams would benefit from standardization capabilities with a shift-left on the time-to-value, reduction in costs, and rollouts happening as rapidly as possible. This is where the EML comes into play. The EML is a predefined, preconfigured template based on SAP best practices, allowing organizations to consume and execute their processes within these templates immediately. The EML helps global enterprises with subsidiaries in multiple countries immediately start the fit-to-standard activities and identify further individual needs with SAP Activate as the implementation methodology. The following snapshot depicts the scope of the content offered by the EML for the project teams to jumpstart their greenfield journeys.

Enterprise Management Layer for SAP S/4HANA

Functional Coverage

Procurement	Sales	Supply Chain	Manufacturing
Invoice Management Operational Procurement Procurement Analytics Sourcing & Contract Management Supplier Management	Order & Contract Management Sales Force Support Service Operations & Processes Service Master Data & Agreement Management	Inventory Warehousing	Production Engineering Production Operations Production Planning Quality Management

Finance	Service	Asset Mgmt.	R&D
Accounting & Financial Close Cost Management & Profitability Analysis Enterprise Risk & Compliance Financial Operations Treasury Management (basic)	New Customer Management Multi-Channel Interaction Center Solution Business	Maintenance Management	Product Engineering

Scope Options			
	Advanced Cash Management Advanced Compliance Reporting Advanced Receivables Management Lease Accounting Group Reporting	Advanced ATP Advanced Variant Configuration Warehouse Management Ext. Production Planning and Scheduling Enterprise Contract Management	Intercompany Processes Project System for Accounting

Figure 9.6: EML content

SAP's EML comes with additional documentation that describes the value of the multinational template compared to the classical SAP Best Practices packages. While the EML comes with a predefined standard scope, this scope can be individually enhanced based on optional scope items. With this, every enterprise can tailor the template to its individual needs. The template addresses the complex accounting and reporting requirements that multinational corporations face when they need to follow both group and local accounting principles and business practices.

The following section will focus on a few more accelerators – this time around, related to the technical implementations of the landscape. It helps to shift the technical activations for the IT teams left to provision for the UX strategy your organization has put forward for adoption and the accessibility required for the new S/4HANA systems.

The UX strategy

We have discussed the customer experience in *Chapter 4* and how it affects the top and bottom lines of the business – how customers interact with, engage with, perceive, and buy into the promise you are making, and how you deliver on this promise throughout the customer life cycle will determine the lifetime value of the customer. With technological advances in mobile device capabilities and the influx of the Internet of Everything with 5G and the ability to render content on demand, customers can engage with your company on any preferred device and channel. As a result, businesses can no longer dictate what channels the customers use.

Today, businesses need to adopt the channels customers prefer and create the experiences the users want, of being able to engage with your organization at any given point in time and place. Engagement can happen on the web, on social media, via voice digital assistants, or via messaging conversational assistants. These technological and consumer shifts have strong repercussions for two of your most important audiences: your internal customers (employees) and external customers (the end customers/consumers of your products). Your UX strategy and the underpinning UX frameworks (such as SAP UI5, React.js, Vue,.js, and Angular.js) should be capable enough to serve the content anytime, anywhere, on any channel, and on any device. Framework selection principles on which framework would best help which channel, with design guidelines and tools to develop consistent experiences across organizational customer and employee touchpoints, are defined by your UX strategy. Let's understand why all this is important for a successful outcome for your business.

Importance of a UX strategy

A successful UX is underpinned by a strongly articulated and easy-to-understand UX strategy. Your organization invests millions in the system's implementation, deploying the best of processes on best-of-breed platforms and services with lightning-fast UI responses to serve the right data for a user touchpoint. However, suppose the UX is not intuitive and requires a lot of getting used to – for example, a cognitive load to train. In that case, adoption dwindles and may not result in the expected traction among consumers, customers, or employees.

No matter how intelligent, performant, and promising your systems are, if the adoption fails, all the effort of putting these systems and processes together will not yield desirable business outcomes. Therefore, it's crucial to have an enterprise-wide UX strategy for channels, across devices and enterprise or customer systems, prescribing the overall information architecture and creating visual design concepts and assets. Detailed wireframes for various features and user scenarios can be developed into an interactive prototype, for the key features that emerge for different customer or employee journey scenarios. Alongside this, design templates, style guides, and specifications need to be created. This unified design language becomes fundamental to maintaining the brand identity and customer retention on all channels. This is true for customer-facing and employee-facing UX requirements. The UX goals and a design brief that will guide the UX team in creating a vision for the new and existing platforms with a target UX need to be clearly articulated.

S/4HANA projects that overlook UX typically do so by just focusing on the processes, data, and integration. Even though SAP Fiori takes care of the UI and the frontend framework, if not appropriately planned, "tile shock" may occur due to an overwhelming number of applications and amount of information on one screen being released to all employees – presented as an endless number of boxed tiles onscreen.

Therefore, getting into the details of what personas will be accessing (which processes and touchpoints, and the current bottlenecks that they experience) and then translating this into a selected set of Fiori applications controlled via Fiori Catalogues, driven by business roles and levels of authorization, will help with better adoption. *Chapter 7* covered in detail the use of customer journey maps and models, which can be combined with UX strategy input. Moreover, if a process spans beyond the remit of one organization, such as having e-commerce touchpoints on mobile and desktop or having conversational UX interactions, it will require user research activities at the beginning of the project via interactive design workshops, which will help identify the primary customer, consumer, and supplier personas in question – for example, for a portal solution. This is followed by identifying any unmet needs within the day-to-day interactions involved in their processes and transactions, and any other insights that will help create useful design solutions.

For consumer-facing applications and touchpoints, user research techniques such as interviews, surveys, discussions, and usability testing could be used to arrive at findings and analysis. Again, these customer UX vision and design requirements must be planned for any transformation. Nevertheless, SAP Fiori comes with a set of best practices and accelerators to help with the enterprise-wide UX challenge regarding the adoption of new S/4HANA systems.

SAP S/4HANA uses SAP Fiori for its UX. SAP Fiori offers business users a unified and uniform UX across all LoBs, devices, and deployment choices. The visual design, information architecture, colors, and interaction patterns specified in the design guidelines make up the SAP Fiori design. The latest iteration of the SAP Fiori design language is SAP Fiori 3. SAP Fiori streamlines company operations based on user roles and business processes and eliminates complexity to establish a uniform, corporate-level UX standard, which gives users control over their day-to-day operations by providing them only with what they truly need. In the next section, let's get conversant with some accelerators that will help shift an implementation left and rollout timelines for SAP Fiori adoption and activation.

The Fiori launchpad

The SAP Fiori launchpad can be a single-entry point for your enterprise-wide UX when accessing SAP systems. It allows you to combine standard and custom Fiori apps – transactional, embedded analytics with real-time insights and reporting – alongside trusted classical UIs, such as GUI transactions or Web Dynpro. This lets you pace the change from old to new, respecting the capacity of your users and rolling out more value over time through continuous improvement phases.

SAP continues to release new apps and improvements upon earlier releases of S/4HANA to bring the latest innovation to new releases. Adopting and activating the new content is a choice you can make based on your evolving requirements. The employees from your organization can consume innovative business processes, such as group reporting, central procurement, or predictive MRP. Ready-to-activate use cases for intelligent technologies, such as situation handling, ML, and **robotic process automation (RPA)**, are also made available through the Fiori launchpad.

Here are some key recommendations for accelerators and tools to simplify the implementation of SAP Fiori apps for the S/4HANA UX:

- Fiori UX and embedded analytics are key to unlocking many of the innovations in S/HANA. They offer you access to a post-transactional world with insight-to-action and exception-based handling. Therefore, it is essential to evaluate your use cases early in the project and plan your scope accordingly. Then, incorporate regular maintenance and upgrades.

- To help accelerate the selection of relevant apps per LoB, business role, industry, or type of S/4HANA release, your teams can use the SAP Fiori Apps reference library. It is a comprehensive library with details of each app with its technical data, installation details, and configurations, covering GUI-based and Web Dynpro applications.

- Fiori App catalogs determine which apps the users can launch. You can derive groups based on the catalogs, which define the initial Fiori launchpad content. Ensure that the roles and authorizations associated with the catalogs allow access to the apps required.

- If unsure of what would be the most useful apps from the library for your business situation, you can use the **SAP Fiori Apps Recommendation Report** (**FARR**), which inspects the current usage data for SAP GUI transactions to derive the relevant Fiori apps based on other transactions that fall under that area. It tries to match the Fiori app that is closest in function to the transactions identified from the data provided.

- SAP Fiori lighthouse apps are a smaller selection of top recommended Fiori apps that deliver the maximum value and are the best available apps for a given role. They help you get an idea of what's possible for a particular business role and where to focus your effort within an S/4HANA project. You can find a selection of these available in the Fiori Apps reference library by business role.

SAP Fiori Rapid Activation

SAP Fiori Rapid Activation is another accelerator that helps you quickly provision the SAP Fiori technical components and apps. It uses automated task lists. Task lists help configure the communication arrangements between the frontend and backend servers. When you execute a task list, the system guides you through configuring the subordinate tasks included in the task list. You would typically provide the required information in the scope definition and preparation steps, where available, and then carry out the automatic configuration.

Rapid Activation works when your SAP S4/HANA system is in embedded mode, which means your Fiori frontend server is deployed as part of your SAP S4/HANA system. If you are using standalone mode (central hub), where your Fiori frontend server is separate from your S4/HANA system, you need to use a different task list for that deployment. Typically, the implementation teams use Rapid Activation in a sandbox system to start with. It is usually used to explore the content that SAP offers for a fit/gap analysis of what we want to use.

As mentioned previously, running the activation tasks lists reduces your time-to-value by shaving off weeks to bring it down to under a day. Your teams need to be sure which roles should be activated as intended, as you don't want to activate surplus apps and consume system resources. There are a few other task lists for automating custom content generated by your organization, such as Enterprise Search or Embedded Analytics. It's recommended to run a quick activation task list in your SAP S4/HANA sandbox/dev solution with change management transports to capture the changes and optionally specify a test, used to help you test the activated business role in the Fiori launchpad. Let's understand the options your teams have next and the considerations when deploying the Fiori **Front-End Server** (**FES**) for your SAP S/4HANA stack.

Embedded and central hub deployment for your FES

Before you activate the Fiori content, it's key to understand which deployment option will serve your landscape and business requirements, scalability, and security. Each option has its pros and cons and should consider the number of SAP ERP components (S/4HANA and ECC), other SAP components such as SRM and CRM that need to be accessed by the Fiori FES, the intended performance, the reuse of existing backend components, and so on. Extensive help documentation and recommendations are available on this topic.

SAP Fiori FES, which is the SAP Fiori frontend UI component, has deployment choices concerning the location of the backend components. When a new SAP S/4HANA system is set up, the following alternative options are possible:

- (Cloud/on-prem) SAP Fiori frontend UI components are deployed and installed alongside each other within the same SAP S/4HANA system stack (embedded deployment)

- (On-prem) SAP Fiori frontend UI components are deployed and installed on a separate system, away from the SAP S/4HANA system (central hub/standalone)

- (Hybrid) The SAP Fiori launchpad and (custom) Fiori UIs on SAP BTP (Cloud Foundry) are used so that OData requests can either be handled by SAP FES (in the same way as for the on-premises setup) or the OData provisioning service on SAP BTP through Cloud Connector:

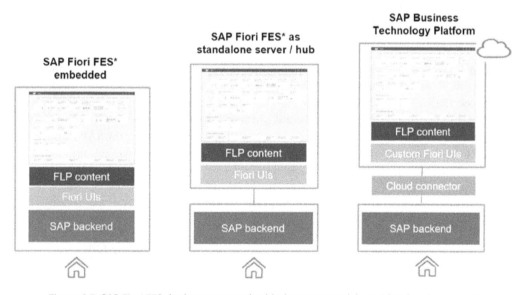

Figure 9.7: SAP Fiori FES deployments: embedded versus standalone (cloud and on-prem)

Your user adoption is also influenced by the ease of access, usability, and number of entry points the users have to complete their day-to-day operations. Therefore, reducing any hindrances and collocating business-critical apps for ease of access on devices preferred by the users with security built into these access points is critical. Let's see how SAP Launchpad Service or SAP Workzone enables this in the next section as an option for your organization if you have a number of business-critical applications using different UI technologies.

SAP Launchpad Service on SAP BTP

Another option is to access your Fiori apps through a central access point on the cloud for your SAP landscape of content and applications. SAP Launchpad Service on SAP BTP enables a streamlined digital experience by establishing a central and secure point of access to SAP (such as SAP S/4HANA), custom-built apps, with UI Integration for Cards, various UI technologies, and third-party applications and extensions both on the cloud and on-premises. It is available as a free-tier service in the BTP trial and is included under the BTP credits for the RISE with SAP offering.

SAP Launchpad Service offers a role-based launchpad for personalization and branding following the SAP Fiori 3 design guidelines. Business users can utilize their inbox, other integrations with central SAP BTP services, and cloud identity services for SSO into connected systems. Access to business tasks, notifications, workflow items, and reports, all relevant information, is made available in one place. It has an extensible framework, with key user adaptation and customizations using shell plugins also offered. Features such as Enterprise Search and Web Assistant are available. Each connected system or solution can evolve per its life cycle, business content, roles, and authorizations. The user can access each of the connected systems and their relevant apps under the content assignment and roles through the local entry point or its home page on SAP Launchpad Service. It is recommended if your focus is essentially on content and application access and collaboration between your employees is handled outside SAP via tools such as Slack, Confluence, or Microsoft Teams.

Mobile Start offers employees an optimized mobile UX for your organization's SAP Launchpad Service content. This is offered through SAP Mobile Start, available on iOS and Android devices. Users can still access the SAP S/4HANA FLP using Fiori Client for accessing a specific system and apps as provisioned for their role. The Fiori Client and the Mobile Start apps can co-exist on one device if required, although this is unnecessary. Users can access all apps directly using the SAP Launchpad Service URL on supported browsers. SAP Mobile Start does not need a separate subscription. It is included in the SAP Launchpad Service subscription.

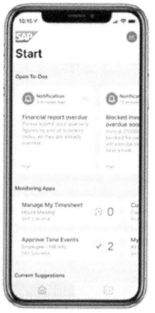

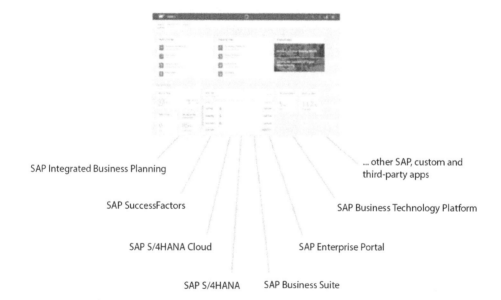

SAP Integrated Business Planning

... other SAP, custom and third-party apps

SAP SuccessFactors

SAP Business Technology Platform

SAP S/4HANA Cloud

SAP Enterprise Portal

SAP S/4HANA   SAP Business Suite

Fig 9.8: SAP Launchpad Service with possible connected systems
Mobile Start using SAP Launchpad Service

> **Note**
>
> Prerequisites: for on-premises deployments, check that your S/4HANA version is S/4HANA On-premise 2020 or above with embedded FES on SAP NetWeaver Application Server for ABAP, version 7.55 or S/4HANA Cloud 2108 or above. Please ensure you are on the latest SPS/FPS stack and have the latest updates for SAP Mobile Start.

SAP Workzone on SAP BTP

If you want your users to access the content, applications, documents, and collaboration features on a central platform with a single-entry point, then SAP Workzone makes its case. This portal product offered by SAP provides a central entry point to SAP and non-SAP sites and also simplifies the creation of your own business sites. With the UI Integration with Cards feature, you can display personalized content from any connected system, also including features for active collaboration with knowledge databases, access to document repositories, and establishing discussion forums within your organization. Users are offered SSO to third-party systems and can be authenticated by your organization's identity provider. For example, your employees want to apply for leave from the SAP Workzone site to SAP SuccessFactors, approve requests in backend SAP systems through the Fiori launchpad, access documents on Microsoft SharePoint, or share their experiences on discussion forums all through the same portal – SAP Workzone is the holistic platform your use case. Moreover, SAP Workzone is also offered through the native mobile app for Android and iOS.

When it comes to ease of access with the least cognitive load, natural language and voice processing scale better than any other UX. SAP has a few tricks up its sleeve when it comes to conversational UX – let's see what options we have here.

Conversational UX

If your enterprise has a multichannel strategy for its customers and wants to reuse most of the data and processes to drive customer and employee touchpoints, the use of **SAP Conversational AI (CAI)** is suggested to make interactions simple, execute complex processes through automation, and deflect traffic from support teams and the front office to other channels to increase customer and employee satisfaction. In addition to a high-performing **natural language processing (NLP)** technology and low-code features to ensure quicker development, SAP CAI offers a single intuitive interface for training, building, testing, connecting, and monitoring chatbots embedded into SAP and third-party solutions or different channels.

Your employees and customers alike can request information or trigger automated processes using simple commands with tailored human-like conversations and support for multiple languages, which makes it more accessible to any demographic across geo-specific and language-specific requirements. Using a low-code platform, development teams can move quickly from design to deployment with reduced development costs and efforts across support teams to expand usage within enterprises.

In summary, the right mix and balance of the UX choices discussed here will help your adoption. A new SAP UX is one of the fundamental changes your enterprise users will see in their day-to-day life. It has all the features and capabilities for users to personalize it and make it accessible per their personal preference. These changes are easily absorbed by intuitive and delightful designs in SAP Fiori 3, although the same principle cannot be assumed across other elements of change that may be part of the transformation. The following section deals with organizational change management aspects of your transformation and how to prepare for a successful outcome.

Change management

Change is a constant in the transformation journey. S/4HANA is a major cornerstone when it comes to digital transformation, impacting an organization's core processes and data. You will introduce several innovations, new processes, and essentially a changed or new TOM, which affects people, processes, and technology as pillars of change.

At the start of *Chapter 4*, we discussed several paradigms of change that an organization needs to start bringing in to create synergy across the three pillars (people, processes, and technology) right from inception – almost predicting what needs to change and working toward managing that change, with a change strategy throughout the transformation and post-rollout. This includes cultural shifts in how work gets done to propagate the value the enterprise intends to create for its consumers and how it is delivered on the field.

It's imperative that your organization's transformation teams understand the vision for why your organization is undergoing this change and what the value drivers are and that it's reinstated, time and again.

Having this clarity at the level of executive leadership and involvement from key stakeholders, business partners, and IT keeps sponsors bought-in, bakes in the vision, and communicates progress across the program during the execution of the next milestone that brings us closer to our goals – it's fundamental to keep much-needed focus and funding going.

These top-down and bottom-up handshakes will ensure there are no gaps in terms of the direction and purpose of travel. Supporting this transformation are your CBM heat maps, tools and platforms, value accelerators, agile delivery methods, and a hybrid cloud mindset. Several gauges for your organizational change and executive dashboards need to be monitored, controlled, and governed. Every organization is different and has its own change verticals and horizontals – functional, non-functional, technical, and non-technical. Captured here are some key change drivers and topics that should be considered when it comes to your S/4HANA transformation journey:

- **Shift in standards**:

    An emphasis on moving toward industry best practices, the standardization of the process models, and moving away from old legacy processes may be hard to accept at first for key users, process owners, and operational teams. However, this can be absorbed more easily if teams appreciate the benefits of keeping the core clean, and how embracing innovation as early as possible and automating commodity processes will help the business in the short and long term. Day-in-the-life scenarios showing how new processes will help ease friction in day-to-day operations can be discussed in customer and employee persona journeys workshops to get early buy-in.

- **Organizational design**:

    Some organizational design changes may be necessary for TOMs, as an organization may want to pivot to nearshore or offshore support models and centralize shared services, finance, and HR operations. It may bring in new onshore support and front-office arms for customer service, or could change sourcing strategies and reverse logistics as part of a circular economy where suppliers have particular ESG goals. Sustainability will be a crucial player in any organization from now on and how that affects each of the organizational units, teams, and processes needs to be understood. Your company needs to be prudent and aware of industry regulations and additional organizational structures that will govern and improve your ESG standing in the long run.

- **Role changes and optimizations**:

    With changes to our ways of working, certain roles and jobs will not be done manually anymore or made obsolete due to standardization, RPA, ML, or self-service. Organizations recognizing these changes earlier improves the chances to transform the workforce by retraining, upskilling, and then deploying these roles during UAT in systems and dress rehearsals of how local, internal, or central teams will work with new processes and systems – this will help ease the acceptance of the change. Onscreen assistance using tools such as SAP Enable could be used to tailor generic training materials to fit the needs of a specific role. Several training tools on the market can be of enormous value to help get end users up and running in no time.

- **Technical roles and authorization**:

    When implementing SAP Fiori, the major decision ahead of you is the scope of your target business roles and your to-be process; the changes and authorizations that need to be mapped to the PFCG roles, groups, and catalogs assigned to business roles; and testing them out. Adjust them in UAT and small launch pilots within specific user groups. Understanding which roles are impacted by changes to processes and how to preempt any challenges to allow your users access to business-critical tasks will help achieve your desired business outcomes. It is recommended to involve your users during Discovery Workshops or as-is employee journey maps, capture problem statements, and understand the as-is reality. Take into account a few other role design considerations, such as whether the users are front office, back office, or plant/factory staff, what their most important and frequent tasks are, and whether they are casual or regular users or key users.

- **Operational readiness**:

  Process owners, operational teams, plant managers, and suppliers need to be brought up to speed as to how upstream and downstream processes will be carried out in the new world. These personas may have been operating in silos in LoBs internal or external to the organization while the new world will provide visibility into their actions to help move the process faster and more efficiently. How systems and technologies will support them throughout the change, how tasks will change onscreen, and process dependencies need to be called out. Explaining the KPIs and how these are affected by every action within the process will help you appreciate how each participant in the E2E process plays a key role. How will you conduct day-to-day operations within the new systems for increased visibility? How will off-system processes and offline paper-based jobs be eliminated or substantially reduced in the new world?

- **UX changes**:

  We discussed tile shock and how overwhelming the end user with all the possible apps for a role can be controlled if they are gradually brought in through workshops/connections with the business. A limited number of apps allows the users to grasp how to operate their new UX and personalize their preferences. Once they are well versed with the SAP Fiori design language, it will be easier to improve apps with every release incrementally. As explained in the previous sections, tile shock can be avoided using the SAP Launchpad app selection to highlight apps and features that bring immediate value to the roles in question. Embedded analytics scenarios, intelligent solutions, reporting requirements for output forms, notifications, Enterprise Search, and SAP CAI integration, all of which help drive business outcomes, are some of the options to be agreed upon and designed with end users in mind in the discovery and design stages.

  For accessibility and access to the new SAP S/4HANA UX, the enterprise IT landscape and systems need to be assessed across teams participating in the process, devices, and the associated enterprise security policies. Here are some considerations along these lines:

  - Select your to-be UX, remembering that the SAP Fiori launchpad lets you create your ideal mix of new SAP Fiori apps and older classical ones so that you can decide the pace at which you want to change over time from old to new, based on the apps released by SAP and those that support the process PPIs.

  - Assess whether a field worker or road warrior would carry out a particular function or use a particular set of apps to consider which tasks are required for mobile access. The need to react faster, collaborate, or delegate will dictate choices on entry points, inboxes, and notifications.

  - Note which mobile device type, iOS or Android, the organization allows under BYOD policies, or if only enrolled devices are provided to employees by the enterprise, SAP's Mobile Device Management solution with its Appstore will enable users to download apps to access the S/4HANA Fiori launchpad on mobile.

- Another prerequisite often overlooked is browser compatibility – as in, which browser versions are used across the organization, contact centers, the offshore back office, or any other suppliers accessing part of the process using Fiori. The SAP Fiori 3 support notes and help on browser compatibility will dictate the features and UI elements that can be used and avoid any surprises towards the tail end of the project. Being aware of your S/4HANA version on the cloud and on-premises and which browsers are best supported for the best UX should be constantly monitored by the design and development teams on the project.

- **IT support and organization**:

    You are moving your workload deployments away from enterprise data centers with cloud adoption. This also entails the need to have a cloud support team. What are the new skill sets required for support on new future systems, platforms, and services? Do your current IT teams require upskilling or do you need to bring in more cloud-native expertise from the market? The size and right mix and balance of SAP on-cloud, on-premises, and hyper-scaler skill sets are recommended. Security, DR, HA, and the support SLAs offered by SAP under RISE with SAP should be considered when deciding the headcounts. Involve your IT and support teams in deployments, right from deploying a sandbox to deploying production environments with SAP and/or implementation partners. This ensures a good appreciation of the decisions taken during the implementation and post-go-live. Shadow support and the reversal of this shadow support during the pilot and post-go-live support are critical for steady-state support. Here are some other points to consider:

    - **Cutover planning**: Manual cutover activities, such as addressing outstanding account balances and delta transactions that were made on the old system and not migrated to the new, business continuity data capture forms from the field and back office, and so on, need to be planned and put to the test in dress rehearsals of the cutover data migration and support simulations. All business stakeholders, including the operational staff, should be aware of the BCP guidelines.

    - **Dual maintenance**: It may be required to maintain both the old and the new IT landscape to be run – dual maintenance until such a point in the future when all the required data and processes have been migrated and old systems can be decommissioned. Plan for a gradual transition from the old to the new support structure, data archival, and decommissioning activities.

    - **Continuous improvement**: In transformation involving Control Tower dashboards with BPI, you can measure the KPIs for processes as the new process and its changes are released. The performance gauge helps you measure the improvements to help you fine-tune your processes to be resilient and ready to respond to any challenges the business faces.

- **Business networks**:

    We dealt with the change levers that your organization needs to monitor, control, and govern within your organization as the transformation unfolds. However, there are key personas beyond your organization that you cannot overlook. They are also part of your change and will significantly contribute to the success story as they are and will be part of your value chain. With S/4HANA, we are traversing the boundaries of processes limited by application areas into intracompany to intercompany interconnected processes that span several LoBs, third parties, and partners. With extensions based on SAP BTP intelligent workflows, we can go beyond the remits of one organization to share data, process flows, and visibility with our partners, suppliers, manufacturers, distributors, and service providers.

Although it is impossible to have a full view across your external network actors, this may restrict the desired visibility into an entire web of networks. This results in limited collaboration across trading partners, when required, to change the sourcing of required services, raw materials, or logistics. It is a challenge to discover new trading partners and stay resilient. This is where the SAP business networks embedded in the RISE with SAP offering can help. While SAP S4/HANA optimizes processes internal to the organization, SAP Business Network incorporates external networks to connect them and collaborate efficiently to provide visibility – for example, into E2E supply chains, customers, and trading partners.

This will underpin a robust sourcing strategy, fulfillment prediction, and execution strategy. This connects buying, manufacturing, selling, transportation, and service through one business network. Ultimately, you can expect much higher resilience. Still, it also translates into tangible LoB benefits such as, for example, fewer stockouts, higher revenue and margins, lower operating costs, higher asset uptimes, less risk, fewer enterprise challenges outside the core competencies, and better use of working capital. More details on how SAP Business Network can help accelerate your sustainability goals, such as responsible sourcing, carbon footprint management, and ESG compliance, are covered in the next chapter.

A few other progressive cultural changes that your organization and leadership should help foster, encourage, and sponsor so that new ideas are adopted for innovation in the business and Process Excellence will be discussed in upcoming chapters. For now, in the next section, let's understand how we iteratively promote the changes to higher environments and get the MVP ready for your pilot rollout.

Getting ready for the pilot

The previous sections discussed methodologies that deliver the S/4HANA transformation based on agile practices to provide a faster time-to-value and time-to-market. IT operations cannot rely on the waterfall approach when the business is agile to deliver the changes and the new improvements in increments to the production environments, especially when dealing with hybrid multi-cloud environments.

To cater to this agile way of pushing changes from dev to production, the IT DevOps teams need to have dynamic, automated CI/CD pipelines set up for their SAP and non-SAP content. We will be dealing with how CI/CD operations can be activated using the SAP BTP **Transport Management Service** (**TMS**) and the central Change Control Management and Transport Management components within SAP Solution Manager or CALM in the upcoming sections to orchestrate and manage your cloud and on-premises changes to be released in perfect harmony through a single control plane.

Adopting DevSecOps takes a lot of different steps, moving away from traditional practices to a hybrid cloud platform approach. The DevOps culture must be instilled within teams to exploit the advantages of the cloud with the right tools. Changes are delivered incrementally towards an MVP build ready to be released after the change management mechanisms are in place. Once the MVP is released, your teams need to start delivering additional features to production incrementally. In a hybrid cloud landscape, you will release content, development artifacts, processes and data, and related customization changes in parallel to the cloud-based systems. In *Chapter 7*, we discussed Side-by-Side Extensibility for SAP BTP and other options such as Red Hat OpenShift and other hyper-scalers. The two tracks of changes – in the cloud and on-premises – need to move in tandem to production environments to avoid mismatches in releases and avoid production issues. In this section, we will briefly introduce the different **Change and Request Management** (**ChaRM**) systems on-premises and on the cloud and run through the scenarios to explain how they can be used in combination:

- **Central Change and Transport System** (**cCTS**): Transport has been an integral part of the SAP landscape when delivering changes to applications through the SAP landscape to production. They are bundled into ChaRM to manage the releases that deliver fundamental changes to production and launch new functionalities.

  These have been further developed and equipped to handle and orchestrate changes and releases across SAP BTP and on-premises (the hybrid SAP landscape). SAP's cCTS enhances the classic CTS with functions for complex, heterogeneous system landscapes, allowing you to centrally control transports within a transport landscape. The cCTS provides a technical infrastructure for enhanced flexibility functions in Change Control Management.

- **SAP BTP TMS** (**SAP BTP TMS for the Neo and Cloud Foundry environments**): This is the life cycle management tool for SAP Cloud development on SAP BTP. It controls content transport between different tenants on SAP BTP. Suppose you have both on-premises and SAP Cloud applications in your landscape (a hybrid landscape). In that case, you can use ChaRM and Quality Gate Management with SAP Cloud TMS to manage the transport processes for SAP Cloud development.

- **The enhanced Change and Transport System** (**CTS+**): This has been available for many years to transport on-premises non-ABAP content (such as the SAP NetWeaver Development Infrastructure) via the ABAP CTS. With CTS+, you can now model your non-ABAP systems as virtual systems in your transport landscape and connect them via transport routes as depicted in *Figure 9.10*. The illustration shows how we can combine SAP Cloud TMS, SAP CTS+, and CTS to have controlled releases to the target environments managed centrally by the SAP cCTS:

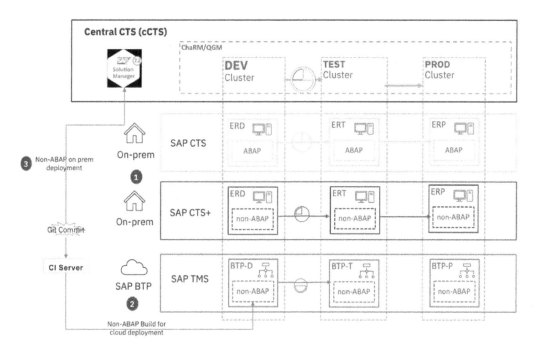

Figure 9.9: Scenarios for hybrid and on-premises technical change management with Solution Manager

Scenarios for the use of TMS + CTS for on-prem deployments

- **Frontend and backend release on-premises**: Content is released through the transport route to the respective environment using ChaRM. The non-ABAP (SAPUI5) frontend component is deployed via CTS+, and the ABAP components are deployed via parallel change documents in their respective environments.

- **CI for cloud deployments**: TMS handles the transport of development artifacts and application content in the SAP BTP sub-accounts. The code commits on the frontend code repository trigger a CI build to push the **Multi-Target Archive** (**MTA**) file onto the SAP BTP dev subaccount and trigger the pipeline through SAP TMS to deploy to other subaccounts – such as quality, pre-prod, and production in the transport route connected via SAP TMS.

- **CI for hybrid deployments**: These change deliveries are typically a SAPUI5 application (to be deployed in the cloud) and served with an ABAP backend on-premises. Development teams can use SAP BTP **Business Application Studio** (**BAS**) on SAP BTP for low-code developments to develop the frontend and very often make use of CI processes by storing the development artifacts in a central source code repository such as Git. Upon committing a change to this source code repository, a CI server such as Jenkins is triggered to run a CI pipeline, which involves steps such as building the development artifacts. The CI server then uploads the content (the frontend – SAPUI5) to SAP TMS. It pushes any additional frontend content and extensions for on-prem systems through the change document in Solution Manager through CTS+ to trigger the release. The backend (ABAP) is released and is synced with the TMS and CTS+ releases to the respective backend components through the transport routes set up for the on-premises S/4HANA environments.

Transport management with SAP CALM

SAP CALM was introduced in *Chapter 4* as an application life cycle management tool and is the de facto choice for technical change management for SAP S/4HANA Cloud deployments. The usage rights are included in the S/4HANA Cloud, public and private editions and with the RISE with SAP Offering. SAP CALM, paired with SAP Activate, provides the implementation and operations framework for cloud solutions for a cloud-centric customer.

SAP CALM is recommended for S/4HANA Cloud public deployments to manage the implementation and its subsequent operations. Although there is no parity between SAP CALM and SAP Solution Manager, the latter assists you with more control and flexibility across your landscape (hybrid or cloud). SAP Solution Manager is also recommended if you have moderately to highly customized (custom code) on your source SAP ERP and want to move to S/4HANA implementations on the cloud (private edition) or on-prem deployments.

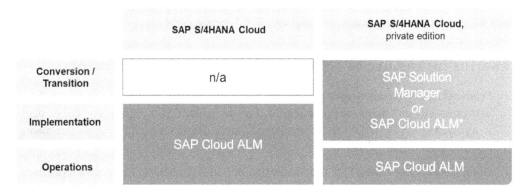

Figure 9.10: SAP CALM versus Solution Manager usage spectrum for S/4HANA cloud deployments

SAP CALM becomes a weaker recommendation for S/4HANA Cloud, private edition if your transition's custom code footprint increases. However, you would be well off in terms of the costs if your transition choice were a new implementation on a S/4HANA public cloud with fit-to-standards adoption for processes using SAP Activate, with automated testing and managing your deployments to higher environments while consuming cloud updates and ensuring their adoption. On the operational side, SAP CALM offers alerting and monitoring capabilities, allowing for the root cause analysis of the defects as they happen. SAP CALM is also open for integration with cloud services or third-party ALM tools via open APIs in SAP API Business Hub so that you can invoke test automation with tools such as Worksoft or Tosca. For post-transformation, steady-state operations, SAP CALM can be used for both variants (private and public) of S/4HANA Cloud deployments to leverage advanced capabilities such as event management, which can lead directly to automation and AIOps if that's the direction of IT operations for S/4HANA. SAP CALM is recommended for use in harmonized, content-driven implementations of S/4HANA Cloud.

Here are two scenarios for the use of SAP CALM for transport management:

- SAP CALM supports the integration of CTS (on Solution Manager) for SAP S/4HANA Cloud, private edition, and SAP NetWeaver Application Server for ABAP on-premises.

- To use the transport capabilities of SAP CALM in conjunction with SAP Cloud TMS, you must establish a connection between the two.

Here are some recommended options for SAP CALM:

- A cloud-centric S/4HANA transformation uses SAP CALM – it can combine the backend ABAP on-prem transports if required. For operations on the cloud, SAP CALM is preferable over SAP Solution Manager, as it doesn't need diagnostic and host agents deployed on connected systems such as S/4HANA to collect diagnostic and monitoring information.

- If your deployments are on-premises-centric, using your existing usage rights on Solution Manager for technical change management for an on-prem and cloud landscape can be combined with TMS and CTS+. You can bring SAP CALM into the mix if required. Solution Manager can also be deployed using the SAP **HANA Enterprise Cloud** (HEC) service offered by SAP as a managed service on the cloud, or you can deploy it on your own data center (on-premises, on a hosting partner, or your hyper-scaler) by procuring for Solution Manager, which may turn out to be cost-intensive for longer durations.

- Start with a hybrid landscape and move to cloud-centric operations. You can begin with Solution Manager (if available in your usage rights) and, post-implementation, move to SAP CALM for operations for operating public and private cloud services, as well as ABAP-based on-premises systems, if you still plan to run SAP Solution Manager for implementation in parallel.

Bringing it all together and the pilot rollout

In this section, we bring together all our learning from previous chapters and sections to provide a high-level walkthrough of the different activities an organization (or hypothetical organization) would typically go through for a S/4HANA transformation. The set of tasks explained here is not exhaustive and has several activities within each of them with specific prerequisites to start both technical and functional tasks. These are to provide you with an overview and help you foresee the different stages the program teams will go through when moving from the Discover stage to the Deploy and Run stages of the S/4HANA transformation using SAP Activate Methodology:

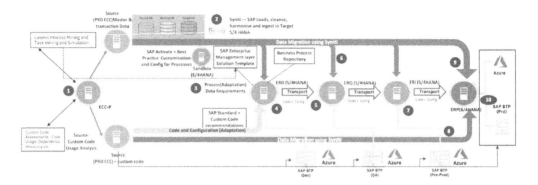

Figure 9.11: Overview: how we get from ECC to S/4HANA

> **Note**
>
> The S/4HANA boxes in the diagram are generic for any deployment choice on the cloud or on-prem. Some activities may vary depending on your organization's architectural choice and deployment choices but won't differ much from the common critical path, which will be the backbone of your transformation. The preceding diagram assumes a greenfield implementation for S/4HANA Cloud, private edition. Azure is used as a representative hyper-scaler platform service and its applications constitute an outer-ring component of the landscape, not a recommendation. The following tools mentioned are not mandatory to be used and are just options relevant to certain phases or activities within a S/4HANA transition, and readers have the choice to go with any of the tools and third parties at their disposal at the time of project implementation:
>
> - **Celonis Process Mining and Code Usage Analysis**: These tools were connected and deployed on the source **ECC Production** (**ECC-P**) environment since the program was signed off by the CxO office to be undertaken:
>
>   - The teams have been quick on the ground and turned on the required connectors and accelerators for the data and insights to flow into the respective engines for further analysis.
>
>   - Process Mining reveals the as-is process inefficiencies, reflected by KPIs and PPIs that are non-conformant. Monitoring the code usage demonstrates how much of the actual custom code in production is utilized by the business processes.
>
>   - The tools are left running for two quarters, including quarter ends and any planning activities that come with it. The prebuilt accelerators on Celonis offer dashboards for playing with the different variants discovered and slicing and dicing the data to visually discern inefficiency and improvement opportunities.

- The data extractors made available from Syniti were deployed on the production in the early discovery stage to allow the infrastructure teams to open the correct ports and network connections for the tools to connect, which were deployed on the cloud:

- This provided an opportunity to look at the data health as early in the Discover phase as possible to then devise strategies around data quality and start cleansing quality checks and agreeing upon transformations to the target data model in the process of discovery and design workshops per the signed-off target processes.

- An S/4HANA sandbox environment with activated SAP Best Practices and standard processes has been provisioned. The sandbox, through the automated task lists, has also activated some key business process role-based Fiori apps for the business users and the owners to experience SAP Fiori 3 UX firsthand.

- The findings from the Celonis process and task mining dashboards were used in Discovery Workshops to playback process efficiencies and friction to help optimize the top five variants of each process:

  - These were then mapped to SAP Best Practices (or SAP EML) templates that were imported into the S/4HANA dev environment, and a Quad A exercise was carried out. Based on the business's stakeholder agreements, the target's to-be processes were modeled with any updates to the process repository within the organization or SAP Solution Manager (BPH) to be referenced in the future, and the related config for process adaptation was initiated in the dev box.

  - Changes were made with SAP Best Practices process templates used as a baseline; per the gaps found after a fit-to-standard assessment, they were accepted as is, marked in for further changes, and identified as needing to be filled in by extensions.

  - The Discovery Workshops also included findings around the code and data quality for decisions about what to take forward or leave behind. Business owners were allowed into the Syniti staging environment to start addressing the data quality issues flagged by the data models supporting the target, to-be processes.

- The customization and adaptation of the target processes were tested with the data ingested from the Syniti load in dev to test the hypotheses of the process design, and the development teams tested the extensions required that have been modernized from old implementations and adapted to the SAP S/4HANA Extensibility framework (In-App and Side-by-Side on the SAP BTP platform, or the Developer Extensibility options):

  - Other integrations, the API's availability to customer-facing applications, and the extensions required to support the customer journey were included as part of the development pipeline. Evolving process designs were tested with initial sets of data that were made available in the dev box from initial extracts from the Syniti staging environment to make the relevant data available.

  - The business, data, and development teams do a joint exercise to test the extensions together and ascertain whether any changes to the process design are required. The identified process automation, intelligent workflows, and ML add-ons and models are tried out with some small PoCs, along with extensions and processes.

- This calls out any changes required to the standard content released by SAP and whether it needs further changes to cater to business needs. The cloud mindset used in SAP Activate governs what degree of change to the standard is acceptable and how it is to be done.

- The first set of targeted SAP S/4HANA processes that have been customized and optimized, the Side-by-Side extensions on SAP BTP, other dependent extensions, and integration with customer-facing apps on hyper-scalers are prepared for a move to the next environment – that is, QA:

  - The existing ChaRM request setup (change requests from Solution Manager) is established for the release landscape on SAP S/4HANA Cloud, private edition. This also can be combined with the synchronized release of the Side-by-Side extensions with SAP Cloud TMS for BTP extensions.

  - The DevOps teams have set up Jenkins as the CI server to help trigger the release pipelines on the frontend components, backend components, and integration components to be synced to their respective environments.

  - The CI server also manages the releases in sync with outer-ring components such as Azure, which contains customer-facing content and integration through SAP Business API Hub.

- The readiness of the QA environment is tested, with the first set of process customizations being pushed:

  - Syniti performs data loads (provided, pre-loaded data is validated by business users and signed off) to the QA environment for business users, and the data migration teams perform spot quality checks

  - The DevOps teams move the extensions and the integrations to the QA environment and run functional tests to validate that extensions work in unison with the proposed process execution

  - Automated functional test scripts (using Worksoft, Tosca, or Tricentis) based on the standard processes and data are carried out to accelerate the testing of the processes

- Similar readiness checks are carried out for the pre-production environments, with Syniti pushing more refined and enriched data based on the adjustments made to processes from the QA testing to this environment:

  - Extensions are moved in to sit along with the processes and data, ensuring that all the connected on-premises/cloud applications respond to the ping tests. Integration testing with E2E process execution is carried out.

  - A time-sliced, quality-checked, and enriched dataset (production-grade) is pushed into the built-up pre-production systems for UAT. This helps reconfirm with business stakeholders that the processes are per their business requirements and can be signed off and that there is no deviation from what is expected.

- This also gives actual users of the systems the confidence and first-hand experience with what UX they will use for their day-to-day operations. UAT sign-offs are requested from key stakeholders to move to the pre-cutover activities.

- The pre-cutover activities and run books with checklists are initiated for the interfaces of the connected system, and dress rehearsals for the final data loads are carried out:

  - The time-sliced, production-ready data is pushed to the target S/4HANA production environment provisioned on a private cloud. The change capture features delta transactions and data from the source systems are turned on after a cut-off data.

  - The customization, roles, and authorization of signed-off processes and the master data with historical transactions based on the time slice selected for the production load are loaded, and extensions and integrations are then released to the provisioned production environment.

  - Business units, stakeholders, and representation of the user group are requested for a go/no-go. SIT, UAT, performance tests, and pre-cutover dress rehearsal results are played back for technical green flags, to review system health, and to ensure security (roles and authorization), and the connections to connected applications are confirmed to be responsive as expected.

- The required BCP plans and cutover activities for the IT teams, business, and operational teams are reiterated and fully understood:

  - The production environment is technically ready, but only a few business user groups are allowed on there to carry out some spot processes and play with chosen data. A few critical transactions with dummy data are carried out to validate operational stability.

  - The function of security roles and authorization is tested by test users from each of the organizational units and teams accessing the systems. Infrastructure teams carry out automated performance/load tests, and security posture assessments are carried out on the new environment, which is not yet released.

- During the final cutover, the set of TRs, which will activate the complete set of SAP Fiori business roles and user logins to make it fully operational, is initiated:

  - The business operations on old systems are halted over the weekend. The outstanding data over and above the cut-off window is not moved through the usual data load route, and the Change Data Capture functionality is used. The delta data is pushed in during the downtime on the source systems.

  - The system is released to users and goes live in countries agreed upon as per the rollout plan. The Hypercare teams kick in with high observability of the system's stability and performance, capturing new support requests and addressing them per the SLAs agreed with the business units.

The pilot phase scope can be a small user group in a specific business unit or an entire business unit with a rollout to a couple of countries. A small-scale pilot provides insight into what works well. Providing early insights into what corrective actions are required when rollouts to other countries or new business units start will become part of the new S/4HANA Cloud systems. Adjust your plans accordingly to include feedback from countries where the rollout has happened.

This also reduces the risk compared to a big bang approach – releasing all functions across the entire organization and countries in one big release. The business users/stakeholders from these countries can then become the brand ambassadors for the change going forward to advocate for its adoption and the efficiency it brings to operations. This sets a clear pathway for future improvement and innovation. This approach is instrumental when launching a new product or service to restrict and damage control and test the markets in a controlled environment. A "fail fast and learn faster" ideology is realized by this phased approach.

Local marketing, sales, and service teams can plan how they want to use the launch of new processes, innovations, and automation, which offer flexibility and best-of-the-breed processes, to their full advantage. A successful pilot provides an implementation template (a golden template) to be reused and improved and assures consistency and repetitive success for rollouts in other countries. Moreover, localized requirements can be addressed by the out-of-box country versions with country-specific languages and tailor your business operations per country on S/4HANA Cloud. Further using Localization Hub and its toolkit helps manage localization across heterogeneous landscapes and rich extensibility features, covering languages, best practices, legal requirements, statutory reports, and globalization features, thus equipping your organization to run locally and compete globally while laying down the foundations for the next phases in the digital transformation.

Summary

To summarize, in this chapter, we have focused on the implementation and migration aspects of your S/4HANA transformation. We covered how your teams would go from choosing the SAP S/4HANA deployments based on your point of departure to understanding how SAP's tools, methods, and accelerators help get you move through the implementation phases. We learned how, while doing so, you shift your project timelines left using agile delivery underpinned by SAP Activate Methodology and the latest and best of the migration tools, such as Syniti. Furthermore, we gained an appreciation of why and how UX strategy plays an important role in the successful outcome of your SAP S/4HANA transformation and what some of the technical choices that could help navigate this challenge to increase adoption are. In line with the idea of adoption, we looked at some considerations for change management for your organization while undergoing the transformation and what tools SAP provides for cloud and on-premises technical change management. To conclude, we brought all our learning together by looking at a hypothetical organization undergoing an SAP S/4HANA transformation with a pilot rollout.

In the next chapter, we will see how wider rollouts are carried out, how a battle-hardened template can now become the blueprint of your success, and how improved organizational processes and data are scaled and rolled out with innovations to newer markets and geographies. How do we handle updates to your S/4HANA system, as there will definitely be a couple of them during the timeline of your S/4HANA implementation?

We will also see how all business units and in-country teams hop onto the RISE with SAP rollout with tighter integration of your organization's external business network, including suppliers and partners; how you can use business networks to execute E2E business processes, working closely with business partners; and how utilizing a business network opens up new opportunities to help your organization reach your ESG and sustainability goals to address business challenges that you were unable to with your old legacy SAP ERP.

> **Note**
>
> All the generally available online accelerators mentioned in this chapter are available for general use without licenses for SAP customers, although it is advised to check the latest licensing terms for the usage of the accelerators with your SAP Account Executive before you do so. The third-party and SAP-branded tools and products mentioned are licensed separately unless covered by your existing license agreements or covered by the RISE with SAP licensing.

10
Going All In: A Leap of Faith

In previous chapters, we described how a potential SAP implementation will have passed through the necessary design and build phases of functional activation, process adoption, and solutions extension, all in line with clean core best practices, using, for instance, **SAP Business Technology Platform (SAP BTP)** services, which surround and enhance the core S/4HANA solution. The solution will have gone through rigorous and extensive testing phases to meet both the functional and **Non-Functional Requirements (NFRs)**. However, the implementation is not quite over yet. Now, we have reached the point in the implementation plan that includes the activities required to deploy into production safely and securely, following clearly defined business readiness and acceptance criteria. In addition, important tasks in terms of transferring knowledge and transitioning to the future **Application Management Services (AMS)** remain, which is the support organization responsible for ensuring the operational integrity of the new SAP solution. All the transition activities need to be executed based on the final solution design. Finally, the operational readiness needs to be checked, both in terms of the operational acceptance of the system to ensure it meets NFRs such as availability, performance, and scalability, and also corporate policies and standards around IT cybersecurity and regulatory controls. All of this happens in the run-up to the final cutover preparation stage of the implementation program, in which teams prepare for the successful go-live of the new SAP solution. As you can imagine, this is quite an active and intensive period within the implementation for all teams involved.

Once the system is live and operational with real transactions, interfaces, business events, batch jobs, operational analytics, and reports running through it, the implementation teams quickly shift gear into Hypercare mode (or early life support) for a predefined period – for example, 4-8 weeks – during which time the production SAP system is monitored intensively as users begin their operational activities based on what they have been trained to do within the business change workstream. This Hypercare team quickly resolves any production incidents through a well-defined incident management process – for example, using the SAP Solution Manager Incident Management capabilities – while subsequent deployment rollout teams kick into action and begin the deployment of the SAP solution across the business entities in scope for the implementation – so, enterprise **Lines of Business (LoBs)** by region, country, or territory, or by functionality, such as core finance. Meanwhile, the Hypercare team is monitoring user adoption to ensure that the new system is used productively and effectively, and therefore helps the business teams track and quantify the realization of business benefits.

In this chapter, we will focus on the deployment and rollout of the SAP S/4HANA solution by covering the following topics:

- What defines a Global Template solution design for S/4HANA?

- What are the factors that define the S/4HANA instance strategy?

- How do we successfully roll out and deploy this template in each of the country locations and/or **Business Units** (**BUs**) that are in scope for deployment so that they can start to take advantage of expected business benefits from the new S/4HANA solution?

- What are the factors that drive efficiency for either a distributed or single-instance strategy?

- How do we drive continuous innovation across a globally deployed SAP ecosystem?

By the end of the chapter, you should have gained a good understanding of how to adopt different global deployment approaches and instance strategies in order to meet your business objectives, while enabling a good balance between a global template and localization requirements as the enterprise enhances the SAP solution with future roadmap innovations, functionalities, and features in line with its long-term transformation agenda.

S/4HANA deployment patterns

To recap, as of 2022, SAP S/4HANA comes in these patterns (note that SAP S/4HANA Cloud Extended Edition is no longer positioned for new customers as of 2020):

1. SAP S/4HANA Cloud, previously called **Essentials Edition** (**ES**). This is SaaS public cloud.

2. SAP S/4HANA Cloud Private Edition

3. SAP S/4HANA On-Premise Edition, managed by SAP with their **HANA Enterprise Cloud** (**HEC**)-managed services

4. SAP S/4HANA On-Premise Edition, deployed in an on-premises data center (often managed by an IT-managed service provider) or managed by cloud provider hyper-scalers

Only the first and second patterns here are delivered through RISE with SAP, which uses a consumption subscription model. The other two are delivered through the classical perpetual licensing model based on user numbers.

What is RISE comprised of? There are many features, as described in previous chapters, but to summarize, RISE offers a simplified contractual model for clients to use to migrate to and adopt the S/4HANA core, along with a consistent set of **Technical Managed Services** (**TMS**) delivered by SAP (or by IBM under the premium supplier option) and multiple tools and services to enable extensions to S/4HANA using BTP via the **Cloud Platform Enterprise Agreement** (**CPEA**), with credits provisioned for developers to accelerate innovation on BTP.

In addition, there is the starter pack for SAP Business Network that allows enterprises to reimagine how their business can collaborate across a network of trading partners. Finally, there is the **SAP Business Process Intelligence** (**SAP BPI**) solution, with which clients can use the capabilities of SAP's acquisition of Signavio to offer Business Process Management solutions, whether discovery, modeling, governance, insights, optimization, intelligence, or process management, to continually assess, optimize, and standardize their core business processes in line with the clean core principles. The following illustration – sourced from the standard RISE literature from SAP (`https://www.sap.com/uk/documents/2022/03/90674e29-217e-0010-bca6-c68f7e60039b.html`) – highlights these key features:

Figure 10.1: Core components of the RISE with SAP offering

With respect to these S/4HANA adoption patterns, whether it is through RISE with SAP or using SAP S/4HANA On-Premise Edition, you need to define the Global Template design that will be used as the foundation for deployment across your enterprise. This also includes defining the SAP instance strategy and subsequent rollout deployment model. S/4HANA customers need to address the following:

- **Global Template** – Understand the operating model and identify common global processes with global data definitions and standards

- **Instance strategy** – Establish an SAP landscape strategy and establish a governance system to manage global template development and rollouts across various regions/geographies

- **Deployment strategy** – Define a roadmap for global and/or regional template deployments

Focusing on defining the Global Template

What do we mean by Global Template design? This is a business-led strategy that describes what is to be configured and set up in the SAP S/4HANA core that best meets the business requirements with the broadest possible solution that meets central, regional, and local business needs. It is designed in a way that maximizes business value, reduces the **Total Cost of Ownership** (TCO), and increases user adoption through a *fit-to-standard* mindset adopted during the implementation project.

The guidance on best practices from SAP states that the S/4HANA core should be built by adopting standard configurations for business processes and data structures – for example, master data whenever possible. However, where there is a clear need to adapt the solution based on legal, fiscal, auditing, or localization requirements, then this is done by adopting clean core principles, where any customizations, extensions, and enhancements are delivered as in-app extensions within the S/4HANA core solution and/or SAP BTP as described in previous chapters – all of which is based on a well-defined business process hierarchy defined in the S/4HANA core. This needs to map neatly to the target operating model for the organization, which depicts how the business will consume the new functionality in line with a new hierarchy, in line with the organizational structure, and the topology of decision-makers in that organization.

Naturally, there are some key design decisions needed to design the Global Template properly – for instance, how it should be configured and structured according to geography, LoB (e.g., brand), functional domain (for example, HR or finance), technology platform (e.g., Azure, AWS, or strategic SaaS-based solutions), legal entity, cost or profit center, general ledger and **Chart of Accounts (CoA)** structure, and supply chain relationships between upstream suppliers and vendors, the enterprise, and downstream customers (all of whom may have local, regional, or global representation). Each of these factors determines how *thick* or *thin* the Global Template design is going to be. The chart in *Figure 10.2* shows the relationship between the Global Template design and local template design requirements:

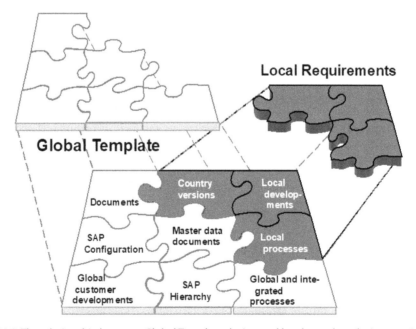

Figure 10.2: The relationship between Global Template design and local template design requirements

The Global Template needs to align with the target organization structure and hierarchy so that it is relevant to all countries and legal entities that are in scope for the S/4HANA deployment program. This strategy defines how to represent the system or instance approach to support the target operating model. The business goal is for S/4HANA to be the modern digital core, in which all transactions are captured in one SAP system, enabling efficiency on a global scale. However, there are several patterns commonly adopted and each has its pros and cons, as shown in *Figure 10.3*. Key considerations include defining what the common processes to support global businesses are, how common master data is defined, how you achieve a single view of data and information, and how you minimize the TCO. All of this has to be tempered by technology and its scalability, business risks, and speed of deployment:

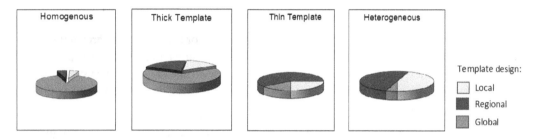

Figure 10.3: Types of Global SAP Template design approaches

The following points describe the different types of Global Template designs, as illustrated in the previous figure, that are possible within S/4HANA:

- A **single Global Template** underpinned by a single global instance of SAP ERP (with tightly coupled application components): In this model, the business will have agreed on a common process, data, and technology template for its entire deployment – across legal entities, organizations, BUs, and geographies. It will have a single primary core business with similar business processes that are universally adopted. Process changes in these areas will have less impact on revenue-creating activities and, therefore, are lower risk than changes in operational areas, such as manufacturing and logistical operations. The corporate culture and policy definition is centralized, with a strong corporate HQ and policy dictated at a corporate level and globally enforced. Companies that include highly independent businesses, in which the culture is based around local decision-making, will face a significant challenge following a single global instance approach, which effectively moves the balance of power from the business to centralized governance/change control. For a transformation program to try and move a company with this culture to a single instance, strong executive sponsorship at the CEO level is required to drive this forward. With this model, businesses aspire to operate as truly global companies with "one face to the customer." They already operate with or plan to standardize a common set of business processes across all BUs. In this case, such a company is well positioned to achieve a global single instance. The consequence of this model is that the IT strategy delivers a single dev instance and a single production instance for S/4HANA, which enables an optimized and maximized **Return on Investment** (**ROI**) and the reduction of the TCO. Therefore, a fully harmonized single template would have these features:

- A global/centralized business transformation
- Centralized configuration and development
- A central program with parallel rollout teams
- Local requirements included in the core template
- A single development track
- A high success rate for a single instance

On the other hand, companies operating as multinationals or those that have grown through mergers and acquisitions over time may be operating with a different set of business processes for each BU. They will have difficulties running all these businesses on a single system with harmonized business processes, so a single Global template would be a major challenge, but alternative options exist.

- A **thick template** is a Global Template in which all agreed global processes are configured, tested, and deployed together so that all deployment countries and locations receive the same consistent solution at go-live. From an instance strategy perspective, the solution may be delivered through multiple development instances (which are built via a set of **Business Configuration** (**BC**) sets from the Global template, and local customization/development is added on top) and then deployed to multiple production instances aligned with the corresponding development instances. Note that BC sets are a part of the SAP best practices, which are delivered in the form of preconfigured business settings that can be used to assemble either a prototype or a development system. The user can choose the pre-configuration to be used for the implementation of a business scenario via the installation roles. This way, enterprises increase their ability to be more flexible around local businesses in terms of rollouts, upgrades, local configuration, and so on, and also reduce the level of change control (although the global template is subject to global governance). A thick template can typically comprise the following:

- Significant business changes
- Many global parameters and config elements
- A single global program with parallel rollout teams enabled to make minor modifications by country (legislative only)
- A single dev track managed through the template concept (e.g., BC sets used to feed local dev systems for localized work)
- A single instance can be achieved with central governance

- A **thin template** is a documented set of principles for a smaller set of global parameters, allowing for increased variation from the core design in localization developments. From an instance strategy perspective, this may be delivered through multiple development instances (which each have their own build for global/local configs, with the global config following a set of documented guidelines for global parameters, such as customer and product hierarchies). This configuration is deployed on multiple production instances aligned to the corresponding dev instances. This option maximizes flexibility and reduces the level of governance and change control. However, it does increase the TCO (many builds, increased infrastructure, increased support, etc.) and minimizes integration and its potential business benefits. The companies that follow this approach (e.g., global pharma/life sciences companies due to strong local/ regional governance rather than corporate global governance) typically find that each of their instances gradually diverges significantly over time, which makes consolidation very difficult. The characteristics of a localized template that adopts certain standards, our thin template, include the following:

  - Business "compliance"

  - Few global parameters

  - Multiple projects with local autonomy within global parameters

  - Managed through standards and configuration scripts and design reviews

  - The risk that systems gradually become out of sync over time

  - A single instance will be very challenging

- A **heterogeneous template** is an approach involving diverse, heterogenous systems in which there is no commonality across businesses, and each does what they want in their own local/ regional systems, with the only requirements being for consolidation at the financial level – for example, the SAP Central Finance or Group Reporting solutions. Typically, this option is not encouraged, as it minimizes the overall business, IT, and financial value of deploying S/4HANA. In terms of the balancing act of "benefit" versus "risk," this will obviously negate some of the risks we have covered, but also minimizes the business or IT benefits. The characteristics of a heterogenous template include the following:

  - Highly localized and independent templates

  - A high degree of local business autonomy

  - No global/regional parameters

  - Multiple parallel project teams with a carte blanche to alter the enterprise structure, key configuration, and design details

  - No consistent approach to design

  - Not suitable for a single instance

The following illustration shows the factors that drive the Global template design, where common standards, processes, data, and technologies drive how thick, thin, or heterogenous the template should be:

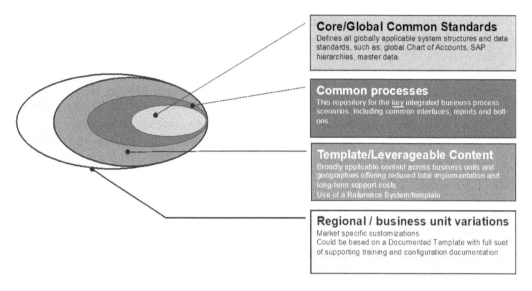

Figure 10.4: Considerations for a global SAP instance/template

Figure 10.5 shows the degree of commonality often expected in a thick template, where the higher the percentage, the *thicker* the template can be. Typically, a regional/global instance needs consistency across global standards, processes, and data (e.g., 80%), with local variations (e.g., 20%) to address local legal and fiscal requirements, while a local instance involves every business process being performed locally:

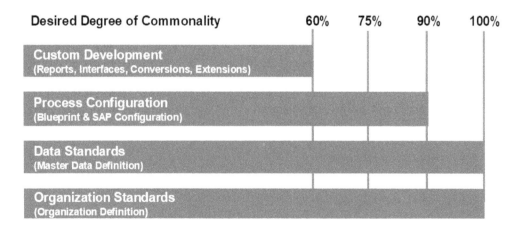

Figure 10.5: Degree of commonality across code, processes, data, and organizational structure

From a business transformation perspective, drivers include the need to achieve process standardization and functional harmonization, to enable a data-driven enterprise with integrated and automated processes that operate end to end.

The business needs to take these strategic decisions upfront in the program design phase to reconcile a highly diversified, decentralized company, striving for maximum commonality using the power of S/4HANA to do so. The following table shows an example of selected factors to be considered when arriving at that decision, as this drives the S/4HANA instance strategy:

Business goal	Heterogeneous	Thin	Thick/Single instance
Generate consumer demand	• Brands are planned and managed at the BU level, including operational marketing	• Operational marketing is done at the BU level, but planning and management are global, including brand profitability and investment	• All aspects of a brand and its associated marketing operations are planned and executed at a global/regional level
Service the customer	• Customers are owned and serviced by the individual BU	• Customers are owned and serviced at the country level, including, for example, one invoice, shared logistics, etc.	• Accounts can be managed at a global/regional level, including the ability to take orders that cross BUs and countries

Business goal	Heterogeneous	Thin	Thick/Single instance
Optimize the supply chain	• The supply chain is planned and executed at the individual BU level • Different customers and suppliers • Different supply chain practices • Global, 24x7 manufacturing ops (lack of downtime)	• Supply is planned and managed at a country level with factories supporting multiple BUs with shared procurement, logistics, etc.	• Supply is planned and managed at a global or regional level, with focus factories or contract manufacturers supplying all BUs. This means more use of common customers, common suppliers, and common materials, but multiple manufacturing and distribution locations for the same products.
Standardize finances	• Finance organized to support individual BUs with local currency ledgers supporting local COAs and accounting standards	• Finance organized as a shared service across BUs within a country	• Finance is organized globally/regionally – for example, as a European shared service center with one CoA providing financial information by country, category, and function

Business goal	Heterogeneous	Thin	Thick/Single instance
Cohesion of corporate structure	• This tends to imply a long history of local acquisitions and local decision-making. Changes are made independently between countries and the global organization. • There are no common shared services but this results in a lack of visibility. • Clearly, there is a need for global best practices across disparate account practices that operate globally and a need to reduce their IT operations costs.	• Here, there is a common approach toward growth through acquisition, but regional divergence is permitted based on legal/fiscal constraints and broader business benefits	• Here, the enterprise has already consolidated large divisions through global record systems such as SAP, with the largest systems already supporting a large number of users. There may be the possibility of divestiture in the future as part of a global company strategy.

The ideal solution is that the global template is designed and built at the outset and that the remaining changes are local legal and fiscal changes that are specific to the business being deployed. The issue is that as more and more end markets and countries are rolled into a Global Template solution, the more difficult it becomes to apply fixes and patches and to deploy new release functionality without disruption, particularly if changes are invasive (i.e. changes to global processes, hierarchies, or data). For instance, every system change, be that a patch or new functionality as part of a release, needs to be assessed for its level of invasiveness and whether it is mandatory or optional for BUs to adopt. This will impact subsequent regression testing efforts to maintain the integrity of the global template functionality.

Localization requirements

The instance strategy that is integrated with the target operating model is underpinned by S/4HANA as the system of record in any of these patterns we have covered. Most customers embark on a transformation program that benefits all levels of the organization, covering business, people, processes, data, technology, and tools. The key motivation factors stem from the combination of the need to remove technical debt from an IT perspective and the need to achieve competitive advantage from a business perspective.

At the same time, we need to allow business changes driven by localization requirements, such as the following:

- Country-specific legal regulations
- Meeting the accounting standards
- Local tax, audit, legal, fiscal, and trade tariff regulations
- Sustainability standards – for example, non-financial disclosure standards
- Reporting in the local language

It is important to ensure that the Global Template solution is designed in such a way to allow localization needs to be met as part of the rollout deployment for a given country. This means that the solution architecture for the core configuration in S/4HANA needs to be loosely coupled, and one way to achieve that flexible architecture is to adopt SAP BTP Extensibility features so that localization requirements can be delivered through augmented, enhanced, and enriched features of the S/4HANA core processes in line with clean core principles.

Design authority governance

In all major SAP implementations, there is a need for functional integrity between the global template and localization requirements. This affects how the overall template is then rolled out in each country. The question is how you do that in practice. This is where a strong **Design Authority** (**DA**) team needs to ensure the integrity of the Global Template design while working with business stakeholders.

As the DA operates within the enterprise governance model, it needs to address the following key requirements of the program:

- The requirements encompassing the following dimensions:
  - Processes
  - Master data and standards governance
  - Policies/standards
  - The data quality framework
  - Organization structures
  - IT tools (functionality and solutions)
- A unique regional end-to-end process to manage the master data life cycle
- Clear roles and responsibilities in the different instances (local, regional, and global)

- Information ownership/stewardship

- Information and standard committees

- One regional policy and standards definition and communication

- Operational discipline – process control and visibility (KPIs)

- Data quality throughout

- The user workflow orchestration layer with supporting systems synchronized and integrated

The DA needs to support the target template design and act based on the choice of the Global Template. For example, the following chart shows how a strong DA can enable the establishment of a global single instance with common centralized standards and ways of working on S/4HANA – such as through a global template, single global template, or thick template. However, if an organization is highly federated with a distributed DA, then the S/4HANA solution will either have regional instances or a Thin Template model.

An effective DA team will be a small focused team of experts across solution design, business process functions, technical architecture, security, and application development, as well as with links to business and program/project management to ensure that the integrity of the global template is maintained throughout the solution's architectural design. The DA needs to be empowered to make recommendations and decisions to ensure the integrity of the solution across the transformation program and beyond:

Figure 10.6: This table shows how reporting is impacted by instance strategy

In the end, the goal of the Global template is to enable businesses, people, and technology to transform according to a consistent design that is well architected, adheres to the industry's best practices, and delivers a high ROI within the shortest possible time scale. The following illustration depicts the classical challenge that clients face when developing a Global Template design – how much of the design is the core and how much room should be allowed for legitimate localization requirements?

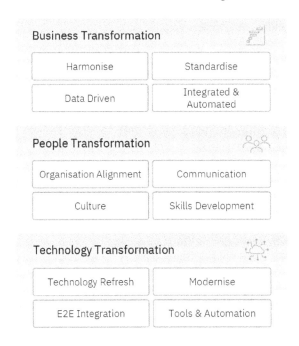

Figure 10.7: Typical set of outcomes driven by an S/4HANA implementation
across business processes, people, and technology

For many customers, this means they need to address complex, internal business architectural challenges head on. For example, they may start with an objective analysis of the business culture that needs to be honed, covering factors such as how governance, business, and regional autonomy will work in the target landscape. The use of central shared services, funding security, and legislation are all factors that influence the ability to trade or expose data from specific countries (e.g., restrictions on operations in embargo countries), or where there are significant security/legislative demands (for example, defense and pharma).

Defining the instance strategy

Now that we have defined the Global Template, the next thing to focus on is the SAP instance strategy. This relates to the configuration of production (and non-production) instances of SAP S/4HANA in line with business organization structures. It is also a physical consequence of the template design in terms of how a live, operational, and productive SAP application is established and configured for each of the BUs. This is tightly bound with the Global Template design.

With the growing adoption of RISE with SAP, we see a tremendous opportunity to innovate at scale using a combination of the S/4HANA core and SAP BTP and the broader shift to the cloud. Architects and developers have to contend with a new set of NFRs, from establishing "loosely coupled" IT architectures to maximizing business value through the adoption of technologies that enhance user experiences, optimize processes, standardize data, rationalize applications, and integrate all of this using an underlying technology layer comprising both hybrid cloud platforms (on-premises and cloud) and hardware infrastructure systems. By enabling loosely coupled architectures, you maximize your business flexibility and business agility to adapt to both internal and external changes and priorities.

So, does this mean that you can adopt a Global Template yet easily allow for localization requirements? In principle – yes, but only if you adopt clean core principles, as described in *Chapter 4*. What this means is that you can safely introduce solutions to localization requirements with SAP's recommended approach – using SAP BTP's Extensibility features, which are based on a loosely coupled architecture that supports a standard clean core system and balance the need for standardization with continuous innovation and differentiation through localization. As we move to a new mode of operating with richer user experiences, the global template and instance strategy need to be flexible enough to allow for localization requirements to be delivered – and this means alignment on solution architecture principles that guide how the solution will develop over time – something that the DA will be responsible for:

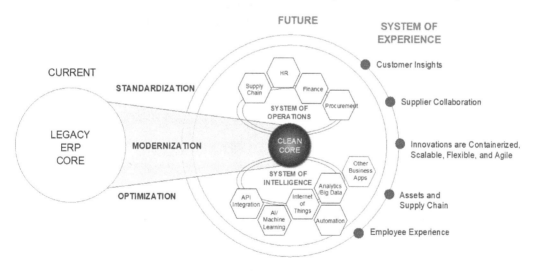

Figure 10.8: Clean core foundation used to define the future operating model

The following figure depicts how Extensibility features in SAP BTP allow S/4HANA to retain integrity through its standard functionality and ensure data quality standards while differentiated features are extended using BTP to introduce process variants. Legal, fiscal, auditing, tax, and regulatory requirements can be delivered using these Extensibility features and capabilities:

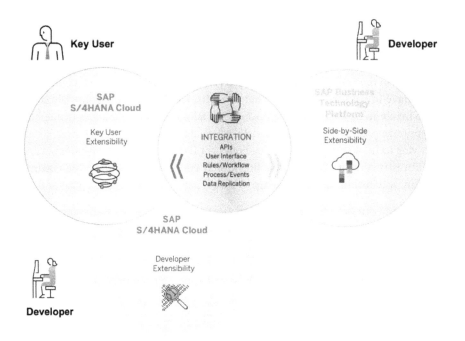

Figure 10.9: Extensibility options in SAP BTP (Reference site: `https://extensibilityexplorer.cfapps.eu10.hana.ondemand.com/ExtensibilityExplorer/`)

All these factors influence how to define the global instance. For example, here are a few different models of what an end-state S/4HANA landscape might look like given the application, data, integration, and technology of the enterprise. Here, we see how the path to production is represented by the type of template in action:

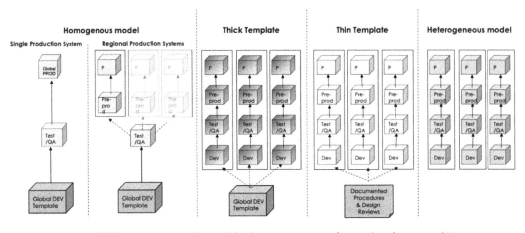

Figure 10.10: SAP instance strategies and deployment patterns for prod and non-prod instances

This figure represents the different global template deployment patterns for SAP ERP typically seen across large clients. With RISE with SAP, clients can adopt the public cloud, where the number of instances is restricted to starter edition, dev/QA, and prod, which aligns with a single production instance model. With S/4HANA Cloud Private Edition, clients have the option of additional non-prod and regional prod instances depending on the choice of Global Template design, but this will incur additional costs when both deploying and supporting these instances.

This diagram represents how deployment by country is driven by localization requirements, which are included in the Global Template to ensure a consistent and predictable data model before go-live for a given country:

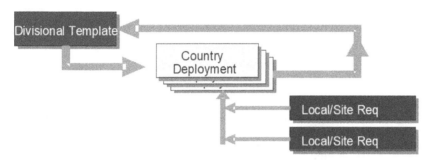

Figure 10.11: The feedback loop to drive local requirements into template design

The following example represents another way S/4HANA could be deployed – in this case, by company division or market segment, or a regional model. Each business must decide on the parameters used to segregate the SAP landscape based on organizational factors, as well as the target operating model and the business architectural vision for the SAP transformation program. Each model here has advantages and disadvantages highlighted to inform decision-makers on the right choice of Global Template and instance strategy:

Figure 10.12: Example of SAP instance strategies based on organizational and functional structures

SAP Instance Strategy	Advantages	Disadvantages
Flagship Platform Model	• Business process harmonization • Harmonized shared services • A global system for the main LoBs • A global system for financial reporting	• Integration complexity of SAP and non-SAP systems • Significant time spent on process alignment across divisions/regions • Risk of losing agility to change an established process • Reduced downtime window
Divisional Model	• Centralized group to define divisional business processes • Autonomy for changes • Easily scalable to bring new countries into the template	• One plant caters to multiple divisions for a few smaller markets
Market Segment Model	• Small/medium-sized markets and non-MFG sites can easily be brought to the template	• Global, division-level complexity for large markets

SAP Instance Strategy	Advantages	Disadvantages
Regional Model	• Autonomy for regional business processes • Adaptable to local requirements	• Division-level complexity remains across a region
Global Instance Model	• Single face to the customer • Preserves tight integration of end-to-end processes • Drives a strong, centralized organizational culture	• High effort initially to align standardized business processes across an enterprise • Risk of losing agility to change an established business process • Reduced downtime window
Functional Model	• Ease of adapting a shared services model per function • Autonomy of changes at the BU level	• Complex integration • Redundant distribution of master data across systems

The choice of template is further influenced by the "potential to harmonize" business processes across all the operating divisions and geographies, with an analysis of the common and differentiated processes that apply across the enterprise.

Transitioning to SAP S/4HANA is an opportunity for clients to also rethink the landscape strategy and take advantage of the opportunity to consolidate it, even into a single-instance strategy. In general, the criteria for defining the best production system strategy have not changed. With system consolidations, you reduce the number of SAP instances required, thereby lowering the barrier to implementing additional digital functions while reducing the TCO and enabling greater efficiency across business processes and data.

The consolidation and harmonization of the SAP system can involve either system consolidation and process harmonization, data center consolidation, server consolidation, or a combination of all three.

With system consolidation (and process harmonization), multiple ERP systems are collapsed into fewer, larger systems based on a common design that serves more users over a broader geographic or business area. This consolidation has the highest cost but also delivers the greatest benefit and ROI to the customer.

Data center consolidation involves collapsing multiple geographically dispersed data centers, hosting ERP systems in fewer larger data centers (or virtual clouds), and serving a larger geographic area. This option has moderate costs but delivers only moderate benefits.

Server consolidation involves collapsing multiple instances of ERP within a data center onto fewer, larger servers or a virtual cloud, reducing the TCO. This consolidation has lower costs and lower benefits than the other options.

The next port of call is to establish a prioritization framework to inform the ERP roadmap, balancing the benefits of ERP consolidation with the associated investments and efforts required. For example, it's crucial to understand the capabilities in scope and the characteristics of each country's deployment requirements:

- Is harmonization of the business processes/data/user interface required?
- Can the business adopt industry-standard processes where they are non-differentiating?
- If a single instance is to be achieved, the processes in scope must be harmonized and where possible, standardized.
- If a component is to be removed from ERP, it shouldn't be heavily interconnected.

The following axes can be defined and used as part of roadmap prioritization to inform the deployment options:

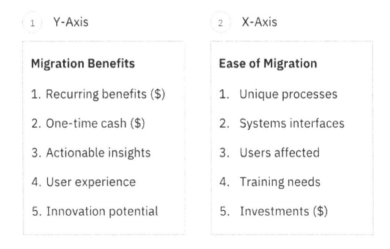

Figure 10.13: Key factors in terms of migration benefits and ease of migration

The following is a map of migration benefits to determine the instance strategy options:

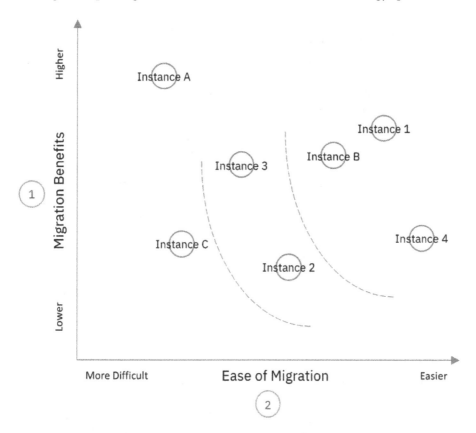

Figure 10.14: Mapping migration benefits to determine the instance strategy options

Next, you need to analyze numerous value pools with the potential to drive improvement in revenue, operating margins, and asset efficiency, and then apply these to country-specific deployment options. Functional drivers can include the following:

- Process harmonization and execution

- Internal versus abstracted processes (linked to the discussion of process harmonization and orchestration)

- Global processes that influence strategy (e.g., Cross-BU **Availability-to-Promise (ATP)**, planning, and the supply chain)

- Highly sensitive processes with stringent NFRs (e.g., manufacturing, replenishment, and **Point of Sale (POS)**)

- Intrusive processes (e.g., locking updates)

- Process orchestration where it is appropriate

- Harmonized/commoditized processes versus specialized/differentiating processes

- Data architecture and data models

The following chart illustrates the example business process value pools used to develop the business case for an SAP S/4HANA transformation – with factors driving revenue growth, improved operating margins, and improved asset efficiency:

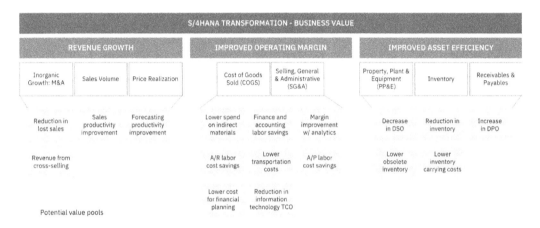

Figure 10.15: Value pools assessed that drive business benefits through S/4HANA adoption

This way, we can leverage industry insights from a vast body of experience in ERP transformations, as well as proven ERP assessment frameworks and sample ERP roadmap deliverables. The following chart shows how we can use industry insights to consolidate ERP using broad experiences and knowledge of what major industry players have done to modernize and consolidate their own SAP instances into S/4HANA. It shows the pathway others have taken to move from legacy, local instances to strategic global instances:

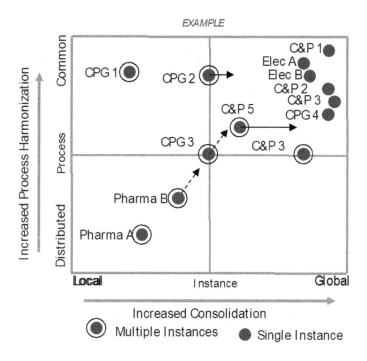

Figure 10.16: How industry insights can be used to transition to S/4HANA

Indeed, when defining a single-instance strategy – shown in *Figure 10.17* as a move from **MODEL 3** to **MODEL 1** – there are multiple decision points driven by the degree of process harmonization in question:

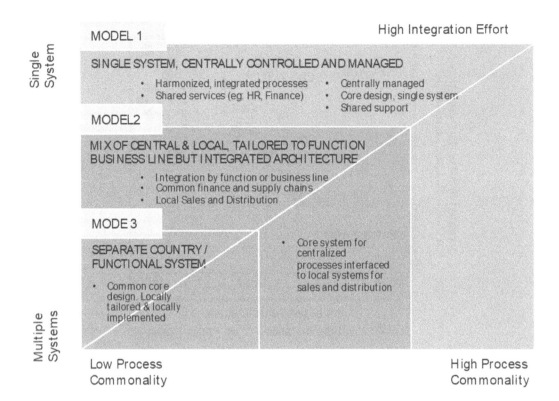

Figure 10.17: Using evaluation methodologies for ERP consolidation,
including evaluation criteria and assessment frameworks

The following is a list of NFRs that can be considered when it comes to defining your instance strategy and meeting the system demands (non-functional) of the business. Modern ERP engagements involve hybrid applications (on-prem and cloud applications) with their own release timelines and governance. Key questions that need to be answered include the following:

Domain	Key questions
Functional	These are the global processes that influence the strategy (e.g. cross-BU ATP, planning, and the supply chain): Which processes need to be harmonized for execution? Which of these are internal and which ones are abstracted processes? Are there any highly sensitive processes with stringent NFRs – for example, manufacturing, replenishment, or POS? Which processes are invasive and critical to other processes (e.g. locking updates)? Where should process orchestration be performed? Which processes are harmonized because they are commoditized processes versus which ones are specialized because they are differentiating processes? Analyze the degree of differentiation versus the degree of commoditization of any given capabilities. • Is harmonization required for all business processes/data/user interfaces? • Can the business adopt industry-standard processes where they are non-differentiating? If a single instance is to be achieved, then the processes in scope must be harmonized and standardized where possible. If a component is to be removed from ERP, it shouldn't be heavily interconnected.
Data	This is about how we set up master, configuration, and transactional data, including selective data migration (e.g., open items) or total data migration from the legacy system into the target system while applying business rules to ensure data quality, and reconciling and remediating erroneous data that is important to the business for operations, auditing, and compliance. Where are data standards defined and how will data governance work? Selecting a more homogeneous instance strategy will force a common data model across all geographies and LOBs.

Domain	Key questions
Integration	Analyze the degree of integration/interconnectivity between capabilities/processes.
	The more connections identified indicate a higher tendency toward being in the core ERP system.
	Standard versus specialized interfaces – rationalizing the system landscape can provide opportunities to remove the duplication of interfaces.
	Are there government, legislative, and other security requirements for interfacing data? Multiple system instances may be required to meet these requirements.
	What are the expected maintenance and support costs and how are these calculated? The number of interfaces on the system may influence this. In a consolidated system landscape, these points of integration can decrease the number of interfaces at play and, in turn, reduce support costs.
	Consider the future integration roadmap (e.g., the move to the cloud) – the speed of adopting the future roadmap has a direct correlation with the simplicity of the landscape.
	Undoubtedly, there will be many interfaces required for exchanging data into and out of S/4HANA. You could adopt standard interface Application Programming Interfaces (APIs) using, for example, Open Data Protocol (OData) services, which could be adopted from SAP API Hub: `https://api.sap.com`.
	Other interfaces may need to be specialized, but, again, rationalizing the system landscape can provide opportunities to remove the duplication of interfaces.
	Meeting business, government, legislative, and other security requirements for interfacing data may require multiple system instances.
	SAP (and other) instances with different data models will increase the complexity of integration.

Domain	Key questions
Release management	Ideally, in a single-instance model, all regions should have a common release/maintenance plan and the planned release calendar for the year should be published prior to the start of the year (e.g., the last quarter of the previous year). Many enterprises work on a single instance in the third quarter of the year to prepare the release plan and publish it early in the fourth quarter.
	As the system is accessed across the globe, there may be a very limited window within 24 hours a day to make any unplanned changes. Exceptions may be required for smaller markets/geographies in which a time zone window could be considered for unplanned releases.
	All SAP transports and Functional Support Packs (FSPs) need to be delivered at the speed of change across the ecosystem – this is one of the key aspects of keeping the systems in good health and avoiding any unplanned downtime. If we move from an SAP multi-instance to a single-instance strategy, the release and maintenance of the SAP system become more challenging but, in return, bear some key benefits, such as reduced maintenance costs and a uniform system used across geographies.
	• Here are some implications of the instance strategy:
	• Reduced maintenance costs with a single instance
	• Uniform systems used across geographies
	• Common changes deployed for all countries/markets operating on the system
	• The speed of change for ad hoc releases reduces as we move to a single instance

Domain	Key questions
Technology	While defining the instance strategy, the following operational aspects need to be considered and, accordingly, will influence the instance strategy decision – for instance, whether the Recovery Time Objective (RTO) and Recovery Point Objective (RPO) are key aspects influencing the instance strategy. If the RTO and RPO are very low-value (near zero), then the following points need to be considered: Data volume – If the data volume is very high, say, in the order of >20TB, then we need to check whether the system can be restored within the stipulated RTO; otherwise, it may be a constraint to have a single instance for the enterprise. Transaction volume per sec – A high transaction volume may impact the log shipping capacity and recovery in case of failure and will demand a near-zero RPO. Backup policy – If the volume of data to be archived is very high, this needs to be checked so that for a single instance, it can be restored without compromising the Service-Level Agreement (SLA) of the system. Here are some implications of the instance strategy: • If the platform moves toward having a single instance, then the platform has to adopt the strictest region's RTO/RPO and build the most expensive solution for a bigger single-instance platform. • The single-instance system needs an aggressive archival policy in place to ensure the data growth is managed in line with mandatory data objects and their retention periods. • Ensure that data is accessible across the hybrid cloud, availability zones, regions, and networks. • Considering these NFRs may mean funding higher SLAs to meet these requirements.

Domain	Key questions
Data archival	The archival policy dictates the online volume of data. To have a more performant and economical system, it is always recommended to archive data that is old and not required to be online from functional and regulatory/legal perspectives. For a single-instance system, an aggressive archival policy may need to be in place to ensure the system performance meets its NFRs and reduce OpEx costs for cloud infrastructure. A major enterprise that has a single instance may need to adopt an archival solution to archive as much data as possible. While S/4HANA Cloud is a SaaS solution, there are data prevention, data life cycle management, data retention, and data residency requirements. You need to align data volume management with the transactional and analytics needs of your business. This includes considering the architectural topology (business, data, application, and technology) and how to deal with data sensitivity issues in line with the GDPR requirements. Limits on the level of information that can be accessed outside the country border in accordance with local cybersecurity laws must be imposed.
System size	As we orientate to SAP on the cloud, the size of the system becomes a key consideration, especially for large customers due to current (scale-up and scale-out) constraints on cloud architectures. Traditionally, this includes both user-based and throughput-based sizing, but with SAP S/4HANA Cloud, we size based on another metric called Full Use Equivalents (FUEs) and on T-shirt sizing to define both normal and peak volumetrics and load statistics that drive our performance requirements. Regular capacity forecast models are needed to build on the initial system sizing to ensure that the system scales to meet user expectations. This means continuously forecasting based on country-specific deployments, with a defined period to allow for scaling up the system capabilities to take on the new workload.
Maintenance and support costs	This is calculated based on the number of interfaces at play. A consolidated system landscape can decrease it and in turn, reduce support costs. As we define the future integration roadmap, we can determine how the speed of the adoption of the future roadmap has a direct correlation with the simplicity of the landscape.
Security controls	This is about ensuring compliance with policies and cybersecurity threat protection measures, covering the perimeter of the enterprise into the infra, database, application, data integration, and user experience layers.

Domain	Key questions
Performance	This is about ensuring an end-to-end performance that meets both SLAs (including for the network) and supports the overall user experience. This needs to consider the last mile from the server within the SAP S/4HANA cloud to the user device (mobile, tablet, or desktop) so that the user experience is consistent and the system is highly responsive.
Extensibility	By adopting SAP BTP Extensibility capabilities, you enable clients to keep the core clean while extending, enriching, and enhancing functionality around the core S/4HANA Cloud solution using the latest SAP BTP platform services (which continually evolve and mature).
Change management	What we define today as the starting point of the journey will be continuously re-assessed during program deployments and roll-ins. Shifting to DevSecOps with CI/CD and continuous release approaches is now possible using SAP Activate, SAP Solution Manager, and SAP Cloud ALM.
Instance strategy	This requires deep analysis of the options to ensure clients select the right long-term models to align with their businesses while also accommodating the NFRs. SAP S/4HANA Cloud, as a SaaS, ensures continuous alignment with the NFRs, including scale-up, scale-out, high availability, and future upgrade options (e.g., NZDT solutions for SAP).
AMS operations	This is about how we introduce continuous improvements that drive both business and operational value through automation techniques, such as AIOps solutions for continuous monitoring and minimizing system disruption. With RISE with SAP, this technical monitoring is part of the SAP TMS as defined in the RACI for services. However, even with that support from SAP, the AMS team needs to monitor the application processes and data.
Sustainability	Merging ESG-related frameworks, standards, and regulations will mean that the application layer addresses supply chain solutions, shifting to more localized networks to minimize the impact of carbon emissions, while the infrastructure layer needs to apply green IT principles to the enterprise architecture, the process architecture, development, and operations so that the S/4HANA target solution is sustainable by design.

Domain	Key questions
Geopolitical drivers	Regional conflicts continue to impact CXOs' decisions around business operations – for example, global supply chains being impacted by COVID-19, the war in Ukraine, or tensions between China and Taiwan, all resulting in countries looking to secure long-term energy and supply chain protections, driving more and more work at the source – for example, new initiatives to develop the latest semiconductor technologies in the 2022 CHIPS bill in the US.
Global market economics	These directly influence the business and economic confidence and climate, so new business structures can trigger divestments and mergers and acquisitions – for example, exiting the Russian market and dealing with the risk of managing stranded business operations, data residency, and data security issues.
Sustainability in the target operating model	As clients adopt cloud-centric business models, they are shifting to a more platform-centric business architecture, embracing SaaS and the hybrid cloud in order to drive more customer intimacy – for example, B2B/ B2C, a faster time-to-value, and business agility, with richer user experiences that wrap around new products and services. This drives business growth across the quadruple bottom line of people, planet, prosperity, and impact. What we define today with S/4HANA Cloud will be the starting point of that transformation journey, and this will be foundational to country-specific deployments and roll-ins.
Application landscape and modernization – move to the cloud	As we move to more hybrid applications between SAP and cloud-native best-of-breed solutions, the use of SAP will change over time with the adoption of new technological innovations, such as solutions using the blockchain, AI/ML, advanced analytics, process automation, the IoT, edge analytics, and RPA. Clearly, the evolution of cloud capabilities (ever-increasing TB size, availability, and NZDT), and loosely coupled architectures that use containerized, modern, and fully supported application landscapes will determine how fast the business can grow and thrive.

Now that we have gone through the non-functional technical parameters that drive our choice of SAP instance strategy, we should have enough information to determine the landscape for the S/4HANA implementation – either through a big-bang go-live or pilot-led deployments and rollout. We can start with SAP Activate Methodology to guide clients and their system integrators to follow the best practices with a well-defined, proven set of methods that can scale.

Methodology

To ensure best practices, we recommend the adoption of a well-defined, proven method that scales across industries and the S/4HANA solution patterns we have covered. For that reason, we adopt SAP Activate Methodology. This describes all phases from project implementation to cutover/go-live and from Hypercare to AMS operations. The following diagram illustrates the phases we go through using SAP Activate Methodology to drive the Global Template design to then enable a deployment rollout in line with the overall business rollout plan:

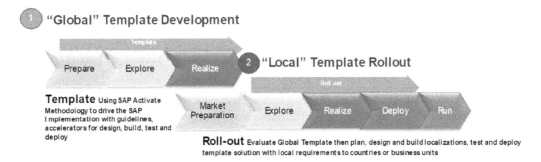

Figure 10.18: Using SAP Activate to develop the Global template as the baseline for the rollout

Why use SAP Activate? It is SAP's standard best practice methodology for an S/4HANA implementation and deployment rollout. With its stages, phases, activities, tasks, deliverables, and detailed guidelines, this set of methods provides guidance on how to actually produce S/4HANA relevant deliverables throughout, with tasks making them easy to consume when they are needed. The deliverables and tasks are listed in sequential order based on the activity starting time. However, parallelization might be necessary to expedite the implementation. Activate Methodology comprises the following phases: **Prepare**, **Explore**, **Realize** (build and test), **Deploy**, and **Run**. If we focus on the last two phases, they cover go-live, Hypercare, and operational support as we begin the rollout deployment phase.

In the **Deploy** phase, the production system is ready for cutover/go-live. Users are mobilized onto the system as part of organizational readiness, and the switch to new business operations is enabled, as well as the completion of all scheduled end user training and final business change activities, while business benefits are tracked.

Meanwhile, during the **Run** phase, the system is further optimized in line with the NFRs and SLAs. The operations team monitors and supports system operations, supports continuous change management, supports users through continuous learning, and initiates continuous improvement initiatives through release cycles.

The rollout approach

An important key decision will be the nature of the go-live – either through a pilot (based on geographic location, legal entity, or business capability) or a big-bang go-live across all geographies, legal entities, and/or BUs. This decision is often based on how the business stakeholders want to realize the benefits of the newly configured S/4HANA solution. This means having a clear view of its functionality, how to deploy the solution, and when to deploy the solution across the business enterprise across legal entities, geographies (countries, territories, regions), and/or business capabilities.

The following diagram shows a three-tier approach to organizing the global deployment rollout. It is typically comprised of a global core team, supported by global delivery teams as part of the S/4HANA implementation for the pilot country, with regional and local teams who work with the AMS team to deliver changes into the productive S/4HANA system through change and release management processes:

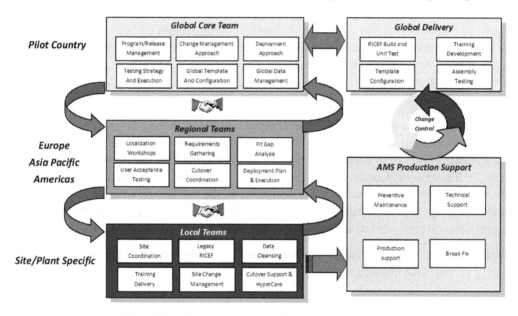

Figure 10.19: Global, regional, and local deployment teams

This three-tier approach leads to lower risks and lower overall costs for the rollout program while enhancing the global acceptance of the solution by connecting a greater number of regional and local resources to the project. It also provides more efficient leverage of "scarce skills," as localization workshops are run for each region (these are process experts) and better enables the setup of regional CoE teams, global process owners, and the superuser network. All the configuration and development is done at the core level, enabling tighter control over the global template/design, and this improves the preparation of local sites by providing a dedicated site team. This way, local teams are much more agile since they are only responsible for site change management, delivering training, and data cleansing/reconciliation. Note: for reasons such as cost optimization or the limited availability of skills/resources, it is possible to scale this back from a three-tier model to a two-tier model with no regional team coverage.

Any rollout deployment strategy has to be business-led, based on a careful analysis of what the business priorities are at a given point in time, although these need to be defined upfront during the project's Explore phase, with deployment plans integrated with business change initiatives during the Realize phase of the program.

For enterprises that have a simple, function-based solution that is additive to existing business capabilities, such as central finance, then a big-bang go-live could be feasible where rollback and/or business continuity plans are well defined, readily available, and can be executed.

However, most enterprises prefer to take risk-mitigated options with pilot go-live options, then evaluate their impacts/benefits, apply the lessons learned, optimize the cutover plans, and mitigate risks before rolling out to downstream geographies based on an agreed rollout deployment schedule. This way, they can show that the target solution works with the lowest possible risk with a selective pilot. It will have a less business-critical impact within the marketplace yet be positioned for success and representative in terms of being the right size of the business, with broad coverage of the business processes and with the availability of skilled local resources (internal and external) to enable a successful outcome.

With a successful pilot, core business processes and their supporting data models and technological enablers are proven to work. This can lead to the next step, which is confirming the first release. Typically, for release 1 (post-pilot), the goal is to generate an ROI to sustain the execution of the program. The focus of release 1 is to ensure full benefit realization (an immediate ROI) and alleviate any technical debt by eliminating any application/technology-related burning platforms. The release scope is tailored to the business imperatives and serves as the foundation for the scalability of an enterprise's template for a global rollout. The release will mitigate and contain business risks while also ensuring that local resources (internal and external) are fully deployed to support go-live.

These **Critical Success Factors** (**CSFs**) are essential for realizing the benefits and mitigating the risks following an S/4HANA implementation:

- Timely access to information and data in order to make timely decisions at critical points that can benefit the business.

- Access to key ERP stakeholders and securing sponsorship alignment and buy-in to build ownership in order to make rapid decisions through the empowerment of business process owners and project leadership.

- Discipline with program governance and commitment to target dates. This requires a three-tier model: global core, regional, and local teams perform distinct tasks and have dedicated team members – the best/brightest of the business and IT to ensure the effective execution of the milestone plan. This is facilitated by frequent and collaborative teamwork sessions between core, regional, and local teams.

- Everyone on the project is fully engaged with balancing the big picture and the implementation details to ensure the execution is in line with the business vision and roadmap.

- Local ownership with a commitment on the part of local management to both readiness and deployment and superuser engagement to build a knowledge base and complete key activities.

- Business change management working closely with business users to enable focused process changes at each individual location with a structured tailored process- and role-focused training program.

- A harmonized data model with clean master data, data governance, and a standardization process, supported by early data cleansing and overall data stewardship throughout the business.

Now the solution has been built to quality standards and thoroughly tested through multiple test cycles – technical unit testing, functional unit tests, end-to-end system integration testing, user acceptance testing, operational acceptance testing, performance testing, cutover/rollback testing, and, finally, deployment into production through a well-organized cutover/go-live implementation. With a successful go-live, the solution is ready for global deployment across countries/regions and ready to be scaled out across the enterprise in line with the deployment plan.

Deployment

Many factors of deployment planning are covered in this section. Strategic deployment planning needs to be started as early as the Explore phase in SAP Activate Methodology. It's made up of the following:

- Release management

- Cutover management

- Readiness of the solution

- Readiness of people

- Readiness of the business

- Deployment and transition to AMS

- Monitoring progress to go-live

- Hypercare with the post-pilot global deployment

- Go-live

- Rollout post go-live with localization

Many best practices for global deployments ought to be included as part of deployment planning. They include the following factors:

- The pilot selection needs to match the broad scope of the template but with less risk.

- Design an industrialized release strategy that has support from key stakeholders.

- Reduce the number of go-lives across the deployment program to minimize business disruption – for example, minimize disruption to integrated shared services and the supply chain.

- Avoid breaking up each deployment release into major SAP functional releases, as this may not maximize business value. It's preferable to weave functional changes into each planned release and ensure effective regression testing for each release, so for live countries.

- Reduce the number of enhancements (fit-to-standard) where possible or bundle them as part of each major release.

- Avoid overlapping parallel building and testing during regional/local deployments so that the path to production has a clear line of sight from a dev instance to prod.

- Evaluate the legacy application and maximize the retirement of non-strategic applications in line with an S/4HANA implementation in order to achieve a shorter time-to-value and greater agility.

- After the first major deployment, ensure the main lessons learned and benefits observed are maximized as part of the next release.

- After the first major deployment, the core Global Template should be a fit of 80% or more, which will facilitate a faster time-to-value and increased business benefits through more clustering of countries. The key to this is starting the data process early for future releases.

The following chart in *Figure 10.16* shows a typical example of a deployment rollout plan by region, wave, and year. This will vary from one enterprise to another but shows how deployments can be sequenced depending on business priorities, constraints, regional/local readiness, and budgets.

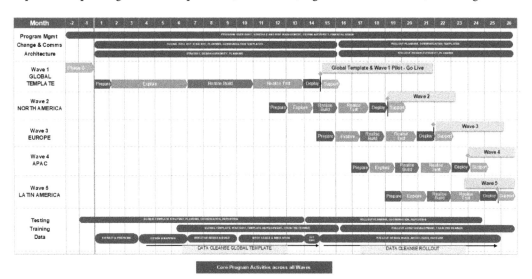

Figure 10.20: Example deployment plan by wave

Now, let's cover how release management factors need to be considered as part of the deployment strategy.

Release management

The definition and management of the program release scope encompass people, processes, and technology. The following are the key inputs and outputs:

Release management – inputs	Release management – outputs
• Number of users impacted • Geographical locations • Business processes in scope • Change impact • Interim processes for co-existence scenarios • Decommissioning/archiving scope • Business blackout periods • Solution release management	• Release scope (locations, function, go-live, and users) • Deployment governance management • Go/no-go criteria by release • Decommissioning scope/archiving scope by release • IT change management board • Technical and business go-live management • Interim process start/end by release • Manage hardware and device dependencies

Typically, during release management, we follow a phase-gate process to ensure quality outcomes in each phase. We recommend a minimum of five phase-gate reviews for SAP implementation projects. For complex projects or first-of-their-kind projects, more phase gates may be required. Within agile projects, periodic retrospective reviews across teams are recommended. We ensure that phase-gate reviews are organized/planned early in each phase so that each review includes adherence to project standard processes and the quality control of deliverables.

Now, we will focus on the cutover process itself in the next section.

Cutover management

This is a meticulously planned and highly coordinated set of activities required to discontinue business processes and operations on a legacy system and resume business operations on a new system, such as S/4 HANA and SAP BTP. The key input and deliverables required to perform successful go-live include the following:

Cutover plan – inputs	Cutover plan – outputs
• Trial conversion of data and sharing plans and results	• Dress rehearsal plan (scope, environments, and activities)
• Introduce data freeze periods and legacy system freeze periods in line with the business agreement	• Cutover approach (logistics, comms, timing, scope, and reporting)
• Define business roles and cutover activities	• Cutover plan (detailed activities)
• Technical cutover activities (new and legacy systems)	• Legacy system cutover plan
• Environment planning as part of the mid-level plan	• Business cutover plan and processes
• Rollback options in the cutover to protect production	• Deployment communications
• Business ramp-up/ramp-down	• Rollback plan

The cutover is jointly the remit of the business, superuser, and deployment teams in terms of the planning, coordination, and execution of the activities, both business and technical, needed to move from the legacy system to the new system, and includes all the associated business processes and data activities. There are dependencies between tasks, which can include handoffs between the project team and business users.

The cutover plan is a single, integrated plan that is managed centrally, which holds the master list of cutover activities: one plan – one version of the truth. Activities are assigned to specific owners within the different workstreams who are responsible for feedback on the completion status against the integrated plan. The activities under specific workstreams are executed by specific activity executors.

The cutover execution starts with the formal execution of activities as per the owners, times, and dates captured in the detailed cutover plan. This phase usually starts approximately 3-4 weeks prior to go-live. The cutover execution phase covers the pre-blackout period activities, in which existing business activities continue in the legacy systems alongside the cutover activities. This allows teams to start preparing the live production SAP S/4 HANA system – transports are moved to the production environment, along with manual configuration and other system setup tasks being completed. This way, the final production data load activities start.

The cutover lead can use a deployment framework model that comprises the following:

- Solution readiness – Is the technical solution ready for go-live?

- People readiness – Are the people involved ready, willing, and able?

- Business readiness – Is the business ready?

- Deployment and transition readiness – Are the support structures in place for go-live and beyond?

Daily status meetings of all teams confirm the status of the activities to complete that day and involve discussion of any issues encountered. Daily emails on activities due are sent to relevant executors and owners. Cutover execution dashboard status reports are issued twice a week to the project and leadership team.

Who is involved? Typically, this is an all-inclusive process so that no program-related data points are ignored. This means the cutover lead is obliged to engage all teams. They orchestrate data collection and normalization and work with each team to define every critical path activity, along with the task executors from both the project and support teams. We can use a range of tools to support this activity. They include the following:

Cutover tools/components	Cutover milestones and deliverables
<ul><li>Final detailed cutover plan trackers</li><li>Cutover execution dashboards</li><li>Cutover status reporting templates</li><li>Email templates for due cutover activities</li><li>Cutover and Hypercare support matrices</li></ul>	<ul><li>Transports moved to production</li><li>Final Hypercare support approach</li><li>Go/no-go meetings</li><li>Cutover plan activities completed</li></ul>

Now that the cutover plan has been prepared with the right team supporting its execution, we can look at the next step with the solution readiness checks.

Solution readiness

The goal of solution readiness is to ensure the preparedness of the technical solution delivered by the program, specifically that the following applies:

- The system has been developed and configured in a way that meets the functional and NFRs described by the business

- The solution has been tested with data and any outstanding defects have been accepted by the business

- The interim processes between releases have been identified, planned for, and agreed on

- The preparation activities have been undertaken to ensure the solution is ready to be switched on at go-live

- Integration with legacy, strategic, and third-party applications is in place within a joined-up environment plan

- Desktop, mobile devices, and IoT devices have all been checked and are accessible for go-live

- The infrastructure security is in place in line with corporate standards

Next up, we can check the status of the business users for the go-live with people readiness.

People readiness

The goal of people readiness is to ensure that people within the business are prepared to receive the solution in that the following applies:

- They understand how changes associated with the release will affect them due to effective communication

- They understand how their roles and responsibilities will change as a result of go-live

- They have been adequately trained to effectively perform the duties required

Next, we can check the status of the overall business operational readiness for go-live.

Business operational readiness

The goal of business operational readiness is to ensure that the critical business preparation activities for adopting new ways of working, systems, and tools are complete or on track:

- Business transformation changes and communications are in place.

- Business role changes have been confirmed and interim processes have been defined.

- External consultations/notifications have taken place; there is a **Business As Usual** (**BAU**) support model in place for the new solution.

- There is geographical readiness in terms of the site and location physical facilities and the integration of IT with the core template.

- Data preparation, with a final data load based on clean data, is complete.

- Hypercare and AMS support models are in place with processes to support operations.

Now that we've checked in with the business users and their operations teams, we need to check the readiness of the AMS support teams for the planned go-live and ensure the knowledge transfer has been successfully completed as part of the transition to AMS using operational acceptance criteria.

The readiness of AMS for deployment and transition

The goal of deployment and transition readiness is to ensure you are prepared to commence and run deployment and that the required structures are in place to support the landscape post go-live:

- Cutover plans, business transition processes, and support structures are in place. This includes access to the agreed incident management, ticketing system, and resolver queues to ensure tickets are monitored and resolved quickly.

- Legacy solutions are ready for cutover and decommission or archival.

- IT BAU support structures are in place to support the solution at the conclusion of the program.

Now that we have transition readiness, we need to check that teams are ready to perform the cutover execution and get ready to activate critical business process workflows, interfaces, and system monitoring in line with AMS processes.

Monitoring progress to go-live

The goal of monitoring is to ensure that every critical path task and activity is fully tracked with transparency and control. This requires detailed criteria to enable effective tracking and governance as part of the deployment readiness matrix and scorecard. This includes clearly defined criteria that have an associated **Red, Amber, Green** (**RAG**) definition. These criteria are reviewed and the RAG status is tracked weekly and supported by multiple stage-gate meetings that can be planned to review readiness, as well as a formal stage gate to approve entry into cutovers and go-live.

Go-live

This is the actual cutover execution window, which is an agreed business and technical outage window. This follows the cutover plan meticulously. Naturally, the immediate period after the go-live period is business-critical and requires intensive care from all support providers. During this period of intensive care, all aspects of change management will be assessed to determine the effectiveness of the cutover, including final user acceptance. Typically, we monitor the processes to ensure the design is working as planned.

Hypercare

Hypercare is the group of support activities including both preparation and execution that will happen after go-live for a limited period. These are the key inputs and outcomes that are typically expected:

Hypercare input	Hypercare outcomes
• Release scope • Key support rosters • First-time use scenarios • Deployed defects • BAU support processes • Transition plans	• The Hypercare approach (duration, governance, and exit criteria) • The Hypercare operating model (resources, logistics, and triage)

Stabilization and Hypercare – post-go-live support and incident management

We know that a successful operation depends on the ability of the operational staff to support the solution. We will take the following steps to ensure a smooth handover from project Hypercare to AMS support. Hypercare is the group of support activities that happen after go-live for a fixed period to enable the stabilization of the solution before handover to BAU:

- Typically, 10 weeks, including 2-month ends, which involve superusers, the project team, and the BAU support organization.

- Ensuring that the business will have adequate support in the transition to S/4 HANA as part of the deployment.

- Support businesses with operational stabilization and embedding new ways of working.

- To enable Hypercare, a series of preparation activities are performed by the project team:

  · In the detailed design phase, we will create training plans for the project team, key users, and support team.

  · We will ensure training starts as early as possible and is finished by the time the transition phase starts.

  · Resource plans and Hypercare organization charts will be built to ensure we have the correct skills to support the business teams at all sites.

  · A tool is set up to capture all technical incidents. This tool is used by the project team and superusers. The project team will be assigned to Resolver groups, to provide solutions and close all incidents.

- Logistics for Hypercare team rooms, hotlines, and so on are all set up – this will also include any virtual requirements in light of the current home working environment.

- Communication distribution lists are agreed on to ensure the flow of information to all people/groups involved.

- Knowledge is transferred between IBM and the BAU support team to provide primary and secondary support to the project and BAU teams during Hypercare.

The following chart shows an example timeline for Hypercare for 10 weeks, usually providing coverage over a critical business event – for example, the end of the month – to ensure that the system performs as expected and that any incidents have been quickly resolved.

Figure 10.21: Example of the Hypercare model

Rollout post go-live

Following Hypercare, the RISE model allows the project implementation team to transfer knowledge to AMS support. This enables the main project implementation to continue with the deployment of the solution across legal entities defined by countries, regions, or processes/functional scopes – such as finance templates. The following chart highlights the key considerations for subsequent deployment principles, where any delta localization requirements can be delivered through country deployment plans, but where the Global Template design and solution integrity are maintained at all times:

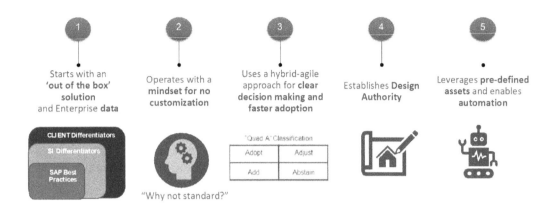

Figure 10.22: How a cloud mindset enables the right deployment outcomes

The following points describe some of the best practices that can support the rollout deployment of the solution while retaining control over the Global Template design's functional integrity:

- **DA governance** – Ensuring solution integrity throughout requires effective governance with representation from different countries. For example, in a two-tier deployment model, the central enterprise DA, sometimes referred to as a technical review board, comprises designated representatives from core business process leads, solution architects, and enterprise architects. Meanwhile, deployment countries can manage localization requirements through a local DA that has decision-making authority to extend, enhance, or enrich, but not change, the core functionality of the core template to retain the clean core principles, as well as alignment with the five golden rules for both public and private cloud editions of S/4HANA.

- **Service provider roles and responsibilities** – With RISE with SAP, the application delivery and project implementation, AMS support, and TMS are separate groups of activities delivered by different **System Integrators** (**SIs**). TMS can be delivered directly by SAP or subcontracted by an SAP partner – for example, a regional supplier. With the Breakthrough with IBM option, IBM can deliver additional value-adding propositions, services, assets, and value-adding accelerators on top of the core SI services. Furthermore, with the Premium Supplier option, IBM can also deliver TMS services on IBM Cloud, which is certified to deliver SAP workloads so that IBM takes the risk of all services under RISE (except software provisioning, which remains with SAP). It's important to mitigate the risk of working with suppliers, as there may be challenges with scale-up/scale-out or lead time issues.

- **SLAs and NFRs** – The RISE offering provides a comprehensive RACI describing the services that can be expected from SAP for TMS and what the SI provider has to do. The only firm SLA is to ensure users can access the SAP system. For example, S/4HANA Cloud, public edition has 99.5% system availability for prod and 95.0% for non-prod. Server provisioning has 99.5% system availability. Enterprises accustomed to higher levels of SLAs with their SAP workload located in on-prem data centers may have to purchase additional SLA levels – for example,

99.7% system availability or 99.9% system availability for prod applies if purchased by the customer and identified in the order form. Understanding the availability SLAs during rollout is important as the system has to be sized and scaled to enable additional workloads and capacity.

- **Pilot and subsequent deployments** – For the deployment approach, choosing a bilities" pilot needs to be done in a way that will convince other markets that the global template solution will work, then incentivizing and motivating other countries to adopt the global template design as a solution. This way, they can get on the bandwagon, and it can be a self-fulfilling prophecy in terms of global mobilization and deployment. This means designing the template so that country core requirements are built in. By taking input from strategic deployment countries/entities, you can build with future needs in mind.

- **The duration between deployments** – It's important to estimate how long to spend before going to the pilot. If the solution template is not federated and if the pilot is accepted, then it's important to build it out as quickly as possible, so that it is easier to deploy into a new location. It's important to build momentum and predictability so that, regardless of the platform, the deployment's momentum ensures a smooth delivery and supports a positive and constructive psychology that maximizes the business benefits.

- **The pace of change** – Is the business keeping up with the rollout strategy and does this help ensure that all stakeholders are onboard and reaping the benefits of the solution and seeing successful outcomes? The key is not to leave any country behind (rescheduling a deployment may be OK, but this is something that a business has to decide, not IT). Recognize that the core template does not need to change so fast – brand management may change more frequently but finance/procurement will largely be stable.

- **Localization** – Working with local teams is crucial to making the solution work, as is capturing localization requirements early (legal, fiscal, audit, global/local regulatory, and industry) by working with the next market team. Choosing which market follows which – for example, MVP/Release 2/3/4 onward – is dependent on ensuring the solution includes the right level of localization from the outset. Also, the solution template needs to justify how much local configuration is required. For some regions such as Germany, you need to consider works councils and EU regulations as part of any pilot or template in which German localization needs to be included. For localization plans, it's important to have a clear view of functional/process impacts first and then data, application, and technology. Deployments can be accelerated and enabled by a cloud development model but it's important to ensure the core functionality of the template retains its integrity and is controlled by a well-structured DA team.

- **Integrations** – Each country will have its own global and local integration requirements that need to be included as part of the deployment scope. Consider inner-ring/outer-ring integration with SAP PI/PO or SAP BTP Integration Suite to drive referential integrity with the SAP S/4HANA core while alternative/existing integration PaaS solutions may be used to enable wider enterprise-wide integration – for example, Kyma or MuleSoft integration models.

- **Global template design** – Consider how homogenous the template is – for example, whether we use models and industry cloud solutions from SAP or whether the template is highly configured with extensive updates and WRICEFs. If the latter applies, then changes may be required to introduce the template into each deployment, as it may not be aligned with SAP industry best practices. With S/4HANA Cloud, public edition, the adoption of a standard global template is easier due to a fit-to-standard mindset, while allowing for localization using the data, integration, and Extensibility features of the SAP BTP layer. You need to consider levels of differentiation, harmonization, standardization, and interconnectivity here.

- **Global instance strategy** – Consider N and N+1 landscape to support a regional or global single instance of SAP. This means making transport paths clear for release/change methods for the SAP core, integration layer, and legacy applications. We have described this previously.

- **Legacy application and modernization** – How are legacy applications (non-SAP and SAP) going to be treated? What are the treatment patterns for modernization? How many will be sunset due to S/4HANA; refactored, rehosted, or redeployed onto modern applications (for example, containerized on the cloud); replaced with SaaS; or retired and sunset out of the landscape? What happens to the integrations that existed in the legacy system – are these data integrations relevant to S/4HANA? What are the business change implications between the legacy and SAP systems? What are the implications of a legacy application holding up deployment – for example, if a given legacy application is business-critical to a given deployment country/region? All these questions will drive the approach to modernizing legacy applications. This topic has to be addressed as part of the S/4HANA deployment plan.

- **Global and local politics on deployment** – With complex stakeholder maps and cost owners/profit centers, it's easy to see how politics can drive behavior when stakeholders consider their position in the new target operating model. While politics is an emotional fact, there can be legitimate concerns that it could manifest itself as delays in stakeholders making decisions and users accepting the target solution. Again, early stakeholder management, including celebrating successes and quick wins, is key to neutralizing political impacts. It's important to invest in building a representative business during deployment planning – to ensure all stakeholders are engaged properly. It's important to stay close to decision-makers so you can access those who drive corporate strategy.

- **AMS support teams** – Secure early engagement. As part of the project's phases, we build what we need based on the scope and requirements. During Realize and Deploy, it's important to secure full support on what needs to be done.

- **Geopolitics** – Supply chains are going local, where due to sustainability drivers and the move away from just-in-time supply chains, more sourcing, planning, execution, and shipping is performed locally, resulting in improved ATP metrics with more confidence in meeting customer expectations. Also, a big driver of a single-instance strategy was to reduce the TCO and manage costs, but there are more ways to achieve that – for example, cloud flexibility options. This gives more options to diverge, merge, or divest – for example, moving away from Russia/China into regional instances or divesting completely and addressing data residency rules. An uncertain geopolitical world fractures our globally aligned, cohesive template.

- **In-flight upgrades** – Most of the time, clients have no direct business case for upgrades during deployment, so an upgrade is not built into the plan. However, with the pilot, there may be no chance to implement any upgrades, although there may be legitimate requirements – for example legal, fiscal, auditing, and security requirements. With S/4HANA Cloud, public edition, clients have quarterly releases to contend with, while the private edition requires upgrades within a 5-year window to ensure the currency of the application and auditable reporting. However, watch out for upgrades to partner apps – for example, with SAP, we fix SPAU/SPDD fixes, which cover the majority of changes, but we also need to look at the impact on tightly coupled applications such as OpenText, SAP SuccessFactors, SAP Ariba, SAP Concur, SAP Qualtrics, SAP Fieldglass, and other SaaS solutions, as these are not in scope for upgrades, but the data flow can be impacted – for example, an IDOC structure with integrated apps.

Summary

In this chapter, we covered all of the different factors, features, and capabilities required to deliver a successful go-live, including pilot and global rollout considerations. Following the deployment and rollout plan, a business can start to realize the benefits of the S/4HANA solution in terms of people, processes, data, code, and infrastructure.

We discussed how a well-defined Global Template, instance strategy, and deployment model allows businesses to rely safely on a system that is based on solution integrity with extensibility and flexibility. A clean core and fit-to-standard mindset will yield the maximum benefits for customers who define a strategy and implement it consistently throughout the implementation program.

In the next chapter, we will describe how the move toward continuous innovation increases the agility of the solution and its ability to scale, using the latest SAP BTP offerings and citizen development tools such as SAP Build for low-code/no-code, rapid application development to augment process automation. We will also discuss how we can extend S/4HANA using cloud-native capabilities with Web 3.0 and Industry 4.0 – for example, using digital twins to move toward the vision of being a sustainable, intelligent enterprise.

11

Innovation Unleashed: The Hunger Games

In the last chapter, you learned how to smoothly transition from a pilot rollout to a wider, global adoption of your golden template, gaining a whole new appreciation of the deployment and instance strategy and how it helps scale your integration and extend your clean core, propelling your organization toward its business vision. Once your organization has got the ball rolling for its digital transformation, there is no stopping or slowing it down. Your organization's leadership should fuel the fire to keep the verve going. The success of one part of the organization will rub off on the other units that have been more inactive and motivate them to follow the tried and tested template that has worked for other teams: using the golden template, accelerators, and the new **User Experience** (**UX**) with simplified data and processes. It all contributes to the adoption. The idea is that your organizational units join the mainstream of the S/4 HANA transformation and don't create another version of the siloed landscape from which they are emerging. That would defeat the point of reducing costs and operationalizing your sustainability goals – for example, reduced carbon emissions, including your data center and infrastructure footprints. System consolidation and the opportunity to have modern, harmonized processes across your organization offer synergy at scale in operations, including IT operations and maintenance costs. Moreover, it gives all employees an E2E view of the process and allows for tighter collaboration and appreciation of any additional ideas for new changes being introduced in the future.

Among many crucial decisions, the choice of using a single instance versus multiple instances is a difficult decision you will encounter in the initial stages of your S/4 HANA transformation. However, the processes of a unified and uniform digital core, barring a few variations, can be extended or changed using the extension platform, so even if you end up having a multiple-instance strategy, there will be a standard template to help optimize the change effort across the landscape over a lifetime and yet be hyperlocal in terms of the in-country/regional extensions hosted on hyper-scalers or SAP **Business Technology Platform** (**BTP**). In addition, the edge deployments your organization will have introduced to distinguish itself will help with the overall landscape sanity, performance requirements, and data privacy restrictions for certain countries – especially in data creation activities, data-in-transit security requirements, and retention. Moreover, the security posture is more robust with a standard core and differentiation at the edge, separating critical systems that govern your processes and data from systems that orchestrate them and manage the UX in terms of performance and scalability at the edge. In the following sections, we discuss future outlooks and considerations beyond your digital core on how other non-tangible and tangible levers of your organizations will help accelerate your journey toward your business goals.

It's time for Spark4Life to capitalize on the recent global roll outs, best in class user experience, harmonized processes, and hybrid cloud technologies to create a competitive advantage and to venture into new business domains and offer new products and services in existing and new geographies. The innovation streak that was unleashed during the implementation phases should be carried on. This is where they are planning to bring about some changes in their culture, ways of working, at times by getting industry experts in to do live webinars or talks to help their organization teams to think big, learn fast and fail faster. We will discuss these required changes in upcoming sections which Spark4life adopted bolstering and further improving their continuous innovation culture.

This chapter will cover the following main topics:

- The cultural shift to innovation
- Rewiring an enterprise for agility and scale
- Web 3.0
- The future of work
- Business and commercial models
- Industry 4.0

Let's begin!

The cultural shift to innovation

An S/4 HANA transformation is based on several shifts in process discovery and the execution and rollout of changes. This requires several small steps in the ways of working within the IT and the transformation teams and moving away from a waterfall mindset to a cloud mindset, with iterative improvements to adapt to markets and respond with agility. While these are the efficiencies introduced within an organization, external efficiency includes releasing new features and improving the current product with updates to keep the product and service relevant as customer needs evolve. This engages customers by incorporating their most requested features into subsequent releases. This has a considerable advantage in terms of buy-in, customer confidence, and brand loyalty. Your product will be valued more than perfection if you consider reviews, feedback, and surveys from your internal and external customer base. Waiting for the most comprehensive, excellent product or service for your customers to appear on the market will delay the launch, impact your first-mover advantage, and then lead to you playing catch up with the market or, worse, your competition. As this gap widens, panic sets in, and soon you will find yourself emulating market leaders in your industry. Therefore, the role of transformation is to bring about a cultural shift in how the organization evolves, with its new innovative products and value to the customer underpinned by technology and platforms. To achieve success, this cultural shift should encompass operations, the employees in the front, middle, and back offices, in plants, your field force, business users who use your solutions at the edge, and not just the transformation teams responsible for your digital core.

The digital core and the ecosystem levers it enables should move in the right direction to achieve accelerated synergy. These key business actuators have first-hand knowledge, are directly involved in delivering your organization's promises to customers, and get real-time feedback. If these actors are made aware of the art of possibility, they can bring up use cases that are quick wins and also of significant impact and value to your customers. Making them aware, training them with the essential tools, and then creating a platform for them to voice their ideas and opinions is required. Your organization should encourage discussion platforms and collaboration hubs and support use cases for sponsoring and funding the most voted-for services, products, or changes in the process. The following section will review frameworks for getting the ball rolling within a culture that spurs and fosters new ideas.

Sponsored innovation hackathons

More often than not, staff in the field come up with great ideas to solve the problems the customers face. They also have a wealth of practical information on what needs to change to turn a situation around. If your front-line employees have great ideas, they should be incentivized to come forward and make their vision a reality. The journey from ideation to realization for any new service or product should be encouraged, supported, and, most importantly, funded by the organization. At any given time, the organization should have a backlog of potential ideas that have been scrutinized through lenses of practical implementation, commercial feasibility, and market need. This is what allows you to differentiate yourself on the market, rather than waiting for a competitor to come across a gap that your employees have already identified and requested that the management considers in the next change release. The goal is to enable cultural agility and promote an environment of encouraging new ideas in which "good" is an acceptable starting point, rather than having a well-developed and perfect idea. Creating an organizational framework to develop further, improve, and realize commercially viable ideas is vital.

These frameworks for transforming your teams to think in an Agile, cloud-first, and digital mindset should be accessible to every rung of your organization. Employees who feel included and heard and contribute to organizational goals tend to strive harder to achieve personal and organizational goals more rigorously. Invite new ideas in collaboration forums (such as SAP JAM) within your organization. Ask employees, management, and the CxO office to vote on the top 10 to 20 ideas and invite proponents to a time- and cost-funded innovation hackathon. The teams or employees who contribute to these ideas should be allowed to work on their development and mature them with supporting squads from development, design, IT, operations, and marketing and sales teams to be involved in coming up with viable business models for these ideas.

Targeted training and code weeks help foster the adoption of technologies, which will help the company in general but has a positive side effect on the entire industry – enabling your employees with sponsored breaks from their daily operations to work on ideas while allowing them to learn and apply their learning to develop new ideas further. Arranging for technology evangelists to showcase the art of possibility and talking about where we are headed in terms of technological innovation will help open up the minds of your teams to think beyond what they know. Allowing supporting squads to evolve the initial idea into the first MVP will give your teams an appreciation of all the stages the product or service needs to go through before it is made available to the customer, thereby securing buy-in around what the company stands for, why certain decisions have been taken in the past, and what will be taken in the future. Employees who graduate from this hackathon break will become ambassadors and spread their thinking and verve to encourage wider audiences in the company to come forward, participate, and learn about new technologies. Technology should pervade throughout the organizational layers and be the key driver to transform your ways of working, enable agile delivery, and quickly and efficiently realize your business values.

Once you have a backlog of the most valuable ideas worth investing in, and they have been matured and scrutinized for commercial viability, encourage proponents to pitch their concepts to the organization's decision-makers, like in Dragons' Den. Fail fast, learn faster, and improve quickly should be the mantra. It should be permissible to work on a mediocre idea to change it into a market-leading idea. Building innovation is an iterative process that involves a business model, technology, the definition of value, and alignment with the business goals.

Innovation awards

The encouragement, enablement, and support of the organizational leadership are key here. Have a special career track for employees who promise and intend to learn more and become better versions of themselves day by day. Nothing fires up your organizational teams like an underdog story from the shop floor to the top floor, where smart, collaborative work and embracing technological growth are rewarded. The organization could also throw in award ceremonies or annual events to reward teams and employees who have shown great promise in hackathons, have been fearless when pitching their ideas, and have been open to learning. Again, a cultural shift will not just happen overnight; it takes its own time, as it is a process driven by motivated individuals who want to see change. Mindsets will shift toward iterative innovation – failing fast and learning faster – accepting that not all MVPs are perfect to start with and then incrementally delivering additional features to mature your product from being an initial concept to emerging on the market while scaling faster.

Now, having enabled and motivated people to drive technology-based business ideas, let's see how you can further accelerate the "idea-to-market" journey for your teams with platforms, governance, and technical and organizational frameworks that will help teams reach their goals faster while building the competency required.

Rewiring the enterprise for agility and scale

What used to take years can now be delivered in a few months or days and incrementally improved to be more reliable and successful, with repetitive patterns deployed on market-making platforms. The life cycle of applications and platforms evolves faster with cloud-native approaches and workloads on the cloud. It requires agility to cope with new ways of operating. IT can no longer be focused on controlling and constraining teams but rather enabling and governing them with the right tool sets to allow them to design and develop at their own pace within the given guidelines and support them during rollouts. Scaling the transformation, your organization will need to not only change its culture but also its development and delivery practices, with **Continuous Integration/Continuous Deployment (CI/CD)** to accelerate the time-to-value.

Not all of the workforce across the organization will have the development skill sets, and the existing development team's pros may not be enough to cope with the ever-exploding demand for changes from operations, front-line staff, and the overall business. Nor is it simple for an organization to hire the roles with the right skills within an already resource-starved market on demand, and retaining them is even more challenging. The need is to adopt more open technologies, with interoperable platforms for training, cross-training, and putting the power to develop simple to complex apps within reach for business users. This is where we enter the world of **Low-Code and No-Code (LCNC)** development, enabling functional business users to be citizen developers and improve the productivity and velocity of developers. You can weave their work into the control fabric of DevOps through automated CI/CD pipelines monitored by pros in the development community, supported by IT and platform experts to stage-gate what flows through these pipelines to production.

Citizen developers

As technology becomes pervasive within the organization, work and delivery will change rapidly. The adoption of cloud- and SaaS-based products and accessibility to data via mobile and 5G networks have helped democratize how the non-tech workforce leverages technology. Industry trends show the massive adoption of LCNC platforms within LoB and cross-industry solutions. The ethos of LCNC is based on the enablement of people with little to no coding experience to build and modify applications, allowing business users to be citizen developers to create and modify applications on demand. In the wake of this democratization of the technology trend, conventional development practices are being disrupted to allow anyone with sufficient IT skills to innovate and add value to the business. They create a complimentary yet key-value pool within your organization that supports the tactical changes required as the need for them emerges. Pro developers are focused on mission-critical and market-making platforms and processes. Dependence on a workforce of core developers and whichever technology drives the business outcomes do not overshadow the outcome itself. However, this approach to scaled LCNC mandates strong governance, which will ensure harmony between pro-code and citizen developers, unleashed with LCNC tools. This way, there are fewer hurdles in the way of innovating and getting solutions enterprise-ready. These LCNC platforms, when instilled within the DevSecOps framework, provide a robust set of processes and code checks, automated testing, and a deployment framework for continuous innovation and management.

In short, closed complex enterprise systems and processes are opened out by providing a level field to consume data, and the underlying processes are propelled further by standard APIs and LCNC tooling. A whole new class of employees can tap into these enabling tools and platforms to deliver new customer experiences and address opportunities themselves with minimal involvement from the IT teams. These technology enablers democratize development and operations thereon, equipping non-technical employees to tap into creating solutions for the enterprise and broader ecosystems. The following figure depicts experts from multidisciplinary competencies within an organization helping to create Agile squads that can collaborate, integrating DevSecOps practices when developing an idea rather than retrospectively introducing them after the product or solution is developed. Providing complete support to your business innovators either via teams on the ground or via governance tooling with LCNC is key:

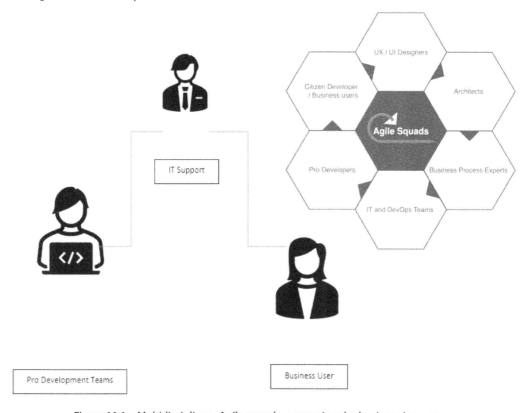

Figure 11.1 – Multidisciplinary Agile squads supporting the business innovators

Ease of use and development is addressed by these LCNC platforms. The acceleration and realization of business outcomes can be achieved by uncovering the value trapped in heterogeneous applications within a hybrid-cloud landscape and using an API-first approach to put this value within reach across the internal and external technical ecosystems of an organization.

Multi-layered APIs

With all the system and business process APIs offered by SAP S/4 HANA, new intelligent workflows, and events generated by processes, applications, and custom solutions, if you do follow some of the architectural principles covered in *Chapter 7*, your organization will end up with a library of reusable APIs. These open APIs (RESTFUL, SOAP, GraphQL, and event-driven) need to be discoverable and classified into experience APIs. The following layers are in line with how MuleSoft defines API-led connectivity and demonstrate the ease of maintaining and scoping them for external and internal use:

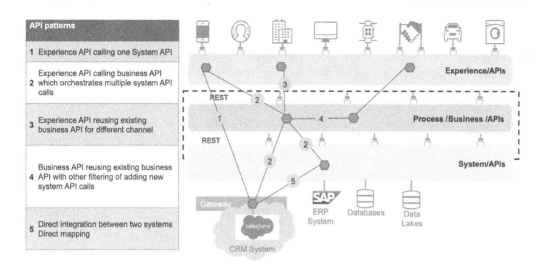

Figure 11.2 – Layered APIs lead to an API economy with inner-ring and outer-ring logical separation

Let's briefly discuss the main APIs:

- The system APIs typically expose the system of record processes and data. The organization typically has SAP ECC, S/4 HANA, customer and billing systems, critical databases, and data lakes sitting in this layer of APIs.

- The process APIs either extend the value of the system APIs to add value to expose it as new APIs. This is where multiple processes can be orchestrated – a layer in which intelligent workflow APIs fit well, which breaks down silos across LoB applications. A single process API can orchestrate between multiple system APIs or process APIs.

- Experience APIs provide the refined value and business context unlocked from the system and process APIs. They can call multiple business APIs or connect directly to the system APIs. They are typically consumed by customer-facing applications such as e-commerce, mobile apps, and enterprise or partner portals.

Democratizing and making these APIs discoverable will encourage reuse across the organization. The APIs can be further monetized by exposing them through an API gateway to third parties, customers, and partners based on the business model established. However, the key focus here is making these APIs readily available to LCNC platforms and citizen developers. All APIs must have appropriate controls built in to protect their data and must be treated as products, with portfolio and life cycle management processes managed centrally through the API management platforms. The APIs available from vendor-managed SaaS solutions such as Salesforce, Ariba, and SuccessFactors can then be classified under the different strata as explained here and scoped for internal or external usage, depending on the business requirements.

Security-as-a-Service

Making security infrastructure more easily consumable, such as using prebuilt components with built-in security, focuses on ease of adoption and implementation for the consuming applications. SSO, OAuth, or CORS mechanisms are handled at the API gateway/service mediation layers. These enterprise-enabled options are driven by trade-offs in terms of ease of use and the level of control and are made available either directly in LCNC offerings or by a team of dedicated IT support that focuses on the go-to-market products and services for the innovating teams. This results in increased developer productivity, with teams focused on creating reusable assets and services that can be broken down into components and used in other projects and products. Organizations are set on a path of exponential value creation, maximizing the return on investment and easing the demand on central IT teams when professional skills are hard to find. Security-as-a-service became the foundational accelerators that increase an organization's innovation quotient.

Let's summarize:

- Provide a support framework for citizen developers by embedding them into core development squads and scrum teams, which include business analysts, architects, and pro-code IT teams, to take the idea to market in a more collaborative way. This will help incorporate insight from outside-in customer experiences and combine it with an inside-out view of process expertise to tailor solutions to the business needs.

- The role of the IT organization and the CTO leadership is to encourage a culture of innovation within teams coming up with new ideas, developing and funding them through evaluation mechanisms such as a Dragons' Den scenario within the LoB, where the most valuable ideas are supported, tested, and taken to market.

- Create a governance model that not only prescribes security and architectural standards and enables teams to adhere to them but also democratizes data and processes on an iPaaS to create secure API service endpoints. This framework will become the bridge required for the LCNC applications to be adopted at the enterprise scale as they evolve and mature rapidly to match IT demands.

To further ease the development journey, when you have a uniform design and branded look and feel across all the applications that are being produced at scale, it is advisable to have a library or repository of all prebuilt assets and UI components that the developers – pro and citizen – can leverage to build prototypes. These visual frontend components in the library can be easily integrated using drag and drop and can consume the underlying API libraries. Every new project that creates a new component can contribute after it has been through code, design practice, and security reviews, and these components become available for other enterprise developers to consume. Most LCNC tools use open source technologies and architectures to allow interoperability with other frameworks on the market, so an organization's internal marketplace for all the reusable frontend components can host open source and proprietary features available to all developers to use as is or as a starter template. In the following section, we will briefly cover SAP's LCNC tooling to realize some of these concepts.

LCNC in SAP (SAP Build)

To keep pace with the technology trends and the demand for innovation, every organization is pushed to maximize the potential of its employees and enable them with the right set of tools to deliver innovation – such as enabling your citizen developers along with your pro developers. SAP Build was recently announced by SAP, which is the evolution of the LCNC development tools and services offered on SAP BTP. It brings together several products related to process automation, SAP workflows, and application development for mobile so that you can build LCNC portals or business sites under one unified development experience. The following LCNC solutions are packaged together as SAP Build on SAP BTP to enable pro and citizen developers to turn an idea into a working app swiftly for the extension of business processes, integration, or available frontend apps:

- **SAP Build Process Automation (SAP Workflow Management + SAP iRPA)** provides an intuitive no-code development experience for building workflows (SAP Business Application Studio) and automates tasks using Process Flexibility to create process variants without any code changes. It allows you to find new content packages for processes released by other LoBs or external partners in the API Hub marketplace. It uses Process Visibility to provide real-time insights into event-driven processes and instances while leveraging easy-to-use business rules, which are easily maintained in the cloud to be accessed by any applications via predefined APIs. RBAC to Inbox allows users to carry out the tasks assigned to them.

- **SAP Build Apps (SAP AppGyver)** is a visual low-code development platform that enables everyone to build sophisticated frontend applications using drag-and-drop functionality for building portals and mobile apps that are device-agnostic. It hosts a frontend component library that consists of open source prebuilt assets, or your developers can add their own for others to consume within enterprise-ready applications. It makes it easier to integrate with standard OData services, open APIs, third-party APIs such as Weather and Exchange Rates, and prebuilt connectors into SAP and non-SAP systems.

- **SAP Build Work Zone (merging the SAP Launchpad service + SAP Work Zone)** unifies two products into a single offering, empowering business users to build and publish business sites. It leverages the power of SAP BTP to deliver dynamic experiences, including but not limited to personalized, guided experiences for employee and manager productivity, such as leave management, the integration of business and partner sites – for example, for workplace safety, vaccine distribution, and management – and even employee training and learning experiences. We discussed the two products extensively in *Chapter 9*. The following are the current offerings:

  - **SAP Start** is the central home page for all SAP public cloud solutions, built on SAP Work Zone foundations with no extensions allowed (it was in beta when the chapter was written).

  - The SAP Build Work Zone Standard Edition (the SAP Launchpad service) provides a central personalized entry point for content and applications across the enterprise. Connectivity is available for cloud and on-premises systems with the possibility to integrate extensions and the ability to build custom navigation menus.

- SAP Build Work Zone, advanced edition (SAP Work Zone) creates and publishes business site content, mashes up external sites and unstructured data, and consumes SAP prepackaged premium content directly through these business sites. Business users can create team workspaces and integrate them with collaboration tools such as Microsoft Teams.

SAP Build
Create and augment enterprise apps, automate processes, and design business sites, all visually

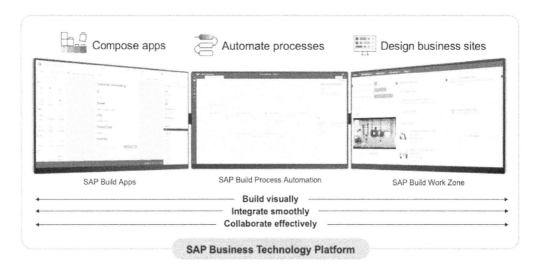

Figure 11.3 – SAP Build unified developer experience offering on SAP BTP

All these tools leverage a common project registry and artifact repository, sharing a common life cycle, and the deployed SAP BTP destinations and services secure access to business application data from S/4 HANA and the common, in-app content store. This content store has access to the largest amount of prebuilt content for process automation and workflows. SAP Build also offers strong collaboration capabilities for business and development teams so that they can define specific project teams in which people can vote and contribute. Business teams can use components developed by pro developers in Business Application Studio and apply them to their ideas or proofs-of-concept. SAP Build also provides governance and life cycle management across all the development artifacts, giving IT teams visibility and confidence that all apps deployed by the business meet the necessary security and governance requirements. To kickstart SAP Build within the free tier, refer to `sap.com/builders`.

- **Pro-code and low-code development with SAP Business Application Studio** allows professional developers to easily create and extend frontend Fiori applications to backend serverless logic (in Java, JavaScript, and Node.js), which can be deployed on Cloud Foundry using the **Cloud Application Programming** (**CAP**) model. It has several built-in plugins to accelerate the development to deployment cycle, with inbuilt integration to several data sources such as OData from S/4 HANA, SAP HANA, and other APIs from API Hub.

- ABAP Cloud, in line with the principle of a clean core (as discussed in other chapters), allows your organization's ABAP developers to create state-of-the-art, upgrade-stable, and cloud-ready ABAP extensions for S/4 HANA (using a **RESTful Application Programming** (**RAP**) model) directly in the S/4 HANA stack or on ABAP Cloud on SAP BTP. They can leverage S/4 HANA public APIs for S/4 HANA data and functionality and use public extension points for SAP objects that can longer be modified. When the extensions are switched to ABAP Cloud, compatibility with the ABAP compiler will enforce the rules of ABAP Cloud. Developers can use Eclipse ABAP Development Tools for RAP development with ABAP Cloud.

With the LCNC suite and all its prebuilt templates, SAP provides pro developers and business users with the tools that make the best of their respective skill sets without long lead times on training. Another service worth mentioning that makes the data across your SAP landscape centrally available through a common data model is SAP Graph, so let's briefly understand the features it offers.

SAP Graph and SAP One Domain Model (ODM)

To avoid a spaghetti tangle of integrations, with a point-to-point connection within in-house systems, development teams need to transition to a simpler integration middleware with a shared data model that takes care of the data mapping for the exchange of data, as not all applications in the cloud or on-premises will use the same data model to represent a business entity or the master data. For example, for customers, products, orders, and so on, SAP has introduced SAP ODM to simplify this, using **Core Data Services** (**CDS**) to adopt a domain-driven design approach to creating a shared ODM and facilitating all systems to speak the same language across an intelligent suite. No mappings are necessary and SAP BTP integration services such as Master Data Integration can distribute the data to all connected systems and/or E2E business processes. This supports the "write once, read many times" principles that we discussed in the *Data-to-value transformation* section of *Chapter 7*. With an incremental set of business data entities added to SAP ODM every quarter by SAP, it can be used across hybrid and pure-cloud landscapes through SAP API Hub.

The API through which SAP ODM is being consumed is called SAP Graph. It speeds up developer productivity on SAP BTP, creating an abstraction layer between the underlying landscape complexities, consolidating data models across several SAP hybrid-cloud and on-premises systems through a unified API, and tapping into SAP ODM in the cloud. It uses a business data graph under the hood to semantically unify all the enterprise business objects and their relationships under ODM to hide where the data is located, what security protocol is being used, and how to connect to these systems using the graph-like API. It uses OData v4 open standards with the OAuth protocol for any consuming customer or enterprise application – for that matter, extensions built using SAP CAP are compatible with SAP AppGyver and the events used in SAP Event Mesh. Check out SAP's Graph Navigator (`https://navigator.graph.sap/entities`) to explore the latest entities that are available for consumption.

LCNC tooling, the availability of data and events, and embedded security in the APIs enable citizen developers and pro developers alike to focus on delivering value with faster time-to-market.

In the past two sections, we focused on an inside-out, technology-enabled cultural shift; in the following section, you will see some of the outside-in forces you need to be conversant with in terms of technical shifts impacting your organization that you cannot ignore.

Web 3.0

The world wide web started as static, read-only content. Then, the era of interactive web technologies such as JavaScript and HTML facilitated the creation of interactive web platforms such as YouTube, Facebook, Wikipedia, and many more, and added more on-demand data with dynamic content and video streaming. Unknowingly, information related to our choices and interests was stored in cookies. These web technologies were then restricted by data privacy laws, which now require consent given that data has previously been monetized by being sold to companies who can tailor advertising to what users search for or base it on our personal interests, encroaching on our personal privacy. Later, social networks and the production of user-generated content flourished since data could be distributed and shared between various platforms and applications whose data was hosted, owned, and centralized by big companies. Today, we are at the inflection point of the evolution of the web.

Web 3.0 is a giant leap in the internet's evolution, using **Artificial Intelligence** (**AI**) and blockchain technology to run innovative programs to enable near-human intelligence to process data and provide appropriate choices to users. Key characteristics of Web 3.0 are that it is trusted, open standard, ubiquitous, and permissionless.

While the blockchain decentralizes data, Web 3.0 brings confidence to the virtual world that you can retrieve metadata and contextual information based on its content. Data about data and the data itself can be stored in multiple places, and minimizes the monopoly enjoyed by big internet giants such as **Metaverse** (**Meta**) and Google; more power is given to the people, breaking down the massive databases that these giants host and control. This could genuinely democratize the right to free speech and the expression of your ideas and opinions without censorship on your preferred platforms. This means that consumers of content and producers of content can interact directly without requiring permission from prominent social media giants, trusted intermediaries, or governing bodies. You would no longer need to accept cookies and provide consent. Reliable trust based on your pre-selected choices will be established by Web 3.0, giving each user control over their own data and resulting in a richer overall experience.

AI and **Machine Learning** (**ML**) will be part and parcel of and embedded into every interaction with Web 3.0. The semantics of the web, expressed through words, images, and emoticons, will be sufficient for interpreting information as we would when interacting with people. This would also equate to search engines accepting pictures, emoticons, jargon, and natural language (of your choice) to serve you the right content based on semantics and provide more relevant content. With the giant steps taken by governments and private ventures (such as SpaceX Starlink) alike, the availability of 5G and high-speed internet across the globe is becoming a reality. The ubiquity of the internet will fast-track the move toward the Internet of Everything, in which humans and machines will be connected in a myriad of ways, either through biological implants for remote healthcare, wearable devices for **Virtual Reality** (**VR**)/**Augmented Reality** (**AR**), or connected appliances within smart cities, operated using voice or gestures. This would offer a more personalized experience and more intelligent and human-like assistance. In a nutshell, the internet will become more intertwined with our daily lives when Web 3.0 arrives.

Moreover, Web 3.0, also known as the Spatial Web, will blur the line between the physical and the virtual world with the use of CGI and 3D graphics technology, creating AR or completely virtual worlds. The recent popularity of Pokemon Go, in which you searched for virtual creatures, was proof of the Spatial Web profoundly engaging people, who even risked their safety at times. The gaming industry is deeply connected to this concept. We already have some market-leading platforms and graphics rendering engines, such as Unreal Engine 5, pushing the boundaries to blur the line between VR and reality further. Smart glasses technologies, such as Oculus Lens, when matured in terms of human-machine interaction, will help provide immersive experiences not only in the gaming world but real life with AR applicable to real estate, health, e-commerce, sales, and service domains.

With **Natural Language Processing** (**NLP**) and the capacity of algorithms to close in with more than 99% accuracy, humans and machines can interact and process data at closer levels of cognition (with the help of AI) with contextual and semantic understanding. Interoperability between the decentralized blockchain, AI, the IoT, and digital assets will allow for smart contracts to be exchanged autonomously and captured as transactions on decentralized ledgers for a new Web 3.0 economy in the virtual and real world. With this explosion of technologies, companies such as Meta, Google, and Amazon are still discovering potential use cases. The exciting part is that we are just getting started with Web 3.0. New business models will emerge, and data sovereignty and the democratization of these technologies will make it more personal with richer, immersive experiences. Now, this is quite invigorating and promising, but can this be applied to any part of our organization? How do we enter the target markets, starting small and scaling after testing our needs?

In the following section, we will tinker with these ideas to see how they could be applied today at the forefront of the adoption of Industry 4.0.

The future of work

With all these technological enablers such as Web 3.0 and automation AI, our lives are being transformed in front of our eyes. We are at an inflection point in which the boundaries between the virtual and real worlds will blur and form a spatial internet. The digital twins of everything and everyone will be interconnected to get work done in ways never thought before. During the pandemic, we saw shifts in how work was done, from staff being collocated in a physical location to working remotely, with tools that enabled virtual collaboration. Meta promises even more immersive experiences by allowing you to design your avatars and meet and collaborate in the virtual world. This is also true for your customers and consumers alike being able to form communities, meet, collaborate, and share ideas and feedback in customer meetings and during product announcements, or use remote services while still interacting face to face. To accommodate and adopt these shifts in work and how work gets delivered, the HR and organizational culture will need to move towards a more skill-based (and more digital) resourcing approach to the workforce. When we talk about the real world, we talk about people and their talent, the skills they bring to your teams, your team's skills, and how these skills help achieve a task or complete a process.

When discussing human capital and how we manage our skills, we have traditionally been talking about domestic labor pools, as well as offshore and shared services labor pools. A third arm is now emerging in this model – the digital workforce consisting of digital beings. These digital beings, either process automation/transactional bots or virtual avatars, are digital extensions that augment your capabilities in the digital or virtual world. Your human workforce needs to be introduced to and understand how it can augment its capabilities to make it more effective, smarter, and more efficient by tapping into the capabilities of the digital workforce. To make use of its support and assistance and, in turn, train them to complete business processes, train them on cases where they didn't perform well, improve their capabilities, and manage their life cycle from onboarding to decommissioning in order to introduce a new version of an improved process. In short, HR needs to be cognizant of managing the digital workforce and should have systems and organizational controls for the digital workforce managed by the human workforce. Today, the digital workforce for the front, middle and back offices is more software-based as we make exponential progress in maturing our AI and ML algorithms. For the field workforce, production lines, or shop floors, the digital workforce is physically available to carry out the most rote tasks and chores in warehouses and delivery centers, do stock accounting, quality-check, and move goods, with intelligence injected into them based on the advancements of computer vision, classification problems, and autonomous mobility.

Once your company embraces these principles of workforce diversity and equality for digital beings and the human workforce, it becomes possible to operate in a gig economy where we recruit the right workforce (with the right skills), scale per our requirements for the right amount of time, and share expertise across LoBs or companies – for example, end-of-the-month/end-of-the-quarter closures where accounts receivable/accounts payable, with automated clearing and matching payments to accounts, is a crucial task. An AI-based bot can complete tasks such as these within a few minutes and pass on any tedious exceptions to the human supervisor managing the month-end closures for further action. The marketplace for this gig economy can offer the workforce (with protected IP) as a service to other companies or within other organizational arms to complete this routine work. A fleet of these bots can focus on specific tasks (OCR scanning), processes (raising work orders), or advanced reasoning (learning and unlearning the root cause for failures on service tickets), leading to decisions that help users execute their tasks more efficiently, reducing errors. Again, this advancement in AI and robotics and its adoption is not about replacing people; it's about augmenting the human workforce and allowing it to focus on tasks and jobs that require experience and higher skill sets. The tag teams formed within an organization will help to generate more reliable, compliant, and predictive outcomes with higher success rates.

Once you have got this digital fabric of human and digital workforce weaved in, you will have a workforce that can ramp up to any skill level at short notice, as AI-based assistance will be available for anyone newly joining or moving into a new process, which will help when carrying out E2E business processes. Work can then be mapped to skills rather than a specific team or team member. The best part is that the digital workforce will gain from experience and share this same experience with someone entirely new so that a novice can operate with the help of a digital entity with 20 years of experience. The human expert/business owner trains the ML model on the job and, at the same time, also trains the bots, who can then execute the same tasks if the situation arises. Once you have mastered this, a business model emerges in which you can offer the skills of the digital workforce as a service on the cloud, if you choose to, within your industry. Bots become highly skilled at specific tasks and can be ramped up and down when demand spikes rise and fall as other companies will be doing the same in other parts of the business, resulting in a skills economy that's very similar to the gig economy. This is possible today when you start to unlock the value of the SAP S/4 HANA processes, accelerated by RPA and underpinned by ML-based decision-making, and make these skill sets available to your people via Conversational AI to trigger and complete E2E processes.

Delivering these bots and combining them with intelligent workflows as the backbone is the key – for example, in a life insurance application, your teams may think to add intelligence to analyze patient records to provide a better life insurance solution, as medical underwriters are hard to find and are highly skilled and valuable individuals. This dilemma has all the characteristics of something that can be solved by an intelligent workflow, bringing in data from many different doctors' practices and disparate data sources, which are inherently in different formats. You can apply ML to extract considerable value from the content to drive most routine work and allow medical underwriters to focus on crucial tasks that make the most of their capabilities. You can use simple automation to reduce the number of mouse clicks, improve efficiency, and use ML instead to filter out the more routine cases and enable humans to focus on high-value tasks.

There are several key advantages of a digital workforce:

- A digital workforce is available 24/7 and is infinitely scalable because it is cloud-based, and you can have as many conversations with them as possible

- Digital entities are permanent employees and have no attraction to competitors

- There are a lot of AI components that involve human experience, such as NLP; they learn from every single interaction, so they get better at their job by interacting over time

- Contact center operators leaving the front office during the pandemic and remote support becoming unreliable for your customers are problems that can quickly be solved by deflecting most telephone conversations to a chat-based or CGI-based digital workforce

Think about the future in terms of how it will change the UX and the underlying economics of the competition. Essentially, when you are subscribing to, building your own, or buying a digital provision such as this, you are purchasing a scalable asset rather than investing in a linearly scaling cost center of HR.

The spectrum of automation and digitalization

The automation of business processes, transactions, and tasks can be applied to different degrees, whether semi-automated, completely automated, or intelligence-driven. A day-in-the-life scenario for the digitalization of a paper-based process that precedes a transaction in a business application could be field workers who take notes on their rounds and then enter the readings or observations into a business application on their return to the office to trigger a service order. Semi-automating the process, the field worker could use their mobile device to point their camera at the readings to auto-populate the readings using ML and dictate notes (speech-to-text) to their phone to create a ticket, which means being more productive at work, completing more rounds, and focusing on what matters the most. This service order, on the back of the mobile data being synced, will be triggered immediately to help reduce overall business process times.

Another common automation scenario is the digitalization of a semi-automated process. Approval processes are managed over email by the approving manager for purchase requisitions going through cycles of clarification, getting stuck in overflowing inboxes, or ending up in the wrong place. Unfortunately, this is an error-prone process with uncertain cycle times that can be hard to audit. A clearly defined digital process flow helps you collect the required information and follow business rules to route to the correct approvers, accelerate cycle times, and improve governance. If the digital purchase requisition process is integrated with procurement, approval can automatically trigger a purchase order without requiring the requestor to enter the information again. The following diagram depicts the automation level and infusion of intelligence, if at all, at each level of this kind of process. Each of the points along this spectrum involves different patterns of work that digital beings do – from pure basic automation to highly sophisticated business process execution with the help of AI decision support.

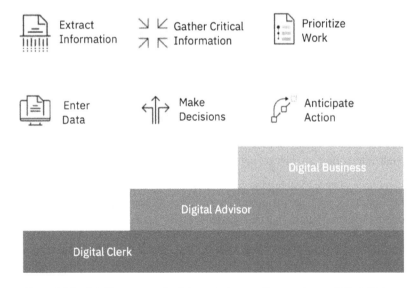

Figure 11.4 – Intelligence can be integrated across the spectrum of digital labor

Let's look at each in detail:

- **Digital Clerk**: This is an RPA bot that completes a set of repetitive tasks. It typically sits in the front office or sometimes in the back office, but humans usually do this repetitive mundane work. A typical example is offices as they are feeding documents to an OCR mechanism to extract structured data from the documents. The trade-off is reliable, high-quality data extraction versus the cost of deploying a human resource. What you are looking for is to extract the semantics and key-value pairs out of what's in the document.

- **Digital Advisor**: You have knowledge bots who augment your knowledge with advice or recommendations so that a worker doesn't have to search through millions of documents to discover something or look back through historical searches, for example, for every single auto claim you have ever taken. The employee or consumer has somebody or something that gives them advice. Digital augmentation facilitates intelligent decisions, insights, and recommendations to help and augment a person's daily tasks. A good example would be a digital assistant gathering information for a service engineer whom it is assisting to figure out the context of the trouble ticket; they have to dig down into a myriad of data to figure out what the problem is that needs to be addressed to resolve the ticket. If this is infused with intelligence and automation, the service engineer can get the key data points to interpret the information they have about the ticket and what other engineers have done in the past. This is in the middle of the spectrum of automated intelligence.

- **Digital Business**: The other end of the spectrum is when an advanced intelligence bot (or bots) executes the E2E business process. With this inside-out labor transformation, your organization can turn your customer into your back office to capture data and initiate automated processes. This kind of transformation allows you to change your business model and requires the automatic execution of tasks, ML, and critical flows that understand your business goals. It provides the ability to prioritize and follow the best action for the situation. For example, a certain kind of alert pertains to a certain kind of problem, and an intelligent bot will act and make something happen on your behalf in response. I have seen this kind of pattern before. 95% of the time, we offer a service to the client in this situation, and the problem is resolved. The assistant to the business user will recommend that you repair or replace assets as appropriate, creating a feedback loop that drives your business processes. That's what automation with intelligence is all about.

Digital employees

Technology is only valuable if people can adopt it quickly and easily, serving humanity and accelerating its purpose. The UX should be simple when using AI. Its comprehension of human conversation, be it text- or voice-based, scales exponentially, and so does its adoption. Conversational interaction becomes more relatable through emotional and contextual connections to the user. The following section discusses some of the possibilities when creating UIs for AI and how this translates to the UX, which was never thought of before.

Several digital/human AI companies have given faces and personalities to digital beings. Soul Machine is one such company, which simplifies interaction with customers with empathetic, smart conversations in natural language, democratizing the creation of intelligent, emotionally active avatars, which are autonomous and can think and react based on personality skills and are empathetic to your experiences, with the digital brain reacting in real time in a highly personalized way. Besides a synthetic voice, a digital avatar and conversational AI, if trained for most customer touchpoints and situations, can be autonomous, tapping into its training, knowledge base, or the vast amounts of data that can be looked up from the internet, as Google or Siri does.

Brand ambassadors

The brand's customer experience is an important asset for any company in the digital and transactional world. Most powerful brands have relational properties and not just transactional ones. Customers buy from brands aligned with their values. Creating an empathetic connection is vital. How do you acquire a customer, retain them, and make the relationship more valuable? The way the digital being responds and the tone of the voice defines how empathetic the being seems. Creating human-like conversations remains an immensely complex task. The conversational content and AI algorithms determine the best response, and the NLG technologies help improve how an answer is communicated. Your employees, as a brand, will always want your customers to have a specific experience and for it not to vary across different channels, so technologies such as AI assistants, chatbots, and the digital workforce are brand ambassadors. They need to provide the same brand experience and inspire loyalty and customer retention, as customers form connections with digital beings if the digital entities can emote and express themselves in ways they can relate to. This enables companies to provide customers with an experience that achieves a high NPS score; people want to return and experience it again.

When you design the brand ambassador, consider fundamental aspects such as what do they look like? What do they sound like? What is their personality? How will the digital employee represent the brand and the product to the customers, and how will they represent the values of the company, the same as real people do in the real world? This is a lot of what real-world behavior and demeanors communicate, transposed to the digital world. Digital brand ambassadors could be your first digital employees with personality and life-like characteristics.

While relying on digital employees, companies must also consider the ethical use of digital workers when interacting with customers and employees. With the implications and data privacy, companies must think about coming to the grips with cookie-less marketing, for example. Government regulators govern how private and personal data is used. We are on the cusp of an era in which companies have to start thinking about how they take responsibility for customers' personal data – for instance, the ethics of deploying a digital workforce. These considerations apply to digital entities as well as human employees.

Teams of digital employees can be of different genders and from different age groups, and speak different languages. The customer can then choose the personality they want to talk to, maybe choose a being of the same age, opt to speak in German rather than English, and align their interests with an applicable digital employee. This is how we should start thinking about how the workforce comprises a mixture of different skills and how they are delivered to the customers it serves, so the whole concept is way beyond just implementing a chatbot. The way you and your customers interact and use these technologies will be above the level of a chatbot. Some key functions for digital employees include, but are not limited to, HR onboarding, application training, and upskilling people with new skills and capabilities. Interact directly, request feedback, and act on the data you collect from the engagement to personalize and consume more information.

By combining digital faces with Conversational AI today, we enable digital beings to respond to users in their chosen language to enable customer engagement while creating a brand following or a new type of community, which leads to new opportunities opening up and new ways to connect your customers to your brand both personally and at scale.

Futuristic retail experiences

A fundamental thing missing from e-commerce is an in-store experience in which you are greeted by someone who engages with you consistently in line with the brand identity. The way they interact and greet people, this personality, represents the brand – for example, intelligent, quirky, friendly attributes – as do the skills needed for the job, such as guiding customers through the store using virtual glasses and assisting them in making selections per their taste and liking. An avatar can be personalized to the customer's preference. Hence, this all gives the experience of visiting a store with a friend who explains the features of the product and the pricing details and knows your likes and dislikes – meanwhile being secure enough to protect your data. These different skills must be built upon and improved to obtain better coverage of all possible situations and a better understanding of the semantics that Gen Z in particular use to express themselves. Moreover, there must be elegant handoffs to human staff and feedback from onsite staff or the customer on what went wrong in the case of failure and how the interaction could be improved during the next visit.

Further, for e-commerce sites and customer portals, you can plug these digital humans as digital assistants rather than just chatbots to interact in a customer-preferred language – for example, to guide people through available assortments, selections, sizes, and variants of products or apparel; answer queries on order statuses; provide information on the latest fashion trends; and virtualize how a particular clothing pattern would suit an occasion using intelligent suggestions on type and color using either personal data or pictures of the customer. The knowledge base for this kind of skill set is enormous. It needs to be curated based on conversational content from history, personal preferences of the customer, and FAQs, and should be ready to look through purchasing records and infer deals that would be most enticing to close sales. These experiences can be rich and immersive, 2D on simple screens, or completely virtual if you have a retail space in the metaverse.

Suppose your organization doesn't want to take the leap with these unique digital human interactions. In that case, you can start small with voice-based or text-based digital assistants such as Google or Alexa. This provides a digital assistant for your employees to do some commodity tasks for employee productivity and for critical tasks such as processing all approvals with voice commands to initiate automated processes or intelligent workflows based on the context and the intent of the conversation.

As mentioned at the start, voice scales, and so does the option, dropping the user interaction barrier to have any specialized training to operate or interact with the digital assistants.

The following diagram depicts how these interactions would look in the SAP S/4 HANA space using Blue Prism or any other automation platform such as Automation Anywhere, UI Path, or SAP iRPA. The following example diagram is just an example – you can substitute the products or services available in your IT landscape:

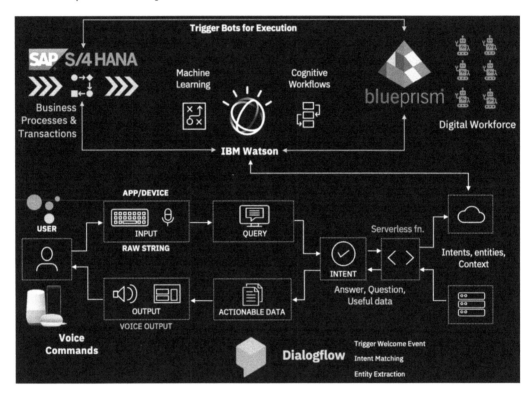

Figure 11.5 – Using Google as Conversational AI: voice-based interactions for business process automation

Business and commercial models

With all these technologies at your disposal, your people are enabled and motivated to deliver value at scale. The industry best practices that the S/4 HANA digital core, with in-memory data, has to offer within the hybrid cloud landscape prepare you to expand to new markets, create new revenue streams, and introduce new products. How does your organization offer these services and products to customers with palatable commercial agreements? The supporting TOMs and associated costs define your top and bottom line. The customer experience, combined with marketing campaigns, will help open a lead funnel; converting it into sales involves commercial considerations and the right price points for variants and add-ons, making your offering *good value for money* from the customer's perspective in simple terms. In the following section, we will weigh up several commercial and business models that your organization can consider. We will discuss some of the industry trends and consumption patterns that aim toward an on-demand economy, which are a win-win from a customer affordability standpoint and foster sustainable practices for organizations.

A subscription economy

The pandemic saw a rise in subscriptions with Amazon Prime, Netflix, Apple, and so on. People stuck at home accentuated this pivot from one-off sales to subscription-based services, with the ability to buy online and get things delivered. A subscription-based business model creates a direct ongoing relationship between the OEM/producer and the customer; it's about creating long-term relationships with customers and staying relevant to their ongoing needs and wants. It involves moving away from discrete, one-off sales to ongoing recurring transactions and identifying opportunities to expand engagement to gradually grow the customer base instead of having to constantly find new customers. Subscription models allow a company to build a lot of data around the consumer. Leverage that data on usage and purchase behavior to personalize the offering and services and deepen existing relationships. Subscriptions also translate into a brand loyalty philosophy. More importantly for an organization, the transition to a subscription-based business model requires a change in mindset from how to make discreet sales to how to cultivate relationships.

On the flip side, too many subscriptions result in subscription fatigue. Cineworld had a subscription model for a Cineworld pass, typically a monthly or yearly subscription, allowing movie lovers to watch as many movies as possible for a subscription fee; in recent years, it raised the fees, which felt like throwing away money during the pandemic, as it was prohibited to be in public places in groups. Nor did the subscription offer any on-demand streaming options on existing platforms as a stop-gap arrangement for subscribers. As a result, the subscriptions dropped, and there were no repeat subscriptions, as viewers didn't see the value of sticking with a subscription and moved to stream via on-demand services. Another variant of a similar shortfall in subscriptions was that of Netflix, as subscriptions plummeted post-pandemic with an increase in competition due to the lack of new, exciting, and relevant content and the frequency at which content was being dished out. Another twist in the changing dynamics of consumption patterns applies to the BBC, which has seen declining budgets and UK citizens deciding that they don't require a TV license subscription mid- and post-pandemic as the masses flock to on-demand services. This is aggravated further by the cost-of-living crisis that the country is currently undergoing.

Delivering relevant experiences to the consumer at a good cost, conveniently, and with a discernible value was the historical driver of purchasing behavior and how to build better customer relationships that would drive customer retention. Now, it is more driven by value and purpose, while other additional dimensions, including choice (competitors), apply. What do subscribers identify themselves with? Sustainability, equity in the workplace, and responsible sourcing are some critical aspects that younger generations relate to. Whether the customer's values align with the purpose of a company offering a subscription dictates whether they identify with the brand.

A 2020 consumer study revealed that Gen Z and Millennials are more likely to have subscriptions than older generations and are more interested in trying them if they don't already have them. Looking at the data, Gen Z and Millennials already have close to 60% of the potential to absorb more subscriptions than the older generation in the customer segments depicted here: `https://www.ibm.com/thought-leadership/institute-business-value/en-us/report/subscription-business-model`.

The fundamental change for any organization is to move from the number of units sold to the **Average Revenue per User** (**ARU**) in subscription terms and the number of active users, which define the revenue potential. Revenue recognition in subscription-based models is always less than the one-off sales achieved by your organization. Still, the overall predictability and reliability of future revenue streams are much higher, which results in a higher valuation of your brand amongst shareholders and customers alike. For example, Apple decided to stop reporting on the number of units sold for iPhones to shareholders, switching to reporting the average revenue per subscriber and the number of subscribers that apps had, which was a significant shift in the way revenue was being recognized. This is paying back now as Apple has a vast number of subscribers, and this makes a positive impact for shareholders in terms of earnings per share.

With the subscription model, it will take longer to recoup the initial investment or costs of the goods. For example, if the cost of manufacturing a car is $20,000 and it is sold at $25,000, the profit would be $5,000. If offered as a subscription model at $1,000 per month, over a period of 36 months, it will yield $16,000 more than a one-off sale within the transaction model, but take 20 months to recoup the costs of manufacturing.

Revenue recognition

Subscriptions are not just operational add-ons. Companies must rethink how they will account for revenue, assess the capabilities required to manage ongoing relationships, and transform to deliver a subscription model. The revenue recognition model will be impacted quite significantly, so setting up the model and the financial infrastructure to support that and how well your organization is prepared to react to the market feedback as it shifts its revenue to accommodate a different model is important.

There is a complete switch in the metrics the organization will need to adopt to measure value and success. Data analytics are required to understand which KPIs would work for your subscription model, so your teams have to lay this approach out right from the design stages to define the KPIs that will measure your outcomes. Rethink the business process, not just technological and operational solutions, and the talent and skills required to define and extract the data points from the data collected. Companies skilled at subscription-based business models measure the success of their customer relationships by tracking metrics such as the following:

- Number of subscribers
- Number of **Monthly Active Users** (**MAU**)
- The **Average Revenue Per User** (**ARPU**)

- The **Annual Recurring Revenue (ARR)**
- Rates of churn and retention
- The **Customer Acquisition Cost (CAC)**
- **Customer Lifetime Value (CLV)**

Now, let's look at some of the business models and the revenue models that you can realize when moving to a subscription economy with some examples in the following section.

Subscription-based business models for sustainable Consumer Packaged Goods (CPGs)

The consumer industry has a high throughput economy; more stress falls on sales than product reuse, repair, and recycling. Many products, including electronics, garments, and food packaging, that fall under this category end up in landfills or offshore, where the cost of dismantling and extracting valuable resources, from e-waste, for example, is low, although it is fraught with health and safety concerns, creates pollution due to the extraction process, and dumps heavy metals in the soil. Humanity is ignorant when moving its waste from one part of its home to another – it still has to be taken care of sooner than later, and the boomerang effect will affect us all. This is where all industry sectors and leaders must introduce the design for circularity concept to reduce waste and circle back to the value in sourcing and production lines to become responsible, sustainable businesses with **Environmental, Social, and Corporate Governance** (**ESG**) in mind.

The high churn of electronic products due to the new versions of the hardware and the software being released every 6 months makes most devices obsolete within 3-4 years, resulting in mass production, energy consumption, and high levels of extraction of rare metals. The recent Right to Repair movement in the electronics industry led to a law being passed in the US to allow local repair shops and authorized service centers to repair with the right components from the OEM and recycle most electronic devices. With this movement spreading across the globe, producers, consumers, and supply chain operators must work hand in hand to improve the effectiveness of the levers that will help circular design mitigate environmental damage effectively.

Changes to business are inevitable with design by circularity, to incorporate more regenerative and restorative circular models and extend the value of manufactured products. Giving a second or third life to a product after sales and service processes with modular, upgradeable, and serviceable parts or offering the product as a service with the service life cycle being maintained by the manufacturers are some of the shifts that are required. To support the way that entire business systems and processes (from sourcing to recycling) are designed, subscription-based models such as on-demand, community sharing, or leasing are required, which endorse circularity and initiate more novel business models to move away from high throughput to high usage.

- **Product as a service (fixed revenue)**: For a specific duration, the latest and best products can be offered as a product-as-a-service or pay-per-use installation at specific locations in an office building. This reduces the focus from CAPEX to OPEX for your customers or consumers – for example, many multi-function office printers and pieces of copying equipment can be offered as a service to large companies; with the asset maintenance and servicing, replacements of modular components being carried out by the OEM or a partner who manages the entire service. This model is a win-win for the customer and the manufacturer, as the customer gets the best service and is hands-off in terms of maintaining and servicing the equipment. The best part is that the customer doesn't have to worry about upgradability and repairability or the depreciation of the assets. On the other hand, the manufacturer can collect data to improve reliability and innovation for the product to offer more suitable products. Circularity through reverse logistics and recycling processes is more easily managed by supply chain partners.

- **Sharing services (one-off or hybrid)**: This values access over ownership and facilitates a circular economy. This is offered by distributors or partners in every region across the globe on products that rent out products or services to consumers and customers based on rental fees and can result in other complementary business models with other service partners – for example, DIY and power tools are offered as a rental, and service technicians are trained in using the tools to get the job done as an add-on offered to the rental service. This also applies to heavy machinery such as earthmovers. A software or app service could be extended to partners or owners of these tools and equipment on a platform so that the owners can rent it out to other prospective buyers or ad hoc users. This provides a good return on investment, and the commercial value-to-depreciation ratio is better over the life cycle of the product for the owner as a result. Users of these types of equipment can try out the equipment for infrequent use as a "taster," which may result in purchasing decisions if their needs increase. The manufacturer may then offer buy-back services with discounts on upgraded equipment based on the residual value of the returned product. The manufacturer can then deploy the circular models to refurbish, reuse, repair, or recycle components and materials. The logic is simple – the more infrequently you build new products, the smaller your carbon footprint, contributing to a sustainability agenda and your organization's goals. The ESG aspects of sustainability significantly focus on decarbonization and the reduction of energy emissions.

- **Community sharing (consumption- and usage-based revenue)**: In this model, the manufacturer funds an entire communal setting and its appliances, with equipment such as the washing machines at launderettes, and communities – private or public – either pay as they go or take a monthly subscription of certain bundled services as suits their requirements. These are situations in which the OEM can provide a more reliable service using refurbished or recycled appliances. Any value-adding services, such as extra provisions in launderettes, also generate additional revenue streams.

- **Pay-per-outcome (outcome-based revenue)**: This is focused on the delivery of necessary capabilities, outcomes, or services required by users with uptime agreements, without the need to purchase a product. These are continuous, ongoing, no-interruption operations. Examples of this could be office copiers and printers that the OEM maintains, as well as providing consumables, such as printing paper of all sizes and ink cartridges, and ensuring the uptime of the service as per the contract. Customers don't need to worry about replenishing the stock of consumables or any maintenance. This model also pertains to providing customer segments with premium products such as luxury cars without the need to maintain or purchase them, available on demand to drive for a month and swap for another the next. In this way, they pay for the outcome – 24/7 availability of the services and products they want. Some of the services are asset management – for example, keeping a plant running; they don't just keep the production lines running but also operate without interruption, so with maximum uptime. This invites service models for production, repair, onsite inspections, and predictive maintenance for continuous no-interruption operations. Other examples are delivery-as-a-service for logistics providers and mobility-as-a-service from auto manufacturers with a fleet of self-driving cars to get people around. In this example, when you make a one-off sale of a car, you may earn $3,000. However, if you look at the vehicle's life cycle, the car requires annual servicing, tires being changed, spare parts, and labor to keep it going without breaking down, which may amount to a $30,000 profit pool over the vehicle's lifetime. The CAR OEM can step back and understand how it can provide subscription services to cash in on this profit pool. Understanding the E2E need and understanding how a subscription and service model will meet that need is essential.

- **Tiered licensing (data-based revenue)**: Some data providers, such as weather data providers and OEM manufacturers, can offer APIs based on this model to customers such as Apple for weather requests made by Apple's users that are hyper-local, logistics companies planning optimal routes, and ride-hailing companies predicting surges in demand in bad weather. The data provider and aggregators of the weather data may allow a tiered subscription service – bronze, silver, gold, and platinum. They will allow a set number of API calls per month against permitted numbers and types of APIs based on the tier chosen. The metering, throttling, rate limiting, and provision of the latest API versions available are ensured by the API management and associated account management services offered by the service provider. OEMs for appliances or cars can monetize the anonymized data collected from devices connected to consumers and service history so that it can be used by other service providers interested in cross-selling, value-adding services. This also applies to energy companies interested in analytics and data science investigations on the usage of energy, with a similar ecosystem of freelance developers and third parties who want to create specialized home energy monitoring solutions and services.

Shifting from product ownership on the part of customers/consumers to a subscription-based system defines a circular economy that is reflected by the product design (with product design taking the modularity of components into account so that they can be replaced), the business process design, the supply chain, the take-back and decommissioning processes, and the refurbishment and recycling processes. Governments and regulatory bodies tracking the ESG goals within an industry incentivize the OEM to design a product to allow easy software and hardware upgrades and extend a product's life cycle. The recent release of Fairphone 4 smartphones is an excellent example of modular, upgradable, repairable design, making it easy for users themselves to replace or swap any critical modular parts with others. This is the first wave of sustainable smartphones hitting the market. A whole host of people is coming up with ideas and ways to become more eco-friendly and quickly adopt a circular economy.

Other considerations for subscription models

Supply chains within a subscription-based economy need to be thought of to adopt changes when moving from a transactional model to a subscription-based one – for example, the rental model for power tools, or, for major high-street brands, getting products ready to be shipped out for a rental duration, reclaiming the product after it has been used, cleaning and maintaining the product, and repackaging it to be shipped to different customers again. This involves a process for depreciation, inventory decay, managing membership, and also billing. Therefore, the overall process of moving from transaction-based sales to a subscription model requires several changes within the operational supply chain. A supply chain generates so much data that contains the potential to increase revenue by streamlining and optimizing whole processes. Unfortunately, supply chain processes and systems haven't seen the light of day despite recent technological advancements in the past decade. When you think about the supply chain, the employees who plan it, the truck drivers, the people who unpack boxes, and quality checkers, many of these processes can make use of ML elements to aid decision-making, make processes more efficient, and increase performance in your subscription economy. The concepts and the frameworks we discussed in *Chapter 4*, *Chapter 7*, and *Chapter 9* (process mining, intelligent workflows, and adopting the industry best practices) will help define robust subscription, billing, delivery, service management, and, importantly, process automation systems in the long run, putting your organization and its teams in a better position to tackle the high churn involved in subscribing, unsubscribing, the changes to data that ensue, and the deactivation of services.

Likewise, a lot of data is generated about the subscriber – what they buy, how they use your products, and their preferences. How you tailor what you offer to them for a more personalized experience involves data analysis and skilled data science. How do you leverage that data to retain customers? How do you extend that relationship to cross-sell and upsell opportunities, promote responsively, and continuously deliver the desired experience and meet evolving needs? You will also need a modern data and AI infrastructure, as explained in *Chapter 7*. With the help of AI, you can predict customer wants and needs for tailored services and recommendations, providing insights to build subsequent new offerings. Design for relevance – rethink with data, analytics, and AI.

Before you jump on to the bandwagon of subscription models, please consider asking yourself some of the following questions:

1. Why do you want to use a subscription model? What's in it for you, and what's in it for your customers? It is recommended to mine your data, understand customer behavior patterns, and use it to inform design decisions and features before you decide whether the subscription model works for the product or service you have to offer. Understanding the need and whether you can provide your customers with a product or service that addresses that need is fundamental to the success of a subscription-based model. A design thinking session or facilitated workshop would be a great start to the whole discussion required to answer these questions – undertake consumer research, learn about the need, understand the opportunity, and you can serve the market broadly.

2. Do you have the capabilities required to deliver a subscription model? This should be assessed for all the partners in your ecosystems. For example, you provide an experience. One of the biggest problems is overpromising despite supply chain issues or procurement issues, but companies don't think about the entire customer journey E2E and identify the pain points for frictionless delivery. Think through all the bits and pieces that ensure the journey is frictionless and delightful.

3. Managing a continuous subscriber relationship will require the customer relationship and management teams. The customer expects new features to stay engaged, necessitating a transition from a traditional waterfall model to frequent updates and agile models to deliver innovations incrementally. Are your teams equipped with the right tools, systems, and training to take on ongoing CRM activities to support the subscription model – for example, quarterly updates and upgrades being pushed to central vehicle management consoles for OTA updates?

4. Involve key stakeholders and partners in the design discussions to streamline the processes, which allows for easier adoption of the subscription model within the underlying enterprise processes. Leveraging the moments that matter within the UX and designing processes to reduce friction while delivering the service reduces the attrition rates and increases the retention of monthly subscriptions. Once systems and processes are deployed, continuous monitoring and improvement will be undertaken until you fine-tune the optimal working efficiencies.

Start small, learn fast, and improve incrementally, bearing the MVP in mind for agile delivery.

To summarize, the vision of a circular economy also includes changes to marketing and sales methods to think beyond one-time sales and ensure customer lifetime value – for example, pay-per-product models, recurring revenue through repeat sales, after-sales service contracts, value-adding services, and cross-selling opportunities. Profits are gauged by outcome-based performance indicators agreed upon in terms of service. Likewise, many other SLAs allow OEMs to better weather supply and demand fluctuations in uncertain market conditions. We have discussed the KPIs to look out for when your organization moves to a subscription-based commercial model for revenue recognition, bearing in mind that it takes longer to recoup costs. Lastly, there are a few aspects to consider before your company decides to adopt a subscription model with a circular design at the heart.

In the first few chapters, we introduced a business case for Spark4Life, a hypothetical company that needed to transform to survive the market turmoil and changes to industry trends, with shifts toward more sustainable business models and new revenue streams. The following section will elaborate on some proposed changes, applying Industry 4.0 technologies to introduce new products and keeping the sustainability goals in mind to realize the outcomes the company wants to move toward while offering its customers value and a delightful UX.

An Industry 4.0 lens

With hardware miniaturization outpacing itself every 2 years (Moore's law), we have seen CPUs and GPUs cramming billions of transistors onto chips that are nanometers big. The availability of highly performant computing comes at a cost, although production at scale has democratized the use of this technology in our daily lives. The explosion of cloud computing and its ease of adoption through intuitive software have powered everyday items such as smartphones and wearables, which are smaller yet more powerful than supercomputers from 5 decades ago. That said, the past decade has seen exponential growth in the availability of high-end sensors that sense their environment to process data and act (edge computing) or transmit data over purpose-built protocols, securely and reliably over longer ranges at radio frequency. This data can be relayed over 5G or the internet to data centers for further processing. With analytics and data science, we try to make sense of this data to derive further insights through AI and ML in real time. All of these advancements have brought Industry 4.0 to the fore, helping manufacturers use all these technologies to make their factories smarter, more efficient, and more automated. Furthermore, combining the operational data from production lines with enterprise data (combining IT and OT) provides elevated levels of visibility and insight for better decisions that your organizations can put into action for a competitive advantage. Essentially, Industry 4.0 underpins sustainability, as ESG requires this technology backbone.

We discussed the idea of digital entities being digital twins of real people. The same is true for equipment – we can create digital replicas of equipment, production lines, factories, manufacturing processes, or, for that matter, supply chains. With the **Industrial Industry of Things (IIoT)**, manufacturers can simulate and improve OT to introduce new products to the market or improve their capacities by monitoring and recalibrating production lines quickly. Avoiding downtime with predictive maintenance, using AI-driven visual inspections to reduce defects and quality controls, and using robotic trained arms to accelerate critical assembly that is done manually provide the flexibility and predictability for any manufacturer to respond to market dynamics as they play out. These concepts can be applied across any industry, whether discreet or process-based manufacturing, mining, or renewables. Smart factories use simulation with digital twins and automate the entire production line to manufacture goods on demand, making any custom changes per the product design. Propelling this move forward is 3D printing technology, which makes custom manufacturing a reality and has taken the construction, food, and medical industries by storm – sustainable houses can be built to order, beverages and pizzas are made on demand, and regenerative medicine is advancing faster toward creating artificial bones and body parts for animals and humans alike. The possibilities are vast.

Speaking of regenerative medicine, these technologies also make life more sustainable. AI exponentially matures by the day and shows huge promise to contribute to human well-being. Progress in the capabilities of ML and deep learning has seen many applications, whether autonomous vehicles, predicting weather patterns, scanning medical records, diagnosing cancer earlier, or pushing the boundaries to discover novel anti-cancer drugs. Applying AI to a business application is entirely objective. It handles discreet, tangible business problems by classifying images, predicting outcomes, or extracting the key-value pairs from incoming invoices. The reliability and accuracy of an ML model depend on how clean and accurate your datasets are and whether the models are fit for purpose. As IBM CEO Arvind Krishna states, *"you can't have AI without the IA"* – **IA** being **Information Architecture**. Previous chapters have stressed the importance of data architecture and creating data stores for specific functions in order to build ML models for data science. Streaming data and analytics have gained more traction with IoT connectivity and the proliferation of connected devices, with higher computing available at the edge and in the cloud. Deriving insights from big data, used as inputs to train the new ML models and improve them by the day, hones the accuracy of their outcomes.

We will now discuss some possible Industry 4.0 applications that can help with TechTronix's challenges in launching operations and manufacturing processes for new products, and how technology solutions to ongoing challenges and futuristic plans can move Spark4Life toward its ESG goals.

Dealing with after-sales service issues

Human visual inspection is slow, often expensive, and can present quality risks. Spark4Life produces washing machines that require welded drum assemblies and drum bearings sourced from different vendors. The drum assemblies need to be inspected for a range of washing machine products and checked for defects such as cracks, inconsistent welds, and surface imperfections. Moreover, any vibration not within an acceptable limit must be observed when installed with bearings. Accepting the quality of incoming components is critical to extending the life of motors, as they spin at high RPMs. Therefore, escape rates (the proportion of defective parts that might slip through the cracks) can cause a rise in recalls and, more importantly, warranty claims, which also impacts the NPS. Traditionally, much of this inspection was done by human experts on production lines, but this isn't optimal and can present unwanted quality risks. This makes intuitive sense; people typically don't perform well at tasks that require focused attention for an extended period, where the probability of a notable event is very infrequent. Moreover, judgments will vary from person to person, and the time of experts is expensive too. Therefore, visual inspection AI was used on real-time images and videos of incoming deliveries from vendors. Sensors for the vibration levels were deployed for quality checks when testing assembled goods. This solution automates visual inspection tasks using image classification models and computer vision technologies that enable Spark4Life to transform quality control processes by automatically detecting product defects. The quality of the machines delivered to the market has reduced the number of service calls and warranty claims and helps increase the lifespan of appliances.

Spark4Life settles approximately 500,000 service call-outs and warranty claims for defective or damaged components. Traditionally, customers would seek repairs by calling authorized independent service providers, which were then used to send estimates and settle claims. This was prolonged and often involved disputes on whether the replacement of a particular component was warranted. This led to disagreements about charges and delays to repairs while customers were disadvantaged due to long waiting times. Spark4Life has released a new mobile app that allows customers to answer a set of questions about their problems and upload images and videos about an issue. NLP, followed by image classification, makes assessments using convolutional neural networks to provide more reliable diagnoses and request replacements with the correct spare part. There has been a dramatic improvement to first-time fix rates in these service visits, and the costs of repair (for the components) are pre-authorized in 90% of cases. Repair turnaround times have dropped from 5-7 days to 1-2 days, as less or no human intervention is required to talk to customers, coordinate with third parties, and settle balances when completing service requests. The intelligent workflow manages most of the comms, with notifications sent to the customer on the intelligently scheduled visits and timings with first-time resolution rates exceeding 90%.

The futuristic outlook of Spark4Life

As part of COP 27, Spark4Life is a key member at the table of industry majors, has pledged to net zero emissions by 2030, and has plans to introduce more sustainable practices into the production, supply chain, and circularity of its products. The aim is to work with companies to operationalize sustainability E2E by integrating and automating quality ESG data into daily workflows in a robust and auditable way. Some of the key initiatives to meet the sustainability goals that Spark4Life has defined involve launching new products and services, as elaborated here:

- **Connected community sharing-based launderettes**: Spark4Life has recently launched some pilot sites, first-of-their-kind launderettes-as-a-service, which allow consumers to try out the latest product models released by the company at a minimal subscription fee. The launderette sites are equipped with other older models for the community to book to use or subscribe to use monthly, with billing depending on the service tier. Subscribers can book their slots online and visit the launderette at specified times. The launderette also offers other complimentary services such as deep dry cleaning and ironing using the company's products. With this approach, the sustainability posture of the company has improved dramatically, as the company manages all the machines and ensures the health of assets, recycling, and pre-emptive maintenance. The whole site is operated using clean energy from solar panels and has become a community spot for social hangouts, building community trust and buy-in from all customer demographics. Marketing campaigns are run for a portfolio of products from time to time to promote the company's products and early launch offers.

- **Retail stores with VR glasses/wearables**: To appeal to Gen Z demographics, Spark4Life has enabled VR experiences across their retail stores in pilot regions. Every customer gets a pair of Oculus Lens 3D glasses, which allows the customer to experience VR, with a Spark4Life brand ambassador to help them with the information, queries, pricing, and other comparative studies of the product that Spark4Life offers against the competition.

- **After-sales service and support**: The AR app available for every customer of Spark4Life allows them to point at an appliance or product to enable a demo by the brand ambassador, who can also explain the optimal conditions to run and maintain home appliances. This has reduced the number of calls to the contact center, as many of the FAQs and service requests can be logged and answered by the digital assistant available on the mobile app. The data relating to the issue, or fault codes, are quickly relayed by the IoT sensors on the machine to mobile apps to raise a service request automatically, so the service turnaround times are minimal and more accurate when dispatching the right technician or repairing with the right components.

- **Armbands for the aging population**: As a part of a new health-as-a-service offering, Spark4Life plans to offer a portfolio of health monitoring wearable devices with diagnostic and advisory consultation from expert doctors, offered as a subscription. As connected devices and wearables from the company have become more sophisticated, they expose more data and services OTA, with 5G connectivity to improve patient safety, reduce costs, and improve the health of populations. This improves the patient's experience of care (including quality and satisfaction) and reduces healthcare costs for older and younger adults. The initial pilot offers wearable devices, such as wristbands and smart watches, as part of a CSR initiative, allowing sponsored councils in the region to run the campaign for free for 1 year for all older adults. This will enable continuous, accurate data collection, subject to an individual's agreement, for patient management and care, symptom management, medical research, clinical trials, treatment monitoring (tracking pill consumption and times), and predictive health monitoring. The data collected is also a source of information or insight that is monetized where appropriate. The added advantage of these wearables is also to track and help guide patients with dementia back to their homes and alert local authorities if they cross certain perimeters to send a pickup van to help them return to their home addresses. All the patient records and events are logged and stored in a blockchain with complete control over who accesses the patient's data, with appropriate controls offered to patients to give permission where required through mobile apps.

- **SmartBins-as-a-service**: As part of a new launch of products in certain regions as part of a first pilot rollout, Spark4Life plans to launch SmartBins across all local councils as a contribution toward a greener smart city. The SmartBins are equipped with sensors to indicate how full they are. They relay the information over the LoRaWan protocol to the nearest control towers, allowing autonomous bin collector trucks to plan an optimal route daily. Moreover, citizens are incentivized to empty their food and dry recyclable waste into the correct bins and are given vouchers after a set number of compliant actions by homeowners, tracked through smart contracts. SmartBins are also located at prime spots in shopping centers, takeaways, and other community spaces, with the council leasing these SmartBins for several years, after which time the bins are planned to be recycled to make way for new, upgraded versions being made available. Spark4Life has ensured the circularity of all the components, which are sourced from sustainable resources.

Furthermore, Spark4Life is focused on establishing and implementing governance and architectural principles for their organization around processes, automation, and AI practices. It is advisable to have a **Center of Excellence (CoE)**, with experts focusing on one single domain, which could be automation, iRPA, or CoE teams seeking out ways to optimize processes to influence KPIs, add more value, or replace them altogether after a while. Demystify concerns around automation and understand how it can accelerate work. Here, a data science CoE churns out and trains the ML models, making them available for enterprise developers to consume easily via APIs and maintaining a balance with open standard, pre-trained ML models developed by open source communities and the data scientists within the organization. The CoE is quite active in educating and training the teams on the latest trends and best practices when implementing new ideas and developing the proofs-of-concept or MVPs for selected and sponsored products.

Adopting sustainability in every aspect

Sustainability is a massive challenge for our generation and will also affect future generations. It's centered around how data points are translated into action using technology to derive data insights – right from your installed bases (OT) at physical locations, serving customers with products and services under your new business models, to the IT you use to manage and monitor the installed bases remotely. Also, consider the supply chain that underpins the delivery of these products and services promptly to customers and how it should contribute to your sustainability goals. It's a lot more than meeting regulatory requirements or tickbox exercises for reporting purposes; your organization should be fearless when implementing the new ideas supported by shifts technological and cultural shifts that we discussed in previous sections. Reporting and adhering to regulations will be the natural outcomes of your efforts. Moreover, these practices reflect that the brand is more ESG-aware and responsible, which has massive appeal for Gen Z and Millennials.

Moreover, embedding sustainability into your products, services, and offerings doesn't mean completely overhauling your IT, people, and technology and rather should be planned as a slow, incremental introduction, with IT support and risk and compliance teams that will work in parallel with any transformation being undertaken and improve on it continuously. As such, it can be a natural extension of your organization's processes. There are several cloud portfolio products from SAP for holistic management and reporting, such as SAP Sustainability Control Tower for climate action and SAP EHS for health and safety. Combine this with Ariba Network and SAP Business Network and you have E2E visibility into your ESG score and the controls to take necessary preventive actions to improve your KPIs alongside your extended partners, suppliers, and customers. When considering these products, try to answer these questions: how do you decarbonize? How do you make your net-zero transition? How do you measure your progress against the KPIs?

ESG scores

An ESG score is an analysis framework for measuring and quantifying how sustainably an organization is operating in relation to others across industries or sectors. It is a score or a metric that is used by a wide variety of stakeholders such as customers, investors, shareholders, or governing bodies to assess how responsible an organization is and how it is moving toward critical practices and taking accountability in terms of ESG. There are several frameworks, such as the **Carbon Disclosure Standards Board (CDSB)**, the **Global Reporting Initiative (GRI)**, the **World Economic Forum (WEF)**, the **Sustainability Accounting Standards Board (SASB)**, and a few others to measure how your organization fares compared to standards or other industry players. An ESG score can be used by the CxO office to understand how they are performing in terms of the ESG factors relative to their peers, or by internal LoBs so that they can compare themselves against their own annual performances or against other business units within the same organization.

Summary

After you have been through your transformation, success may not look how you expected it to when you set off on this arduous journey. You will have learned a lot from what worked and what didn't and will emerge stronger. There will be intangible benefits, such as a cultural shift and the agility to meet market demands with a fail-fast mindset, and a few tangibles ones, such as the new services or products on the market, your turnaround in terms of your NPS score, or changes to the perception of your brand. These intangible outcomes will go a long way in catapulting new and existing tangible outcomes in the right direction. Again, it's a journey, and allowing time for teams to mature digitally will help in the long run. The skills and mindsets of your teams lay down the foundation for repeatable, successful outcomes in the future. Rushing through with unclear goals and half-baked skills and leaning toward a solely technological transformation in the hope that the change will be accepted only invites more unknowns and presents new challenges to your organization – so start small, fail fast, and scale faster.

In this chapter, we covered how you can inspire a hunger for innovation and excellence within your organization, nurture healthy competition, and motivate employees to learn about new technology. This new verve is supported further by rewiring your organizations, making IT teams take on the role of enablers to support new ideas, and using LCNC platforms supported by organization-wide API layers to help your business users and innovation teams alike realize their ideas quickly and efficiently to enable transformation at scale.

Then, we covered the opportunities that Web 3.0 opens up, how it will transform the future of work, and how it be delivered by emerging technologies working together. We spoke about how we leverage new subscription-based business models to create new revenue streams, enable the circularity of products, and serve our sustainability goals. Lastly, we went through a few examples of how the Industry 4.0 revolution has changed the way new products and services are delivered, looking at the business case of our hypothetical company Spark4Life, its current set of business challenges, and its future outlook as it leveraged technology and subscription models to emerge as a sustainable digital brand loved by the masses.

We will briefly cover where to start on sustainability initiatives in the next chapter, how to make sense of the data you are capturing, and how to measure your progress to ensure you are on track for your net-zero emissions or carbon neutrality goals. The progressive motive is to leave the blue planet greener and better, environmentally and socially, for future generations.

12
Digital Supremacy – the Path to Sustainable Growth

In the previous chapter, we learned how SAP brings to the fore some of the solutions that will make it easier for businesses to measure, analyze, report, and act on their business ambition and vision to become an intelligent, sustainable enterprise.

We learned about how trends such as the cultural shift to innovation are enabling businesses to increase their agility, flexibility, and responsiveness to both internal and external events. We saw the potential of Web 3.0 for the future of work with new innovative business and commercial models powered by Industry 4.0 themes.

For Tektronix, this means embracing the major industry trends as part of their S/4HANA solution and reaping both quantifiable and non-quantifiable business benefits that justify the initial business case for transformation. They can now look at the decisions that were needed to realize their vision of being a sustainable intelligent enterprise. Fundamental to achieving a tangible return on investment is how the user community has adopted the new solution. Measuring the outcomes achieved can help direct the business with new growth opportunities.

With the new S/4HANA digital core and RISE with SAP surrounded by ever-increasing SAP **Business Technology Platform** (**BTP**) capabilities covering data-to-value, integration, extensibility, and **artificial intelligence/machine learning** (**AI/ML**) process-oriented innovations, Spark4Life now has the benefit of a radically new ERP platform for driving innovations and business value powered by process simplification, optimization, and automation.

In this final chapter, we will cover the following topics:

- Looking into the rear-view mirror, we will *reflect* on the salient points made in each of the previous chapters that have led us to this point, covering the factors driving the business transformation of Spark4Life.

- We will *envision* the future by looking into what could be coming up next, describing the outlook and opportunities that lie just over the horizon, where the business can exploit new differentiating capabilities and new SAP features and bake these into their transformation roadmap and target operating model to become an intelligent, sustainable enterprise that delivers business growth.

- We will *initiate* the process, starting with incremental steps, then moving at pace along your transformational highway using a collaborative engagement model and a Garage structure starting with Design Thinking techniques, then moving on to a **minimal viable product** (**MVP**) concept, and finally scaling up into a continuous delivery model. We will wrap up with the final points to inspire ambition into action.

Let's begin!

Reflections

The following sections help us to weave a golden thread using the key points from each of the previous chapters. That way, we can layer new SAP capabilities onto the technology foundation that we use to realize the future business vision for Spark4Life.

Chapter 1 reflections

As we reflect on the key takeaway messages from *Chapter 1, Truth and Dare – The CXO Challenges*, we identified the eight levers of business change. Many of them are external, yet some are internal to the organization. The **chief experience officer** (**CXO**) suite needs to be able to proactively respond to market threats and challenges, yet take proactive steps to seek out new opportunities to differentiate their company in the marketplace, by driving more customer value, increasing profitability, reducing operating costs, and ultimately, increasing market share and shareholder value. This points us to one fact: business transformation is not only constant, but it is also inevitable, relentless, and needs to be well-managed with continuous stakeholder engagement right across the 360 degrees of the organization at every level. Everyone should have a vested interest in its success.

The last few years have been unprecedented in terms of geopolitics, economics, climate, technology, and social trends. We have witnessed how many nations are dealing with the impacts of a series of unexpected global economic events:

- The aftershocks of the COVID-19 pandemic from 2020, which continues to rage in many parts of the world, required massive fiscal interventions by central banks and governments to shore up their respective economies in order to survive the impact of waves of lockdowns.

- Broken global supply chains resulted in stockouts, delays in deliveries, unavailability of spare parts and raw components, and peak demand for commodities.

- The tragic war in Ukraine in 2022 and its geopolitical and economic consequences.

- The consequential rises in global energy prices during 2022, and the unfortunate doubling down on fossil fuel investments, even if it is to maximize short-term profits for those energy companies.

- The rise in the cost of provisioning fertilizers and raw materials for the agricultural industry has affected food and grain prices across all global markets.

- The curtailment of fiscal quantitative easing measures in 2022, which were first started by central banks following the 2008 financial crisis.

- The debt to GDP ratio has increased for every major economy to over 98% of GDP.

- To top it off, we also have the climate crisis that is now bearing down on all countries. Many low-income countries are suffering the most, yet they did the least to create the crisis in the first place. Extreme weather events, disruption to normal seasonal trends, and huge biodiversity losses are steadily underway across the planet.

The combination of these factors drives up inflation and, therefore, the overall cost of living for many millions of people globally, resulting in industrial strife and the breakdown of public services. One could argue that we are in dire straits in terms of international geopolitics and economics. So, what does all this mean for our CXOs? It is in this global economic context that CXOs must decide whether to, how, when, and where to deploy their new upgraded system of record with S/4HANA, given the inevitable end of life of SAP ERP ECC6. Why is this important? This is not just about IT or managing internal processes better. The fact is that 77% of all worldwide business transactions touch an SAP system. Typically, SAP ERP is the foundational system for the majority of enterprise core processes and so it is the backbone of the enterprise, covering finance, the supply chain, logistics, procurement, HR, and more. It's only with a modern digital core, with access to real-time data, faster simpler processes, and a modern technology platform that businesses can survive this onslaught of relentless change driven by threats and opportunities.

Chapter 2 reflections

In *Chapter 2, Faith of Four – Vision of the Masters*, we described the pressures and opportunities that lie in front of four master personas – the CEO, CFO, CIO/CTO, and CSO, and their business growth ambitions around the top line, bottom line, and now with the focus on sustainability, the green line. Given the latest technology opportunities that drive innovations, the four masters can now readily achieve deeper customer insight and engagement and refresh their IT through modernization plans as part of their journey to the cloud. They can focus on increasing the business process automation scope and drive towards sustainability with a lower emissions footprint, integrated as part of their overall business vision. They can adopt business transformation powered by SAP S/4HANA through, for example, the RISE with SAP offering, starting with a journey starter and value advisory service from their system integrator, or indeed from SAP directly. The idea is to help the enterprise take its corporate strategy and vision and translate this into a business and technology transformation roadmap. That way, it can take a sure-footed approach toward an intelligent, sustainable transformation mission. With a clear business vision underpinned by a well-defined business case, the selection of the right

S/4HANA adoption scenario, a clear methodology such as SAP Activate that uses best practices, and the adoption of an Opex-based contractual model such as RISE with SAP, the business can transform into its target operating model founded on Clean Core ERP such as S/4HANA with clarity, confidence, and certainty.

Chapter 3 reflections

In *Chapter 3, Eureka Moment – Missing Link*, we explored how RISE with SAP offers deeper and richer capabilities starting with new features, functions, adoption options, benefits, and opportunities. Applying the lens of the CXO personas from *Chapter 2*, each of them must make key decisions on the type of S/4HANA model they want to adopt. As it is a decision for the long term, careful qualification and selection of the right S/4HANA adoption path and deployment option are critical. The key is to secure executive alignment with tangible, quantifiable, and non-quantifiable business benefits. With RISE with SAP, both business and IT can innovate with differentiated value with a Clean Core S/4HANA system. With CPEA credits from the RISE contract, clients can exploit SAP BTP capabilities to deploy extensibility features, integration, and data-to-value capabilities. The simplicity of RISE with SAP means businesses can benefit from a completely technically managed service from SAP, with their chosen system integrator partners providing implementation services and/or application-managed services as needed. This way, the new ERP solution is fully managed through the Opex model, and consequently, this results in a lower **total cost of ownership** (**TCO**) while providing faster access to business benefits.

Chapter 4 reflections

In *Chapter 4*, we discussed how intelligent enterprise and sustainable design are foundational. We described how disruption and crisis could act as a catalyst for significant business transformation. This is powered by the new SAP S/4HANA core, such as a solution supported by ever-increasing technology capabilities in SAP BTP – all provisioned through the RISE with SAP offering with a specific focus on industry use to enable that holistic transformation. This journey starts by defining core principles such as automation – first and a shift – left mindset that requires a clear-eyed view of capabilities to drive an insight-driven approach using the capabilities of business process mining and insights that are the foundation of intelligent workflows using process automation. Next, to create differentiated value, we recommend using the extensibility features of SAP BTP to wrap around the Clean Core S/4HANA to provide a future-proof upgradable Core, where you exploit continuously evolving yet standard features from SAP themselves through a **functional service provider** (**FSP**)/ upgrades, which can be delivered with minimal business impact or outage.

Chapter 5 reflections

Chapter 5 was part 1 of 2, where we focused on the topic of the *cloud with a silver lining – busting the myth*. We reviewed the need for a well-detailed business case for adopting the S/4HANA solution, through a RISE with SAP offering or an alternative option. This critical decision has multiple influencing factors, such as understanding the latest industry trends, accelerating the journey to the cloud, system consolidation opportunities, mergers and acquisitions resulting in process and data optimization, understanding the architectural patterns within RISE with SAP, and exploring what is in the art of the possible RISE with SAP as well as other alternative options. We covered the business and IT needs, evaluated how each stage in the business case process worked, and gave examples of questions with their associated scoring model for selecting the right option. The goal is to develop a strong business case based on both global and local business-specific parameters that ensure the solution brings value in dynamically changing market conditions with new operating models.

Chapter 6 reflections

Chapter 6 was part 2 of 2 focusing on the topic of the *cloud with a silver lining – busting the myth*. Here, we continued the focus on the RISE with SAP offering by looking into the standard and tailored editions of S/4HANA, especially when it comes to the bundled cloud services that help you get more transformational abilities. We also examined typical roles and responsibilities for both standard and optional and additional variants. We investigated the approach for handling rollouts and upgrades as part of RISE with SAP. In addition, we covered what should be expected under **application management services** (**AMS**) with RISE with SAP and **cloud application services** (**CAS**) packages for S/4HANA.

Chapter 7 reflections

In *Chapter 7, Back to the Drawing Board: Reimagined Processes*, we covered how data-driven scenarios support data migration requirements while minimizing business disruption when delivering a successful go-live. We covered the options available with different products to provide an effective data migration outcome. We started by examining the process design, simulation, and modeling for future customer and employee experiences, considering how process changes are made or, instead, how new processes are introduced. We looked at data requirements for supporting the new processes and the technology that can help bridge the gaps identified. Specifically, we looked at how businesses can deliver enterprise-scale and experience-led transformation using the principle of a data-to-value transformation model covering the data engineering required across processes. Then, we learned how to use that data to design intelligent workflows putting insights into action to extend the core business processes in S/4HANA and use the amalgamation of automation and intelligent workflows for the intelligent enterprise from SAP BTP. Moreover, adopting cloud-native capabilities from SAP BTP, we showed how to integrate existing hybrid cloud solutions with SAP BTP for extensions and innovations with the S/4 HANA components.

Chapter 8 reflections

We started *Chapter 8, The Exodus – Data That Matters*, by using the **component business model** (**CBM**) to define strategic business capabilities to help define that target operating model. That then drives how we adopt the new S/4HANA solution – whether you choose a greenfield, brownfield, or bluefield (selective) migration, where it is critical to get the data migration planning right. Each of the adoption scenarios addresses the data migration activities slightly differently and this impacts the life cycle of the project. Either way, we need to ensure that the solution has the right data for the business to be able to make well-informed decisions and this requires good-quality data (including cleansing processes) defined at the outset. This means data migration needs data governance, data quality, and data profiling, as well as effective SAP-certified technologies to execute data migration effectively through SAP Activate Methodology.

Chapter 9 reflections

In *Chapter 9, The Pilot – High Stakes*, we learned that the implementation and migration aspects of the S/4HANA solution are proven with a pilot site/location that is representative of business operations yet provides a controlled way to manage deployment risks. We started by recapping best practices and approaches from the previous chapters that help shift left your implementation and migration timelines using the ready-to-use content from SAP or system integration partners. Starting with the **user experience** (UX) strategy, we described how important it is to address business users through a delightful experience, through processing *moments that matter,* and how business change initiatives can maximize user adoption and acceptance through early engagement and training delivered by the transformation project. We covered how iterative release management across hybrid cloud deployments supports the move to the digital core in a controlled way and we explored how **continuous integration and deployment** (CI/CD) mechanisms support continuous product increments of business value. This chapter focused on getting ready for the pilot implementation followed by a global rollout.

Chapter 10 reflections

In *Chapter 10, All In – A Leap of Faith*, we covered how we move on from a pilot go-live to global deployment using a well-defined global template solution design for S/4HANA. We described the factors that define the S/4HANA instance strategy and how we successfully roll out and deploy this template in each of the country locations and/or business units that are in scope for deployment so that they can start to take advantage of expected business benefits from the new S/4HANA solution. We described the factors that drive efficiencies in a distributed or single-instance strategy, and we also covered how to drive continuous innovation across the globally deployed SAP ecosystem.

Chapter 11 reflections

In *Chapter 11, Innovation Unleashed – A Hunger Game*, we focused on the ever-louder drumbeat of continuous innovation that brings with it a tectonic shift in business cultural approaches where stakeholders are more empowered by adapting to relentless change triggered by emergent threats and exciting opportunities. We described the need to rewire the enterprise to increase agility and scale through well-motivated and empowered employees who can consume the SAP solutions on demand, using the power of low-code/no-code application development via SAP BUILD apps on SAP BTP to change the very nature of how work gets done. This also drives new subscription-based commercial models to drive new predictable revenue streams while being able to adopt new powerful capabilities of cloud-native development with Web 3.0 and Industry 4.0. For example, using Digital Twins to model real-world events enables the business to emerge as a sustainable intelligent enterprise.

Envisioning the future

In this section, we describe the *art of the possible* and how new industry trends are driving new growth opportunities and business benefits. What were once considered peripheral and emergent technologies are now very much the mainstream, such as AI/ML, data analytics, automation, the cloud, and blockchain. These can be used to accelerate a new generation of solutions to help businesses with their sustainability goals and ambitions. Tangible business benefits are now within reach once you have established the new SAP digital core with SAP BTP capabilities as wrap-around services.

New horizons

Now that we have S/4HANA providing standard, optimal, and simplified processes across order-to-cash, procure-to-pay, source-to-contract, lead-to-cash, record-to-report, and operational analytics and reporting, you can achieve a lower data complexity and data footprint, which helps with an overall reduction in TCO. More intelligent processes enhance the user experience and productivity. With more efficient processes across S/4HANA and integrated with SAP BTP, you can scale up your innovations and drive differentiated value. This allows the organization to focus on business growth initiatives that address market needs and sustainability priorities.

The following diagram illustrates how businesses can start expanding layers of new capability around the S/4HANA Core ERP. Many businesses can start with sustainability as the first and end goal. How? Move to S/4HANA with sustainability management solutions so that your business is sustainable by design. Next, define, realize, and convert those business benefits into tangible results, fast. All this needs to be integrated with the quadruple bottom line with data and KPIs for people, planet, prosperity, and impact. This can be powered by S/4HANA, SAP BTP with SAP Cloud for Sustainable Enterprises, and SAP Industry Cloud solutions. With the emergent standards around sustainability, compliance and reporting are on the critical path.

How do you meet those emergent requirements? Regulatory standards mean you need to transform real-time insight into action across the whole business process value chain, which means investing in a data architecture that breaks down data silos using SAP BTP data to value solutions SAP HANA Cloud will be used as the database. SAP Data Warehouse Cloud can be used for defining new data models and supporting operational reporting. For data extraction, data transformation, data cleansing, data loading, and data cataloging services, we use SAP Data Intelligence Cloud to allow businesses to move and optimize data from source legacy applications to target SAP systems. Reporting will be handled by Analytics Cloud. These solutions can be easily integrated into SAP **Sustainability Control Tower** (**SCT**) to provide holistic steering and reporting. Finally, how do we reduce TCO and modernize IT? By adopting ccrc, gclean core, responsible computing, and green IT principles into developments to decouple process, data, code, and the platform for maximum agility:

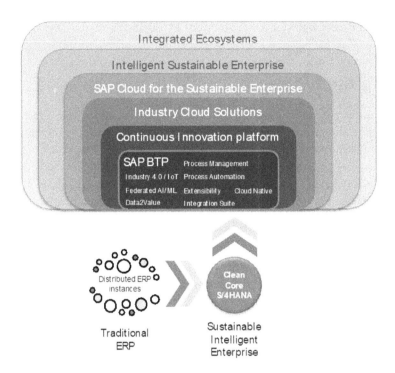

Figure 12.1 – Transforming beyond Clean Core into an intelligent sustainable enterprise and ecosystems

Using DevSecOps to deliver value through iterative agile sprints into product increments, the business can see real growth in new capabilities across their organization. Combine that with the adoption of AI/ML fused into intelligent workflows and businesses can start to convert their roadmap into the reality of innovation-led sustainable enterprise – as this is where it is all headed. This vision helps us to focus on emerging industry and market trends, while at the same time, ensuring an evergreen Clean Core ERP with innovations that extend the core S4HANA solution to go beyond traditional ERP capabilities.

Finally, in the *Initiation* section later in this chapter, we will cover how to get started on the continuous development agenda, describing the initial steps that can be taken as part of the broader SAP transformation roadmap to help enable that business vision and realization of benefits in a well-architected, well-structured, and coordinated way, enabling a positive change culture for the future.

The rise of ESG priorities

In this section, we start to focus on the climate crisis by looking at emissions, waste, and inequality. Many companies define their own **environmental, social, and governance** (**ESG**) objectives as they tackle their own sustainability challenges within their business, industry, and broader society. Their ESG reports now replace traditional **corporate social responsibility** (**CSR**) reports that are still around. With ESG categories, businesses can show which of the UN **Sustainable Development Goals** (**SDGs**) are adopted and are made available to their auditors, regulators, investors, suppliers, customers, and industry commentators, along with industry metrics and data points to compare how the company is delivering on their ESG commitments. In fact, they rely on SAP ERP to serve as a key data source for ESG data, analytics, and reporting to drive insights. They also increasingly rely on SAP capabilities to orchestrate new business processes to drive actions across their business value chains.

Unequivocal climate facts

The UN **Conference of the Parties (COP)** process is the only global mechanism to get governments, industries, and organizations to agree on commitments to reduce **greenhouse gas (GHG)** emissions, help mitigate the risk of the climate crisis, and work collaboratively using international standards and frameworks to enable all countries to lead the way toward a more sustainable model of economic growth that operates within planetary boundaries.

COP21, held in Paris in 2015, resulted in a ground-breaking legally binding international agreement to limit global warming to well below 2 degrees Celsius, preferably to 1.5 degrees Celsius, compared to pre-industrial levels. This agreement established the 2015 DG the SDGs or Global Goals are a collection of 17 interlinked objectives designed to serve as a *"shared blueprint for peace and prosperity for people and the planet, now and into the future"* as per the sdgs.un.org site. These 17 goals are assigned to each of the ESG categories. Most companies typically adopt between 4 and 11 of the 17 SDGs and translate them into their own sustainability ESG ambitions and corporate mission statements. Forward-thinking companies are drawing a clear line of sight between some of these goals and their business objectives and operations, so that they can track progress along their sustainability ambitions, goals, and objectives. The following diagram is a good way to represent how the 17 SDGs can be categorized by ESG:

Figure 12.2 – The 17 UN SDGs, categorized by ESG

The UN **Intergovernmental Panel for Climate Change** (**IPCC**) issued reports stating that globally, we need to reduce GHG emissions by 45% by 2030 to achieve net zero by 2050 to stave off the worst impacts of climate change. This means accelerating the move away from a fossil fuels economy to more sustainable sources of energy such as renewables (wind, solar, tidal, and so on) and considering zero-carbon options such as nuclear fission energy generation. Many argue that the war in Ukraine, resulting in high commodity prices for oil and gas, has meant that many countries are shifting their focus to renewable energy. The ideal solution of course is nuclear fusion, but that is some decades away from becoming available, so doubling down on available technologies today, with innovations around renewables and battery storage is a clear way forward. Indeed, solar power is the cheapest source of energy on the planet. In fact, the cost of energy produced from solar farms has plummeted. With the latest generation of solar panels, there are even higher levels of energy efficiency achieved). Between 2010 and 2021, the cost of a kilojoule of energy has reduced by nearly 90%, and just considering 2021 alone, that cost dropped by 13%! These figures have surprised many industry commentators, and the forecast for the mid-2020s is to see further drops in the cost of energy produced by solar. It is expected that solar electricity will be up to 50% cheaper today than the **International Energy Agency** (**IEA**) had originally projected for 2022 (excluding regional variation) (source: `https://www.theecoexperts.co.uk/blog/is-renewable-energy-cheaper-than-fossil-fuels`). All of this accelerates solar adoption, and with that, the cost of technology matures with continuous innovation, achieving very high economies of scale and making solar the cheapest energy source on the planet.

Tackling biodiversity loss

The human impact on the environment is more than just GHG emissions. The biodiversity losses underway right now are unprecedented. Scientists have analyzed that 69% of biodiversity loss has already happened since the 1970s, caused by a range of factors, and 70% of the world's most vulnerable people depend directly on wild species.

In December 2022, COP15 concluded with a historic international agreement on the Kunming-Montreal Global Biodiversity Framework. This allows for new global goals and targets to be set that are aimed at protecting and regenerating nature for both current and future generations, while also ensuring the sustainability of these assets through investments in green global economy initiatives. This agreement complements the 2015 UN Paris Agreement on climate change (COP21) by outlining the path toward a more nature-positive and ecologically resilient world by 2050 with clearly defined quantifiable targets for both 2030 and 2050. These targets include restoring 30% of degraded ecosystems globally (on land and sea) by 2030 and conserving and managing 30% of areas (terrestrial, inland water, and coastal and marine) by 2030. As a result, the agreement aims to limit the rate of extinction of many species of plants and animals so that by 2050, the result should be a tenfold reduction in the extinction risk and rate of all species. Clearly, there is still a lot of work to do, but it is possible, and the targets are not legally binding, but it's a good step forward in the right direction. Digital technologies are the only way to track progress and convert ambition into real-world action.

These announcements mean that climate action must go hand in hand with action on protecting biodiversity. Enterprises need to reflect these global commitments in their corporate mission statement, goals, and objectives in order to survive and grow in an unpredictable and volatile world, especially since most businesses are integrated into global supply chains.

Start with standards and frameworks to drive compliance and reporting

There are more than 20 global standards and frameworks organizations advising governments, regulators, industry leaders, and businesses on what needs to be reported, when, how, and why. These ESG disclosure and reporting requirements and standards are rapidly evolving worldwide with regulatory, consumer, and investor-driven purposes.

Some standards are global, others are regional and local, and some are industry-specific. Any business must take time to determine which of these standards apply and then identify KPIs/metrics that will be followed to track progress towards sustainability, starting with their ESG objectives. Typically, we have organizations that publish standards and ones that issue frameworks or guiding principles. The point of these standards is that they set a commonly agreed upon benchmark for the calibration of sustainability-related activities. They aim to bring consistency and quality into reporting requirements to allow regulators to compare like-for-like outcomes. They contain specific and detailed criteria using metrics describing *what* needs to be reported (and why). Meanwhile, a framework simply provides more context for defining the direction of sustainability-related actions, but it is not a methodology. It provides a set of common principles for guidance to enable a well-defined reporting strategy so that frameworks and standards complement each other.

Many emerging ratings and rankings organizations act like data collectors who sell datasets to help businesses *score* or rank the maturity of their business based on its publically declared ESG credentials. This information is often volunteered by individual enterprises as part of their non-financial disclosure activities, but sometimes information has been gathered through industry regulators based on regulatory compliance requirements that companies need to provide. Why is this information useful and becoming critical? For many, ESG ratings represent a public scorecard and a statement about the risk of doing business with a given company. Many **chief procurement officers (CPOs)** are dependent on trusted ESG data to define whom to contract as a supplier in their business supply chain activities. As more companies use ESG rating data, the maturity of that data improves so that companies measure, track, and qualify their sustainability-related data for external consumption.

The emerging standards that are now dominant across industries include the US **Securities Exchange Commission (SEC)**, the EU **Financial Reporting Advisory Group (FRAG)**, the **International Financial Reporting Standards (IFRS)**, and the **Task Force on Climate-related Financial Disclosures (TCFD)**, as shown in *Figure 12.3*:

US Securities Exchange Commission

Requires domestic and foreign SEC registrants to disclose qualitative and quantitative climate related risks and metrics

EU Financial Reporting Advisory Group

The Corporate Sustainability Reporting Directive (CSRD) will replace the current reporting directive and is part of the EU Green Deal

International Financial Reporting Standards

The launch of the International Sustainability Standards Board (ISSB) is developing a harmonized sustainability reporting and disclosure standard

And More

Task Force on Climate-related Financial Disclosures

The voluntary recommendations published in 2017, often form a basis for the development of mandatory climate disclosure rules globally

Figure 12.3 – Emergent global standards are setting the agenda for compliance and reporting

Most companies reflect and incorporate these standards in their sustainability materiality assessments, which allow companies to focus on the really important KPIs and metrics they want to use to transform their business. These standards serve as a yardstick that enables companies to perform meaningful like-for-like comparisons using common data semantics, terminologies, and measurements. The US SEC incorporates both the TCFD and GHG, which address the different sources of emissions across upstream and downstream supply chains.

Tackling waste through circularity

It's also about our use of raw materials in the linear economy of the take-make-dispose economic model, which is very destructive to the environment as it accelerates biodiversity losses, increases waste, and increases inequality. By introducing circularity business models with better use of raw materials and being smart about product obsolesce through reuse, repurposing, and recycling, companies are creating new revenue streams and growth opportunities, which have increased shareholder value. The circular economy eliminates waste through a cyclical model: *make, use, recycle*. The circular economy is now driving new opportunities for businesses to capitalize, exploit, and monetize the waste generated from linear manufacturing and production processes.

For example, we see many start-ups in tech hubs across different cities opening circular economy companies, such as second-life clothing companies, or providing digital platforms for the easy reuse and repurposing of waste materials for secondary supply chains. These models are likely to be more common in the future because raw materials are readily available – simply put, making money from waste! In fact, by 2029, Gartner predicts the circular economy will be the only economy, replacing wasteful linear economies as consumer and shareholder preferences rapidly shift toward sustainability.

Tackling inequality through data transparency and action

When it comes to inequality in organizations, this has been a long-term issue that needs to be resolved with better representation across organizational hierarchies and structures through people-focused initiatives that enable diversity and inclusivity and promote talent based on individual merit through capability and expertise rather than traditional policies of longevity within the organization. Triggering outreach programs, diversity campaigns, and celebrating the variety of workforce backgrounds are ways to excite and mobilize talent and increase broader diversity and stronger representation in leadership positions within the organization.

The challenge is to strike a balance between people, planet, prosperity, purpose, and impact. Yet, it's very clear that sustainability is now a mainstream and critical driver for transformation.

Business transformation with purpose

In 2022, the IBM **Institute of Business Value (IBV)** did a study on the topic of transformational sustainability, identifying priorities and challenges for the CEO. In the survey, over 51% of CEOs most frequently identify sustainability as their greatest challenge. Their companies plan to increase and prioritize spending toward the ESG objectives in 2023 because they are under mounting pressure to progress toward more sustainable and socially responsible business operations—and to demonstrate these measures in a robust and verifiable way. To that end, prioritizing spending on ESG initiatives and sustainability technology is now an investment imperative that enables them to streamline operations, reduce TCO, increase process efficiency, and increase both employee and customer experience while enabling the business to be much more responsible and profitable in the long term. ESG is more than just good intentions. It's about creating a tangible, practical plan that achieves real results. *Figure 12.4* illustrates the points from the 2022 IBM CEO study showing that sustainability is now a top priority.

Expected greatest challenges for your organization over the next 2–3 years

Challenges		2021	Trend
Sustainability	51%	32%	→ →
Regulation	50%	51%	
Cyber risk	45%	39%	→
Technology infrastructure	41%	45%	
Supply chain disruption	38%	28%	→
Geopolitical uncertainty	35%	14%	→ →
Market shifts	34%	45%	← ←
Public health incidents	29%	33%	
Cash flow	25%	27%	
Consumer demographics	24%	24%	
The 'anywhere' workplace	21%	11%	→
Industry convergence	21%	11%	→
Fluid workforce	21%	30%	←
Capital raising	20%	29%	←
Diversity and inclusion	18%	19%	
Workforce demographics	18%	20%	
Tariffs/trade barriers	16%	26%	←
The sharing economy	14%	14%	

→ → Increase >10%　→ Increase 5-10%　← ← Decrease >10%　← Decrease 5-10%

Figure 12.4 – IBM CEO study 2022: Own your impact - `https://www.ibm.com/thought-leadership/institute-business-value/en-us/c-suite-study/ceo`

For the CXO, we see the importance of sustainability rising, requiring data to insight and insight to action. Let's look at our CXO – the four master personas and this time we'll add the COO as well, to give us five personas. Each of these key stakeholders is now incentivized to embed sustainability into the core of their business in order to achieve ESG-specific outcomes:

- Innovation and growth (CEO): Business transformation, the creation of new business models, and value propositions for customers, employees, and stakeholders.

- Regulatory compliance (CFO): Simplified data transparency in disaggregated data for ESG reporting, holistic steering, and supply chain transparency.

- Operational excellence (COO): Seamless integration into established processes; convert insights into action to drive sustainability into the business core.

- The pathway towards sustainable enterprise (CSO): Define a clear roadmap that meets the company materiality assessment and business goals and objectives.

- The modernization of applications and platforms (CIO): Adopt green IT principles by reducing data replication, snoozing non-productive or inactive systems, moving towards API economy with event-driven architectures, eliminating technical debt, and modernizing apps with containerization across hybrid cloud platforms.

IBM IBV studies during 2022 revealed the trends that are underway with stakeholder, consumer, and employee expectations when it comes to sustainability. These data points are reflected in the way different industries are responding to the need of the hour:

Stakeholder Expectations

38
Of the world's top 50 economies have, or are developing, environmental impact corporate disclosure requirements.

80%
Increase in share price performance for companies with good sustainability practices

Consumer Expectations

84%
Of global customers consider sustainability important when choosing a brand.

57%
Of consumers are willing to change their purchasing habits to help reduce negative environmental impact.

Employee Expectations

67%
Of people say they are more willing to apply for & accept jobs from organizations they consider to be sustainable

43%
Of people believe their employer could do more to help the environment.

Figure 12.5: Key industry indicators from IBM IBV studies showing the trends toward increasing sustainability expectations in business operations and outcomes. Source:
`https://www.ibm.com/thought-leadership/institute-business-value/en-us/c-suite-study/ceo`

Industry trends

Every industry is now taking action on its sustainability goals and objectives, starting with ESG reporting but moving into transforming the business architecture and toward the intelligent sustainable enterprise powered by SAP at the core. Many industry innovators are focusing on developing assets and platforms to help their sector accelerate their sustainability vision.

For the discrete **industrial manufacturing and components (IM&C)** process, which is a key part of the manufacturing industry's production process, many businesses have started to address the following sustainability priorities using structured and unstructured data. This data is typically of a high volume, velocity, and veracity, usually generated through key business events during the manufacturing process workflow, which can be orchestrated through SAP S/4HANA and SAP BTP:

- **Emissions management**: This is how to offset persistent emissions using emerging **carbon capture usage and storage (CCUS)** technologies, how to accelerate supply chain decarbonization, and how to ensure continuous reporting accuracy using real-time data across GHG Protocol scopes 1/2/3.

- **Circularity**: This is how to reinvent and innovate towards circularity in product design by removing the waste and tracking **life cycle assessment (LCA)** of every material flow through the supply chain at the **stock-keeping unit (SKU)** level. This includes resource optimization in manufacturing and production planning while ensuring compliance with product optimization, then driving insight into sourcing, risk, and how we manage power grids.

- Responsible sourcing and optimization of physical assets and resources during manufacturing and production planning is a key focus area. Additional focus areas include ensuring compliance with product optimization and driving greater insight into sourcing and managing products' carbon footprint starting from source to pay/procurement processes into the rest of the supply chain. This includes risk mitigation for any deviation from target KPIs/metrics.

In the **consumer packaged goods (CPG)** industry, the key focus areas are more around the customer experience and recognizing consumer trends where the following factors are driving changes in behavior:

- **Brand**: Managing customer expectations as part of marketing and reputational impact

- **Consumer insights**: Customers are very dynamic and willing to move their dollar to another more sustainable and reputable brand

- **Ethical practices**: Selecting suppliers based on disclosure data, for example, CDP, but also on those who proactively eliminate human trafficking and exploitation

- **Insight to action**: Analytics, ESG compliance, and reporting

In energy and utilities, we see the obvious move towards renewable energy, but there are other trends underway triggered by the energy crisis witnessed in 2022:

- **Accelerating the switch to renewables**: Supporting customers to move to 100% renewable energy using a flexible platform for load balancing demand/supply across suppliers, consumers, and now prosumers using a scalable digital platform

- **Microgeneration**: Supporting communities with their local renewable power feedback into the grid and monetizing that model

- **EV and E-mobility**: As fleets move to **electric vehicles** (**EVs**), supporting the switch to a charging network and consumption model transportation

As you can see, there is a convergence of business benefits that are enabled by sustainability being woven into the fabric of the enterprise. What we are seeing is that those CEOs that are able to fuse their sustainability goals and objectives with their digital transformation agenda for modernizing business and IT tend to benefit from a significantly higher average operating margin than their competitors in their marketplace. This requires a well-defined sustainability strategy with committed sponsorship, stakeholder support, and funding. These organizations are much better positioned to navigate the ever-changing regulations while delivering solutions that meet new stakeholder attitudes and expectations. This is about going beyond disclosure and compliance with reporting and analytics, but it's about how we infuse AI-powered intelligent workflows to help us with what we buy, sell, and deliver as a closed loop towards circularity in business models and driving the green line right through business value chains.

Challenges to overcome

Yet, as with any other monumental shift, the global economic movement toward sustainability presents significant challenges for industries and businesses. The following list represents some of these challenges:

- How do you break down data siloed across the organization?

- How do you drive the effective execution of sustainability measures with conviction through business change initiatives?

- How do you build a strong technology foundation based on open architectures to drive continuous innovation at the speed and scale necessary to meet your ESG ambitions?

- How do you act on the climate crisis meaningfully? Many companies have committed to carbon reduction or net-zero targets, but their increased voluntary and mandatory reporting requirements don't always align.

- How do you measure progress consistently across the industry? Tracking material flows and carbon intensity across the pharmaceutical industry is challenging, given the varying product types, modalities, locations, complex supply chains, and data security.

- How do you mitigate risks from extreme weather events driven by the climate crisis? There are significant climate change-related risks to all industries, including physical, transition, legal, and regulatory risks, with little clarity on how to go beyond reporting to implement mitigation and adaptation strategies.

RISE with SAP for S/4HANA with SAP Cloud for Sustainable Enterprises

To help answer and resolve these questions and challenges, this is where the new raft of SAP sustainability solutions can help. With the S/4HANA core, you have the benefit of a simplified data model and optimized business processes that make it much easier to access, analyze, and visualize data across core business processes. We know that standards and frameworks are evolving all the time to meet mandate regulatory reporting requirements for mandatory disclosure requirements; new regulations are announced for 2022 and will continue to evolve. We already know that the supply chain is the source of up to 80% of GHG emissions covering scopes 1, 2, and 3 as per the GHG Protocol.

We know that transforming from a profitable business into a profitable and sustainable business is difficult and challenging. Why? First, where can you find the right real-time, accurate data you can trust? Second, how can you change your business processes to drive focused impact to maximize business benefits?

With SAP Cloud for Sustainable Enterprises, you can start to take advantage of both native sustainability features baked within S/4HANA core as well as net new solutions provided by SAP built on the SAP BTP platform. For example, with SAP SCT, you can start to record, report, and act on your sustainability goals, focusing on what you can do using the data and processes you already have in place:

Figure 12.6 – An overview of SAP Cloud for Sustainable Enterprises. Source:
`https://www.sap.com/sustainability.html`

SAP SCT provides ESG transparency, enabling access to data that is recorded in S/4HANA core and SAP cloud solutions such as SuccessFactors, Fieldglass, Concur, and Ariba. This is along with these new sustainability solutions to record real-time auditable data and turn all that into high-fidelity insights using SAP SCT key ledger mapping to a choice of ESG standards such as the **World Business Council for Sustainable Development (WBSCD)**, EU Taxonomy, **Global Reporting Initiative (GRI)**, IFRS, and **World Economic Forum** (**WEF**) KPIs. That way, you can start to report ESG performance across your supply chain. More importantly though is the responsibility that companies will now have to act holistically using this insight from SAP SCT, which offers out-of-the-box integration taking you from averages to actually using automation to accelerate action and measurements.

This way, you can zero in and out of the big three challenges: emissions, waste, and inequality. This brings us back to our first point. We know that existing approaches aren't doing enough, especially when most of the emissions are stuck in your supply chain. With additional SAP components such as Product Footprint Management and Environment Health and Safety, you can now tap into data from every part of your business to measure, manage, and minimize the bottom-up carbon footprint of products that could be lost within your business value chain:

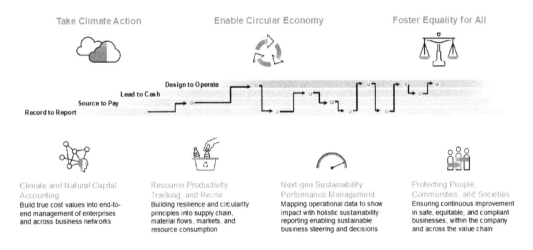

Figure 12.7 – How SAP sustainability solutions operate across business workflows. Source: SAP

Looking at the growing problem of waste, we see that for all of the raw resources we use in production planning or manufacturing, only 9% gets recycled. To eliminate waste, you need to see the whole picture so you can start circulating materials and regenerating natural systems. That's where a circular economy model is essential. Together we can capture data across every element in the packaging layer and combine it with local requirements and tax declarations, so you get full visibility and can act on your zero-waste commitments.

The waste you can see

Finally, the human impact of business isn't visible. An estimated 40 million people are trapped in modern slavery in upstream opaque supply chains, with most of them being part of corporate value chains. You may be making ethical decisions, but your value chain extends to 2,000 supporters and millions of people. With supply chain transparency, we can help ensure decent work in compliance with human rights so you can sustain equitable, responsible business practices that positively impact people and our planet. Becoming a responsible business is hard, but we all have the same goal. With our technology and your commitment, we can achieve a sustainable world, together.

When you stack up the financial impact of inaction or bad action when it comes to sustainability, it starts to add up. Typically, the CFO is focused on meeting financial reporting obligations in line with standards such as **generally accepted accounting principles (GAAP)** and IFRS, which are standards for the finance ledger, and S/4HANA is excellent for this because SAP has industry-leading Cash Ledger and ERP for 24 different industries. However, economic externalities are not captured, thus the groundswell of interest in and adoption of ESG Green Ledgers. Some external costs/revenue (carbon price, cap, and trade credits) and risks (climate impact on assets, risk reserves, and so on) are applied to the finance ledger, but we are seeing a growing focus on climate-related risks and opportunities, 60 of the top 100 firms use TCFD today. Now, the same CFO, combined with the priorities of the other major CXO players, must focus on broader impacts such as brand, compliance, and even the right to operate.

SAP has defined the business value of sustainability by recording, reporting, and acting on insights through its Value Framework, as shown in *Figure 12.8*. While individual KPIs/metrics will define business value (depending on the ESG-related standard that is adopted), businesses will integrate these KPIs/metrics into their own materiality assessment, which is done within the context of their industry and their specific business growth strategy. This results in a symbiotic relationship between **return-on-investment (ROI)**, sustainability KPIs, brand equity, and strategic outcomes:

💲 ROI	CO₂ Sustainability
▪ Lower Energy Costs ▪ Lower Material Waste ▪ Revenue increase from sustainable products ▪ Improved Supply Chain resilience ▪ Lower labor for Regulatory Reporting, ESG processes **Metric: Currency: Revenue, Margin, Asset efficiency**	▪ Science Based Target for overall Carbon Footprint Product (CFP) ▪ % Decrease over baseline year ▪ Product Supply Chain Miles ▪ % of product recycled **Metric: Sustainability Goal Attainment (%), CFP goals (%)**
Brand	Strategic Outcomes
▪ Lower Energy Costs ▪ Lower Material Waste ▪ Revenue increase, sustainable products ▪ Improved Supply Chain resilience ▪ Lower labor for Regulatory Reporting **Metric: Brand Score(s) (e.g., Top 100 Brand Rank, NPS, etc.**	▪ First mover advantage new products ▪ Business Networks for product carbon footprint ▪ New Products supporting circular economy… **Metric: Market share, % Products supporting circular economy, Granularity of carbon footprint estimate**

Figure 12.8 – The SAP Sustainability Value Framework shows a symbiotic
relationship between each quadrant. Source: SAP

Therefore, the impact of the ESG Green Ledger is getting to be as important as the financial ledger because Green Ledgers align with the ESG criteria, with many enterprises starting to report on multiple ESG frameworks, often manually. This takes tremendous effort, time, and money, and also raises questions of audit, providence, assurance, and quality. The CFO has to consider accountability and value creation beyond financial markets, for example, carbon impact on climate change and biodiversity loss as well as social equity. Therefore, externalities have to be measured, analyzed, and improved, and that's why the ESG framework with the Green Ledger has to be the scorecard.

With RISE with SAP, you have the S/4HANA core solution supported by SAP BTP capabilities. With SAP Cloud for Sustainable Enterprise, organizations can take advantage of new solutions built natively on SAP BTP, which includes ESG-specific data models, workflows, and integrations that augment the core S/4HANA solution. These include the following:

- **SAP SCT**: This is a central sustainability data warehouse that enables transparency and management of all organizational ESG-related data. It allows you to set sustainability targets and metrics/KPIs, align sustainability data with established ESG reporting frameworks, monitor progress, and gain actionable insights across the business network. This solution incorporates features of **SAP Analytics Cloud (SAP SAC)**, **SAP Profitability and Performance Management (SAP PAPM)**, and **SAP Data Warehouse Cloud (SAP DWC)**.

- **SAP Product Footprint Management (SAP PFM)**: This solution captures and calculates the environmental footprint of products across their life cycle, using existing business data through procurement of raw materials into production, transportation of materials, energy from production facilities, product use, and end-of-life.

- **SAP Responsible Design and Production (SAP RDP)**: This solution allows you to manage **extended producer responsibility** (EPR) obligations and plastic taxes according to the latest regulations. It also calculates fees and taxes on material and packaging choices in the supply chain.

- **SAP Environment, Health, and Safety (SAP EHS)**: This solution allows you to manage all incidents, waste, occupational health, and corporate emissions, and calculate all types of corporate emissions: hazardous air pollutants, GHGs, and other air or water emissions. It also enables you to collect and analyze operational activity data such as fuel or electricity usage. Also, you can embed operational risk management for a culture of corporate safety and respond proactively to hazards in the workplace.

- **SAP Product Compliance**: This solution assesses the compliance of products against multiple environmental and safety regulations across the globe. It also enables clients with product marketability to show that the product is safe to use and operate.

- **SAP E-Mobility (EV charging, UX mobile app)**: This is a single platform to create, operate, and manage electric vehicle charging networks with the integration of other software solutions such as billing, expense reimbursement, and invoicing.

- **SAP Landscape Management Cloud (SAP LCM)**: This solution allows you to analyze the energy consumption and infrastructure costs of SAP systems. You can also manage the running time of SAP systems through scheduled start/stop procedures.

- **SAP Logistics Business Network Material Traceability**: This is an open network that allows companies to connect with business partners for inter-company collaboration and transparency. It is dependent on the blockchain network and participants within the network. It provides full visibility of every ingredient and component used in a finished product.

- **SAP Ariba – Supplier Risk**: This provides risk intelligence to guide supplier selection, with proactive monitoring to minimize supplier risk in procurement. It consolidates supplier risk information from multiple sources, including news sites, government data, disaster systems, and public and private data sources.

- **SAP SuccessFactors – Human Experience Management Suite (HXM)**: This provides analysis and insight into HR data from a compliance and ethics perspective to ensure diversity of employees and inclusion across the organization.

These are delivered through SAP BTP with integration with S/4HANA Public Cloud (but will be integrated with the SAP S/4HANA AnyPrem edition and SAP ECC6 via BTP Connector). The following diagram shows a typical reference architecture for SAP SCT integrated with multiple data sources, including S/4HANA, SAP ECC6, and non-SAP datasets:

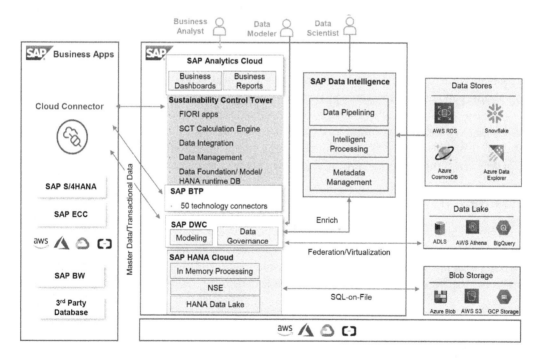

Figure 12.9 – Reference architecture for SAP SCT. Source: SAP

In addition, SAP has made updates to existing solutions on SAP S/4HANA, such as the following:

- **SAP Transportation Management (SAP TM)**: This calculates the emissions quantity and fuel consumption for a freight order, allowing you to plan the most economical and environment-friendly routes through different modes of transportation.

- **SAP Integrated Business Planning (SAP IBP)**: This executes carbon calculation early in the supply chain planning for the mode of transport and logistics suppliers/carriers so you can get better visibility of the GHG footprint of your products and operations – from the start of the execution of the supply network.

- **SAP Extended Warehouse Management (SAP EWM)**: To stock in warehouse and distribution centers from an energy and resource consumption perspective, including waste management.

- **SAP Concur**: This captures corporate travel and expense data with the capability to generate reports related to sustainability, enabling corporations and their employees to make informed travel decisions based on sustainability insights. It is best for corporations with sustainable business travel initiatives.

As a consequence, organizations have a real opportunity to balance quadruple growth and profitability. This is the time for finance to take advantage of technology to drive better profitability. S/4HANA solves many of the financial challenges of the past with the new richer capabilities of the Universal journal as a single source of truth for all financial transactions from accounts payable, accounts receivable, cash and banking, credit management, and the finance supply chain as well as inter-company reconciliation and real-time period close. Now, those processes can be augmented by fusing AI and ML capabilities into core business processes right across the enterprise. For example, we can use SAP Signavio to drive process discovery, insights, optimization, standardization, and automation. When it comes to process execution, all of this can be visualized through a single dashboard depicting key workflows operating in real time across the enterprise's processes. This is a really powerful capability.

Sustainability and SAP enterprise architecture

Successful organizations rely on their **enterprise architecture** (**EA**) team to operate across business units and departments to understand the end-to-end business model (for both the AS IS and TO BE world), then manage the impact of business requirements and change, and articulate risks and mitigations. Therefore, the EA team has a critical role in defining business and IT capabilities while providing control points to drive new solutions into the enterprise that plug any capability gaps that were identified for an organization. That way, new changes are adopted after consideration through an EA framework, for example, **The Open Group Architecture Framework** (**TOGAF**), with industry best practices, so that changes are owned and managed effectively. The EA team can introduce sustainable thinking and action to address both functional and non-functional requirements, and help the business deliver the outcomes at each layer of the EA structure. The following diagram shows how sustainability thinking pervades each of the EA layers, starting with IT and **operational technology** (**OT**) (used for

Industry 4.0 use cases), process and data, capability, and strategic layers. Taking an EA-led approach toward sustainability helps to ensure the line of sight from requirements to solution:

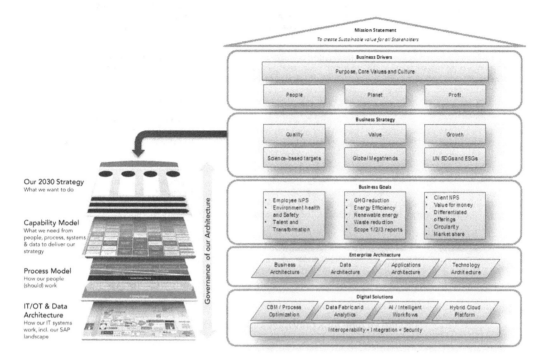

Figure 12.10 – An example of a sustainable EA model

We can see that green IT and responsible computing is about managing the impact of energy and emissions from data centers, which ultimately means managing computational resources, storage, and infrastructure while challenging how we architect solutions going forward. We know big data is expected to accelerate in the coming years, demanding high-end computing resources to execute AI algorithms and analytics and deliver business value at device in real time. Using renewables to source energy for the data center is a positive step, but not enough.

SAP developers, technical architects, solution architects, and functional business process experts developing solutions on top of S/4HANA using SAP BTP need to have sustainability principles and non-functional requirements in order to deliver solutions that are compatible with net zero or ESG objectives. *Figure 12.11* shows some of the principles that need to be considered:

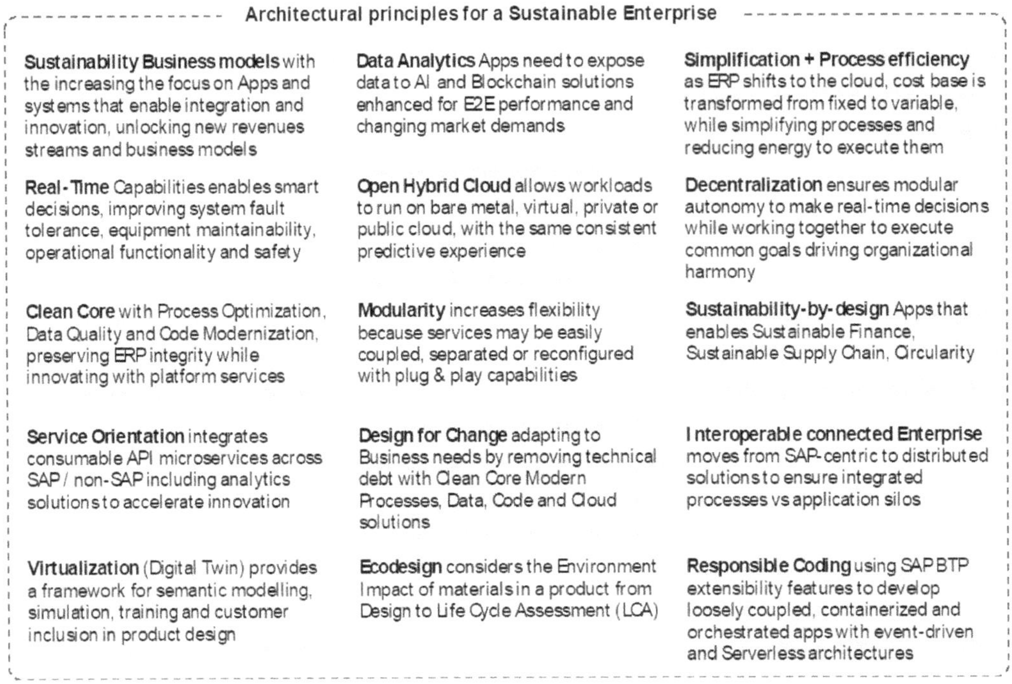

┌─ − − − − − − − − − − − − Architectural principles for a Sustainable Enterprise − − − − − − − − − − − ─┐

Sustainability Business models with the increasing the focus on Apps and systems that enable integration and innovation, unlocking new revenues streams and business models

Data Analytics Apps need to expose data to AI and Blockchain solutions enhanced for E2E performance and changing market demands

Simplification + Process efficiency as ERP shifts to the cloud, cost base is transformed from fixed to variable, while simplifying processes and reducing energy to execute them

Real-Time Capabilities enables smart decisions, improving system fault tolerance, equipment maintainability, operational functionality and safety

Open Hybrid Cloud allows workloads to run on bare metal, virtual, private or public cloud, with the same consistent predictive experience

Decentralization ensures modular autonomy to make real-time decisions while working together to execute common goals driving organizational harmony

Clean Core with Process Optimization, Data Quality and Code Modernization, preserving ERP integrity while innovating with platform services

Modularity increases flexibility because services may be easily coupled, separated or reconfigured with plug & play capabilities

Sustainability-by-design Apps that enables Sustainable Finance, Sustainable Supply Chain, Circularity

Service Orientation integrates consumable API microservices across SAP / non-SAP including analytics solutions to accelerate innovation

Design for Change adapting to Business needs by removing technical debt with Clean Core Modern Processes, Data, Code and Cloud solutions

Interoperable connected Enterprise moves from SAP-centric to distributed solutions to ensure integrated processes vs application silos

Virtualization (Digital Twin) provides a framework for semantic modelling, simulation, training and customer inclusion in product design

Ecodesign considers the Environment Impact of materials in a product from Design to Life Cycle Assessment (LCA)

Responsible Coding using SAP BTP extensibility features to develop loosely coupled, containerized and orchestrated apps with event-driven and Serverless architectures

└─ − ─┘

Figure 12.11 – Selected architectural principles and guidance for sustainable principles

Sustainability and AI/ML

Today, we already have some strong emerging AI/ML features available through SAP BTP and partner ecosystem solutions that augment the SAP process insights and process automation capabilities, for example, with SAP Signavio. With AI, you can curate disparate datasets right across the supply chain to enable better insights around key business and technical events that enable stronger collaboration with partners across the supply chain. Investing in growing AI capability through insight into automation, you get a real-time track and trace capability. From a sustainability perspective, you can combine shipments, increase packaging density, reduce packaging materials, and lower emissions with logistics and shipping. AI naturally combines with ML to consume large datasets to understand, learn, and predict patterns across the supply chain, using data from the edge of the organization connected through sensors/devices to feed real-time analytics, discover patterns, learn from experience, and automate agile and responsive workflows. For the sustainable supply chain, this means proactive process optimization measures can be taken to reduce waste and energy usage.

When it comes to the frontier led by AI/ML, there is the OpenAI project called ChatGPT, which allows you to ask deep and searching questions and get answers in real time that are structured and the articulate and accurate response is obtained using a human conversational AI chatbot. So, what does that mean for a finance department and people looking to perform analytics? It means better use of, for example, natural language that classifies queries, where you can ask questions of your SAP system (e.g. integrate with SAP CoPilot or another suitable AI Chatbot) and get better-quality curated answers that enable immediate actions. The stage is set for businesses to be able to access all of their data and start adopting modern analytics solutions on top of their data. So, imagine if you could ask questions in the context of the way your business performs, namely, "What are my opportunities this quarter?", "What are my challenges?", and "Where am I struggling, and where can I do better?" essentially define the *next best action*. This gives businesses such as Spark4Life a new capability of having much greater profitability and an advantage over their competitors in this space, ultimately delivering better best-in-class shareholder values. Spark4Life can then adopt technology that is sponsored and endorsed by their finance department. Now is the time for AI ML, which is going to drive new possibilities for growth in finance organizations and ultimately lead to more shareholder value through data to decisions in real time.

Sustainability and Digital Twins

We learned about the concept of Digital Twins in the previous chapter, but this time in the context of sustainability, it is just about a digital representation of a physical asset. Going forward, Digital Twins can amplify the *moments that matter* right across the supply chain, so you get a complete understanding of all the key business events, data points, and impacts. These moving parts of the supply chain in action increase transparency, which leads to reporting, insight, and action. This isn't just about data collection; it's about putting data into a more structured environmental context to create these digital twins across the organization, providing real-time insight and opportunities to act with more sustainable interventions and actions.

Sustainability and digital workers

We covered robotics in *Chapter 11*, but with the power of AI/ML and process automation through SAP BTP – now with SAP BUILD Apps – you can extend the capabilities of existing process automation technologies such as **robotic process automation** (**RPA**). The COVID-19 pandemic in 2020 changed entire supply chains to the point where customers now expect nothing but fast, next-day delivery, which stretches the existing capacity of warehousing and last-mile logistics provision to breaking point if it is not designed with streamlined processes. With the adoption of delivery drones, warehouse robotics for pick/pack/dispatch capabilities, and intelligent replenishment processes, we see the optimization of warehouse operations. This leads to streamlined sales distribution, which feeds into finance – all using intelligent workflows in SAP S/4HANA and SAP BTP supported by AI, process automation, and robotics. The outcome is that we can visibly improve workflow efficiency, optimize energy consumption, reduce waste, and reduce transportation fuel usage in the logistics network.

Sustainability, virtual reality, and augmented reality

Going forward, there will be further advanced headset and mobile technology embedded in **virtual reality/augmented reality** (**VR/AR**) capabilities that will superimpose data from core ERP and digital twins into real-world visuals through sophisticated geospatial location data to deliver an extended reality. Using VR, engineering staff patrolling heavy asset infrastructure sites can get real work data augmented to their field of view. This can not only inform, update, and notify them of the status of physical machinery and equipment, but also, with the integration of clever chatbots, for example, SAP conversational AI or the OpenGPT standard AI bot, trigger intelligent business workflows to manage maintenance orders, plans, and safety checks, and spare parts so that preventative maintenance is proactively done before risks become issues.

If we look at manufacturing and the connected enterprise assets, we see how the adoption of localized manufacturing with 3D printing means you don't have to transport prefabricated goods vast distances. Now, we can produce new components and products through *designed-to-order* processes and, therefore, avoid extended wait times between process steps. These components can be manufactured just in time but also locally, reducing time to value and overall distribution and storage costs. This is called **additive manufacturing**, and it allows companies to maintain virtual inventories and manufacture stock on demand. From a sustainability perspective, this 3D printing and manufacturing approach can increase the use of recycled content, reduce single-use plastics, and close the supply chain loop as we get smart about using existing materials for 3D manufacturing. Combine this with edge computing and the **internet of things** (**IoT**) with process automation and predictive analytics, and you get the benefit of the intelligent digitized production planning and execution process for the whole manufacturing industry.

What does all this mean for a business running SAP? Well, they can implement these solutions quickly using SAP BTP by integrating foundational business processes with these innovative technologies and delivering these services with a user interface using natural language, for example, CoPilot integrated with business processes straight to business users. The outcomes we can now expect from a sustainability perspective include reduced energy use, reduced resource usage such as water, reduced waste generated, increased plant productivity, increased process efficiencies, reduced emissions, and much more.

Sustainability and business networks

No individual business operates in isolation. Every business is part of a vibrant, extensive, and dynamic ecosystem operating complex globally distributed and often brittle supply chains. In Sapphire 2022, SAP announced the continued investment in SAP Business Network as a **network-as-a-platform** (**NaaP**) to support underlying mechanisms of global supply chains.

This is where ESG focuses minds to increase visibility, especially when it comes to responsible sourcing and demand planning. For the **chief supply chain officer** (**CSCO**) and CPO, this means that they now need to understand much more about supplier information, where raw materials are coming from, whether there are inherent risks in the last mile upstream in the supply chain from forced human labor, carbon-intensive processes, deforestation, or worse? Can they fulfill the requirement of providing goods and services that do not contravene ESG goals and objectives? If they do, then can they switch suppliers easily? This area has a high focus as it is the start of the supply chain. Therefore, the need is for more data to support better sourcing decisions but also managing scope 3 emissions upstream as this is now getting mandated in various standards such as SEC (proposed for 2023/2024) and EU **Cross Border Adjustment Mechanism** (**CBAM**) (announced in 2022).

There is an opportunity to combine data from digital twins into the green line that runs through the organization, sponsored by the CXO, and then to present the KPIs/metrics internally and externally to ensure that goods, products, and services produced by any given enterprise are *sustainable by design* and operationalize this right across the business value chains of the enterprise – not only for compliance and reporting but also to stand out as a differentiating factor.

Additionally, to collaborate across business networks operating in disparate industries, businesses have the option of adopting more sustainable supply chains. Using blockchain technology – a type of **distributed ledger technology (DLT)** – is particularly useful in its ability to act as a trusted enabler for real-time, reliable, and secure data exchange combined with workflow automation that operates beyond the typical four walls or boundaries of an organization. As the digital platform that underpins transactional activity for any given asset flowing through the supply chain, DLT solutions provide immutability, indelibility, provenance, traceability, and auditability through a *system of trust* across a vast heterogeneous landscape of supply chain participants who can subscribe to the model using permissioned smart contracts, which act like APIs that are empowered to write approved transactional entries into the blockchain ledger.

When we combine DLT with Industry 4.0 technologies such as the extensive use of sensors across business operations, you get an insight into how products and materials are consumed, then accurately track those components used in products, for example, through a bill of materials, and trace these back up the supply chain to reveal their point of origin. That way, we can remove any doubts or concerns around their ethical sourcing, authenticity, quality, and handling in the supply chain. This level of transparency is unprecedented and gives businesses direct insight at any stage across the supply chain. It's not only about greater trust in the data used in the supply chain but also about efficiencies and speed. There are many blockchain solutions available in the marketplace – see SAP API Hub at `https://api.sap.com/package/SCPBlockchainServices/overview`, for example, where we can integrate DLT solutions with SAP S/4HANA via SAP BTP integration suite to achieve processing efficiencies, reducing the time taken to execute supply chain processes that span multiple third parties from days to minutes/seconds, depending on the specific steps and complexity.

More recent, the SAP GreenToken offering combines Digital Twin with blockchain capabilities to provide material traceability to enable increased use of circularity models across industries. This solution enables end-to-end traceability and transparency for raw materials used in supply chains, such as how we track and trace the use of plastics in many industries. SAP's GreenToken is an offering that leverages capabilities such as mass balance certification standards, tokenization, and blockchain for chain of custody to tackle the significant sustainability challenges in the global supply chain network. See `https://www.sap.com/documents/2022/03/c81bc8cb-1d7e-0010-bca6-c68f7e60039b.html` for further information.

Going beyond the enterprise

If we look ahead using 2023 trends as forecasted by IBM, SAP, and Gartner around tech predictions, they all describe emergent technologies over the next five years where all of them have a line of sight to a sustainable outcome. Let's look at the top four focus areas:

- **Industry Cloud Platforms**: We know how to use modern cloud capabilities to run operational transactional ERP workloads on either public or private cloud platforms. While this reduces Opex costs as a tactical benefit, it is not the strategic destination that most businesses strive for. The real value comes from transforming and optimizing that workload by using industry-specific platforms that have customizable and extendable solutions to support industry-specific solutions for retail, insurance, banking, healthcare, manufacturing, utilities, and more. These industry cloud solutions are developed using an open architecture framework on top of SAP BTP. They provide *oven-ready* business processes that comply with best practices, use predefined templates and accelerators that aid rapid adoption, drive faster innovation and cycle times, increase process efficiency, and reduce time to value. By infusing AI, analytics, IoT, and process automation, a business can maximize speed to market with scalability as they respond to new sustainability features, functions, and capabilities (see `https://partneredge.sap.com/en/solutions/industry-cloud/about.html`). Examples of sustainability include the following:

  - Industry cloud for utilities could provide features that track payments to prosumer apps for the microgeneration of electricity through household solar energy when this is sold back to the grid at peak or off-peak times.

  - Industrialized IoT and Digital Twins to model energy from renewable source conversion to green hydrogen to reduce methane use in gas supplies.

- **Superapps**: Here, we already know that the new generation of the working population (Gen C) is fully accustomed to digital native and mobile-first experiences as a given. They expect to perform multiple functions, all within the comfort and ease of a single mobile app experience. For example, ordering a pizza, doing their banking, and starting a group chat all at once. These are not just composite mobile apps. They're built as platforms and provide more personalized experiences through built-in mini apps that cover a broad range of uses. Superapps reduce friction throughout the user experience, increasing value for a larger user base and providing more engagement for customers, partners, and employees. Garner predicts that by 2027, more than 50% of the global population will be daily active users of multiple superapps, and over the next three years, consumers will want convergence of these capabilities on a superapp across different industries, for example, finance, retail, and healthcare, and workforce adoption will gain even more traction. Some sustainability examples are as follows:

  - Sustainability services, offered through the digital banking ecosystem to small/medium businesses, can offer them circularity.

- A unified retail experience through a platform provided by major retailers to provide second household goods using customer sales history data, stock inventory, and end-of-life product data such as on furniture or electronics to minimize waste.

- **Generative AI**: This is where AI learns and changes based on new data conditions and changes in outcomes. This may sound like science fiction, but many customers are using this technique to improve AI modeling in dynamic and volatile conditions such as supply chain disruptions, for example, in the post-COVID-19 pandemic scenario. Garner predicts that by 2026, enterprises that build adaptive AI systems will have 25% more AI models in production than enterprises that don't. So how does it work? Unlike conventional AI systems, this new generative AI can update and modify its own code to respond to real-world events that were unforeseen or unpredicted at the time of originating that AI code. This type of advanced AI learns by applying sophisticated graph analytics to retrain AI algorithms, allowing applications to adapt more quickly and drive better decision outcomes. These systems require that current processes are re-engineered and have a long lead time. So, we start by assessing the readiness of decision flows for augmented or automated decision-making, then build the foundation by complementing the current AI implementations instead of a complete redesign. Once this is done, we can re-engineer those decision flows to make them more flexible and capable of being updated as soon as more information is captured. This is a whole new architectural approach to developing responsive AI based on evolving data models. Some sustainability examples are as follows:

  - Selecting alternative vendors as part of source-to-pay or source-to-contract procurement processes in the event of a vendor deviating from ESG metrics or supply chain instability with sourcing materials. An adaptive AI can reconfigure the process workflow to automate the selection of alternative providers that meet selection criteria, for example, price, availability to promise, ESG, credit checks, and so on.

  - Climate risk mitigation actions using external satellite, weather, geospatial, or traffic data to determine business risk exposure and recommend the next best action for mitigation. For example, rerouting shipment trade lanes or relocating warehouses/factories away from locations that have a risk of extreme weather or geopolitical events.

- **Sustainability technologies**: These will underpin all these previously mentioned trends. This capability isn't just about your IT infrastructure and solutions, which are important, but it's about how you use technology to deliver sustainable outcomes for your organization. Gartner says that 75% of executives will be responsible for sustainable technology outcomes and 25% will have compensation linked to their sustainable technology impact. So this is about ensuring that IT emission costs decrease over time even though the demands on IT increases with the onset of new data, apps, and services. With reference to IBM's survey via Morning Consult (Dec 2023), it resulted in the insight that many companies are planning to build services on top of that infrastructure, including AI (33%), automation (24%), and chatbots (20%). About three in four businesses say that these investments will drive profitability in their business, a key indicator of ongoing investments even as companies face strong economic headwinds. Looking ahead, survey respondents specifically cited digital employees (35%) and generative AI (35%) as the top emerging technologies that will change their businesses the most in the next three to five years (`https://newsroom.ibm.com/image/IBM+-+Global+Tech+Investment+Predictions+Report.pdf`). When it comes to specific SAP technologies, SAP's ambitions for 2023 and beyond will be focusing on RISE with SAP powered by S/4HANA and SAP BTP technologies, which will be foundational for all innovation and differentiation:

- **SAP BUILD**: SAP Build combines SAP Build Apps (formerly SAP AppGyver), SAP Build Process Automation (formerly SAP Process Automation), and SAP Build Work Zone (formerly SAP Work Zone and SAP Launchpad service) into a comprehensive suite. The solutions in SAP Build are integrated for a unified and engaging customer experience.

- **ABAP Cloud**: Now you can do ABAP development using Steampunk (SAP BTP ABAP Environment) to develop modern, cloud-ready, and upgrade-stable ABAP apps and extensions. You can turn these modifications and classic custom ABAP code into upgrade-stable extensions. This is at the center of the Clean Core approach.

- **Integration Suite**: SAP's **integration platform-as-a-service** (**iPaaS**) aims to provide scalable, versatile, dynamic integration capabilities that operate across on-prem apps, hybrid cloud, user experience scenarios, and IoT use cases supporting a wide range of integration scenarios, patterns, approaches, and methods. Integration Suite enables industry cloud scenarios that rapidly reduce development times using common connectors and API/microservices that digital teams can use to quickly build highly integrated digital applications.

- **Analytics and AI**: The focus on SAP Analytics Cloud, SAP Data Warehouse Cloud, SAP HANA Cloud, and SAP Data Intelligence continues to enable insight to action, where data should be behind every single decision and enterprise plan to enable data-driven decision-making. SAP supports the embedding of new AI capabilities into all business processes with AI and process automation features through BTP.

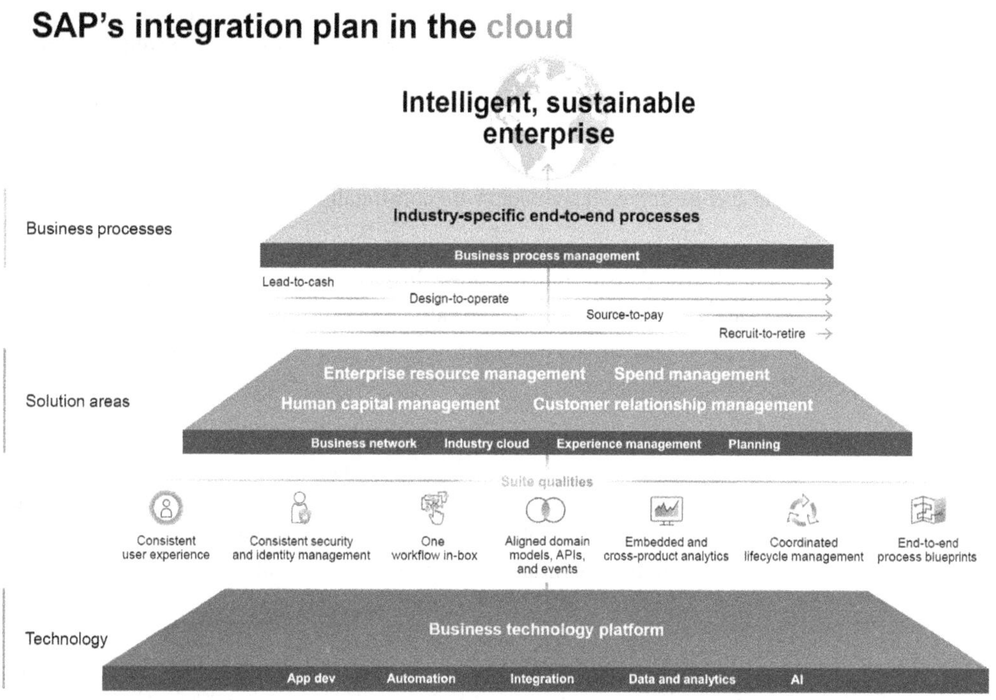

Figure 12.12 – SAP BTP foundation to SAP S/4HANA and sustainability solutions

Initiation

Before we get started, let's get the big-picture view as you think about developing the action plan. Here are some suggestions on how to begin the conversations around not only S/4HANA adoption but with the RISE with SAP construct and the differentiating innovations that can stem from that decision and the journey forward:

- Adopting a Garage-based design approach allows enterprises to act with speed, but the first step is to get aligned on the business case. Using a Garage framework to create co-ideation, co-creation, and co-operation models with all the key stakeholders, you can be outcome-driven.

- This approach helps businesses deliver on the promise of becoming more sustainable enterprises. It's a forum to refine and focus ideas, quantify the value of initiatives on measures of business and sustainability, and get results in weeks, not months or years.

- This approach can also help define use cases and accelerators that have been codified from previous project experiences. Using a Garage approach itself has been enriched with practices focused on sustainability – putting ESG standards at the core of our operating model. With a Garage-led approach, you can get access to a multidiscipline squad made up of design thinkers, data scientists, and software engineers focused on building an MVP. Once that MVP is in the market, the squad monitors its performance and prepares to scale the solution across the enterprise.

- This approach will also bring cohesion to your organization and to many pockets of innovation you may have started. We do this by leveraging the same operating model, working on the same cadence calendar, and engaging with sponsors who continually track our outcomes across the entire business.

- This collaboration and shared accountability among executives, business, and technology teams ensure the garage moves at speed to deliver value. Examples of Garage-led MVPs include blockchain solutions for supply chain challenges to leveraging AI technologies that improve farming yields or reduce water usage.

- Performing due diligence as part of the broader process and solution discovery work can help. Using the IBM Rapid Discovery offering can help break down overall business ambitions, goals, and objectives into clearer functional/non-functional requirements through the process, data, and technical workstreams and help to define the business case for the whole transformation along with a clear approach and a potential timeline for implementation.

So, start by building a business case through a design workshop where you bring in key stakeholders to help define a persona-led transformation agenda. Start by defining industry priorities, leverage the materiality assessments, and ESG reporting priorities, secure early business engagement and executive sponsorship (including funding), demonstrate proof points, conform and define the data and technical stack requirements, and finally, help shape the business case for the strategic transformation plan of action.

Summary and conclusion

What we have done in this book is to tell a story – one that should act as a roadmap, sat nav, or a guide to help companies as they examine the business case for moving to S/4HANA through the RISE with SAP offering. We described the benefits available from the Opex-based transformation engine provided by RISE. The SAP solution naturally has tremendous benefits across process, data, technology, user experience, and security, but also now includes capabilities around sustainable-by-design, which is a major transformation imperative and objective of our time. Adopting RISE with SAP means making your IT organization more agile, responsive to business change, underpinned by a hybrid cloud ecosystem, and yet sustainable at the same time.

It's true to say that RISE with SAP appeared in 2020 and landed with a splash in the marketplace with an eye-opening statement: *"Business transformation as a service,"* but since then, the message has evolved. It's more than just an Opex-led commercial vehicle for enabling transformation. It's more than just an ERP modernization accelerator. It is also safe to say that it is more than just a pathway to the cloud for ERP services. It goes way beyond that original statement around business transformation. SAP would argue that RISE with SAP allows a whole new business model to take shape with Clean

Core S/4HANA surrounded by SAP BTP capabilities. In that sense, it is a business platform that enables new business architectures to be realized – almost a *business operating model as a service* that is designed for tomorrow's world of online, fast, real-time, accurate data insights, with automated and intelligent processes and predictive capabilities that blend together the full capabilities of the cloud, applications, supply chains, and sustainability.

Index

`Packt.com`

Subscribe to our online digital library for full access to over 7,000 books and videos, as well as industry leading tools to help you plan your personal development and advance your career. For more information, please visit our website.

Why subscribe?

- Spend less time learning and more time coding with practical eBooks and Videos from over 4,000 industry professionals

- Improve your learning with Skill Plans built especially for you

- Get a free eBook or video every month

- Fully searchable for easy access to vital information

- Copy and paste, print, and bookmark content

Did you know that Packt offers eBook versions of every book published, with PDF and ePub files available? You can upgrade to the eBook version at `packt.com` and as a print book customer, you are entitled to a discount on the eBook copy. Get in touch with us at `customercare@packtpub.com` for more details.

At `www.packt.com`, you can also read a collection of free technical articles, sign up for a range of free newsletters, and receive exclusive discounts and offers on Packt books and eBooks.

Other Books You May Enjoy

If you enjoyed this book, you may be interested in these other books by Packt:

Architecting Solutions with SAP Business Technology Platform

Serdar Simsekler, Eric Du

ISBN: 978-1-80107-567-1

- Explore value propositions and business processes enabled by SAP's Intelligent and Sustainable Enterprise
- Understand SAP BTP's foundational elements, such as commercial and account models
- Discover services that can be part of solution designs to fulfill non-functional requirements
- Get to grips with integration and extensibility services for building robust solutions
- Understand what SAP BTP offers for digital experience and process automation
- Explore data-to-value services that can help manage data and build analytics use cases

SAP Intelligent RPA for Developers

Vishwas Madhuvarshi, Vijaya Kumar Ganugula

ISBN: 978-1-80107-919-8

- Understand RPA and the broad context that RPA operates in

- Explore the low-code, no-code, and pro-code capabilities offered by SAP Intelligent RPA 2.0

- Focus on bot development, testing, deployment, and configuration using SAP Intelligent RPA

- Get to grips with SAP Intelligent RPA 2.0 components and explore the product development roadmap

- Debug your project to identify the probable reasons for errors and remove existing and potential bugs

- Understand security within SAP Intelligent RPA, authorization, roles, and authentication

Packt is searching for authors like you

If you're interested in becoming an author for Packt, please visit authors.packtpub.com and apply today. We have worked with thousands of developers and tech professionals, just like you, to help them share their insight with the global tech community. You can make a general application, apply for a specific hot topic that we are recruiting an author for, or submit your own idea.

Share Your Thoughts

Now you've finished *RISE with SAP towards a Sustainable Enterprise*, we'd love to hear your thoughts! Scan the QR code below to go straight to the Amazon review page for this book and share your feedback or leave a review on the site that you purchased it from.

https://packt.link/r/1801812748

Your review is important to us and the tech community and will help us make sure we're delivering excellent quality content.

Download a free PDF copy of this book

Thanks for purchasing this book!

Do you like to read on the go but are unable to carry your print books everywhere?

Is your eBook purchase not compatible with the device of your choice?

Don't worry, now with every Packt book you get a DRM-free PDF version of that book at no cost.

Read anywhere, any place, on any device. Search, copy, and paste code from your favorite technical books directly into your application.

The perks don't stop there, you can get exclusive access to discounts, newsletters, and great free content in your inbox daily

Follow these simple steps to get the benefits:

1. Scan the QR code or visit the link below

https://packt.link/free-ebook/9781801812740

2. Submit your proof of purchase
3. That's it! We'll send your free PDF and other benefits to your email directly

www.ingramcontent.com/pod-product-compliance
Lightning Source LLC
Chambersburg PA
CBHW081457050326
40690CB00015B/2829